The Truth about Leo Strauss

The Truth about Leo Strauss

Political Philosophy and American Democracy

CATHERINE AND MICHAEL ZUCKERT

THE UNIVERSITY OF CHICAGO PRESS ⁂ CHICAGO AND LONDON

The University of Chicago Press, Chicago 60637
The University of Chicago Press, Ltd., London
© 2006 by The University of Chicago
All rights reserved. Published 2006
Paperback edition 2008
Printed in the United States of America

17 16 15 14 13 12 11 10 09 08   2 3 4 5 6

ISBN-13: 978-0-226-99332-4 (cloth)
ISBN-13: 978-0-226-99333-1 (paper)
ISBN-10: 0-226-99332-9 (cloth)
ISBN-10: 0-226-99333-7 (paper)

Library of Congress Cataloging-in-Publication Data

Zuckert, Catherine H., 1942–
The truth about Leo Strauss : political philosophy and American democracy /
Catherine and Michael Zuckert.
p.   cm.
Includes bibliographical references and index.
ISBN 0-226-99332-9 (cloth : alk. paper)
1. Strauss, Leo. 2. Political science—United States—Philosophy. 3. Political science—United
States—History. I. Zuckert, Michael P., 1942–. II. Title.

JC251.S8Z83 2006
320.092—dc22   2006002541

Contents

Preface

This is something of an accidental book. A fortuitous conjunction of events led us to a project we had never planned. First, we were invited to deliver a series of lectures on Leo Strauss in Japan, the lectures to be presented in December of 2003. We approached these lectures with a good deal of uncertainty, not knowing what the Japanese knew, or wanted to know, about Strauss. (As it turned out, they knew a good deal and wanted to learn anything more that we could add.) We prepared lectures that we hoped could speak in an introductory way to those who might know little of Strauss and still say something either new or differently to those who might know Strauss well.

Then, as we were thinking about our trip to Japan, we were besieged on all sides with reports about Leo Strauss in the media. When we studied with him, he was known well in a small circle but largely unknown outside that circle. All of a sudden he was being pronounced the thinker behind ever-larger sets of political actors and policies, but most especially he was being identified as "the brains" behind George W. Bush and the Iraq War. Having ourselves sometimes been frustrated by how remote Strauss's thinking usually was from practical politics and policy, we were generally astonished to see that he had become—or was said to have become—a real mover and shaker in Washington. What was said about Strauss in the media coverage made him sound like a very powerful personage, but that image of Strauss was far from the way he presented himself—as a rather detached fellow, by no means uninterested in politics, but not aiming to run the country from the back room.

We thought we had better say something to the Japanese about these rumors and allegations regarding Strauss and Iraq, Strauss and Bush, Strauss and the neoconservatives. Most—perhaps all—of what was said about Strauss seemed to us wrong and misguided, the product of not having read him or not having understood him. So we incorporated into our lectures on Strauss for the Japanese some reflections on the recent deluge of media attention to him. Therein lies the occasion for the book and also the reason for its character and tone. We were moved to "rush in" by a conviction that most of what we were hearing about Strauss was greatly inaccurate and by a desire, motivated by a deep sense of gratitude to him as our teacher and, we must say, by a bit of righteous indignation at the injustice being done him, to attempt to "set the record straight."

This book is a joint product: we have been talking about Strauss and the thinkers and issues with which he busied himself as long as we have known each other. Nonetheless, there was a division of labor involved in the composition. Catherine wrote the initial drafts of chapters 1 and 3, Michael the initial drafts of the rest. All of part 1 was revised and worked over collaboratively, however, so that we no longer can say this is hers and this is his. Part 2 was mostly written by Michael.

Along the way, we have run up many new debts, which gratitude requires that we recognize. We are indebted, first of all, to our Japanese hosts, Professors Shozo Iijima and Yoshihiko Ishizaki, who not only are exemplary students of political philosophy but also were exemplary hosts, and, second, to their graduate students Messrs. Kondo and Tanaka, also students of political philosophy and wonderful tour guides. Since returning to the United States, we have shared many parts of our manuscript with various individuals and have benefited from their reactions. Michael Davis of Sarah Lawrence College; Fred Crosson, Jeff Church, and Alex Duff of Notre Dame; Les Harris and Ralph Lerner of the University of Chicago; Rachel Zuckert of Rice University; and Phil Lyons read all or some of the manuscript and made helpful comments. Finally, two anonymous readers for the University of Chicago Press gave us a careful reading and constructive criticisms that we have taken to heart in trying to improve the book. John Tryneski, the editor at Chicago, has been a great support from the moment we thought we might turn our lectures into a book. Emily Zuckert typed most of the manuscript, no small achievement, and gave us more feedback than the usual typist does. The Liberty Fund hosted us while we completed the book; without the opportunity they provided us as visiting scholars, we could not have written it as quickly as we did. A group of fellows there also joined in a seminar on several chapters and gave us very helpful reactions.

Mr. Strauss Goes to Washington?

A specter is haunting America, and that specter is, strange to say, Leo Strauss. Dead more than thirty years by now, Strauss was a self-described scholar of the history of political philosophy. He produced fifteen books and many essays on his subject. Although well known and very controversial within his discipline, he never achieved public fame. For example, during his lifetime he was not reviewed in places like the *New York Times Book Review* or the *New York Review of Books*. He was not accorded the kind of public notice that other philosophic figures of our age, such as Martin Heidegger, Hannah Arendt, Jacques Derrida, or Richard Rorty, acquired. Although Strauss's books covered a broad range of topics in the history of philosophy—ancients like Plato and Xenophon; medievals like the Arab philosopher al Farabi, the Jewish philosopher Maimonides, and the Christian philosopher Marsilius of Padua; and moderns like Machiavelli, Hobbes, and Heidegger—he gained little acclaim because nearly his entire corpus consisted of studies of figures from the history of philosophy and because he himself therefore rarely spoke out in his own name on issues of political life. Moreover, the character of his studies had limited appeal; they were distant from the concrete issues of politics. He wrote detailed, almost Talmudic interpretative studies, dedicating more space to questions like how often Machiavelli cited the Roman historian Livy than to the substantive discussion of Machiavelli's principles of realpolitik. Such interpretative practices not only excluded Strauss from that broader public recognition attained by an Arendt—whose shared interest in the history of philosophy did not prevent her from pronouncing on issues like the Vietnam War— but it also cut into the acceptance of his work within the more specialized scholarly community to which it appeared to be primarily addressed. Many scholars found his books nearly unreadable, and many others considered them so drastically misguided in their substantive readings of the history of philosophy that he was often dismissed by fellow scholars as an eccentric or, worse, as a willful and distortive interpreter of the philosophic tradition.

Thus, James Atlas observes that "Strauss's work seems remote from the heat of contemporary politics. He was more at home in the world of Plato and Aristotle than in debates about the origins of totalitarianism." Alain Frachon and Daniel Vernet point out that "Strauss never wrote about current politics or international relations. He was read and recognized for his immense erudition about Greek classical texts, and Christian, Jewish, and Muslim sacred writings. He was honored for the power of his interpretive methods." "Strauss," two other commentators conclude, "did not write books in such a way as to be immediately relevant to the policy debates of his day or ours. Rather the reverse." Nearly a decade ago, Richard Bernstein wrote a piece about Strauss titled "A Very Unlikely Villain (or Hero)."[1]

Despite these testimonials to Strauss's remoteness from practical politics, we see claims of the following sort: *Time* magazine in 1996 called Strauss "one of the most influential men in American politics."[2] Before that, Strauss was identified as particularly influential on the Reagan and first Bush administrations.[3] He is held to have really come into his own in the second Bush administration, however, and particularly in that administration's foreign policy, most especially in the Iraq War. In the discussion of the war, it has been nearly impossible to miss "Strauss-in-the-news." The *New York Times*, the *New Yorker*, the *Weekly Standard*, the *Wall Street Journal*, and the *Atlantic Monthly,* to mention only a few of the most mainstream media outlets, have all carried stories about Strauss and his purported influence on the George W. Bush administration. The coverage of Strauss is not limited to American media, either: the *Economist*, *Le Monde*, and *Asia Times*, to say nothing of newspapers and journals in Germany, China, Japan, and the Netherlands, have joined in with articles on the scholarly Strauss.

The claims put forward in this recent literature are quite remarkable. The *Economist* identifies Strauss as the latest in a long list of alleged "puppeteers" pulling the strings of President Bush. Jeet Heer in the *Boston Globe* informs us: "We live in a world increasingly shaped by Leo Strauss, who is 'the thinker of the moment' in Washington." In an article entitled "The Long Reach of Leo Strauss," William Pfaff assures us that "Strauss's followers are in charge of U.S. foreign policy." Even though he is among those who explicitly note Strauss's apparent remoteness from politics, James Atlas takes seriously the claim that the Iraq War "turns out to have been nothing less than a defense of Western Civilization—as interpreted by the late classicist and philosopher Leo Strauss." He cites certain "conspiracy theorists" who believe that "the Bush administration's foreign policy is entirely a Straussian creation."[4] Although Atlas seems reluctant to endorse the view of these conspiracy theorists—which he nonetheless repeats without dissent—he does, in his own name, answer the question "who runs things?" as follows: "It wouldn't be too much of a stretch to answer: the intellectual heirs of Leo Strauss." As evidence in support of that answer, he points to the fact (or alleged fact) that "the Bush administration is rife with Straussians."[5] The *Le Monde* writers identify Strauss as one of two "master thinkers," the "theoretical substratum" beneath the neoconservatives, who, they say, "have marginalized center or democratic center left intellectuals to occupy a predominant position where the ideas are forged that dominate the political landscape."[6]

If one strays from mainline media and consults the Internet, the home of modern electronic democracy, one finds even more extreme claims. Not only does Strauss control the Bush administration, or the neoconservatives, or the Republicans, but he is the *éminence grise* behind the Democrats as well, or at least that wing of the party associated with Bill Clinton and Al Gore.

Strauss-in-the-News

Restricting ourselves for the moment, however, to the mainstream media, it is difficult to draw a consistent picture of what Strauss is said to stand for and thus of what his allegedly immense influence is wielded in support of. Two features of the popular media presentations stand out. The authors are concerned above all to grasp those aspects of Strauss's thought that seem to have some direct connection to the policy positions the authors are attempting to explain. But there is little evidence that the reporters and columnists have "done their homework," that is, that they have read much of Strauss at all, to say nothing of reading him with the kind of care that their own description of his work suggests is necessary for understanding his elusive and politically remote thinking. The consequences are predictable: there is a fair amount of disagreement among the different writers, and the agreement there is appears almost to be deduced from the writers' conceptions of what Strauss must have said in order to produce the policy results they are trying to explain. It is hard to avoid the thought that there is something circular about the literature: the exposition of Strauss's thought is motivated by the desire to find in it the themes that resonate with Bush foreign policy, and the writers' conceptions of the themes that drive that foreign policy are then attributed to Strauss with little independent effort to find them in his texts.

Two broad substantive themes do stand out, however. For convenience' sake, let us call these Straussian Wilsonianism (or Straussian idealism), and Straussian Machiavellianism (or Straussian realism). One, for the most part, is meant to explain the genesis and purposes of Bush foreign policy insofar as Strauss's thought has anything to do with it; the other, the justification for the means by which that policy has allegedly been pursued.

A composite picture of Strauss's Wilsonian idealism would run something like this: Strauss's chief motivation as a thinker derived from his desire to oppose the twin forces of positivism and historicism, which separately and in combination produce relativism in political thinking. Positivism is the theory that says only scientifically (empirically) supportable claims merit the label of truth; all claims of the sort we have come to call values (for example, judgments of what is morally and politically good, right, and just) are pronounced merely subjective preferences, which can never be rationally validated. Only facts and broader theoretical conceptions built upon facts can be rationally established and defended. Values are thus "subjective" and "relative" to their holders.

Historicism goes even further than positivism in a relativistic direction: even truths of the sort positivists are willing to accept as rationally defensible are rejected as being subjective, as being dependent on or expressive of values—indeed, identified as value judgments themselves. In contrast to positivism, historicism, and relativism, it is said, Strauss taught "the immutability of moral and social values." This commitment to what is often technically (though never in the popular media) called "value cognitivism" ran contrary to the "moral relativism" dominant in the 1960s and 1970s.[7]

Moral relativism was not, in the eyes of Strauss and his followers, a merely academic foible; it underlay, among other things, the dominant foreign policy approaches of the era. It accounts for the sense of "malaise" so evident, for example, in the Carter years and the policy of détente pursued in the Nixon (Kissinger) years, a policy based on a notion of convergence of, or even moral equivalence between, western liberal polities and their communist adversaries in the cold war.[8] In place of value relativism and the drifting foreign policy established under it, Strauss and the Straussians affirmed the necessity for "moral clarity," a term one hears fairly frequently from the lips of President Bush and Strauss-influenced political thinkers like William Kristol.[9] Moral clarity, based on value cognitivism, is thought to supply clearer guidance on foreign policy than do the tenets of relativism.

But the bare commitments to value cognitivism and moral clarity in policy say nothing in themselves of what exactly one is committed to. The media writers (mostly) find Strauss committed to liberal democracy. Perhaps the most unequivocal statement of that position came from Strauss's daughter in an op-ed piece in the *Times*. Strauss "believed in and defended liberal democracy; although he was not blind to its flaws, he felt it was the best form of government that could be realized." Frachon and Vernet emphasize Strauss's sober and restrained, yet solid, commitment to liberal democracy; like Winston Churchill, Strauss "thought that American democracy was the least bad political system. No better system has been found for the flourishing of the human being." According to Atlas, Strauss finds "the free society . . . the best man has devised." Writers who are sympathetic to Strauss are the most insistent in emphasizing his stance in favor of liberal democracy. Writing some years before the hubbub about Iraq, Dinesh D'Souza pointed to Strauss's and his students' employment of "the philosophy of natural right to defend liberal democracy and moral values against their adversaries."[10]

Thinkers more hostile to Strauss make the same point. Charles Larmore says that "Strauss repeatedly declared his allegiance to modern liberal democracy. Some of the bitterest opposition to Strauss supposes that he rejected such values . . . but this is a misconception. . . . As a political form, liberal democracy seemed to him a good approximation to the ideal." Paul Gottfried, a self-described "paleo-conservative," finds the Straussian position to be a "defense [of] global democracy or a . . . standing up for 'values,'" a position of which he does not approve, for he thinks it amounts to "managerial tyranny" in practice.[11]

Strauss, according to the consensus of mainstream writers, may have endorsed liberal democracy as best, or at least as good enough, but he also, the *Economist* says, "emphasized . . . the fragility of democracy." "Strauss's influence on foreign-policy decision-making . . . is usually discussed in terms of his tendency to view the world as a place where isolated liberal democracies live in constant danger from hostile elements abroad, and face threats that must be confronted vigorously and with strong leadership," says Seymour Hersh in the *New Yorker*.[12] Strauss's sense of the fragility and vulnerability of liberal democracy is often traced to his personal experience in the 1930s. "As a young man, he lived the dissolution of the Weimar Republic under the converging attacks of the communists and the Nazis. He concluded that democracy had no ability to impose itself if it stayed weak and refused to stand up to tyranny."[13]

Moral clarity—the refusal of relativism—thus means defense of liberal democracy in the face of its vulnerability. The particular version of "defense" is related to one of Strauss's most characteristic themes: "the central notion of the regime."[14] According to William Kristol, one of the most frequently identified neoconservative Straussians in Washington, Strauss has "restored" a political science "that places the regime in the forefront of analysis."[15] The regime, the nature of the internal ordering of a political community, "is much more important than all the international institutional arrangements for the maintenance of peace in the world." The greatest threat comes from states that do not share American democratic values. Changing these regimes and causing the progress of democratic values constitutes "the best method of reinforcing security (of the United States) and peace."[16] Thus, it is alleged, Straussians endorse a Wilsonian agenda of an active, even militant foreign policy aimed at "regime change" and, in principle, universal implantation of liberal democracies throughout the world. "Moral clarity" is taken to mean an unabashed recognition of the difference between liberal democracy and the various less free alternatives it faces and has faced in the world (e.g., Communist dictatorships or radical Islamic theocracies), together with a commitment to act to bring into being a world where the better regimes (those that are liberal democracies) predominate. That action is premised on both self-interest (American security is best achieved in a world of likeminded regimes) and benevolence (peoples everywhere are better off and actually prefer, if they are free to express their preferences, a free and democratic polity).

This Wilsonianism, or militant commitment to the worldwide spread of liberal democracy, is but one-half of the dominant view of the Straussian orientation, as portrayed in mainstream media sources. It is, strange to say, combined with a very hard-edged realism, which tends to be a feature distinguishing it from human rights idealism. Strauss, it is said, may be committed to liberal democracy and its spread, but his is a peculiar version of liberal democracy. William Pfaff, for example, identifies the Straussian theory as "a bleak and anti-utopian philosophy that goes against practically everything Americans want to believe. It contradicts the conventional wisdom of modern democratic society." In the first place, Straussian theory is unabashedly elitist: "There is a natural hierarchy of humans, and rulers must...exploit the mediocrity and vice of ordinary people so as to keep society in order." According to Jeet Heer, "Strauss believed that classical thinkers had grasped a still-vital truth: inequality is an ineradicable aspect of the human condition." Peter Berkowitz identifies the elitism charge as one of the three chief elements in the current set of allegations about

Strauss. Strauss "emphasized...the importance of intellectual elites," according to the *Economist*; a recent study of American conservatives found that "it is hard to be more elitist than the Straussians."[17]

The novelty or uniqueness of the alleged elitism can, of course, be much overstated, for one strain of American political science, going all the way back to the Federalists, has always emphasized the significant role of elites within democratic politics, as have more current writers like Joseph Schumpeter and Robert Dahl.[18] But in the media presentations, Strauss's elitism is different and appears more sinister than other versions of democratic elitism. His elitism is presented as more intellectual: the relevant division between the elite few and the many is the line between philosophers and nonphilosophers. What distinguishes Strauss's elite is not wealth, status, political, military, or economic power, but recognition of "the truth." This truth is hard to face: there is no God, and there is no divine or natural support for justice. "Virtue...is unattainable" by most people. "The...hidden truth is that expediency works."[19] Or, alternatively: "Strauss asserted 'the natural right of the stronger' to prevail."[20]

The truths discovered by the philosophic elite "are not fit for public consumption." Philosophy is dangerous and must conceal its chief findings. Philosophers must cultivate a mode of esoteric communication, that is, a mode of concealing the hard truth from the masses. "Only philosophers can handle the truth."[21] The elite must, in a word, lie to the masses; the elite must manipulate them—arguably for their own good. The elite employ "noble lies," lies purporting to affirm God, justice, the good. "The Philosophers need to tell noble lies not only to the people at large, but also to powerful politicians."[22] These lies are necessary "in order to keep the ignorant masses in line."[23] Thus Strauss counseled a manipulative approach to political leadership. In sum, the media writers conclude, Strauss held that "Machiavelli was right."[24] When read with "a skeptical mind, the way he himself read the great philosophers...Strauss...emerges a disguised Machiavelli, a cynical teacher who encouraged his followers to believe that their intellectual superiority entitles them to rule over the bulk of humanity by means of duplicity."[25]

The Machiavellian side of the Strauss served up in the mainstream media is also readily connected to the Iraq War and Bush foreign policy more generally. Just as the Wilsonian side is used to explain the ends of neoconservative policy, so the Machiavellian side is used to explain the means deployed in procuring consent to the war. The various claims raised by the administration to justify the war—the apparently nonexistent weapons of mass destruction, the apparently nonexistent links between Saddam

Hussein and al-Qaeda—are connected to the Straussian themes of elite manipulation and noble (or not-so-noble) lying.

One of the very difficult questions thrown up by the composite view of Strauss we have just summarized concerns the relation between the Wilsonian idealist side and the Machiavellian realist side. There is, to say the least, a tension between the two. Some attempt to resolve the tension by emphasizing one side at the expense of the other. Thus, there are writers who suspect that the Wilsonianism is mere "exoteric," or public doctrine, and that the hard truth that "expediency is all," or that "natural right is the right of the stronger," dominates and sets the ends as well as the means of political action. But the alternate view holds as well. That is to say, the attribution of either of the two main theses to Strauss is in fact controversial, and the discussion in the media is of little help in understanding what Strauss actually stands for.

Peeling the Onion: Tracing an Urban Legend

Strauss's rise to prominence in the media is as part of a story of connected persons and events: (1) Strauss supposedly influenced a large body of students, who (2) either became or influenced the group called neoconservatives. These neoconservatives (3) entered government and influential media in large numbers and (4) either made policy themselves, or influenced those in the Bush administration who did. Among the policies they devised or promoted are (5) the Iraq War and the broader new strategic doctrine announced in the document "The National Security Strategy of the United States of America," issued in September 2002 over the signature of President Bush. Thus, by a chain of transitivity we arrive at the conclusion: Leo Strauss caused the Iraq War.

Strauss's prominence in the story of the Iraq War, or in the story of the neoconservative ascent to power, remains a puzzle, however. He did not, it will be recalled, write much about practical politics, and certainly not about international relations. Moreover, even if every link in the aforementioned chain were real—which we will argue is not the case—Strauss's rise to notoriety in the media would remain puzzling because, so far as we have seen, those who have been allegedly influenced by him have not paraded his name and doctrines and have not defended or explained their policy preferences by reference to Strauss or his views. Whence, then, comes the connection to Strauss?

The first to suggest a link between Strauss and makers of public policy was, so far as we can tell, the English professor of ancient philosophy

Miles Burnyeat, in a well-known piece in the *New York Review of Books* from 1985 titled "The Sphinx Without a Secret." Although the article was directed more toward Strauss's scholarship and his academic following, Burnyeat did identify at least one policymaker in the then current Reagan administration as a Straussian. Burnyeat did not have a long list, as the more recent writers do, and he did not place the political influence of Strauss-influenced individuals at the center. His claims were thus far less cosmic than those made by later versions of the "Strauss is running the government" literature. Yet one senses that the political implications Burnyeat perceives in Strauss's work are quite central to what motivates him to his scholarly critique of Strauss. As one reviewer of the Burnyeat diatribe put it, "the dispute between Strauss and Burnyeat is, in the end, not a scholarly dispute. It is political."[26] Burnyeat particularly objects to the way, as he sees it, "Strauss's 'ruthless anti-idealism' [leads] to a dangerously aggressive foreign policy." Political concerns drive Burnyeat's critique—he is especially eager to challenge Strauss's interpretation of Plato's *Republic* as the philosophic source of that "ruthless anti-idealism"—but he is operating more in the mode of warning or forewarning. The one Straussian in government whom he identifies is also a classical scholar, with whose work Burnyeat was most likely familiar before he made the Strauss connection to the Reagan administration. He did not begin from the political side and move back to Strauss in search of intellectual forebears of a dominant political clique. Thus, this first explicit linking of Strauss and Washington is limited in its claims and intelligible in its origins: Burnyeat, a scholar, knew the work of Strauss, another scholar, and perceived a political tendency in it, which he saw realized to some degree in the person of another scholar who was a member of the Reagan foreign policy team. Accordingly, although the Burnyeat critique made something of an impression in academic circles, it had no power to draw Strauss into the daily press.

Another commentary linking Strauss to practical politics was an essay by Gordon Wood in the *New York Review of Books*.[27] Wood was reviewing a number of books related to the bicentennial of the Constitution in 1987–88. He identified a cluster of scholars influenced by Strauss and devoted to scholarship on the founding period. Unlike Burnyeat, who treated Strauss's scholarship dismissively, Wood spoke with respect, if not agreement, with the Straussian scholarship. He did note—and dissented from—a tendency he saw in that scholarship to support the doctrine of "originalism" in constitutional interpretation. He did not voice any worry, however, about Straussians running the government. Burnyeat and Wood represent what we might call the prehistory of the "Strauss and Straussians in politics" motif. They made limited claims, and the claims they made are not in any way puzzling, even if one may be inclined to dissent from some of them, as we are.

The number of public allegations of links between Strauss and Washington made a quantum leap with the publication of a 1994 op-ed piece in the *New York Times* by Brent Staples. Although he wrote it during the Democratic Clinton administration, Staples was concerned about conservative ideas that had become or were "poised to become . . . central . . . [to] this country's social policy." He was remarkably ill-informed about Strauss's views, but he asserted quite assuredly that Strauss's "ideas have crept into vogue in American politics." "Strauss," he intoned, "appealed to the conservative elite because he viewed the status quo as an expression of divine will."[28] Staples named two individuals in or near practical politics who bear the mark of Leo. Strangely, the two he named, Thomas Sowell and Robert Bork, had nothing whatever to do with Strauss. He also named two writers of books more distant from politics, Allan Bloom and William Henry, author of *In Defense of Elitism*. Like Bork and Sowell, Henry had nothing to do with Strauss; his book never mentions Strauss or draws on Straussian ideas. Bloom was indeed a student of Strauss's, and his best-selling *Closing of the American Mind* did make use of Straussian thought. This appears to have been a lucky hit for Staples, however, for what he said about Bloom's book does not make one confident that he had read either it or any of Strauss's writings.

Staples's attempts to link Strauss to the politics of the day were also less puzzling than the current wave of such efforts. Staples, like Burnyeat, had a special reason to hit upon Strauss. As he recounts in his article, he arrived at the University of Chicago for graduate studies in 1973, the year of Strauss's death. He was thus aware of Strauss as a Chicago figure and connected him with Bloom, who was returning to Chicago in the years Staples spent there and whose *Closing of the American Mind* became a major item in the culture in the years between Staples's attendance at the University of Chicago and his writing of his op-ed piece.[29]

Staples's screed revealed something of the power of the *New York Times* editorial page, for his assertions were bandied about in both liberal and conservative media outlets, producing the first wave of interest in Strauss in such places. This flurry of interest did not last long, nor was it so widespread as the recent wave of Strauss-in-the-news. Perhaps the coup de grâce was administered to this mid-nineties round of interest in Strauss by a thoughtful, if sometimes inaccurate, article in the *New York Times* by Richard Bernstein. Unlike many of the writers in the wake of the Iraq War debate,

Bernstein did read at least one essay by Strauss, and his reading led him to conclude that Strauss's ideas were "not...especially conservative," nor was his elitism, such as it was, incompatible with democracy.[30]

The character, intensity, and quantity of interest in 2000 and after are thus very different from the earlier interest shown in Strauss's alleged influence on politics in America, as well as being much more puzzling. A clue to the puzzle appears in several of the recent mainstream media essays. In June 2003, after the Strauss craze had erupted in the mainstream media, Robert Bartley published a piece in the *Wall Street Journal* recounting the boast made by a member of the Lyndon LaRouche organization that the media were following LaRouche into what Bartley called "the fever swamps" of anti-Strauss fulmination.[31] Bartley himself was somewhat uncertain whether to credit the LaRouchite claim to have pioneered the Strauss "exposé," but there is evidence to support their claim. In the first place, LaRouche and his people were on the Strauss story well before the regular media got to it. The first irruption of Strauss into the reputable media in the United States (in this round of interest) was the James Atlas "Leo-Cons" article of May 4, 2003. However, Atlas was preceded by the April 19 article in *Le Monde* by Frachon and Vernet. They, in turn, were preempted by a salvo of publications, press releases, and other communications about Strauss, the neocons, and Bush foreign policy emanating from the LaRouche organization. LaRouche wrote an essay dated March 5, 2003, titled "The Essential Fraud of Leo Strauss," which was followed up by a number of essays and press releases by LaRouche himself or members of his group all through March and early April.

The LaRouche materials clearly did not go unnoticed, for Atlas in the "Leo-Cons" piece makes reference to "intellectual conspiracy theorists" who claim that "the Bush administration's foreign policy is entirely a Straussian creation." This is certainly a reference to the LaRouchites, for they are the only "conspiracy theorists" at that time positing a connection between Strauss and Bush foreign policy. The *Economist* in June, shortly after Bartley's *Wall Street Journal* editorial, also identified the LaRouche literature as the origin of the buzz about Strauss and Bush foreign policy.[32]

It is likely, moreover, that the relatively early essay by Frachon and Vernet was influenced by the LaRouche literature, also. One aspect of the chain of writings particularly suggests a link between the LaRouche materials and the Frachon-Vernet essay: the latter identifies the two "master thinkers" of the neoconservatives as Strauss and Albert Wohlstetter.[33] In one of the LaRouche essays predating Frachon and Vernet, the parallelism between Strauss and Wohlstetter is drawn via their twin presence in the background of Paul Wolfowitz.[34] (Interestingly enough, both Jeffrey Steinberg, the LaRouchite, and Frachon and Vernet are more careful in their presentation of the Strauss-Wohlstetter connection to Bush foreign policy than Atlas is in the *Times*; for Atlas identifies Wohlstetter as a Straussian, which he most definitely was not, whereas the others keep him separate from Strauss, except in the influence both had on certain states-men of the day, particularly Wolfowitz.)[35] Beyond the Strauss-Wohlstetter point, another sign of a LaRouche influence on Frachon and Vernet is that all the people identified by the latter as Straussians were so identified in the LaRouche writings, with the exception of a few individuals in the me-dia, who were not discussed by the LaRouchites. Finally, another very clear connection between the LaRouche materials and the mainstream media is the clear dependence on the LaRouchites of Seymour Hersh's essay in the *New Yorker* about the Pentagon intelligence operations allegedly run by a Straussian, Abram Shulsky. Jeffrey Steinberg, in the same essay that highlights Strauss-Wohlstetter as mentors of neoconservative leaders, also discloses the Shulsky intelligence operation, well before Hersh's article.

The conclusion to which the evidence is leading, we think, is that the "story" about Strauss began in the LaRouche camp and jumped from there to mainstream media—for the most part without attribution. This is not to say that the mainstream journalists took over the LaRouche line hook, sinker, and all, for the story changed a fair amount as it moved from the pamphlets and Internet postings of this fringe, if not quite lunatic, political group into the most august venues of international journalism. Nonethe-less, it is a fact worth noting that that is the jump that occurred.

To trace the explosion of interest in Strauss back to the LaRouchites helps settle some of the puzzle surrounding this literature: the mainstream writers came upon the notion of Straussians under nearly every bed in Washington in the LaRouche literature. But that is merely to push the puz-zle back one step: how did the LaRouchites come to formulate the theory of the Great Straussian Conspiracy? The simplest answer is that LaRouche and his followers are given to conspiracy theories and there need be no particular rhyme or reason to any given theory they develop.

Perusing the LaRouche literature suggests there is more to it than this, however. One of the earliest LaRouchite statements, by LaRouche himself, is less about the Straussian Washington connection than about Strauss's way of interpreting Plato. It must be nearly unique in American poli-tics that a presidential candidate—for that is what LaRouche was (and most of the anti-Strauss material was posted on his campaign Web site www.larouchein2004.net)—makes the interpretation of Plato a major issue in his campaign. The fact is, LaRouche fancies himself a Platonist and takes great issue with Strauss's approach to Plato. Indeed, his objections to Strauss as a reader of Plato are remarkably similar to Burnyeat's, for he objects to the presentation of Plato's "anti-idealism." LaRouche is a self-proclaimed "Promethean," a believer in the (infinite?) possibilities of technological progress for the betterment of the human condition. Plato, he believes, underwrites this Promethean project; LaRouche maintains in his Web site that the Socratic dialogue "expresses a principle of knowable certainty of truthfulness,... a method which undergirds the progressive achievement of knowledge, true principles governing the universe, which can then be 'applied.'" The progressive adumbration of knowledge-based technology in turn allows the development of ever more egalitarian and wealthy societies. There are interests in society, however, some material, some intellectual, which put up roadblocks to this progress in knowledge and power.

Strauss's approach to Plato, denying the progressive character of Platonic thought, is one such roadblock. Strauss is thus "a depraved anti-Promethean creature."[36] Strauss "tended to uproot and eliminate the idea of progress, on which all the true achievements of our U.S. republic had depended." Because Strauss stands against progress (and reads Plato as doing so as well), LaRouche wonders whether Strauss is "actually human," or instead a product of some kind of "reversed cultural evolution, into becoming something less than human."[37]

Eccentric as he may be, LaRouche appears to have read some of Strauss's writings and to have had opinions about him prior to the debate over the Iraq War. He had Strauss in his sights before March of 2003 and thought about Strauss in a larger context than most of the mainstream writers did. Of course, when the mainstream media picked up the Strauss theme from LaRouche, they trimmed away most of the bizarre eccentricities and added some theories of their own. So, very little of the Prometheus–anti-Prometheus theme migrated over to the regular media. But two of the chief theses of the LaRouche literature did make the crossing: the strong claim that Strauss stands behind neoconservative thinking, especially on foreign policy and the war, and the notion that Strauss is a Machiavellian or a Nietzschean, a "child of Satan" or perhaps Satan himself, as the title of one LaRouche pamphlet suggests. It is the LaRouchites who produced the long lists of Washington Straussians that made it into places like the *New York Times* and the *New Yorker*.[38]

Characteristically, the LaRouchite version of the carryover themes is stated in more extreme and immoderate language, but the main elements of what the mainstream press promoted as Straussian are present in nearly recognizable form in the LaRouchite statements. In contrast to LaRouche's own promodern, proprogressive, prodemocratic Prometheanism, Strauss is presented as regressive and fascist—even Nazi. According to one of the LaRouchite statements, significantly subtitled "Leo Strauss, Fascist Godfather of the Neo-Cons": "A review of Leo Strauss' career reveals why the label 'Straussian' carries some very filthy implications. Although nominally a Jewish refugee from Nazi Germany . . . Strauss was an unabashed proponent of the three most notorious shapers of the Nazi philosophy: Friedrich Nietzsche, Martin Heidegger, and Carl Schmitt. . . . Strauss, in his long academic career, never abandoned his fealty to Nietzsche, Heidegger and Schmitt."[39]

The LaRouche writings constantly affirm the Nietzsche-Heidegger-Schmitt-Nazi filiation of Strauss, and then they group him with a surprising set of thinkers (mostly fellow émigrés), who allegedly stand for the same "fascist" principles. Thus LaRouche himself associates Strauss with Karl Jaspers, Theodor Adorno, Hannah Arendt, and Jean-Paul Sartre; and to this "gang" Steinberg adds Max Horkheimer, Herbert Marcuse, and Leo Lowenthal.[40] The grouping of Strauss with these others—a diverse group indeed, including some of the best-known leftists of our day, such as members of the Frankfurt School and Marxist existentialists like Sartre—is itself surprising, for Strauss is usually thought of as a man of the right-of-center with little sympathy for the "bedfellows" LaRouche is identifying for him. But the grouping the LaRouchites come up with makes a certain sense from their perspective. All the thinkers they name have in the first instance been influenced by Nietzsche and especially Heidegger, and all have reservations about modernity. From LaRouche's "Promethean" perspective, the differences between these thinkers are less important than their antiprogressive orientation.

Thus Steinberg identifies "the hallmark of Strauss's approach to philosophy" as "his hatred of the modern world, his belief in a totalitarian system, run by 'philosophers,' who rejected all universal principles of natural law, but saw their mission as absolute rulers, who lied and deceived a foolish 'populist' mass, and used both religion and politics as a means of disseminating myths that kept the general population in clueless servitude." Tony Papert, another member of the LaRouche organization, expands on these themes: according to Strauss, "moral virtue had no application to the really intelligent man, the philosopher. Moral virtue only existed in popular opinion, where it served the purpose of controlling the unintelligent majority." Papert attributes to Strauss the nihilist views "that there is no god, that the universe cares nothing for men or mankind, and that all of human history is nothing more than an insignificant speck in the cosmos, which no source began, that it will vanish forever without a trace. There is no morality, no good and evil; of course any notion of an afterlife is an old wives' tale."[41]

These "truths" are so harsh, says Papert, that "the philosopher/superman is that rare man who can face" them. In order "to shape society" in the interest of those "philosophers themselves...the superman/philosopher...provides the herd with the religious, moral, and other beliefs they require, but which the supermen themselves know to be lies...they do not do this out of benevolence, of course."[42] Their public face is all "exoteric" doctrine; they attempt to rule indirectly through "gentlemen" whom they indoctrinate with their false but salutary myths.[43] Although the character of the connection to foreign policy is somewhat vague, the LaRouchites are insistent that there are strong foreign policy implications to their Machiavellian-Nietzschean-nihilistic philosophic stance: "Their policy is to permanently transform the United States, from a constitutional republic, dedicated to the pursuit of the general welfare and a community of principle among perfectly sovereign nation states, into a brutish, post-modern imitation of the Roman Empire, engaged in modern imperial adventures abroad, and brutal police-state repression at home....Raw political power was the ultimate goal."[44]

Although the position is more immoderately and harshly put by the LaRouchites, we see in their writings the elements of the Machiavellian strain we have identified in the mainstream media literature on Strauss and Straussians. The regular media clip off the harsh edge and drop some of the more arcane references (e.g., to Heidegger and Schmitt), but they tell essentially the same story as LaRouche. However, they modify that story in one other way: there is no hint of what we have called the Wilsonian strain of Straussian or neoconservative policy as expressed in the mainstream media. The LaRouchites are more certain that anything that looks like this is pure "exoteric doctrine."

Going Yet Deeper into the Onion: Shadia Drury

Beneath or within the mainstream media treatments of the Straussian invasion of Washington lies the journalistic-political propaganda of the LaRouche movement. A strange bedfellow for the *New York Times* and *Le Monde*, to be sure. But a close look at the LaRouche literature reveals that we have not yet reached the heart of things. LaRouche may have had his own personal views on Strauss as a Plato scholar and an anti-Promethean, but the LaRouchite literature persistently cites and picks up theories from another source, which it adds to LaRouche's indigenous ideas. Papert's essay "The Secret Kingdom of Leo Strauss" relies on the work of Shadia Drury for its explication of the intellectual roots of Strauss's thought. In that context, he refers to her *The Political Ideas of Leo Strauss* as "by far the best book on Strauss." Steinberg in his "Profile" of Leo Strauss cites Drury's other book on Strauss, *Leo Strauss and the American Right*, as the source for his list of Strauss-influenced politically powerful neoconservatives.[45]

Even when the LaRouchites do not cite Drury explicitly, it is clear to those who know her work that they are drawing from it. For example, LaRouche and his faction regularly accuse Strauss of following the triumvirate of "Nazi theorists," Nietzsche, Heidegger, and Schmitt.[46] This is a position originally developed by Drury in her two books, and when she put it forward, it was quite unique to her. Another major thesis in the LaRouche literature is the claim that Strauss finds Thrasymachus to be the "hero" of Plato's *Republic*, and not, as millennia of readers have believed, Socrates.[47] This too is a position Drury pioneered. In other words, the LaRouche treatment of Strauss depends heavily on Drury: behind the eccentric and frequently kooky conspiracy theorists stands Drury, a scholar. The trail thus leads from the mainstream media to LaRouche and thence to Drury.

Drury's influence on the discussion has not been entirely indirect via the LaRouchites. She has a direct presence in some of the literature, especially left-leaning journals and Web sites. In much of this material we find citations to Drury's writings, in particular her *Leo Strauss and the American Right*, the book that (along with Robert Devigne's *Recasting Conservatism*), in a nonjournalistic venue, pioneered the claim of the link between Strauss and neoconservative politics.[48] Several such articles recount interviews with her about Strauss and his purported political influence, and in one case she posted a short essay on the topic on the Web site of an Australian foundation.

Drury stands somewhere behind the eruption of media coverage of Strauss and Straussians, but her own statements in the media are much closer to the LaRouche version than to what we find in the mainstream media. Perhaps her views are most concisely put in the conclusion to an essay she wrote in response to the Atlas and Hersh articles: "It is ironic that American neo-conservatives have decided to conquer the world in the name of liberty and democracy, when they have so little regard for either."[49] Drury dismisses the dual emphases we have noted in the mainstream media—what we have called the Wilsonian and the Machiavellian strains of the Straussian position—by referring to the distinction between "the surface reading," appropriate for public dissemination, and "the 'nocturnal or covert teaching,'" suitable for the Straussians themselves alone, but the true core of their thought and policy prescriptions.[50] In her rendition, the Wilsonianism is surface, the Machiavellianism the covert or true doctrine. She rejects the Wilsonianism attributed to the Straussians by Hersh and others in no uncertain terms: "Strauss was neither a liberal nor a democrat"; therefore his followers are most definitely not crusaders for the worldwide spread of liberal democracy.[51]

Drury's account of Strauss is not necessarily more accurate than that found in the mainstream media or in the LaRouche material (we will argue that she is far from accurate), but it must be said that her account is at least informed by a serious reading of Strauss's works. She is recognized as a major scholarly voice on Strauss, having written two books on him and his followers and a third book in which he plays a prominent part. Her voice has therefore been taken to be particularly authoritative by media writers and has had an undeniable impact on public opinion.

Although her first book, *The Political Ideas of Leo Strauss*, was critical of Strauss, it was also marked by respect for the man. Strauss was, she said there, "an important philosopher worthy of study."[52] She admits to having learned from him, despite her ultimate dissent from his views. By the time she became a participant in the current more popular discussions, her tone had substantially changed. Although she is slightly more nuanced about it, she is the source of the ideas expressed so often in the LaRouche literature and sometimes suggested in the more mainstream literature that Straussian thinking is fascist or Nazi in character. She is the source of the notion, now frequently repeated, that Strauss was a student and follower of the triumvirate of Nazi thinkers: Nietzsche, Heidegger, and Schmitt.[53] Thus, in her public writings she has made such strong claims as these: "Hitler had a profound contempt for the masses—the same contempt that is readily observed in Strauss and his cohorts. But when force of circumstances made it necessary to appeal to the masses, Hitler advocated lies, myths and illusions as necessary pabulum to placate the people and make them comply with the will of the Fuhrer. Strauss' political philosophy advocates the same solutions to the problems of the recalcitrant masses."[54]

Drury's interest in Strauss of course predated the current efforts to connect him to the Iraq War. She has been an important voice in this effort because she wrote an earlier book, well before the Bush presidency, tying Strauss to the "American right," complete with a list of important alleged Straussians—many of whom, by the way, had nothing to do with Strauss at all. Her book followed the lead of Brent Staples's earlier attempt to link Strauss and conservatives in politics, but her effort was infinitely better informed, far more concrete, and in general more powerful. Although her work was not inspired by the Iraq War, she did not hesitate to jump on the bandwagon that she had, in a certain sense, started up, or at least inspired. In her recent public statements, she has enthusiastically and in an ever-more-extremist manner connected Strauss to Bush policy. She informs us that "the Straussians are the most powerful, the most organized, and the best-funded scholars in Canada and the United States. They are the unequalled masters of right-wing think tanks, foundations, and corporate funding. And now they have the ear of the powerful in the White House." Strauss is "the inspiration behind the reigning neoconservative ideology of the Republican party."[55] His students, "a cultish clique... have left the academy in quest of political power." Being "poorly trained" for the academic life, Strauss's students are "held in contempt" in the universities, even though they are "the most powerful" group of scholars in Canada or the United States. Therefore they left to seek power, or were hounded out as incompetents to run the Republican party, think tanks, corporations, the government of the United States, and no doubt the United Nations. (Her charges remind one a bit of the old claims about the trilateral commission and the UN's black helicopters.)[56] Strauss's students "aspire to action," not the scholarly life. They are moved by their own quest for power.[57]

She has no difficulty connecting these omnipotent incompetents to Iraq. For one thing, they believe in the need for "perpetual war." "Perpetual war, not perpetual peace is what Straussians believe in." They therefore support "an oppressive, belligerent foreign policy." Strauss believes that political communities require "external threats" in order to be stable and unified. "If there is no external threat, one has to be invented." In her mind, this is what Iraq represented.[58]

Since the war was fought for reasons of this sort, it had to be sold to the public on other terms, for no sane group of people would conduct a policy built on such views. This was not difficult for the Straussians to do, for "they are compulsive liars." They, following Strauss, are "very preoccupied with secrecy."[59] Being "compulsive liars," they had no difficulty mounting a deceptive defense of their war. Although the Iraq War was really sought as part of their attachment to "perpetual war," "public support" for it "rested on lies about Iraq's imminent threat to the United States"—all that business about weapons of mass destruction and Iraqi links to al-Qaeda.

Although Drury's statements as part of the recent public attention to Strauss and the Straussians are on the whole more polemical and exaggerated than in her earlier books, the main line of her comments follows the argument of the books. Strauss, according to what she has said in both her scholarly and her popular statements, is no kind of Wilsonian, for he is no partisan of liberal democracy. He is in fact an enemy of liberal democracy. He and his followers seek "to turn the clock back on the liberal revolution and its achievement."[60] He has a "hatred for liberal modernity." He had "a profound antipathy to both liberalism and democracy," but "his disciples have gone to great lengths to conceal the fact."[61] (This, we suppose, is why they always speak as defenders and partisans of liberal democracy; only Drury can see through the pretense).

Strauss, as is well known, is a partisan of "ancients" (e.g., Plato, Xenophon, and Aristotle) over "moderns" (e.g., Machiavelli, Hobbes, Locke, and Rousseau), but, according to Drury, Strauss has an idiosyncratic, not to say unique, reading of the ancients: he reads them as Machiavellians, or even Nietzscheans. Thus Drury strongly endorses (is actually the ultimate source of) the other half of the media image of Strauss, Strauss the Machiavellian. Drury's Strauss is a Machiavellian of a peculiar sort, however. Her Strauss favors the ancients, who agree with Machiavelli in all respects but one: they are atheistic and amoral, like Machiavelli and Nietzsche, but are critical of the moderns for openly admitting these things. The truth, according to Drury's Strauss, is that there is no God, no divine or natural support for justice, no human good other than pleasure. Her Strauss, in a word, is a nihilist. These truths are too hard and too harsh for the ordinary person. Only philosophers are capable of facing or living with them. Thus philosophers must conceal the truth from most human beings and communicate it secretly or esoterically to each other. In place of truth, they must tell the people lies; they must give the people sugarcoated myths that will console them and make them fit for social life. These myths include teachings about the gods, the afterlife, and natural justice or natural right. The philosophers manipulate the masses with lies and deception.[62]

The philosophers tell themselves (or others) that this manipulation is for the good of the people, but, Drury insists, it is more than anything for the sake of the philosophers themselves. It caters to their desire for power. The Straussian philosophers see themselves as "the superior few who know the truth and are entitled to rule."[63] They affirm no natural right but the "right of the superior," by which they mean themselves.[64] However, she also has Strauss endorse the quite different claim raised by Thrasymachus in Plato's *Republic* that "justice is the right of the stronger," that is, the thesis that might makes right.[65] The Straussian philosophers seek to rule indirectly, via their influence on the gentlemen, that is, ordinary leaders like George W. Bush or Donald Rumsfeld, who can be manipulated to manipulate the masses.[66]

Her Strauss therefore rejects all the elements of political morality we associate with liberal democracy as defended by modern philosophers like Locke or Kant. There is no "natural right to liberty"; the doctrine of natural equality is rejected; instead Strauss labors to establish the view that "the natural human condition is not one of freedom but of subordination." His chief book "is a celebration of nature—not the natural rights of man . . . but the natural order of domination and subordination."[67] The people are "intended for subordination," and in the final analysis the lies the Straussian elite must tell are for the sake of concealing this unpleasant fact from the people. The people need to be fed religion, and thus the Straussians have "argued that separating church and state was the biggest mistake made by the founders of the U.S. republic."[68]

In sum, Drury is an extremely important voice in the current conversation about Strauss, Straussians, and American liberal democracy. She is the source and presents the best-informed, most articulate version of the anti-Strauss case that is now circulating in the general media. As the author of three Strauss-related books, she has been an obvious quick source for deadline-pressed journalists to consult. And the picture of Strauss they get from her is surely not a pretty one.

About This Book

Where there is so much smoke, must there not be some fire? That is the question we mean to explore in this book. Not to hold the reader in suspense for too long, we are going to argue that most statements about Strauss in the media and in places like Drury's critiques are caricatures of Strauss's political thought and of his relation to current policies and policymakers. Mistaken as these presentations of Strauss's position have been, we argue that it is at least somewhat intelligible that misunderstandings of these sorts have arisen. On the one hand, Strauss is well known for his cryptic writing style, in which his own thoughts are unobtrusively intermixed with or presented via his detailed commentaries or interpretative studies of earlier philosophers. On the other hand, and substantively more significant, Strauss has left behind a complex and tension-ridden set of views about America and liberal democracy that make it easy to misunderstand his position. The most significant task of this book is thus not to sort out the claims and counterclaims to be found in the *New York Times* and the

Wall Street Journal, the LaRouche pamphlets, and Drury's various screeds, but to attempt to clarify Strauss's complex and difficult understanding of and mode of advocacy for contemporary liberal democracy. That task will require that we explicate Strauss's work as a philosophic project as well as a political one and that we explore with care his relations to postmodernism, to thinkers like Nietzsche and Heidegger, with whom he is often associated in the recent literature.

We also wish to explicate how Strauss's thought has been appropriated or applied, not only by those who are involved in public policymaking, but even more by those who have remained in the academy and have devoted themselves to the study of American liberal democracy. As Gordon Wood pointed out more than a decade ago, Strauss's students have made considerable contributions to the study of America and are generally recognized as some of the most significant scholars of the American founding, the American regime, and American political thought in general.

It is also well known that Strauss's "disciples," as Drury likes to call them, by no means form a unified phalanx. There are public and sometimes acrimonious disagreements between several of the so-called Straussians, many of which are often accounted for in terms of personality conflicts or in other subtheoretical terms. Our argument is that the differences among the Straussian scholars or factions are not nearly as trivial as that, but derive from thoughtful and often penetrating attempts to cope with the tension-ridden legacy Strauss left behind him. We see two dimensions of tension around which Straussian schools have formed. The first concerns the dualism of Strauss's project: it was in part philosophic, in part political. One school takes more seriously the philosophic and depreciates the political. This group is sometimes known as East Coast Straussians. Another faction, the so-called West Coast Straussians, do the reverse.

That distinction only begins to define the issues among the Straussians, however, for crosscutting it is the set of tensions particularly relevant to Strauss's stance toward American liberal democracy. Simplifying a great deal, we might identify the three following propositions as comprising the core of Strauss's approach to American liberal democracy:

1. America is modern.
2. Modernity is bad.
3. America is good.

Readers of Strauss have had a difficult time understanding how he holds these propositions together, and the literature on Strauss reflects this difficulty. Those influenced by Strauss have had the same trouble, and it is our thesis that the different schools of Straussianisms form around three typical solutions to the dilemma posed by Strauss's three propositions. Each school typically rejects, or at least downplays, one of the three. The West Coast Straussians reject the claim that America is modern, whereas a third group, Midwest Straussians, are less convinced that modernity is bad, and East Coast Straussians are more inclined to emphasize the deleterious modern elements to be found in American liberal democracy. None of these schools endorse the politically monstrous views attributed to Strauss and Straussians by Drury or LaRouche.

Thus we have three chief goals for this volume:

1. To explain Strauss's way of holding together his philosophic and political projects, which include his advocacy of a "return to the ancients" in philosophy and the endorsement, qualified, to be sure, of modern liberal democracy.
2. To explain and assess the work on American liberal democracy by those who have been influenced by Strauss, especially to elucidate the important cleavages among contemporary Straussians.
3. To assess the public buzz about Strauss and his so-called followers, who allegedly are behind much recent public policy, especially in the international arena.

Although our book is otherwise very different from Anne Norton's recent *Leo Strauss and the Politics of American Empire,* our main topics to some extent overlap with the driving thought behind her book. She distinguishes Strauss himself from his students and both from groups she calls "the Straussians," whom she explains are "the political Straussians," those who have gone into government and the media and who stand behind Bush foreign policy. The main thrust of her book is to deny that "the Straussians" are authentic followers of Strauss, for whom she expresses great regard, or of the students of Strauss, whom she counts among her teachers and friends.

Our three goals in effect pick out the same three sets of individuals. We differ from her, though, in withholding the label "Straussian" from the last group, for we find that the case for a connection between Bush foreign policy and Strauss is much weaker than the media have made it out to be. Indeed, we wonder why Norton uses this terminology when her own argument more than anything challenges the Drurian notion that there is a real link between the authentic Strauss and the Washington "Straussians." The fact that some of those in Washington who have been involved with

Bush policy once studied with Strauss or with students of Strauss, or once knew someone who shook hands with a cousin of someone who studied with Strauss, is not a sufficient reason to identify that person as a "Straussian" or to connect his or her policies and political activities with Strauss. We are perhaps in a stronger position to make this judgment than Norton was, because we devote the bulk of our book to an exploration of Strauss's political thinking. This gives us a solid basis on which to demonstrate that the media vision of Strauss and the Straussians bears little relation to reality and that the policies of the neoconservatives, whatever may be their merits or demerits, show little influence of and certainly do not derive from Strauss's political thinking.

We spend most of our space exploring Strauss's political thinking. We approach Strauss in the context established by the current discussions of him, but we attempt to go beyond that context to present a broader introduction to his thought, especially as it bears on the question of the character of American democracy. It is not a book narrowly focused on the recent Strauss controversies, then, but neither is it the book we might have written in some other context for some other purpose. We do not believe this is the last word on Strauss; after all, there have been several entire books written on individual essays of his. We have not attempted that kind of depth. We have aimed more at an overview, but even in that we have been selective. We do not, for example, dwell much on Strauss's writings on Maimonides, the thinker Strauss was arguably most concerned with over his entire career. Nor do we explore his writings on Plato, the thinker he admired most, except as we are led there by our own particular themes. We do not claim to have gone as deep as might be required to probe the full depth of Strauss's philosophic position. For example, we discuss his response to the thought of Martin Heidegger, but we have not attempted the book-length study that would be required to explore the way Strauss sought his way—a different way—back to the prephilosophic, as Heidegger before him did. We have thought of our audience not as those who have immersed themselves in Strauss's writings, but rather as those who know his work slightly or perhaps not at all and have become interested in him either as a result of the recent media attention to him or because some initial acquaintance has led them to seek to know more. At the same time we hope that those who know Strauss's work better will find some insight here that they did not have before. At the least we are fairly certain that those who know Strauss well are likely to find an interpretation or two they will disagree with—a sign that we are not saying merely what everyone "knows" about Strauss.

About the Authors

We were both students of Strauss, and before that of his students Allan Bloom and Walter Berns. During our years at the University of Chicago we also studied with Joseph Cropsey and Herbert Storing, two other students and colleagues of Strauss. Many of our best friends are "Straussians." Our own scholarly work has been, loosely, in the Straussian tradition. We retain a great sense of gratitude to him as a great and generous teacher, and we find that we still agree with much, although not all, that he said. We do not believe that we qualify as "orthodox Straussians"—whatever that may be. Indeed, one of our objects in this book is to challenge the idea, so prominent in some of the literature, that there is a Straussian "line," a Straussian "common front," and a Straussian "cult." If there is such a cult, we have been left out of it. We intend to defend Strauss from the great misrepresentations recently purveyed about him, but this task does not commit us to underwriting all that he thought. We consider Strauss to be a thinker of great power, originality, philosophic depth, and significance. We would like to free him from misrepresentations so that thoughtful readers—and we emphasize *readers*—can consider his unorthodox and controversial thinking in its own proper terms.

PART I

Strauss

CHAPTER ONE

The Return to the Ancients

AN OVERVIEW OF THE STRAUSSIAN PROJECT

Leo Strauss was born in 1899 in a town in rural Germany, north of Frankfurt. He was brought up in an orthodox Jewish home where, he reported, "'the ceremonial laws' were strictly observed, but there was very little Jewish knowledge." In the gymnasium (high school), he recounts, "I became exposed to the message of German humanism. Furtively I read Schopenhauer and Nietzsche. When I was 16 and we read [Plato's] *Laches* in school, I formed the plan, or the wish, to spend my life reading Plato, breeding rabbits while earning my living as a rural postmaster."[1]

Things did not work out quite that way. Strauss went to university and at age twenty-two earned a PhD at Hamburg. He continued his studies for three years at Freiburg and Marburg, where he met some of the then and future giants of German philosophy: Edmund Husserl, Martin Heidegger, Hans Georg Gadamer, and his lifelong friend Jacob Klein. In 1925 Strauss began working at the German Academy of Jewish Research in Berlin on an edition of the collected works of Moses Mendelssohn, one of the German Jewish humanists. In 1931 a grant from the Rockefeller Foundation enabled him to do research in France and England. When his grant ran out, he decided not to return to the newly established Third Reich. Instead he went to New York, where he obtained a position at the New School for Social Research. He stayed there until 1948, when Robert Maynard Hutchins brought him to the University of Chicago. As president of the university, Hutchins hired Strauss directly without consulting the department of political science. Contrary to what has been said in recent media coverage of Strauss, he did not found Chicago's Committee on Social Thought.[2] In fact, although many of his students received degrees from the Committee, he never had an appointment on it. After retiring from Chicago, he taught briefly at Claremont Men's College in California and then ended his career at St. John's College in Annapolis, Maryland. The most significant part of his career, as it turned out, was spent not as a rural postmaster, but as the Robert Maynard Hutchins Distinguished Service Professor at the University of Chicago; rather than raising rabbits, he wrote scores of articles and books and became the much-admired teacher of a large coterie of students.

Strauss always described himself as a student—and teacher—of the history of political philosophy. He had an undeniably large impact on that field, contributing to a major revival of interest in a subject that had been increasingly held to be moribund.[3] In retrospect it seems there were two main aspects of Strauss's work that led to his making as much of a mark on the field as he did. In the first place, political philosophy was under attack—or, even worse, being ignored and set to the side—within political science as a nonscientific or prescientific enterprise that had little to contribute to the effort to transform political science into a "real science." Strauss, while appearing to be an old-fashioned kind of political theorist who had not gotten the message, was instead a thinker who came to the American political science profession armed with the most advanced European thinking on the nature of science and its relation to the study of society. Strauss had studied under Ernst Cassirer, one of the leading neo-Kantians of the twentieth century, and had then gone to work with Edmund Husserl, whose phenomenology represented an alternative to the positivism and empiricism characteristic of Anglo-American philosophy of science. His early contact with Martin Heidegger and his subsequent study of the latter's *Being and Time*, another great critique of, and alternative to, the reigning models of social science, also contributed to his reservations about the way in which American political science was attempting to transform itself. He thus launched a powerful counterattack on the scientism of postwar political science. He not only engaged in a strenuous and serious rereading of the great political philosophers of the past; he also went on the offensive, making a powerful case that the positivist scientific study of politics was a misguided effort to understand political life, because it inevitably missed the essential character of political life as the attempt to determine and achieve what is most important in human existence. Strauss's strong defense of the enterprise of political philosophy, especially his insistence on the necessarily normative character of political study (and thus his rejection of the fact-value distinction) was one source of his large impact.[4]

The second source, we think, was the range, novelty, and depth of his presentation of the history of political philosophy. Strauss wrote and taught about political philosophers from Socrates to Heidegger, including, it seemed, almost every philosopher of note in between. His readings of the

Islamic and Jewish medieval philosophers contributed to the reshaping of the study of those writers. His reading of Plato has had a large, often unrecognized influence on the study of ancient political philosophy. His readings of Locke and Rousseau, Nietzsche and Weber, have attracted great attention from other scholars. One reason his confrontation with past philosophers was so influential was the great novelty of what Strauss had to say about them. A large part of his charm arose from his repeated claim that we only presumed we knew what the tradition contained; it was, when read properly, much different from what it was believed to be. The result of his novel readings was a sense of finding great freshness and unexplored depths in thinkers who seemed to have gone stale and whose thought seemed to have been adequately captured and addressed in textbook or encyclopedia renditions. Strauss exploded such notions and led many of his readers and students to believe that there was nothing fresher, nothing more "cutting edge," nothing more worth pursuing than the reappropriation of the philosophical texts of the past.

Strauss's reinterpretation of the tradition has thus spawned a large, ever-growing, new scholarship on those thinkers. Many of his students, or those influenced otherwise by him, have gone on to become important scholars in their own right. There is a thriving "school" of Platonic studies influenced by Strauss, some of the leading members of which are Seth Benardete, Stanley Rosen, Allan Bloom, Joseph Cropsey, Christopher Bruell, Michael Davis, Ronna Burger, and Mary Nichols. Another subset of scholars have pursued the new paths in medieval philosophy that Strauss opened up. These include Mushin Mahdi, Ernest Fortin, Ralph Lerner, Joel Kraemer, Charles Butterworth, Miriam Galston, Remi Brague, Hillel Fradkin, Joshua Parens, and Christopher Colmo. Others, like Harvey Mansfield, Clifford Orwin, and Vickie Sullivan, have followed Strauss into the wilds of Machiavelli. Still others, like Victor Gourevitch, Richard Kennington, Hilail Gildin, Hiram Caton, Roger Masters, Thomas Pangle, Pierre Manent, David Schaefer, Nathan Tarcov, Robert Faulkner, Robert Kraynak, Jerry Weinberger, Arthur Melzer, and Christopher Kelly, have been spurred on by Strauss's readings to give new interpretations of early modern political philosophers such as Montaigne, Bacon, Hobbes, Locke, and Rousseau. Yet others, like William Galston, Michael Gillespie, Susan Shell, Richard Velkley, Steven Smith, Laurence Lampert, Gregory Smith, and Peter Berkowitz, have approached later modern, especially German, philosophy with a perspective shaped to some degree by Strauss. He has, in other words, an undeniably large presence even now, more than thirty years after his death, in the study of the history of political philosophy.[5]

Strauss's Philosophical Project

From reading the popular press (or, to speak more precisely, semipopular press) like the *New York Times* and the *New York Review of Books* in the thirty-some years since Strauss's death, one would think that he had attained prominence in the United States primarily as a conservative political ideologue.[6] Although he was a Jew who emigrated from Germany to flee the National Socialists, Strauss has even been castigated as a Nazi.[7] Despite the portrayal of Strauss as the intellectual source of the "neoconservative" foreign policy of the Bush administration, he said and wrote very little about American politics. He did express his opinion that liberal democracy was much better than the totalitarian alternatives confronting it in the twentieth century; but as an émigré, he often stated, he was not really qualified to comment on American politics. Also, his chief concerns lay elsewhere, with the question of the character and fate of philosophy. "He rarely left the esoteric world of high thought, preferring to construct a history of political philosophy."[8] And that, we maintain, is where Strauss's significance primarily lies. He presented a novel diagnosis of what is often called the crisis of the West but which could also be dubbed the end of philosophy. He tried not merely to revive but to reform this distinctive form of intellectual activity, which, he argued, defines Western civilization.

Strauss's signature idea was his call for a return to the ancients, his appeal for a reconsideration and reappropriation of the political philosophy of the classics: the writings of Plato, Aristotle, Cicero, and so on—a group of writers Strauss thought of as "Socratics" because they followed the path of thought opened up by Socrates.[9] Strauss did not begin with a commitment to ancient philosophy, although, as his youthful attachment to Plato indicates, he was seized by an admiration for them, or at least for Plato, from an early age. It was only when he was well along in life, sometime in his thirties, that Strauss concluded that a return to the ancients was both possible and desirable. Like most German students of philosophy of his day, he began as a student of modern philosophy. Having studied with Ernst Cassirer and Edmund Husserl, Strauss met and came to admire Martin Heidegger, who later became the founder of existentialism. He also read Friedrich Nietzsche very seriously in his younger days. His attempt to return to the ancients represented a break not only with these particular thinkers, but with modern philosophy in its entirety.

The important story about Strauss is the story of his call for this return—how he came to formulate it as a philosophic project, what he saw to be the barriers to such a return (barriers that made the very idea of return unthinkable to most of his contemporaries), what he meant by calling for return, and what the chief consequences of his call for return were. His main impetus for returning to the ancients was a growing dissatisfaction with the various manifestations of modern philosophy, including dissatisfaction with the great modern critics of modern philosophy, Nietzsche and Heidegger. In response to that dissatisfaction, he came to a new or at least very untraditional understanding of the ancients; he rediscovered an older and very nonstandard tradition of Platonism, which, in his opinion, contained a superior understanding of ancient philosophy. It also opened up an understanding of ancient philosophy that was immune to the critiques to which it had been subjected by modern thinkers, from Machiavelli in the sixteenth century to Heidegger in the twentieth. Their criticism of ancient philosophy failed, he came to believe, because they never understood correctly the doctrines they were criticizing. The ancients to whom Strauss wanted to return were thus very different from the ancients as depicted in the textbooks.

The first and perhaps chief consequence of Strauss's recovery of the ancients was therefore a reconceiving of the entire philosophic tradition. Not only did he come to understand the classics differently from the way they had been understood, but he also radicalized a commonplace distinction between ancients and moderns. With the emergence of modern philosophy, Strauss believed, there had occurred a cataclysmic break with the older philosophy, a break of such magnitude that all that came after was simply a working out of the implications of that break. In the Straussian frame, the difference between ancients and moderns became decisive; Strauss sided with the ancients and traced the ills of modern philosophy and many of the ills of modern politics to that break with ancient philosophy and the consequences of that break.

Part of Strauss's new grasp of the ancients was an appreciation of political philosophy, of politics, and of the relation between politics and philosophy as a central theme of Socratic philosophy. Strauss had noted already that the greatest philosophers of the first half of the twentieth century, those dominant when he formulated his philosophic project (Henri Bergson, Alfred North Whitehead, Edmund Husserl, and Martin Heidegger), all lacked a political philosophy or any serious philosophic reflections on politics.[10] Another way to formulate Strauss's signature doctrine, then, is as a call for the rebirth of political philosophy. In this reborn political philosophy, a philosophy that took its bearings from Socrates, not Nietzsche or Heidegger, Strauss believed he had discovered a far more adequate grasp of politics than that prevalent in the academy (social scientific political science) or in political life (ideologized politics). The reconceptualization of the philosophic tradition was thus to be at the same time a reorientation of thinking about politics. Strauss's project was, to say the least, ambitious.

Although Strauss has recently become famous, if not infamous, the world was slow to take notice of him. One reason the significance of Strauss's work is only now coming to be properly or truly appreciated in the United States is that many American intellectuals became aware of the arguments against which he positioned himself, in particular the thought of Martin Heidegger, only after Strauss's death. Living and writing in America, Strauss wanted to respond to Heidegger, but he did not want to propagate Heidegger's thought by explicating his turgid prose. As a Jew who had fled Hitler's Germany, Strauss was all too aware of the unsavory political associations of Heidegger's Nazi-sympathizing thought. Strauss therefore directed his arguments against what he called "radical historicism," by which he meant Heidegger.[11] Few of his American readers understood whom or what Strauss actually had in mind.

Strauss's Departure from Heidegger and Nietzsche

Strauss opposed Heidegger, at least in part, because, as he saw it, he and Heidegger had begun with the same philosophical problem or source—the challenge posed by Friedrich Nietzsche. In classes at the University of Chicago in the mid-1960s, Strauss suggested that the best introduction to Heidegger's thought was to be found in his lectures on Nietzsche, first published in German in 1962. Whereas most others would look to *Being and Time*, Strauss thought Heidegger's confrontation with Nietzsche was most revealing of Heidegger's project.[12]

Strauss himself had been enthralled at an early age with the author he had read furtively in gymnasium. Indeed, Nietzsche exercised a powerful intellectual influence on him for quite some time. In a letter he wrote to Karl Loewith in 1935, Strauss stated that "Nietzsche so dominated me between my 22nd and 30th years, that I literally believed everything that I understood of him." By the time he wrote to Loewith, however, Strauss had discovered that he agreed with Nietzsche only in part. Like Nietzsche, Strauss "wanted to repeat antiquity...at the peak of modernity." Like Nietzsche, that meant, Strauss wanted to revive a truly noble form of human existence.[13] But Strauss had come to believe that the polemical character of Nietzsche's critique of modernity had prevented him from realizing his intention. Strauss came, moreover, to have a very different notion of the peak of antiquity, or the most noble form of human existence. Whereas Nietzsche praised blond beasts and Caesar with the soul of Christ, Strauss tried to revive Platonic political philosophy and the Platonic hero, Socrates, who was not a great favorite of Nietzsche's. In contrast to Nietzsche, Strauss never praised ancient generals and statesmen such as Pericles or Caesar, nor their modern imitators such as Napoleon. He wanted to revive ancient political philosophy, not ancient politics.

Strauss came to question not only the adequacy of Nietzsche's understanding of the ancients, but also his analysis of the modern crisis. The date at which Strauss says that he ceased to believe everything he understood of Nietzsche coincides roughly with the publication of his own first book, *Spinoza's Critique of Religion* (1930).[14] Strauss's study of Spinoza led him to conclude that the early rationalist modern critics of scriptural religion had failed in their effort to prove that revelation was false, because revelation had never claimed to rest on, or be available to, human reason; and human reason had never been able to generate a comprehensive account of the whole that left no room for the biblical God. "If one wished to refute orthodoxy," Strauss maintained, "there remained no other way but to attempt to prove that the world and life are perfectly intelligible without the assumption of an unfathomable God.... Man had to establish himself theoretically and practically as the master of the world and the master of his life; the world created by him had to erase the world merely 'given' to him."[15] Merely showing, as Spinoza had done, that statements in the Bible were contradictory or anachronistic did not prove that they were not the word, or accurate depictions of the acts, of an omnipotent and unfathomable God. To show that miracles were impossible, modern rationalists had to give a systematic explanation of everything that had occurred or could occur. Unable to do so, Enlightenment thinkers had attempted by means of mockery "to 'laugh' orthodoxy out of a position from which it could not be dislodged by any proofs supplied by Scripture or by reason."[16] By the twentieth century modern rationalism in the combined form of natural science, progressive politics, and industrial technology had shown that it could not describe or remake the world in completely rational form. In Nietzschean terms, Strauss's study of Spinoza had convinced him that God was by no means necessarily or evidently dead, either as a philosophically disposed-of entity, or as an object of human attachment and belief.[17]

Nietzsche had insisted that the denial of God was a requirement of intellectual honesty, or probity, which, he thought, was our last virtue. Probity constituted a kind of spiritual courage or, in Heideggerian terms, resolution to face the utter meaninglessness of human life and the world. But, Strauss objected in his 1935 book *Philosophy and Law*, if the world is utterly meaningless, if there is no truth, then there is no basis for Nietzsche's obligation to declare it or to live by it.[18] According to Nietzsche, the intellectual probity that required him to posit and declare that God is dead was a product of the Christian conscience turning against itself. However, Strauss again pointed out, if there is no God, there is no ground or reason to have, or to listen to, such a conscience. Nietzsche's own philosophy was based on the same scripturally derived morality he himself had declared to be invalid once the ground of that morality, faith in God, was eroded. Strauss thus attempted to move beyond Nietzsche, for Nietzsche's philosophy was paradoxically grounded or generated by the very commitments he renounced. Nietzsche was, in this sense, deeply incoherent.

The antagonism to religion characteristic of modern philosophy that Nietzsche had made manifest was not a result simply of the demands of reason, Strauss concluded. The late modern philosophical critique had established, if anything, the limits of reason, and that conclusion made even more incredible the claims of reason to disprove revelation. Rather than constituting a logical conclusion, modern philosophical atheism rested on an act of will. Modern philosophers, even those prior to Nietzsche, had insisted that there was no superhuman, independently existing order or source of morality, because they wanted to improve the human condition. To improve that condition significantly, Strauss maintained, they thought it would be necessary to manipulate nature, even to transform it entirely. But nature would not and could not be manipulated so long as it was regarded as the product of a divine creation. To remake the world, modern thinkers were led to deny the Creator God.

Strauss thus began to suspect, as Heidegger was to argue later, that the core or essence of modern philosophy was technological.[19] But, whereas Heidegger argued that the technological grasp of beings was a necessary result of a fateful dispensation of "Being" itself, Strauss saw it to be the result of a fateful choice. The crisis of modernity was not so much scientific in origin as it was moral and political. The modern attempt to improve and elevate human life threatened to end, as Nietzsche had so powerfully shown, in the utter degradation of human life in the "last man" or in mass society. Once human beings ceased to recognize any superhuman goals or standards by which their efforts could be judged, they stopped striving for anything beyond comfortable self-preservation. As a consequence, their lives lost all nobility. The early modern political philosophers had made the acquisition of power a means to the end of relieving the general human condition; the acquisition of virtue was no longer viewed as an end in itself, and the ancient conception of human excellence as the form of human life worth living had been lost.

Strauss's Analysis of the Contemporary Crisis

The point of departure for Strauss's call for a return to the ancients was the congeries of ill effects of modernism that he called "the crisis of our time." The crisis was both announced and partly provoked by Nietzsche and his successors such as Heidegger. As Strauss understood it, the crisis was constituted by the triumph of "radical historicism," which he thought to be ultimately another name for nihilism. Radical historicism was radical not merely in reductively insisting that all thought reflected its age, or that no thought could escape the limitations inspired by its historical situation. It was radical also in denying that there were any permanent realities whatever. The consequences of this denial were very grave, Strauss thought. On the one hand, there was the contention we now identify with postmodernism: the denial of "foundations" for knowledge or truth. That denial meant the end of philosophy as it was known from Thales to the twentieth century. The "end of philosophy" meant the replacement of the quest for truth with the positing of conventions, or the consensus of "communities" of "knowers," or mysterious dispensations of fate, or poetry, or pragmatic effectiveness as the measure of a "truth" that could only be written in quotation marks. On the other hand, Strauss thought, the "crisis of our time" was more narrowly political and moral; because it heralded the "end of philosophy," it also produced a deep-going relativism, denying the possibility of trans-historical truth with respect to moral phenomena. The loss of faith in moral and political truth had two apparently opposite but intimately connected and unfortunate consequences, as Strauss saw it. One was that it encouraged a kind of decisionism, such as is found in many continental philosophic movements of the twentieth century, existentialism for example. In the face of the groundlessness of moral and political choice, what counts is "commitment," the decision itself, not the substance of what is decided for. Intrinsic merits of political and moral choices were held to be beyond debate: justice, moderation, and sobriety, traits once held to be sine qua nons of responsible action, were not merely no longer favored; they were positively disfavored as signs of lukewarmness or weakness of will. Understanding them to be responding in this way to "the crisis of our time," Strauss was not surprised to see great thinkers at the "end of philosophy," like Heidegger, support Hitler and the Nazis.

toleration

The other political and moral outcome of radical historicism was loss of faith in any moral truths and the adoption of a passionless lack of commitment to anything but toleration. Strauss never denied that toleration was a virtue, but he shared, in this case, Nietzsche's revulsion against the "last man," who said "we invented happiness" but who knew nothing of striving, of the search for excellence, of sacrifice or commitment to anything beyond reality T.V. or Monday night Football.[20] This lack of commitment, which Strauss's student Allan Bloom called "flatness," not only emptied human life of its higher callings, but also endangered the societies that fell prey to it, because life poses challenges not well met by those who look no further than comfort and entertainment.

Strauss came to see that this crisis, in both its philosophical and its political aspects, derived from modern philosophy's great act of rebellion against classical philosophy and biblical religion. The founders of modernity, thinkers like Machiavelli, Hobbes, and Spinoza, set mankind on a path that, via an almost inexorable dialectic, produced the end of philosophy and the "last man" as announced and diagnosed by Nietzsche. If modernity was at the bottom of the problem, then, Strauss concluded, the proper response was a retreat or a return to premodernity. Strauss's first efforts at return were to call for a return not to the ancients themselves, but to the "medieval enlightenment," as developed by the Jewish thinker Moses Maimonides, to whom he paid abiding and recurrent attention throughout his long scholarly career. Strauss's turn to Maimonides proved, however, to be a step on his way to Plato and Socrates.

Strauss's Way Back to Ancient Political Philosophy

Strauss recognized that by arguing that Spinoza and other representatives of the modern Enlightenment could not disprove revelation with reason, he had, in one sense, proved too much. The argument that insulated revelation from reason on account of the nonrational foundation of revelation effectively insulated any form of orthodoxy or, we might say, any explicitly nonrational commitment from rational criticism.[21] Seeking an understanding of the world and human life that both admitted its limitations vis-à-vis the claims of Scripture and yet claimed to be based entirely on reason, Strauss turned away from the atheism of Spinoza and Nietzsche to investigate the character and grounds of the premodern rationalism of Spinoza's great predecessor, the medieval Jewish philosopher Maimonides.[22] Strauss's study of Maimonides led him to read the works of Maimonides' teacher, the Islamic philosopher al Farabi. Strauss's studies of Farabi brought him, in turn, to a very untraditional understanding of Plato, which caused him to suggest a new interpretation of the Western philosophical tradition in opposition to those thinkers—Hegel, Marx, Nietzsche, and Heidegger—who had argued that it had, in one way or another, come to an end.

When he wrote his Spinoza book, Strauss later revealed, he had not believed a return to premodern philosophy was possible.[23] In his first book on Arabic and Jewish philosophy, *Philosophy and Law*, Strauss himself stated some obvious objections to an embrace of premodern rationalism. He identified three concerns that seemed to speak against a return to the rationalism of a thinker like Maimonides:

1. Is not the enlightenment of Maimonides the precursor and model of the Enlightenment of the seventeenth and eighteenth centuries? If so, how can one get beyond the modern Enlightenment by returning to its source?
2. Does not the philosophy of Maimonides and Farabi rest on the unrestorable cosmology of Aristotle? Like Christian medieval thinkers, Maimonides and Farabi found it difficult to reconcile Aristotle with Scripture, especially the account of creation in Genesis. Modern natural science poses a similar but perhaps even more insurmountable barrier, for it makes it all but impossible to accept Aristotle's view of the eternity of the world and the species, or his natural teleology.
3. Is not Maimonides' rationalism undercut by his dubious allegorical method of interpretation, which treats any nonrational element in Scripture as an image or metaphor? The so-called higher criticism presented a much more scientific, historically grounded account of the discrepancies in the text of the Bible.

Strauss's answer to all three of his own questions was, eventually, no.

Even in the 1930s Strauss had a ready and relatively easy answer to the first objection: the enlightenment of Maimonides was not the forerunner of the seventeenth- and eighteenth-century Enlightenment, because Maimonides did not require or endorse an attack on religious faith in the name of reason.[24] On the contrary, Maimonides attempted to show rationally that the teachings of the Bible, for example, the Ten Commandments, constituted the necessary grounds for establishing and maintaining the kind of society that makes not only moral but also intellectual virtue possible. Maimonides interpreted the first five commandments, or the first "table," as an order that people should come to know God to the best of their ability; he understood the second set of commands, or second "table," as a specification of the moral requirements for the preservation of any kind of human community. Since not everyone received an immediate revelation, most people would learn about God by following the law, as it was explicated by others who had more opportunity for study. The Maimonidean enlightenment did not produce the critique, nor aim at the thorough-going reformation of public opinion and reigning morality, nor foster the technology, which together had constituted the ill consequences of the eighteenth-century Enlightenment.

Strauss found it more difficult to overcome the second obstacle to a return to Maimonides' enlightenment, the impossibility of resurrecting Aristotelian cosmology in the face of modern natural science. It took him many years to work out a complicated response.

Unlike some of his students (or his students' students), Strauss did not try to resurrect Aristotelian natural science by showing that it is compatible with modern natural science.[25] He came to think that would not be necessary, even if it were possible. Further study of Maimonides and Farabi convinced Strauss that they were not so much Aristotelian as Platonic philosophers. They did not deduce the characteristics or qualities of the best human life from an understanding of the natural order as a whole. Nor did they propagate Plato's doctrine of the ideas. They adopted Plato's political presentation and function of philosophy and adapted them to their own circumstances.[26] At first they appeared to suggest that the philosopher needed to justify his search for wisdom to the authorities by showing how it could improve the life of the community as a whole. But in Farabi's *Plato*, Strauss observed, the justification for philosophy did not depend finally upon such service. Philosophy, as represented by Plato's Socrates, constituted a fully satisfying form of human existence that could be enjoyed by private individuals in less-than-perfect regimes. Based entirely on reason, Socratic philosophy nevertheless involved something less than a claim to full knowledge.[27] Insofar as Socrates' wisdom consisted in his knowledge that he did not know the most important things, it did not require him to deny the existence of any superhuman powers or divinities. Socratic rationalism was thus different from modern Enlightenment rationalism. Explicitly lacking knowledge of the most important things, Socrates did not affirm the truth of any particular account of the cosmic order, although he did have to be able to show why no available account was entirely satisfactory in order to maintain his paradoxical claim that he *knew* that he did not know. Since modern natural science also explicitly provides less than full knowledge of the whole, Socratic philosophy was compatible with it in a way Aristotelian cosmology was not.[28]

In *Philosophy and Law* Strauss had concluded that Farabi and Maimonides began with an essentially Aristotelian understanding of the
cosmos and reinterpreted Islamic and Jewish law in light of that understanding in order to establish and preserve the conditions, especially the
moral beliefs, necessary to maintain political order. He later came to see,
however, that Maimonides' teacher Farabi had followed Plato, not Aristotle, in thinking that philosophy consisted in the search for wisdom, not
in contemplation of the eternal beings. Farabi, moreover, had followed a
Plato very different from the Plato normally understood in the Western tradition, which had been influenced by neo-Platonism and then by the Christian appropriation of Plato and Platonism. The "traditional" Plato is the
Plato familiar in introductory philosophy presentations. He is a believer
in suprasensible, disembodied "forms" or "ideas," which are the true beings, of which the beings we experience are mere reflections or imitations.
He is a believer in a soul separate from the body. He is the advocate of
the rule of philosophers and the devotee of an extraordinarily high-minded
moral doctrine. This traditional understanding of Plato appeared to have
support in the Platonic texts; in the *Republic*, for example, the philosophers' knowledge of the eternal ideas is posited as the basis for their claim
to sovereignty.

Strauss's rediscovery of "Farabi's Plato" was based on a subtle analysis
of Farabi's tripartite work *The Aims of the Philosophy of Plato and Aristotle*.
There Farabi argued that happiness is the aim of human life, according to
both ancient philosophers. Since man's perfection and thus his happiness
consist in philosophy, and since, as the fate of Socrates makes clear, philosophy arouses political opposition, Plato taught that it was necessary to seek
a city different from the cities that existed in his time: "the city in speech"
of the *Republic*, where the philosophers rule. At least that was what Farabi
seemed to say at the beginning of his treatise on Plato. But Farabi proceeded to show Strauss that this was but a surface impression. Farabi provided a number of grounds on which to challenge the textbook version
of Plato's *Republic*. Having initially claimed that Plato thought philosophy needed to be supplemented by a royal art in order for human beings
to attain happiness, Strauss pointed out, Farabi then stated that Plato
"teaches that philosophy does not need to be supplemented by something
else in order to produce happiness." Farabi's second statement thus contra-
dicted what he had said at first. Having first suggested that the happiness
of the philosophers, as well as of their fellow citizens, depended upon the
establishment of the perfect city, that is, the city of the philosopher-kings,
moreover, "toward the end of the treatise, Farabi ma[de] it absolutely clear

that there can be, not only philosophers, but completely perfect human beings...in imperfect cities." Philosophers do not need to rule in order to
achieve their end. Philosophers can live and even thrive as members of imperfect regimes.[29]

Nor did Farabi think that the happiness of the philosopher depended
upon his contemplating eternally existing, unchanging beings, as Plato
seemed to affirm. Although he purportedly summarized the *Phaedrus*,
the *Phaedo*, and the *Republic*, Strauss pointed out, Farabi did not mention the immortality of the soul or the unchanging Platonic ideas. Yet
Farabi had claimed to present "the philosophy of Plato, its parts, and
the grades of dignity of its parts, from its beginning to its end." How
then could Farabi leave out topics so prominent in the dialogues he was
interpreting, topics that were apparently so central to Platonic philosophy? Strauss concluded that when Farabi omitted a topic, this meant that
he thought it was unimportant or merely an exoteric (surface) doctrine.
Farabi saw that to avoid being persecuted for impiety like Socrates, Plato
and philosophers in general had to claim not only that they could help
their fellow citizens live better, but also that the philosophers themselves
believed in eternal beings and in an afterlife. Writing in his own name
in the preface to *The Aims*, Farabi thus distinguished "the happiness of
this world" from "the ultimate happiness in the other life." In the central
chapter of *The Aims* on Plato, however, he silently dropped this distinction. And, Strauss pointed out, "in his commentary on the *Nicomachean
Ethics* [in part 3] he declare[d] that there is only the happiness of this life
and that all divergent statements are based on 'ravings and old women's
tales.'"[30]

Farabi could express such impious views without fear of persecution,
Strauss suggested, because as a commentator, Farabi was not explicitly
presenting his own views. Strauss nonetheless thought he could discern
Farabi's own views and his deeper understanding of Plato's views through
his subtle way of presenting the Platonic philosophy. Even as a commentator, Farabi was not simply summarizing what Plato wrote. In the *Phaedrus,*
the *Phaedo,* and the *Republic*, Plato had explicitly argued for the immortality of the soul and hence some kind of afterlife, which brought him very
close to the orthodox doctrines of Farabi's society. That is to say, Farabi
was almost "compelled [by the Platonic texts] to embrace a tolerably orthodox doctrine concerning the life after death." By choosing to attribute another opinion to the philosopher he most highly revered, "Farabi avail[ed]
himself then of the specific immunity of a commentator, or of the historian,
in order to speak his own mind."[31]

Strauss thought that he had learned from Farabi's *Plato* that the goodness of a philosophic way of life does not depend upon the possibility of human beings' attaining complete theoretical knowledge. It was possible, therefore, to revive Platonic political philosophy without insisting on or even affirming the truth of Aristotelian cosmology in the face of modern physics. The model of the philosophic life is Socrates, not Aristotle. In Plato's *Apology*, Socrates tells his Athenian jurors that the Delphic oracle declared him to be the wisest, because he at least knows that he does not know. (Knowing that one does not know is, of course, not knowing nothing; one has to know, among other things, what it is to know.) Socrates recognized that his fellow citizens might find his story about the oracle ironic. All he claimed to know on the basis of his own experience was that the "unexamined life is not worth living, but to make speeches every day about virtue and the other things about which you hear me conversing is the greatest good for a human being." Whether or not Socrates ever attained the knowledge he sought, Plato's presentation of his life represented the contention that philosophy is a way of life, is *the* form of human life that is by nature best. If that claim can be made good, it constitutes a decisive response to Nietzsche and modern nihilism, without requiring questionable metaphysics or cosmology. Plato's depiction of Socrates represents in deed, as it were, the proposition that human beings can discover the right way of life on the basis of their natural reason alone. To provide a foundation or rationale for morality, it is not necessary to appeal to divine revelation, to an Aristotelian cosmology, or to an inexplicable historical "dispensation" of Being or fate.[32]

The third reason the young Strauss had thought it would be impossible to revive the rationalism of Maimonides was Maimonides' purported method of reading the Bible. Having shown that the medieval enlightenment was not the forerunner of the modern Enlightenment, and that the political philosophy of Maimonides and his teacher Farabi did not rest on the unrestorable cosmology of Aristotle, Strauss finally argued that a restoration of the rationalism of Maimonides did not require endorsing the highly dubious method of allegorical interpretation that had been attributed to him. That method involved reading any biblical statement that was contrary to reason or inconsistent with other statements as metaphorical or allegorical.

Strauss's later readings of Maimonides and Farabi convinced him that these medieval philosophers were not simply trying to rationalize the thought of the prophets, who claimed to have been divinely inspired. On the contrary, Strauss argued in his 1952 book *Persecution and the Art of*

Writing, Maimonides and Farabi used a series of complex devices to hide their radical philosophical conclusions from all but the most discerning readers. They did all this in order to maintain, rationalize, and so improve the moral doctrines to which most members of their communities continued to subscribe. Not a dubious allegorical method of interpretation, but what Strauss called "a forgotten kind of writing" was at the heart of the medieval enlightenment.[33]

Nothing has proved more controversial in Strauss's own work than his analyses of esotericism, of secret writing or secret teaching. Strauss's suggestion that earlier thinkers did not state all their views openly has led to accusations that he immorally endorsed lying as well as elitism. Nonetheless, few of his critics would contest Strauss's initial observation that philosophers in the past did not write with the protection of the First Amendment; philosophers often did have reason to fear persecution for their views. As Strauss reminds his readers, Anaxagoras, Protagoras, Plato, Xenophon, Socrates, Aristotle, Avicenna, Averroes, Maimonides, Grotius, Descartes, Hobbes, Spinoza, Locke, Bayle, Wolff, Montesquieu, Voltaire, Rousseau, Lessing, and Kant had all been threatened, if not actually persecuted, for undermining the established order—political and religious.[34] Few of Strauss's critics could contest his further observation that public prohibition and the threat of persecution were not able to prevent some people from thinking thoughts that had been proscribed. The question that divides Strauss from his critics concerns whether, and how, proscribed thoughts can be communicated.

The fact that so many philosophers had been threatened with persecution suggested that their contemporaries suspected that these philosophers did not hold simply orthodox or acceptable opinions, Strauss pointed out. Until the nineteenth century and the emergence of a "scientific" study of history, many commentators had thought that Thomas Hobbes, for example, was an atheist. But nineteenth-century scholars of intellectual history decided that authors' views must be determined solely on the basis of what they said, not what they implied, and that when they said different or contradictory things, what the authors said most frequently had to be taken as most indicative of what they actually thought. Such principles were put forth as the necessary canons of "objective" or scientific interpretation. Commentators then became resistant to the idea that authors did not always express openly and explicitly everything they thought, but sometimes wrote "between the lines." Yet, Strauss observed, one way an author could evade official censorship was to repeat accepted opinions frequently and then only occasionally indicate that he did not agree with them. To be sure, the reader who suspected an author of unorthodoxy would face the same difficulty as the censor in attempting to prove it. Writing and hence reading was an art, not a science.

Nevertheless, Strauss suggested two or three rules of thumb for judging whether an author was engaging in esoteric writing. First and most important, readers should not look for writing "between the lines" until they had completely mastered the "lines," that is, not only the explicit arguments but also the organization or plan of the work and its literary form of presentation. If an author wrote dialogues, for example, her or his views should not be assumed to be the same as those of any character. Second, if an author is suspected of having written between the lines in order to avoid persecution, that author needs to have written "at a time when some political or other orthodoxy was enforced by custom or law." Third, if "an able writer who has a clear mind and a perfect knowledge of the orthodox view" obviously contradicts that view, its necessary presuppositions, or his own restatements of that view, readers have reason to look "between the lines."[35] Although Strauss and his students have frequently been accused of giving "ahistorical" readings of past authors, the mode of reading Strauss recommends requires the student to look at, but not surrender to, the context in which an author wrote. What Strauss refused to concede, and more "historical" commentators tend to assert, is that works by the greatest minds merely reflect, or are addressed solely to, the opinions and concerns of their contemporaries.[36]

Persecution was, however, only the first and not the most fundamental reason Strauss thought past authors had concealed or misrepresented some of what they believed to be true. There were two others. First, philosophers in the past had tried to soften, if not to avoid, the corrosive effects philosophical questioning could have on the foundations of public morality. Second, Strauss maintained, following Socrates in Plato's *Phaedrus*, thought cannot actually be directly communicated in or by writing. What the greatest philosophers attempted to do in their writings was not merely or even primarily to present doctrines; rather they were trying to provoke their readers to think the problems out for themselves.[37]

A century after Nietzsche proclaimed that "God is dead" and that "we have killed him," it would hardly seem shocking for a student of the history of philosophy to observe that questioning the truth of widely held opinions can have serious effects on the foundations of public morality. Pre-Nietzschean philosophers had not always said or written everything they thought, Strauss believed, not merely to protect themselves from persecution but to preserve the healthy beliefs that make public order possible and life more meaningful for individuals.

Since it has been Strauss's suggestion that philosophers did not merely perpetuate salutary public opinions but even, like Plato, composed "likely stories," "noble lies," and "myths" that has aroused the most hostility in recent years, it is important to note that he distinguished between ancient and modern philosophy in this respect. Modern political philosophers like Hobbes and Montesquieu attempted to veil from public censors, if not entirely to hide, their own lack of orthodox Christian belief. Because they were "Enlightenment" philosophers who also thought that public order would be more, not less, secure and just if people held true opinions, these modern philosophers attempted to publish as much of the truth as they thought they safely could. Ancient philosophers saw things differently. "They believed that the gulf separating 'the wise' from 'the vulgar' was a basic fact of human nature," which could not be influenced by any progress of popular education. The gap was not merely a result of differences in natural aptitude, although these existed. People also needed to have the leisure provided by a certain amount of wealth and the opportunity, skills, books, and teachers to acquire the education required to engage in philosophical investigations. As Alexis de Tocqueville also observed, most people have to act on the basis of opinion, not knowledge, about most things most of the time. Few have the leisure or inclination to examine their own fundamental beliefs; most find it unproductive and frustrating when they or others do so.[38] This frustration often gives rise to anger, if not to hatred of philosophy. Even the greatest thinkers, who have devoted their entire lives to determining whether there is a god or a soul or an intelligible ordering of the universe, have not been able to agree with one another on answers to these fundamental questions. Philosophy thus can appear to be useless and ineffective, and the fruitless shaking of belief to be destructive.

"Every decent modern reader is bound to be shocked by the mere suggestion that a great man might have deliberately deceived the large majority of his readers," Strauss acknowledged.[39] But, he suggested, what is stridently called lying might as well be described as acting, or writing in a socially responsible manner. Thinkers should not undermine, much less destroy, healthy beliefs if they cannot replace them with even more beneficial opinions. They ought to exercise this kind of responsible self-restraint, because it is impossible for large numbers of people to possess or act on the basis of knowledge, strictly speaking. The "deceit" in which some philosophers engaged thus consisted in not openly challenging views conducive to the preservation of social and political order. It did not consist in a "manipulation" of the masses to get them to think what philosophers wanted them to think or to enable the philosophers to rule. Philosophers are not and never have been media stars; in all times and places they have written for a restricted audience.[40] Nor did the ancient and medieval philosophers who wrote "between the lines" seek to rule. On the contrary, following his understanding of Plato, Strauss insisted that philosophers qua philosophers do not want to rule.[41]

Ancient philosophers did not write "between the lines" to mold public opinion or to attain power, but because the truth cannot be directly communicated. No reader will understand any work of philosophy if he does not try to think the problems and arguments through for himself.[42] No philosopher can simply transmit the truth to her readers. Although Strauss believed that the ancient philosophers were closer to the truth than the moderns, he explicitly recognized that in thinking through a problem, a reader needed to consider all of the possible or proposed solutions. Therefore, he urged his readers to study the conflict or debates between the ancients and the moderns, the philosophers and the poets, and reason and revelation. We learn from studying the great works of Western philosophy, according to Strauss, that our highest knowledge reveals what the insoluble problems are and why they are insoluble. It is impossible to think about these problems without becoming inclined toward a solution, he admitted. But the philosopher "ceases to be a philosopher at the moment at which the subjective certainty of a solution becomes stronger than his awareness of the problematic character of that solution."[43]

Strauss's philosophy is therefore not dogmatic in any sense. In particular, he is far from the dogmatic atheist he is now frequently accused of being. He thought that the vitality of the West depended upon keeping alive the tension between "Jerusalem" (or belief in the truth of Scripture) and "Athens" (belief in reason). "The core, the nerve of Western intellectual history, Western spiritual history, one could almost say, is the conflict between the biblical and the philosophical notions of the good life . . . this unresolved conflict is the secret of the vitality of Western civilization."[44]

Although Strauss conceded that reading esoteric texts poses great difficulties for modern readers, he believed that recognition of the character of esotericism saved the ancients and medievals from some of the more obvious difficulties and objections raised against them. It also supplied the only path back to the true grasp of premodern thought. The discovery of esotericism was, in a sense, both a prerequisite and a consequence of Strauss's project of return.

Like Plato, who wrote dialogues and not treatises, Strauss did not publish straightforward arguments in his own name; rather he presented the debates among the thinkers. The intent in every case was to invite his readers to engage in the argument, to expose his readers to the best possible defense of each alternative, to enable them, if they were willing and able to expend the time and effort, to understand just what the problem or the difficulty was. His aim was not, as some of his critics (Shadia Drury in particular) have claimed, to hide behind the many authors about whom he has written to avoid presenting his own allegedly nihilistic teaching directly.[45] Such critics have ignored not only Strauss's early critiques of Nietzsche, but also his own statements concerning his educational goals.

In an essay, "What Is Liberal Education," in which he explicitly took his bearings from Plato, Strauss declared: "Philosophy is quest for wisdom or quest for knowledge regarding the most important, the highest, or the most comprehensive things; such knowledge, Plato suggested, is virtue and happiness. But wisdom is inaccessible to man, and hence virtue and happiness will always be imperfect." From studying Plato, we learn that "we cannot be philosophers . . . , but we can love philosophy; we can try to philosophize. This philosophizing consists . . . primarily and in a way chiefly in listening to the conversation between the great philosophers or . . . the greatest minds, and therefore in studying the great books."[46] That is what Strauss did and what he urged his students to do. It is the reason Strauss's students have produced so many new translations and interpretations of classic works of political philosophy. It is the reason they continue to argue about whether he was a believer or, if not, exactly what his stance toward revealed religion was.

Strauss's Rereading of the History of Philosophy

A barrier to the project of return to the ancients that Strauss did not mention in his *Philosophy and Law*, but which must have been on his mind, was the common view that the history of philosophy seemed to be progressive and therefore that a "return" in philosophy makes as much sense as a return, say, to the medical science of Galen. As Charles Larmore put it in a response to Strauss, later philosophers pointed out the problems in the thought of their predecessors and then solved them more adequately.[47] Aristotle was superior to Plato, and Descartes to Aristotle. But Strauss's rereading of Plato under the influence of Farabi had led him to take a much less progressive, less determined view of the history of thought. Philosophy was not progressive; on the contrary, something essential had been lost.

Strauss concluded that a wholly new construal of its history was required as a consequence of his discovery of the true meaning and nature of ancient philosophy and, therefore, also for the break with it.

If the Farabian rather than the textbook version was the true interpretation of the ancients, Strauss concluded, we needed to look at the history of Western philosophy anew. To the extent to which modern philosophers like Machiavelli and Hobbes rejected the ancient understanding of politics because of its unrealistic goals, for example, the establishment of the philosopher-kings of the *Republic*, they were reacting primarily to and against a misunderstanding. Machiavelli was not correct to turn his back on all such "imaginary republics and principalities" simply because they were imaginary. Ancient philosophers had presented the limits of politics in light of the higher and ultimately greater satisfactions of the philosophical life and the guidance that life provided for ordinary moral and political life. Not only had modern philosophers misunderstood or mistaken the character of ancient proposals for the rule of philosophers, but these modern philosophers also had a different project or goal in mind. They did not think that the happiness of a few philosophers was enough. They wanted to do more for more people. The only effective political science, they argued, had to be based on the passions common to all. Rather than urge human beings to pursue goals that few, if any, could ever achieve, these philosophers decided it would be better to lower their sights. In other words, they made a fundamental choice. In order to have both a greater and a more sure or predictable effect, they urged political men to take their bearings by what was common rather than by what was exceptional in human beings, a path that would more certainly achieve the desired results, peace and prosperity.

If modern philosophy was a result of a choice to pursue lower goals that were more likely to be achieved rather than higher, nobler but more improbable human possibilities, Strauss saw, the history of philosophy was not a product of a logical process or some other necessity, as Hegel, Marx, Nietzsche, and Heidegger had all argued.[48] Strauss identified Machiavelli as the "founder" of modern philosophy. He thought the nature of Machiavelli's break with the thought of the past was easy to misunderstand, however. In response to those like Eric Voegelin, who argued that Machiavelli's thought (like modernity in general) had to be understood as the result of a historical synthesis of biblical notions and ancient Greek rationalism, Strauss argued that there was very little of the distinctively scriptural in the thought or the politics advocated by the author of *The Prince*. As evidence for his claim, Voegelin pointed out that Machiavelli called the founders of new modes and orders "armed prophets." But, Strauss retorted, Machiavelli emphasized their being armed more than their being prophets.[49] In his claim to bring "new modes and orders," Strauss nevertheless admitted, Machiavelli himself was, like Jesus, an *unarmed* prophet. The *only* insight Machiavelli took from Christianity, Strauss insisted, was the possibility of overthrowing the reigning world order by popularizing a new moral teaching. By secularizing the promise of instituting a new order through spreading the news, that is, his new gospel, Machiavelli became the founder or harbinger of the modern Enlightenment.[50]

Machiavelli went well beyond "Averroists" like Farabi and Maimonides, who had reinterpreted revelatory texts so as to make them conducive both to the maintenance of political order and to the achievement of true human happiness through philosophy.[51] Instead, Machiavelli openly and directly attacked Christianity for its deleterious political effects. He did not concern himself about the fate of philosophy; he explicitly sought to revive the ancient political virtue that had apparently been wiped out by the spread of Christianity.[52] The founders of the modern Enlightenment like Machiavelli, Hobbes, and Spinoza also brought to the fore the fundamentally irrational character of the doctrines of revealed religion. They sought, indeed, to mock and to laugh revealed religion out of existence, since they could not, in fact, rationally disprove its claims about explicitly irrational phenomena like miracles.[53]

Strauss's rereading of the history of philosophy also led him to see that the moderns had introduced a wholly new understanding of the relation between theory and practice. Medieval rationalists, like Aristotle before them, taught that moral and political legislation served to establish the necessary conditions not merely for living, but for living well, both for the members of political communities, taken as a whole, and for the few individuals who had the talent and opportunity to philosophize. Modern Enlightenment philosophers, by contrast, argued that science was valuable insofar as it helped people satisfy their common bodily desires for comfort and safety more effectively. The moderns dropped the distinction between living and living well, as well as the concern with philosophy as the peak mode of human existence. Modern philosophers tended to present theory solely as a means of achieving better practice, defined not in terms of the moral character or relations among citizens, but in terms of the more palpable outcomes of peace and prosperity.

Strauss argued that as a result of the fundamental change in the understanding of the relation between theory and practice, later modern philosophers had lost sight of that form of human life that is truly satisfying and did not sufficiently take account of their own activity as philosophers. The inversion of the ancient understanding of the relation between theory and practice that occurred when the medieval enlightenment was replaced by modern rationalism was the source of its nihilistic conclusion that there is nothing, especially no form of human life, that is worthwhile in and of itself. Rather than constituting an expansion or correction of ancient philosophy on the basis of ideas derived from Scripture, Strauss concluded, the origins of the modern Enlightenment in the works of Machiavelli involved a severe constriction of the possibilities envisioned in both traditions. The character of that constriction was indicated by Machiavelli's use of Xenophon, the only ancient Greek author to whom he repeatedly referred. Whereas Xenophon's own works moved between the two poles or possibilities of theory and practice represented by Socrates and the Persian king Cyrus, Machiavelli took note of only one of the poles. He ignored the Socratic alternative, the alternative Strauss himself tried to reintroduce.[54]

Political Philosophy and Politics

In attempting to revive a Socratic understanding of philosophy as a *quest* for the truth rather than a set of doctrines, Strauss could not but be reminded of the tension that had existed historically between politics and philosophy. The city of Athens had convicted Socrates of a capital crime and killed him. Enlightenment thinkers had hoped to eliminate the phenomenon of the political persecution of philosophy by establishing political order on the basis of the truth. Even these Enlightenment thinkers recognized limits to their enterprise, however. The best possible outcome would be a regime based on true opinion—and opinion, even true opinion, is not the same as knowledge. As opinion, it is more subject to change and is especially vulnerable to the force of the passions. History revealed that the vulnerabilities of liberal enlightenment regimes were even greater than their original projectors suspected.

Having witnessed the rise of both Nazi Germany and the Soviet Union, Strauss thought that no one in the twentieth century could reasonably deny that persecution for questioning official dogma was still a fact of political life. The twentieth century had, indeed, given rise to the specter of an even worse form of persecution than any that had previously existed. Philosophy, as the open-minded quest for truth, might be entirely suppressed and destroyed by rulers claiming to act on the basis of the "true philosophy," that is, the ruling ideology, that they already possessed. Far from solving the problem of persecution, the modern world had made it potentially much worse. "If philosophers were confronted with claims of this kind in former ages, philosophy went underground. It accommodated itself in its explicit or exoteric teaching to the unfounded commands of rulers who believed they knew things which they did not know. Yet its very exoteric teaching undermined the commands or dogmas of the rulers in such a way as to guide the potential philosophers toward the eternal and unsolved problems. And since there was no universal state in existence, the philosophers could escape to other countries." Insofar as they claim to be based on a universally valid truth, modern regimes are not particularistic in the way ancient regimes were. If one of these modern regimes should succeed in making good its claim to universal rule, there would no longer be any possibility of escape. Not only would there be a single empire, but that empire would also have ways of detecting and silencing dissent that the ancient despots could not have imagined. "Thanks to the conquest of nature and to the completely unabashed substitution of suspicion and terror for law the Universal and Final Tyrant has at his disposal practically unlimited means for ferreting out, and for extinguishing, the most modest efforts in the direction of thought."[55] Insofar as Strauss was concerned with the preservation of philosophy, he was necessarily concerned about protecting it from destruction. That meant he had to be concerned about politics. In particular, it meant that he had to oppose—both philosophically and politically—the arguments and the actions of those who were seeking to establish a universal, homogeneous state, as his dialogic partner, Alexander Kojeve, formulated the implicit goal of modern, especially Communist polities. During the cold war Strauss thus became an unabashed partisan of liberal democracy in opposition to Communism, and political in his focus in a way that other leading philosophers of the twentieth century had not been.

Philosophers did not need to become interested in politics merely in order to protect themselves from persecution, according to Strauss. It might seem that philosophers qua philosophers need not be concerned about politics in order to be philosophers. There were, after all, not only the twentieth-century thinkers Strauss had explicitly mentioned as having little, if any, concern with politics; there was also the entire pre-Socratic tradition. Following Cicero, Strauss pointed out that Socrates had "brought philosophy down from the heavens." That is, Socrates had been not the first philosopher, but the first political philosopher.[56] Nevertheless, Strauss thought, Socrates had been correct in seeing the need for philosophy to become political. Philosophers seek knowledge of the whole. The philosopher himself, or more broadly, humanity, is not merely a part of the whole, however; the philosopher is a particularly central or significant part, because human beings are the only parts of the whole that raise the question about the whole. The first commandment of the philosophic life thus becomes "know thyself." Humanity exists first and foremost within social and political orders. To understand themselves, philosophers thus had to understand the social and political life of human beings, and how the life or the questioning of the philosopher relates to this universal and, in a sense, defining feature of human existence.

Strauss did not think that philosophers were interested in their fellows merely as a part of their own search for knowledge, however. Nor did he think that they had to concern themselves about the lives of their neighbors merely as a means of providing themselves with the necessities of life as well as a modicum of legal protection. On the contrary, he observes, philosophers were moved by "a natural attachment of man to man which is prior to any calculation of mutual benefit." Indeed, Strauss pointed out, because "the philosopher is immune to the most common and the most powerful dissolvent" of the natural attachment human beings feel for others, the desire to have more (*pleonexia*) than others do, "the philosopher will not hurt anyone. While he cannot help being more attached to his family and his city than to strangers,... his benevolence... extends to all human beings." Political life may be a prerequisite for the emergence and sustenance of the philosophic life and in this sense a means to the philosophical peak of human existence, but that does not mean that fostering philosophy is all that political life is good for, or that the moral virtue required to lead a successful practical life is only for the sake, and in the service, of the philosophic life.[57]

In his essay "On Plato's *Republic*," Strauss points out, Socrates shows that democracy is, in many respects, the regime most conducive to philosophy. "Democracy... is characterized by freedom which includes the right to say and do whatever one wishes: everyone can follow the way of life which pleases him most.... Hence we must understand, democracy is the only regime other than the best in which the philosopher can lead his peculiar way of life without being disturbed."[58] Yet, Strauss also points out, Socrates does not recommend democracy as the best—or even the second-best—regime. "The reason is that, being a just man in more than one sense, he thought of the well-being not merely of the philosophers but of the non-philosophers as well."[59] Strauss agrees with Socrates that the good of the philosopher is not the whole or even the decisive end of the city, nor does the philosopher's good set the criteria in terms of which political regimes are judged.

Correctly noting that Strauss affirms philosophy as the peak of human existence, Drury is quite mistaken in concluding that he says philosophers have no respect for morality, are not bound by morality, and are not moral themselves. He never said, as she and many others now claim, that philosophers are immune from the requirements of morality. On the contrary, he argued that precisely because political association and the rules of morality needed to maintain it are necessary conditions for the possibility of philosophy, the philosopher above all must respect those rules. Strauss points out that "the Socratic formula for genuine virtue is: virtue is knowledge." In seeking knowledge, the philosopher cannot help, therefore, but seek to become virtuous as well.[60] In the *Republic* Socrates argues that individuals with philosophical natures possess all the virtues as a result of their overwhelming desire for truth. Seeking truth above all else, they are not tempted to be immoderate or unjust by taking more than their share or seizing the goods of others. Recognizing that all sensible things must pass away, they are not afraid in the face of death. The philosopher's overwhelming desire for truth not only frees him from the desires for wealth, power, and status or recognition that lead most other human beings to be immoral. Taking pleasure in his progress toward knowledge, a philosopher takes pleasure in his increasing virtue at the same time. A philosopher does not, in other words, experience virtue—or the attempt to become virtuous—as a constraint on his strongest passion.[61] Strauss does not agree with Drury, however, that the pleasure a philosopher experiences turns him into a hedonist, indistinguishable in principle and practice from the grossest debauchee or sybarite.[62] On the contrary, Strauss often pointed out, the man he took to be exemplary of the philosophical life, Socrates, was extraordinarily ascetic.

Nor, taking Socrates as his model, did Strauss think that the need for philosophy to become political meant that philosophers had to rule. On the contrary, Strauss insisted: "To see the classical view in the proper light, [it is necessary to remember] that the wise do not desire to rule."[63] To be sure, in his essay "On Plato's *Republic*," Strauss recognized, Socrates had argued that evils in cities would not cease until philosophers became kings or kings became philosophers. But, Strauss also pointed out, in the *Republic* Socrates emphasized that philosophers did not want to rule; they would be the only just rulers precisely because they were the only people who could not attain or hope to attain what they wanted by means of rule. Philosophers could justly be compelled to rule only in a city that had provided them with the education enabling them to become philosophers. It was unlikely that they would be externally compelled to rule in any existing city, however, because most people outside the just city would continue to believe that philosophers were at best useless.

Literally, moreover, no one can be forced to rule. Philosophers are just human beings, however, and there is such a thing as self-compulsion. "It should not be necessary," Strauss added, "but it is necessary to add that compulsion does not cease to be compulsion if it is self-compulsion." But would a philosopher in a less-than-perfectly-just regime feel obliged to rule? "According to a notion of justice which is more common than the one referred to in Socrates' definition," Strauss observed, "justice consists in not harming others; justice thus understood proves to be in the highest case merely a concomitant of the philosopher's greatness of soul." He does not do evil, but he is not compelled positively to seek to do good. "But if justice is taken in the larger sense according to which it consists in giving to each what is good for his soul, one must distinguish between the cases in which such giving is intrinsically attractive to the giver (these will be the cases of the potential philosophers) and those in which it is merely a duty or compulsory." In the *Republic*, "the clear distinction between the justice which is choiceworthy for its own sake wholly regardless of its consequences, and identical with philosophy, and the justice which is merely necessary, and identical in the highest imaginable case with the rule of the philosopher, is rendered possible by the abstraction from *eros*."[64]

If philosophers' overwhelming desire to acquire knowledge were taken into account, it would be clear that no philosophers would choose to spend their time attending to public business and hence, of necessity, giving up the leisure necessary to pursue wisdom, their own greatest love. That does not mean that they would not attempt to help their fellow citizens. "There is no reason why the philosopher should not engage in political activity out of that kind of love of one's own which is patriotism." That is what Socrates did when he went to his fellow citizens in private to reproach them for seeking wealth, honor, and safety rather than truth, prudence, and the good of their souls or when he willingly served the city in war.[65] Political activity and rule are not synonymous.[66] Socrates never went into the public assembly or sought to rule. Had he done so, he states in both the *Republic* (496a–e) and his *Apology* (31c–32a), he would not have survived. In *On Tyranny* Strauss points out that, like Socrates, "the philosopher must go to the marketplace in order to fish there for potential philosophers. His attempts to convert young men to the philosophic life will necessarily be regarded by the city as an attempt to corrupt the young. The philosopher is therefore forced to defend the cause of philosophy. He must therefore act upon the city or upon the ruler." But that does not mean "the philosopher must desire to determine or codetermine the politics of the city or of the rulers." On the contrary, "there is no necessary connection between the philosopher's indispensable philosophic politics and the efforts which he might or might not make to contribute toward the establishment of the best regime. For philosophy and philosophic education are possible in all kinds of more or less imperfect regimes."[67]

The classical view of politics that Strauss advocated involved a recognition that since the wise will not rule, government ought to be limited, and those limits should take the form of laws. On the basis of that observation, Strauss concluded that "liberal or constitutional democracy comes closer to what the classics demanded than any alternative that is viable in our age."[68] Strauss defended liberal democracies on the basis of "classical political philosophy" instead of the modern theories upon which the liberal democratic governments of the United States and Western Europe had explicitly been founded, because he thought those theories had been subjected to unanswerable criticisms by later political philosophers. His defense of "liberal or constitutional democracy" did not mean that he thought that it was the best government imaginable; he did not. Nor did it mean that he thought a liberal democracy could be established anywhere or everywhere. Strauss was no "Wilsonian." On the contrary, his experience as a young Jew in Weimar Germany had led him to doubt the viability of liberal democracy— both in Germany specifically, and more generally—as it was defended on the basis of the principles of the Enlightenment. These doubts about certain manifestations and rationales for liberal democracy did not, however, turn Strauss into an opponent of that kind of regime, as is often said in the recent discussions of him.[69]

Modern Enlightenment philosophers, who hoped to establish government completely on the basis of reason, were mistaken. If human beings were completely rational, government would not be necessary. The natural requirements that make human associations, familial and political, necessary are universal, but the natural attractions and attachments that draw and hold particular peoples together are not. There will be, as there should be, a plurality of nations, built in part on particularistic and subrational factors.[70]

Enlightenment philosophers did not have a proper appreciation either of the breadth of political power or of the primary means by which it was exercised. By limiting the ends or goals of politics to the preservation of life, liberty, and estate, modern political philosophers had transformed government into a public means of achieving private, individual ends. They had thereby deprived public life and service of much of its proper dignity and respect. The line modern political philosophers attempted to draw between "public" and "private" is, moreover, not tenable. In fact, Strauss pointed out, the economy, social institutions, and character of individuals living in communities are decisively shaped by the government or "regime." Political decisions and institutions are not merely epiphenomena. On the contrary, they transform subpolitical ethnic relations, defensive alliances, economic production, and exchange into communities held together by a shared understanding of justice, which is enforced by law.

The fact that laws must be enforced means that the meaning and effect of the law depends on the character of those who administer it. But, Strauss thought, just as modern political philosophers mistakenly narrowed the range and goals of government, so they neglected to take proper account of the importance of individual political leaders. Like James Madison, modern political philosophers had observed that "enlightened statesmen will not always be at the helm."[71] These philosophers thought that it would be better, therefore, to rely on institutions than on individuals. Recognizing that laws and institutions did not always have the intended effects, they found it necessary to look at the underlying, often unacknowledged (if not unconscious) drives that impel human beings to act as they do. Political acts were thus reduced to reflections or results of subpolitical economic, social, or psychological needs.[72] Although Strauss agreed that enlightened statesmen would not always be at the helm and that the power of the unwise people who were apt to be elevated to public office should, therefore, be limited by law, he did not think that the character and intelligence of individual leaders could or should be ignored. It takes a great deal of intelligence to determine what policies and institutions will work in given circumstances. Leaders who subordinate so many of their own individual interests and desires to the good of the community also have to have exceptionally good characters. That is why "enlightened statesmen" are so rare. Whether for good or ill, the fact is that the character of the individual leaders has a decisive effect on political outcomes. For example, Strauss observed, "the weakness of the Weimar Republic made certain its speedy destruction." But that weakness "did not make certain the victory of National Socialism. The victory of National Socialism became necessary in Germany for the same reason for which the victory of Communism had become necessary in Russia: the man who had by far the strongest will or single-mindedness, the greatest ruthlessness, daring, and power over his following, and the best judgment about the strength of the various forces in the immediately relevant political field was the leader of the revolution."[73] Likewise, Strauss suggested, the defense of Western liberal democracies from the threat posed by both Nazi Germany and Communist Russia had depended very much on the practical wisdom of Winston Churchill. One, if not the most important, way a philosopher could help his fellows, Strauss thus concluded, was in educating potential political leaders.

In returning to the ancients, Strauss thus attempted to revive not only a Socratic understanding of philosophy, but also an Aristotelian understanding of political science. Whereas modern political philosophers like Hobbes (and the contemporary behavioral social scientists who have followed him) recognize only one kind of science and thus attempt to reform the study of politics so that it will be more like modern physics, Aristotle thought that there were two kinds of science, theoretical and practical or political. This "distinction between theoretical and practical sciences implies that human action has principles of its own which are known independently of theoretical science (physics and metaphysics)." If human action can be studied in terms of its own principles, independently of theoretical physics and metaphysics, Strauss argued, Aristotelian political science can be revived without Aristotelian cosmology. Everything in the world may not have an "end" or telos, but human beings do observably move and are moved by "ends toward which man is by nature inclined and of which he has by nature some awareness. This awareness is the necessary condition for his seeking and finding appropriate means for his ends, or for his becoming practically wise or prudent." Human beings—at least some human beings—can, therefore, become prudent on the basis of an awareness no other animals have or display. "The sphere governed by prudence is thus in principle self-sufficient or closed" and can be studied independently of modern natural science. But, Strauss also observed, "prudence is always endangered by false doctrines about the whole of which man is a part," for example, arguments that deny the observable differences between the human and the nonhuman. "Prudence is therefore always in need of defense against such opinions, and that defense is necessarily theoretical." Strauss's own rereading of the history of political philosophy, especially his critique of modern political philosophy, constituted such a defense. But he insisted that "the theory defending prudence is . . . misunderstood if it is taken to be the basis of prudence."[74] Like Strauss's own work, the defense of prudence consists primarily in clearing away false theories, for example social science positivism, that cover over the principles of good practice.

As many commentators have observed, Strauss himself did not act in politics or address questions of policy. He tried instead to give a theoretical defense of good political practice. He attempted to revive what he sometimes called "the old political science" but more often referred to as "classical political philosophy" in part because he thought that it provided the most solid theoretical foundation for and defense of liberal democratic political institutions and practices. He sought to defend and so to preserve liberal democracy because he thought that the preservation of a variety of different regimes with limited governments was a necessary condition for the preservation of philosophy. Like the political philosophers who embodied the highest human aspirations and achievements, however, Strauss also understood himself to be acting on the basis of the "natural affection" human beings feel for their fellows. He strove not only to support and defend the regime he thought was the best possible under modern circumstances, but also and more generally to remind his readers of the importance and dignity of politics, not simply for the sake of philosophy or his fellow citizens or the people of the West, but more broadly for the sake of humanity as a whole.

CHAPTER TWO

Strauss — Modernity — America

Leo Strauss was a thinker of polarities: he pitted ancients against moderns, Athens against Jerusalem, philosophy against poetry, America against the Soviet Union (in the cold-war era). Although his ultimate stance is debatable, the general consensus is that he sided with the first alternative in each of these pairs—with ancients, with Athens, with philosophy, with America. What is less often appreciated, however, is that the various affirmations Strauss made do not always cohere readily with each other. Let us put things in as stark a way as we can. Strauss made three affirmations central to his understanding and judgment of America:

1. America is modern.
2. Modernity is bad.
3. America is good.

It does not take a PhD in logic to recognize some difficulty in the coexistence of these three propositions. We propose now to explain what each of these statements meant for Strauss and how he tried to hold them together.

Proposition 1: America Is Modern

Strauss himself said little directly and explicitly about America. He has no sustained treatment of the subject, and he drops comments about America only here and there.[1] To say that Strauss had little to say explicitly about America is not to say, of course, that we cannot discover a Straussian position, but that any statement of it must remain somewhat tentative.

When Strauss says that America is modern, he is invoking his well-known distinction between ancients and moderns. Strauss presented what John Gunnell calls an "epic" history of Western political philosophy.[2] According to his "epic" version of that history, political philosophy begins in a discernible time and place in the thought of an identifiable person: Socrates discovered or founded political philosophy in Athens in the middle of the fourth century BCE.[3] He did not found philosophy—that was done in Greece well before him—but he worked such a shift in the character of philosophy that all that came before him has come to be known as pre-Socratic.[4] As Strauss understands it, Socratic, as opposed to pre-Socratic philosophy, is above all political philosophy.[5]

The Socratic tradition lasted a long time, in many variants to be sure.[6] It was challenged by the rise to dominance of the three biblical religions in the Middle Ages, but it reappeared in some form in all three by making accommodations of sorts with those religions.[7] It survived until one man, Machiavelli, broke with the Socratic tradition and founded a new kind of philosophy, called by Strauss "modernity" or "modern political philosophy."[8] Machiavelli was followed by an illustrious body of pioneers of modern political philosophy, among them Bacon, Descartes, Spinoza, Hobbes, Locke, and on down to the present, or nearly to the present.[9]

The present situation—forecast with great prescience by Strauss—was named by him "historicism" but is now more widely known as postmodernity. At this moment in the history of philosophy, philosophers proclaim the philosophic agenda not merely incompletable but unworthy of continuance, because philosophy, as the quest for what is true, is impossible. Nor is there such a thing as the simply best political order, the object of pursuit for political philosophy in the narrow sense. According to historicists, there is nothing eternal and therefore no eternal truth.[10] All "truth" is historical; therefore the tradition of philosophy begun by Socrates must be pronounced dead. Strauss rose up to oppose this position.

So in Strauss's "epic" history we note the following four moments: pre-Socratic; Socratic, or classical philosophy; modernity (with various "waves"); and historicism, or postmodernity. This history of philosophy is meant by Strauss to be an alternative to Martin Heidegger's account of philosophy as the course of the disclosure (and concealment) of Being in the history of the West, or to Friedrich Nietzsche's account of the course of philosophy as in his sketch of "How the True World Finally Became a Fable." Strauss's history has obvious parallels to Heidegger's and Nietzsche's, but the differences seem more striking. For Strauss, there is, first, the great divide between ancients and moderns. According to Nietzsche and Heidegger, modern philosophy is a modification of ancient philosophy but stands in *essential* continuity with it. Philosophy is one fundamentally unified tradition. According to Strauss, however, at two key moments, the Socratic and the Machiavellian moments, philosophy changed dramatically, and with it the relation of philosophy to human practical life; with the latter change, the character of practical, political life itself was altered.[11]

Second, Nietzsche and Heidegger both see the end of the philosophic tradition as the working out of its own inherent possibilities. The limits or even impossibility of the philosophic enterprise become visible precisely because of philosophy. The death of philosophy is essentially a suicide. They and their postmodern followers thus see the death of philosophy as a move forward, hence to be embraced.[12] For Strauss, the movement into historicism or postmodernism is a decline, to be neither embraced nor cheered. It is not the playing out of philosophy per se. Rather, it is the end result of modern political philosophy. Strauss thus attempts to show that Socratic philosophy (i.e., the classical tradition) is immune from the autodestructive movement of modern philosophy. However, it is immune if and only if it is recovered in its true character. That recovery is, as we have seen, Strauss's main goal.

Strauss's aim is nothing less than to preserve philosophy (and with it, healthy politics) from the claims, raised ever more loudly in our day, that philosophy is dead—and good riddance to it. This is, of course, a very large agenda, and a very difficult one, made even more difficult by the fact that in the country where he did most of his work—the United States—the ultimate targets of Strauss's philosophic action, especially Heidegger, were barely known during Strauss's lifetime; and he was therefore little able to make his project clear in that environment.

When Strauss says that America is modern, he means that it is a nation shaped to a large degree by the ideas that emerged within modern political philosophy. To understand this claim properly requires understanding something more of what Strauss had in mind when he spoke of modern political philosophy. Strauss argued that modern political philosophy differed from the Socratic tradition both in its view of the relation between philosophy and practical political life, and in the substance of what it understood to be the truth of the human situation and the human good.

Classical political philosophy was, in Aristotle's terminology, a practical science; it was meant to speak to political life itself, to give guidance and advice.[13] But classical philosophy never meant to refashion political life root and branch. It was not "radical" in this sense of the term. Classical political philosophers may have attempted to reform public opinion, but they never thought they could entirely replace opinion as the basis of political life. Their main goal, to the extent that they worked on regnant opinion, was to moderate the aspirations (some) men brought to political life.[14] Insofar as human beings have aspirations that go beyond the fulfillments possible in political life, the classical tradition urged, philosophy is the only properly transpolitical life. This emphasis became modified in the medieval era, when it was attached to religion. That which transcends the limited possibilities of the political is essentially private and spiritual or intellectual.[15]

Modern philosophy modified this stance drastically. It aimed at a reorientation in thought, comprising a new understanding of the nature of human existence; at the same time it sought to refashion practical life on the basis of this new understanding. What is needed, in other words, is Enlightenment, that is, the spread within society of truths discerned by philosophy and the replacement of old opinions, understood now as mere prejudices, by these new truths. Philosophy thus becomes particularly eager to have an effect—to remake the world. As Strauss puts it, philosophy, while not giving up its aspiration to truth, also becomes propaganda, the conscious effort to reshape opinion through public teaching.[16]

America was founded by men who were heirs to this project. They indicated that fact to a degree by the Latin motto they adopted for the nation: *novus ordo seclorum*, a new order for the ages. Thomas Jefferson described the meaning of the American founding this way: it was the triumph of "science" over "ignorance and superstition." As he said, "all eyes are opened or opening to the rights of man."[17] The new truths of science are spreading in society and remaking political practice.

Even though Strauss agrees that rights come to play a central role in modern political philosophy, he does not agree with Jefferson that they are defining for it. According to Strauss, *the* founder of modernity is Machiavelli, and Machiavelli has no doctrine of human rights. The doctrine of natural rights is understood by Strauss to be natural justice as redefined and newly understood on the basis of Machiavelli's innovations. The keynote of Strauss's interpretation of the Machiavellian transformation, and thus of modernity per se, is the theme of "actualizability." Classical philosophy culminated in what Machiavelli called "imagined principalities and republics."[18] Classical political philosophy takes as its task the adumbration of a doctrine of the best regime—what is simply best, what is the heretofore-unknown fulfillment of all our aspirations for politics. But that best regime turns out to be impossible, according to Strauss. "It is impossible because it is against nature."[19] For all *practical* purposes, then, Strauss agrees with Machiavelli that the best regime is an imagined commonwealth.

Machiavelli grew impatient with this outcome for reasons having to do with the way Christianity distorted political life and deflected the power of ancient philosophy to supply a remedy. Machiavelli sought instead "the effectual truth," that is, the truth that can be made effectual.[20] Machiavelli's thought is driven, says Strauss, by the striving for the effectual; what is held to be true is determined according to effectualness, and not vice versa.[21] Machiavelli "limited his horizons to get results."[22] Ancient philosophy fell short of the effectual truth, because it aimed too high. It took its bearings from a vision of human excellence, understood as the perfection of human beings as rational and social beings.[23] Such excellence is a rare and difficult achievement, in part because it depends on very favorable social and political conditions.

The ancient goal is so rarely achieved because it aims at the development and rule of what is best or highest in mankind, human reason. Reason may be the highest, but, Machiavelli insisted, it is not most powerful, at least in most men most of the time. Far more effective in most men most of the time are the passions. In contests between reason and the passions, the latter win nearly every time, as witnessed by all the foolish, harmful, and self-destructive things human beings do, even when they seem to know better. Machiavelli concluded that the effectual truth about politics must be one that is in accord with the passions and their goals. That meant, in Strauss's memorable phrase, that the goal must be lowered so as to be more likely to be attainable, or, as Strauss used to say, following Winston Churchill, one needs to build on the low but solid things—the passions.[24] The idea of reorienting social and political life around the passions was a very potent weapon in the hands of Machiavelli and his successors. It led to a number of innovations in their political science. Instead of moral education through law as the core of politics, we see a great new role for political institutions; we also see a great new emphasis on political economy, that is, on the organization of society to produce and distribute material goods. "The modern project . . . depends decisively on institutions, political or economic, as distinguished from the formation of character." According to Machiavelli, said Strauss: "The task of the political art consists . . . in so directing the passions and even the malignant humors that they cannot be satisfied without their satisfaction contributing to the common good or even serving it. There is no need for a change of heart or of the intention. What is needed is the kind of institutions which make actions detrimental to the common good utterly unprofitable and which encourage in every way such actions as are conducive to the common good." As Strauss put it in another place, "restraint of the appetites is replaced by a mechanism whose effect is humane."[25]

Although Machiavelli himself was not a natural rights thinker, that theme soon emerged as important within modern political philosophy. Natural right, what is right by nature, had been understood by the ancients in accord with their understanding of the aims of political life—human excellence (virtue) as the perfection of man as a social and rational being. With the jettisoning of that goal, a new way of speaking of natural right came to the fore. Strauss saw this new rights doctrine emerging in Machiavelli's English successor, Thomas Hobbes, who wrote about a century after the Florentine.[26]

Hobbes represents the first step in the effort to moralize Machiavelli. Hobbes reintroduced the notion of natural right on a Machiavellian basis; *natural* right is that to which the strongest and most indefeasible passion, not reason, points us.[27] Natural right becomes the right of preservation, from which follows logically the right to the means of preservation. In Hobbes's hands natural right meant no less than (and no more than) the moral blamelessness of seeking that which conduces to preservation. Natural right by itself is very expansive; every individual must be his own judge of what contributes to his preservation. Under some conditions at least, every individual would be justified in considering every other person as an enemy or potential enemy.

The new Hobbesian natural right betrays its origin in Machiavelli in resting primarily on the effectual force of the passions, on the strongest passion, fear of violent death. Hobbes accepts, even insists on, the primacy of the passions, and conversely he rejects the classical orientation around man as the rational and social animal. Strauss reconstructed Hobbes's doctrine in terms of natural law: "What Hobbes attempted to do on the basis of Machiavelli's fundamental objection to the utopian teaching of the tradition, although in opposition to Machiavelli's own solution, was to maintain the idea of natural law but to divorce it from the idea of man's perfection; only if natural law can be deduced from how men actually live, from the most powerful force that actually determines all men, or most men most of the time, can it be effectual or of practical value. . . . Natural law must be deduced from the most powerful of all passions."[28] Natural law thus understood is merely the corollary of Hobbesian natural right.

We are now in a position to see what Strauss meant when he said America is modern, or built on modern political philosophy. Most broadly, he means that America was built on Machiavelli's reorientation of political philosophy, and on the post-Machiavellian affirmation of natural rights. The American Declaration of Independence, for example, consists mainly of paraphrases of the text of John Locke, one of the chief modern philosophers in Strauss's catalog of moderns and a chief articulator of the new doctrine of rights.[29] Likewise, one sees in the greatest expression of the American founders' political science, *The Federalist*, by Alexander

Hamilton, James Madison, and John Jay, two emphases characteristic of post-Machiavellian political philosophy. There is, first, that emphasis on institutions rather than character. Good political order is to depend not on the education and moral training of the passions, as in the ancient republics, but on the indulgence (even unleashing) of the passions in the context of well-designed institutions. The model here is the market as analyzed by Adam Smith. Human selfishness and acquisitiveness, previously considered vices, are recognized as most potent, but capable of being harnessed to produce good results, even to produce the common good, if the structure in which they operate is good enough. All through *The Federalist,* one can see the designers of American institutions applying this principle.[30] Accompanying the institutionalism is an emphasis on acquisition and political economy. Strauss, in one of his few references to an American source, quoted James Madison in the famous *Federalist* 10 on the protection of the property-producing faculties of man as the chief end of government. Strauss sees this affirmation as Locke applied whole.[31]

Proposition 2: Modernity Is Bad

Strauss's earliest thinking on political matters was stirred, he tells us in his important autobiographical sketch, by reflections on the failure of modern politics.[32] Coming of age as a Jew in Weimar Germany, he had firsthand experience of the pathologies of modern politics. The Weimar Republic proved itself incapable of preserving itself against challenges from the fascist right and the communist left. As Strauss saw it, "the centre"—liberal democracy à la Weimar and the French Republic—"could not hold," and the triumphant extremes were abhorrent.[33] Strauss matured as a thinker in the death days of Weimar and in the years when it looked as if the future of the West would comprise a struggle to the death between communists and fascists.[34] Moderate men could champion neither side in this fight.[35]

The events of the 1920s form the backdrop for Strauss's earliest serious thinking about politics. Indeed, we can see his future agenda in a kind of nutshell in two of his early books. His first book, *Spinoza's Critique of Religion,*[36] examined the critique of revelation and the Bible that Spinoza presented in his *Theologico-Political Treatise.* Strauss argued forcefully that Spinoza's critique fell short as rational critique, or, put more strongly, that Spinoza's failed effort showed that rational critique of the Bible could only be question-begging and therefore *must* fail in its own terms, that is, as rational critique. Strauss concluded, therefore, that there was something willed and willful about Spinoza's critique, and by extension about the Enlightenment's turn away from revelation and biblical religion as the guide for life.

Strauss's *The Political Philosophy of Hobbes* contained a remarkably parallel argument. Here Strauss focused on Hobbes as a self-proclaimed reformer of classical political philosophy, especially as a critic of Aristotle. Strauss concluded that on examination Hobbes's rejection of Aristotle was not particularly well grounded. In that book Strauss first put forth the thesis about actualizability. Hobbes sought the actualization of the best regime and reformulated the characteristics of the best regime in order to guarantee, or at least make more likely, this actualization.[37] Strauss went so far as to argue that Hobbes's apparent effort to ground his political philosophy in the new Galilean physics quite misrepresented his actual line of thought.[38] Strauss found no good reasons behind Hobbes's critique of classical philosophy, however. And so, as in his Spinoza book, he concluded that there was something willed about the break with the past.

In these two books, completed by the time he was in his midthirties, Strauss examined the emergence of modernity in the critique of the two dominant intellectual forces in the West prior to that emergence—biblical religion ("Jerusalem") and classical philosophy ("Athens"). He argued in both that the path to modernity had been embarked upon for reasons far from rationally compelling. He emerged from these two books with the firm conviction that modernity (in philosophy and politics) might have been a mistake, an act of will not motivated or justified by *good* reasons. The turn to modern rationalism appeared to him to be, in a deep sense, irrational, for the modern principles were not required by evident or demonstrated failings of what preceded them.

He added to his negation of modernity's negation of premodernity a critique of modernity itself. We must understand that critique in order to grasp his second proposition, "Modernity is bad." The Strauss critique of modernity had two parts. Modernity is bad for social, political, and moral life; that is, modernity is bad for human beings in general in their political-practical existence. Modernity is also bad for philosophy, that is, for what Strauss argued is the highest human capability and the fulfillment of human existence.

THE CRITIQUE OF MODERNITY IN POLITICS

We may identify six main points to Strauss's critique of modernity in politics.

1. Modernity as Reductionist. Modernity is literally reductionist—it "lowers the sights" and therefore reduces humanity.[39] Because of the aim of actualization, the modern moral and political orientation makes peace with the passions and becomes reconciled to man-as-he-is, not aiming at man-as-he-could-be.[40] Not human excellence or holiness, but lower things—"comfortable preservation" or "self-expression" or "recognition."[41] In reconciling with the passions, modernity aims at what is in reach of all (or almost all) and therefore democratizes the moral scene. "Modern philosophy comes into being when the end of philosophy is identified with the end which is capable of being actually pursued by all men.... the modern conception of philosophy is fundamentally democratic."[42] This democratization occurs in terms of the lowest common denominator, and thus we find a steady depreciation of high and rare moral qualities like courage and nobility.[43]

Strauss frequently cited Nietzsche's concern that modernity produces "the last man," human beings with nothing to strive for beyond a house in the suburbs with a patio and a gas-fired barbecue grill, a decent job, and the ability to get their children into good schools.[44] This moral diminution of humanity is bad in itself, as a diminution, and bad in its consequences. Political life requires more than the modern moral orientation produces: the unliberal democratic challengers of liberal democracies from Hitler to Osama bin Laden have been quick to spot and attempt to exploit the "softness" and apparent decadence of modern men. It takes something more than a Harvard degree and a membership in a gym to defend oneself and one's interests in a hard world—and the world remains a hard one, despite the long-term hopes of the moderns.

The "last man" is man weakened. Weak man is vulnerable not only to the strong outsider, but also to the social pressures he experiences all around him. Modernity begins as a movement concerned with freedom, but it opens human beings to an insidious and powerful challenge to freedom in the phenomena of conformism and mass culture. Freed from various external servitudes, human beings become internally servile.[45]

2. Modernity as the Entrenchment of Immoderation. Strauss is less certain than Nietzsche that the "last man" is the fate of modern man, however. He is less convinced than Nietzsche that human beings are so completely malleable. Witness Nietzsche himself, who rose in rebellion against the vision of the last man and called for a return to the morally difficult and challenging. Human beings are not as easily pacified as Hobbes, Locke, and the others assumed. The desire to transcend, to do more than comfortably survive, is unquenchable. As Strauss said in reply to Oswald Spengler, a follower of Nietzsche, "man's highest possibilities cannot be exhausted as long as there are still high human tasks—as long as the fundamental riddles which confront men, have not been solved to the extent they can be solved."[46] But it is Strauss's abiding view that "the fundamental riddles" cannot be solved. The desire to transcend produces a constant countermovement to modernity.[47]

Philosophers, among others, responding to the incompleteness or unsatisfactoriness of modern philosophy, reject the bourgeois life and call for more: Rousseau, Kant, Marx, and Nietzsche are all good examples of those who demand that humanity go beyond the moral orientation of comfortable preservation. But according to Strauss, these men rise up against modernity from within modernity. They go deeper into modernity while rebelling against it.[48] "Going deeper" into modernity has one very concrete practical implication, a highly ironic one at that. The irony derives from the dynamic movement of modern thought. By lowering the sights for the sake of actualization, modern political philosophy raises the hopes for politics. Aiming for less, it aims more intransigently to achieve its goal. In the light of the demand for actualization, the commitment to moderation appears to make peace with the old order, that is, with the practical failure to achieve even what the lowered goals for politics project. Moderation accepts aspects of life that the moderns believe can be overcome. The result is impatience with what is.

In the later waves of modernity—in the post-Rousseauian universe of thought—moderation gets an especially bad name, for it seems part of the low, even morally despicable bourgeois attitude that is to be transcended. The result is political ambition on a grand scale, much grander than the kind of ambition Plato and Aristotle attempted to tame. We have here not merely an ambition to rule (to be the tyrant), but a political idealism with no discernible limits, which leads to one political horror after another in the name of the highest goals: the terror of the French Revolution, the gulags of the Soviet regime, the "racial purification" of the Nazis, the "great leap forward" and cultural revolution of the Chinese, the Pol Pot regime's effort to cleanse itself of all corrupted forces by means of the killing fields.

3. *Modernity as the Ideologizing of Politics.* The dynamic of modernity conduces to an intensified political conflict of a new kind. The movement of thought leaves behind a residue of practical regimes or political movements devoted to opposite and conflicting ideologies, all of which have an inherent aspiration to universality. Strauss saw modern political philosophy as possessing a dynamic character because it was unstable in an important way. Whereas he attributed to the ancient and medieval Socratics a

common political doctrine, he recognized that the moderns were more varied. Thus, in his important programmatic essay "What Is Political Philosophy," he spoke of "the classical solution" but of "the modern solutions" to "the problem of political philosophy." Likewise, in his *Natural Right and History* he presented a composite picture of the doctrine of the ancients in a chapter called "Classic Natural Right," but he portrayed distinct and separate versions of modern political philosophy in distinct and separate chapter segments devoted, respectively, to Hobbes, Locke, Rousseau, and Burke. Modern political philosophy displays much less unity than classical philosophy because it was subjected to a series of critiques, based, Strauss believed, on manifest inadequacies within the various statements of the modern doctrine. Thus Hobbes was compelled to modify Machiavelli, because, among other things, "the revolting character" of Machiavelli's doctrine "robbed it of the efficaciousness it sought."[49] Machiavelli's thought also had "serious theoretical difficulties," which later thinkers attempted to remedy with a doctrine of nature conformable with the new natural science. But Hobbes, in turn, was not able to offer a version of modern political philosophy that was generally acceptable, and so his theory was attacked and revised by a series of successors.

The result was what Strauss calls "waves of modernity." The various versions and revisions cluster together, forming "waves." The first wave begins with Machiavelli and includes early modern philosophers like Spinoza, Hobbes, and Locke. Strauss characterizes thinkers in that wave as having reduced "the moral and political problem to a technical problem"—what we have spoken of as an emphasis on institutions rather than moral education—and as having put forward a "concept of nature as in need of being overlaid by civilization as a mere artifact." The moderns take the view that the movement into society is a movement away from, and in key respects against, nature, in favor of an artificial or rational construct.[50] The doctrine of the social contract in these early thinkers expresses this conception.

Rousseau, Strauss argues, initiates the second wave by questioning both aspects of first-wave thinking. Rousseau thus spoke of "virtue" in a robust way against the debauching and demeaning doctrines of his predecessors. Rousseau also discovered history, or that "man's humanity is due not to nature," which the first-wave thinkers still took for granted, "but to history, to the historical process, a signal or a unique process which is not teleological."[51] The second wave ran from Rousseau up to but not including Nietzsche. It did include the great philosophers of history of the nineteenth century—Hegel and Marx—as well as their intellectual forerunner, Kant.

Nietzsche initiates the third wave of modernity with a rejection of the chief conclusions arrived at by thinkers in the second wave. Rousseau believed that the historical process made men more human but effaced or almost effaced in them the naturally good, the sentiment of existence. One conclusion that he drew was that for those who could return to the sense of the sweetness of existence, a turn away from civilization and its discontents was *the* desirable solution to the human situation. Nietzsche rejected that side of Rousseau by insisting that "the sentiment of existence" was not as Rousseau had it, but rather was an "experience of terror and anguish."[52] Terror and anguish are the "natural," because they reflect the exposed situation of mankind in nature. Nietzsche also rejected that side of Rousseau's solution that found expression in his view of the humanization of mankind through history. That side of Rousseau's thought reached its peak expression in the philosophies of Hegel and Marx, both of whom announced that the historical process, on the basis of objective and unintended laws of history, was working itself out to produce a rational end state. These historical philosophers embodied in the deepest way the modern aspiration for actualization of the highest order: history itself was an agent of actualization. Nietzsche found that end state, in either its Hegelian or its Marxist version, to be degraded and degrading. As we have already noticed, Nietzsche found the "last man," humanity at the end of the historical process, to be man diminished. Nietzsche argued more broadly that the historical process is far different from the way Hegel, Marx, and the other philosophers of history proclaimed it. It is not a "process" with its own laws of development, but "the outcome of human creative acts," even if imperfectly realized to be so until Nietzsche's own moment. Nietzsche recognizes human agency in history, but therewith also undercuts the ability to appeal to any trans-human source of authority. All hitherto existing ideals made such an appeal. After Nietzsche, according to Nietzsche, no such appeal is open to mankind. Human beings must now take responsibility for their own history and formulate their own ideals. Knowing what "values" really are, human makings, human beings can now consciously produce a "transvaluation of values" based on human will and resolve.[53]

Of most immediate relevance to our present discussion is Strauss's observation that in accord with the nature of modern political philosophy, each wave produces a practical political movement based on the thinking of that wave as its "ideology." Thus first-wave thinking inspired liberal democracies of the American sort; second-wave theory, the Communist movement; and third-wave theory, fascism.

The premoderns identified apolitical ways to transcend the bounds of ordinary, everyday life: the ways of philosophy or religion. Modern transcendence, in contrast, is political. The efforts at transcendence retain the defining feature of modernity, the demand for actualization.[54] Transcendence then is not an individual or private matter but becomes a public matter, buttressed and driven forward by philosophy, or theory, or ideology. Political life in its premodern form is inescapably marked by conflict, Strauss maintained; but the ideologizing of politics intensifies and broadens that tendency to conflict immensely. Modern politics becomes a particularly intense battle between philosophically inspired, universalistic, hostile political movements.

4. *Modernity and the Perils of Technology*. According to Strauss, modernity has as its chief aim the actualization of the good order. The point of science or knowledge is thus transformed from what it was in its classical prototypes. "According to the modern project, philosophy or science was no longer understood as essentially contemplative, but as active."[55] Science is understood within modernity to exist for the sake of improving human life: in Francis Bacon's phrase, the purpose of science was "to relieve man's estate." An alternate statement was "science for the sake of power." This new view of the nature of science has implications not only for the sciences of human things, but for the sciences of nature as well.[56] It produces a kind of knowing that is technological through and through, and it leads to the political liberation of this science for the sake of contributing to "comfortable preservation." "Nature was to be conquered for the sake of man."[57]

The result of this transformation and reconception of science is very equivocal, however. Human beings now possess power over nature, which is also power over themselves, that is much greater than had ever been imagined. Living in the nuclear age, the age of terrorism, and the age of biotechnology, it is easy to see what Strauss feared: how easy it is to harness technology for harmful as well as allegedly beneficial projects.[58] Strauss was especially concerned with the very explosive combination brewed up by modernity—highly ideologized politics *plus* technology. He did not believe that humanity (or political life) would ever be fundamentally tamed. He did not credit Kant's hopes for "perpetual peace."[59] More likely is the perpetual possibility of war, ever more harmful and dangerous when conjoined with technology.[60] Strauss thus had very moderate political hopes and expectations. Classical philosophy teaches that political evils will never cease, but modernity pins its hopes on the positings of a Kant or a Kojeve, the latter of whom forecast the coming of a "universal homogenous state." These are dreams.[61] The inherent nature of politics, to say nothing of modern ideologized politics, makes the technological venture a grave threat to humanity. And the technological project does not even achieve what it set out to achieve. It may produce affluence, but "affluence does not cure the deepest evils."[62] Material goods do not satisfy the yearnings of the human soul.

5. *Modernity and the Rejection of Phronesis.* Like Aristotle, Strauss put much weight on the faculty of *phronesis* (practical wisdom or prudence), the capacity of a man of moral virtue to understand practical situations and to act in practically wise ways.[63] It is *the* virtue of the political leader. But modernity in its various forms distrusts *phronesis*, seeking instead a science or theory of decision or rational choice. Thus, American leaders are now trained in schools of public affairs in cost-benefit analysis, game theory, decision theory, and other such intellectual schemes, but they do not hone their practical wisdom by studying history and the deeds of statesmen. Nonetheless, modern politics requires *phronesis* not less, but perhaps more, than it was required in the past. Mass societies and powerful technology mean that the stakes of politics are ever higher and the possibilities and consequences of error ever graver. Yet, already in Hobbes, modernity is at war with prudence, and it remains congenitally hostile to it, considering prudence imprecise, unscientific, and subjective.[64] As a consequence, the powers unleashed in the world are ever greater, and the human capacity to deal with them is ever diminished.

6. *Modernity and the "Crisis of Our Time."* All five of the themes discussed above converge on what Strauss calls "the crisis of our time," or the "crisis of the West." This crisis affects both the character of our political life and the possibilities for philosophy in our day. The crisis that Strauss announced was caused by a loss of faith, or a loss of confidence, in what had become the widely understood purpose and character of the West in modern times. The West had believed in a progressive future, built upon the conquest of nature made possible by modern natural science, and in the coming of egalitarian and just political regimes made possible by modern political philosophy and its offshoots, such as modern political economy. Strauss clearly identifies this Western sense of mission with the Wilsonianism so often attributed to him: "This progress would necessarily be the progress toward a society embracing equally all human beings: a universal league of free and equal nations, each nation consisting of free and equal men and women. For it had come to be believed that the prosperous, free, and just society in a single country or in only a few countries is not possible in the long run: to make the world safe for the Western democracies, one must make the whole globe democratic, each country in itself as well as the

society of nations."[65] The Wilsonian mission is not, as we observed earlier, Strauss's mission. He sees loss of confidence in it as a sign or embodiment of the crisis of the West, but that does not commit him to the attempt to revive belief in that particular mission. He wishes not so much to endorse the Wilsonian project as to diagnose the loss of faith in it.

The Wilsonian mission was not his, for it is the culmination of the modern project about which he had so many misgivings. Wilsonianism is modernity at high tide. Strauss thought it impossible "to return to earlier forms of modern thought," that is, those informing the Wilsonian project, because "the critique of modern rationalism or of the modern belief in reason by Nietzsche cannot be dismissed or forgotten."[66] The loss of faith in the modern project at high tide is, Strauss maintained, a result of modernity itself. The crisis of modernity is the self-unraveling of modernity.

As we have already indicated, Strauss sees a dialectical development, or a series of waves, in the unfolding of modern political philosophy. The end point of this process is the situation Strauss saw coming to dominance in his time—the triumph of positivism and historicism. The first takes its bearing by science and insists on the distinction between facts and values. According to positivism, only facts are amenable to scientific treatment: only facts or alleged facts can be potentially true or not.[67] Values are held to be beyond the range of rational inquiry, discourse, or validation. Positivism was very powerful in American social science in Strauss's day, and it remains so today.

Strauss did not see positivism as the most threatening component of "the crisis of our time," however. More important is historicism, which for the sake of convenience we might, in a simplifying way, identify with relativism. It is a far more radical doctrine than positivism. It rejects the fact-value distinction, because it rejects the claim that science escapes the inevitable subjectivity, variability, and historical relativity of all systems of "knowledge." Put another way, science (or facts) is said to rest as much as values themselves on value judgments.[68]

This culminating crisis is a crisis for politics, because politics is, above all, about "values"—justice, equality, rights, the common good, and so on. But our greatest authorities—modern natural science, logic, and philosophy of science—teach that these value judgments have no cognitive status, that is, no truth-value, or that they have no status other than being posited by human beings. In the environment of modernity, these conclusions about values become part of common opinion. The unfolding of the Enlightenment leads to the occlusion of the belief in rationality that had accompanied and supported the Enlightenment project.[69]

So, every college freshman in America knows how to appeal to the claim "That's only a value judgment" to cut off discussion about issues of the good and the just. Some of the more extreme consequences rise to the surface from time to time. In the 1980s, for example, there was a famous serial killer named Ted Bundy, who was young, good looking, and well educated. He searched out young women on college campuses, impressing them with his knowledge of philosophy, among other things. When caught, he defended his actions in terms of the fact-value distinction. He scoffed at those, like the professors from whom he learned the fact-value distinction, who still lived their lives as if there were truth-value to value claims. He thought they were fools and that he was one of the few who had the courage and integrity to live a consistent life in light of the truth that value judgments, including the command "Thou shalt not kill," are merely subjective assertions.

Strauss was more regularly concerned with another consequence of positivism, however: although there is a human nature, how human beings are and what they do depends to a large degree on how they understand themselves, their situation, and their rights and duties. The human being is the rational and therefore reflexive being. Political society requires that the members of it be committed to it. To be committed requires accepting the "value orientation" of the society, that is, the conception of justice and the good animating it and the principles of legitimacy underlying it. Without this sort of acceptance, one cannot have *citizens*. Strauss was convinced that nations without such a conviction of the truth of what they stand for "can not long endure." In the face of the challenge of Marxism, Strauss saw the loss of faith in these principles to be a serious matter. Politics, Strauss insisted, is frequently harsh and demanding. He traced the triumph of totalitarian regimes in the twentieth century to the crisis spawned by positivism and especially historicism. As Nasser Behnegar astutely observes, "the connection that Strauss emphasizes between relativism and National Socialism and other mass movements is not so much that relativism leads one to embrace such movements [although in its "deicisionist" forms it may well do so] but that it disarms any principled opposition to them."[70]

A nation undergoing crisis suffers in its dealings with others from lack of confidence in the rightness of its cause and of its actions. The manifestations of crisis are internal as well as external. Citizens increasingly forget the common good; they are taught or come to believe that the common good is a myth (an empty "value") and they then feel free to pursue their indubitably real and solid self-interest, often at the expense of others and social needs.[71] Strauss would perhaps point to recent corporate scandals, like the Enron affair, as illustrative of his point.

Modernity is not only problematic for politics; it poses special dangers for philosophy. The modern enterprise, when played out to the end, culminates in the claim that philosophy itself is impossible. Since Strauss died, the rise of postmodernism has brought out many voices proclaiming this very thing. One need think no further than of Richard Rorty or Stanley Fish, two prominent popularizers of the postmodern perspective. To find philosophy impossible is to close off this avenue of transcendence and, according to Strauss's lights, to close off the very highest human potentiality. As we have argued, it was Strauss's deepest aim to defend philosophy from these late modern attacks.

Proposition 3: America Is Good

From all that has come before, one would think that Strauss would be forced to pronounce a negative judgment on America, as do many others who raise serious objections to the "Enlightenment Project" and modernity.[72] Yet on the whole Strauss is positive about America. "A contradiction?" ask Alain Frachon and Daniel Vernet in *Le Monde* in September 2003. "Without doubt," they answer.[73]

However, we cannot merely dismiss Strauss's praise of America as thoughtless contradiction or diplomatic generosity toward his host country. Four different sets of considerations help to make sense of Strauss's puzzling position. We can summarize the bearing of these four considerations by saying that he finds America good relative to the alternatives available within modernity, that he finds modernity not wholly or uniformly bad, and America not wholly or uniformly modern.

1. *America in the Context of the Cold War.* Strauss spoke explicitly of America most often in the context of the cold war. In this context he had no difficulty making a firm judgment: America was certainly good relative to its chief rival, the Soviet Union. Unlike Heidegger, who famously concluded that there was no difference, metaphysically speaking, between Moscow and Washington and who had, equally famously, thrown his immense prestige behind the Nazi regime, Strauss thought there was a very large difference, a difference at the relevant level of politics, between America and these other regimes. Heidegger continually had difficulty speaking in a

sensible way of morality and politics, because he reduced all practical and ethical existence to a token in the great game Being was playing with the world. That was one reason Strauss set himself against Heidegger and fought to revive political philosophy, and with it the perspective of political-practical life, from the destitution into which it had fallen.[74] In the light of classical political philosophy, nay in the light of common sense itself, it was easy to see "the clear superiority of Washington." As Strauss said, "the superiority of liberal democracy to communism . . . is obvious enough."[75]

2. *America in the Context of the Dialectic of Modernity: America as Riding the First Wave.* As we have already noted, Strauss discerned a dialectic or dynamic in modern thought and modern politics. The "first wave" of modernity, the wave ushered in by Machiavelli and containing Hobbes, Spinoza, Locke, and others, was the chief source of the guiding theory of modern liberal democracy. It was under the spell of that first wave that America was founded; its regime was and is a first-wave regime.

The deficiencies of the first wave provoked the second wave, originated by Rousseau in a critique of his modern predecessors. This wave contained the German idealists Kant, Fichte, and Hegel, and also the philosophy of Marx. The Soviet Union was founded under the aegis of second-wave theory.[76] Although the second wave was initiated in order to remedy the deficiencies of the first wave, it nonetheless produced a politics that was in many ways much worse. The second wave broke with the sobriety and modest aspirations of the first wave—and in the process produced politics like the French Terror.

Second-wave regimes, especially the Soviet Union and other Marxist regimes, were worse than first-wave regimes both regarding substance and regarding process.[77] They aimed to accomplish more—genuine solidarity, fraternity, and equality, as opposed to what they saw as the sham solidarity, fraternity, and equality within first-wave theory and practice. Second-wave regimes pinned their hopes to a large degree on their discovery of history; human beings are as they are, not as a result of nature (a premise first-wave theory shared with classical philosophy), but on the basis of history. They have become what they are as a result of a fashioning they have undergone via the "historical process." The principle of this process became visible to second-wave theorists, and they hoped to either engage in conscious refashioning in accord with the possibilities opened up by history (Rousseau), or to take advantage of the path on which history had set mankind (Marx). With the right kind of will and the right kind of social and political order, second-wave theorists believed, a kind of reconciliation, hitherto undreamed of, of man with man and with nature (and Being) was possible.[78]

At the same time, second-wave theorists came to be impatient with the moderate elements of first-wave regimes, elements such as rule of law and constitutionalism, representative democracy, and separation of powers. These were seen as drags on history, or on human power to refashion man and society. Thus the Marxists committed themselves to "real democracy," that is, to the substance of equality, and thought this would best be achieved by passing over merely "formal" democracy, those institutions that required rulers to govern with the consent of the governed.[79] The result was predictable: as James Madison said, if men were angels, no government would be necessary. Stalin did not turn out to be an angel. In a word, Strauss maintained that second-wave theory and practice conduced readily to tyranny, whereas first-wave regimes, especially the American regime, were cognizant of the dangers of tyranny and built more wisely against them. Strauss, unlike Heidegger, had no difficulty pronouncing the judgment that a mode of organizing political life prone to tyranny was much inferior to one that did not tend that way.[80]

3. *America as Redescribable in Classical Terms.* Strauss always insisted that there was a fundamental difference in the ways classical and modern political philosophy conceived the goal of political action. The classics generated a model of the best regime, to be sure, which set a standard for thinking about regimes, but this model was not always a goal to be sought nor a measure of the legitimacy of actual regimes. In place of such a singular measure, the ancients developed a flexible and graduated understanding of regimes. They were not committed to the notion that one particular regime was legitimate and all others illegitimate. They rather taught that what was good and desirable depended very much on conditions and circumstances.[81]

Modern political philosophy was narrower, and it was much less flexible. *The* legitimate regime was the one that secured rights, or the one that socialized the means of production. Since the modern ideal was posited as actualizable, there was much less tolerance for regimes that fell short of the legitimate regime per se.

In the light of classical political philosophy, the American regime could be seen as a very acceptable and good, if not quite excellent, regime. America is a constitutionalist regime, and Strauss said, "Wisdom requires unhesitating loyalty to a decent constitution, and even to the cause of constitutionalism."[82] He suggested, moreover, that despite the self-understanding of the American founders, and of the American people, the American political order can be well and properly seen as an example of the regime Aristotle calls polity in book 4 of his *Politics*. A polity is a mixed regime, most often a mix of oligarchy (rule of the wealthy few) and democracy (rule of the many poor). A variant of this regime is heavily weighted toward the dominance of the middle class. Admittedly, this kind of regime does not reach the heights of the better regimes, but it is more than acceptable. Thus Strauss concludes that "liberal democracy" of the American sort, "in contradistinction to communism and fascism, derives powerful support from a way of thinking which cannot be called modern at all: the pre-modern thought of [the] western tradition."[83]

Strauss is well known as a partisan of the ancients and, in political science per se, of Aristotle. And Aristotle is well known as a critic of democracy. It would seem to follow that Strauss is, as Shadia Drury, Tim Robbins, and others claim, hostile to democracy. Strauss admits, for example, that "it would be silly to deny that the classics rejected democracy as an inferior kind of regime." But Strauss also points out that "the democracy with which [Aristotle] takes issue is the democracy of the city, not modern democracy or the kind of democracy which presupposes the distinction between state and society." Modern or liberal democracy embodies principles of justice that, from Aristotle's point of view, are not democratic at all, but aristocratic. Thus selection for office is based not on lot, an embodiment of the pure democratic principle of equality, but on election. Election is aristocratic, because it embodies the aristocratic principle of justice—merit. As we often say: may the best man, or woman, win.[84] Offices that are not elective are, for the most part, even more clearly aristocratic, in that appointments are to be made on the basis of competence and merit. The Civil Service System is thus often called the merit system.

Aristotle objected to ancient democracy because the democratic selection of officials was, in an important sense, defective both with respect to its justice and with respect to the competence of rule it could be expected to produce. The ancient democracies themselves recognized the limitations of their own principle of justice when, in dangerous situations, they looked the other way and attempted to find leaders based on competence and merit. Aristotle, and Strauss following him, would not have the same objections to modern democracies as they had to the ancient type.

Moreover, the ancient democracies to which Aristotle objected were characterized by the dominance of the poor, who were necessarily the uneducated or much less educated. Virtue and competence, however, were understood by Aristotle, and Strauss following him, to be the result of education, broadly speaking. Although modern democracies give the poor a role through universal suffrage, they are by no means necessarily dominated by the poor and uneducated as the ancient democracies were. The relative affluence characteristic of modern democracies means that the poor are not so resourceless or uneducated as they were in the ancient democracies. Thus, Strauss concludes that a major, or perhaps *the* major, issue between ancients and moderns regarding democracy "consists exclusively in a different estimate of the virtues of technology."[85] The ancients had doubts, Strauss avers, about the technologizing of science, and they consciously chose against it.[86] Once the choice for technology has been made, however, Strauss notes the advantages it makes possible; the chief advantage is the potential narrowing of the gap between democracy and aristocracy in their ancient senses, both of which have a discernible presence in modern democracy. The latter thus amounts to a mixed regime.

In this way Strauss endorses the modern moderate regime, liberal democracy. It is a restrained but genuine endorsement. Given his analysis of the nature of the regime and its virtues—among other things, its openness to virtue, as well as to freedom—Strauss tends to warn against some of the natural tendencies of democratic regimes that would push the regime in a more democratic direction and lose some of its mixed-regime elements. In this Strauss is again following Aristotle, who counseled that statesmanship must attempt to counter the disequilibrating tendencies of regimes to push forward extreme versions of their own principles. It is this side of Strauss's political science that is responsible for his reputation as a conservative. Most often, however, those who level this charge fail to understand the broad analysis that lies behind Strauss's anti-extremist, moderate political stance.[87]

4. America and the Saving Remnants of the Premodern. Strauss frequently took note of the fact that the most important political writing ever produced in America, *The Federalist*, was written by men employing the pseudonym Publius. Publius was a figure from the early years of the Roman republic. Strauss saw that the American founders in choosing that name were consciously harking back to classical republicanism. Their modernist theory may have had no particular place for it, but the Americans nonetheless embodied something of the classical orientation as a residue they carried with them and planted in their modern regime. This residue to some degree countered, to some degree supplemented and elevated, the fundamentally modern commitments of the regime. The traditions planted in America carried along much more than modern philosophy. Older notions survive, such as those embodied in ideas of republican citizenship or moral virtue, sometimes unconsciously and beneath the surface, sometimes not. These older traditions supply a kind of capital for modern regimes, which the modern regimes require and can draw on, but to the formation of which they tend not to contribute.

A second residue on which Strauss placed much emphasis was religion. America was originally settled by peoples devoted to their faith, who came to America in order to practice their religion. Many years after the settlement of America, Alexis de Tocqueville noted that the Americans very successfully combined religion and modern democracy. This combination has remained powerful in American life; America remains the most religious nation among the Western powers, a fact about America that Strauss considered favorable to its political and moral health.

Straussian Ambiguities

We have, we hope, removed some of the paradox from the copresence of Strauss's three affirmations. He had a subtle, nuanced, and complex analysis not only of the history of philosophy but also of the realities of American life, which made America no mere reflex of the march of modern philosophy. Part of the complexity of his analysis, however, consisted in the fact that he imputed a great and perhaps growing role in political life to the march of modern philosophy. Indeed, that was one of the chief distinguishing marks of both modern philosophy and modern politics—how much the former seeks to influence the latter, how penetrable the latter is by the former.

As we explain in part 2, Strauss had serious reservations about the power to persist of those forces that made America better than it would have been had it been simply shaped by modernist philosophy. He warned, for example, that America may yet prove to be another instance of a troubling historical pattern, whereby a nation defeated on the battlefield triumphs in thought.[88] Strauss had in mind the inroads German thought, the most advanced embodiment of the most advanced modern thought, was making on American opinion.

CHAPTER THREE

Leo Strauss as a Postmodern Political Thinker

Leo Strauss is by no means alone as a critic of modernity. An entire movement known as postmodernism shares with Strauss a critical stance toward the modernism associated with the Enlightenment and the political movements, liberalism and Marxism, derived from modern philosophy. Strauss anticipated postmodernism, which he treated in the form of "historicism." Yet his relationship with postmodernism is, to say the least, complex. He is a critic of the movement, but he himself is also, in an important sense, a postmodern thinker. As Stanley Rosen observes, "According to Strauss, modern thought in all its forms is determined by the idea of progress...and hence is rooted from the outset in the Enlightenment. Strauss's critique of modernity is thus a critique of the Enlightenment, similar to that of Nietzsche, but also entirely typical of what has frequently been called postmodernism."[1]

Postmodern is a term much bandied about these days, so it may be useful to begin by defining it more precisely. Literally, of course, *postmodern* means "after the modern," and that is generally how it is used. What is understood to be *modern* differs somewhat, however, from field to field. In architecture, *modern* referred primarily to designs, such as those inspired by the Bauhaus, that were strictly, if not starkly, functional. So *postmodern* signifies a reintroduction of decorative elements that are not simply functional, and a mixture of past styles. In literature, modernism was associated not with function but with nonuse, with purely aesthetic value, as opposed to moral, political, or historical value. Exemplified by T. S. Eliot, modernism gave rise to the New Critical claim that texts ought to be read solely in their own terms, not in terms of their context, biographical sources, or broader teaching.

In philosophy and political theory, postmodern also means that which comes after the modern. But here the modern has a much wider historical and substantive scope, for it includes the entire effort, beginning with Machiavelli, Bacon, and Descartes, to acquire and use knowledge to improve the human condition. Scholars disagree, in fact, about where the modern begins—does it have a Christian element, for example?—and whether its essential characteristic is power-seeking or liberty; but they virtually all agree that it ends with Nietzsche. The collection of essays entitled *Nietzsche as Postmodernist: Essays Pro and Contra* indicates the special status of his thought in this regard; he brings the modern to an end and thus points toward, if he does not himself begin, something new.[2]

The Problem of the Postmodern

What is called postmodern in philosophy, we submit, constitutes a response—or, to speak more precisely, a variety of responses—to a problem first enunciated by Nietzsche and modified or extended in Heidegger's criticism of Nietzsche. In arguing that Strauss ought to be understood as a postmodern political thinker, we must, therefore, first describe the dilemma Nietzsche and Heidegger bequeathed to thinkers in the twentieth and twenty-first centuries. Second, we describe the way in which Strauss responded to the problems, both philosophical and political, posed first by Nietzsche and then by Heidegger. Third, we compare Strauss's response with that offered by Jacques Derrida, a thinker who has been much more frequently characterized as a postmodern, in order to show that, strictly speaking, Strauss is more so. That does not mean that Strauss is either a Nietzschean or a nihilist. On the contrary, Strauss does not merely respond to the troublesome results of extreme modernity (postmodernity); he attempts to counter them.

Nietzsche announced the problem in his very first book, *The Birth of Tragedy*: the search for knowledge or philosophy that has been the distinguishing characteristic of what we call Western civilization culminated in the work of Immanuel Kant. It culminated, in other words, in the knowledge that we do not know, that we can never know the things-in-themselves. We know only what we construct. One of those constructs, Nietzsche argued in his later works, is our notion of the "self." In fact, we are bundles and masses of drives, not all of which are conscious and none of which is, strictly speaking, rational, according to Nietzsche.

If the search for wisdom does not produce wisdom or knowledge, the question arises, What good is it? In *The Birth of Tragedy* Nietzsche takes Socrates to represent the promise that human beings can not only plumb the depths of existence but can also use the knowledge they acquire to correct it. This is the dual promise of philosophy that Nietzsche concludes has proved to be false. The problem does not apply simply to the field of philosophy as understood in the nineteenth and twentieth centuries, moreover. Even by Nietzsche's time, and surely in the twentieth century, modern natural scientists have also had to admit that they do not have knowledge, strictly speaking, of the things-in-themselves. What scientists claim to know is how to produce certain effects, to show what works. The question, however, is, What does it work for? In an essay he wrote shortly after *The Birth of Tragedy*, "On the Uses and Disadvantages of History for Life," Nietzsche suggested that human beings do not seek knowledge for its own sake. We seek to learn how things operate or "what works" in order to improve the human condition. But if, as a result of a century or more of scientific and historical research, we no longer believe that there are natural species, that is, if we no longer believe that there is an essential difference between human beings and animals, we no longer have a standard by which to measure what is humanly useful or beneficial. How can we improve or "correct" human existence, if we do not know what is human?

The outcome or end of the history of philosophy that Nietzsche announced thus appeared to be profoundly disillusioning. Nietzsche himself expressed that disillusionment most powerfully and poignantly in his famous announcement that "God is dead.... We have killed him." Eventually, however, Nietzsche concluded that the knowledge we had acquired— that we knew only that we did not know—need not be deadly. On the contrary, the discovery that all those things we thought we knew were human projections or constructions meant that we could now do consciously and intentionally what philosophers had been doing unconsciously, or at least covertly, in the past—giving meaning to the world and their own existence. He called these new philosophical value-givers "supermen" or "overmen," and he predicted in *The Genealogy of Morals* that their attempts to impose their own values on the world would produce two centuries or more of violent, ideological struggle.

The problem Nietzsche left thus had two parts: First, if it is true, as Nietzsche argued, that the search for knowledge or philosophy culminates only in the knowledge that we do not know, what is the character and value of the Western philosophical tradition? Second, if centuries of philosophical and scientific investigations have shown that we do not know and cannot discover any eternal or necessary order in the universe, how do we avoid the Nietzschean politics of the drive for total mastery of the world that would impose order upon it?

Strauss's Postmodernism: After Nietzsche

By claiming that Strauss is a postmodern thinker, we are claiming, in effect, that his thought ought to be understood as a response to Nietzsche. Strauss himself provides grounds for understanding his thought in this context. In a letter he wrote to Karl Loewith in 1935, Strauss stated: "Nietzsche so dominated and bewitched me between my 22nd and 30th years, that I literally believed everything that I understood of him." At the time he wrote the letter, Strauss no longer accepted all that he understood of Nietzsche, but he continued to believe that Nietzsche had set problems from which philosophy in our age must begin.[3]

Strauss's lifework was a response to Nietzsche's pronouncement that the centuries-long search for wisdom had proved to be fruitless. Nietzsche had associated that problem with Socrates in his first book, *The Birth of Tragedy*; the end of philosophy was the end of the vision or the promise Socrates had in effect made that human beings could redeem existence by acquiring knowledge and using it to correct the given. The search for knowledge served for centuries to justify human existence, that is, to make human life worth living. If the search was fruitless, as Nietzsche pronounced, it could no longer serve to justify human suffering or to provoke further striving. Nietzsche feared that loss of faith in the Socratic project heralded a descent into nihilism.

Strauss responded explicitly to Nietzsche's assessment of the character of philosophy and thereby the value of the Western tradition with a study of what he called "the problem of Socrates."[4] In *The Birth of Tragedy*, Strauss observed, Nietzsche portrayed and criticized Plato's Socrates in much the same terms with which Aristophanes had portrayed and criticized Socrates in *The Clouds*—that Socrates was above all (literally, in a basket in the air) a student of natural philosophy. As a practitioner and a teacher of rhetoric, Socrates was also noted for his ability to make the weaker argument the stronger one. But, in a series of studies of Aristophanes, Xenophon, and Plato, Strauss showed that the Socrates presented by his students differed from the philosopher lampooned by the comic poet in two decisive respects: First, unlike Aristophanes' Socrates, the Socrates depicted by Xenophon and Plato clearly recognized the difference between the human and the nonhuman things. Second, their Socrates also saw the need to preserve the political conditions necessary for the perpetuation of his own philosophical activity. The Socrates depicted by Xenophon and Plato did not differ from the Aristophanic by being simply a moralist, however, as Aristotle suggested;[5] on the contrary, both of his students show that Socrates continued his studies of nature after his "turn" to the study of the *logoi* (speeches or opinions) described in Xenophon's *Oeconomicus* and Plato's *Phaedo*. But Socrates is not shown to possess knowledge with which to reform the world, so much as to be engaged in the quest for knowledge, a quest culminating in the knowledge that he did not know. He did not know the "metaphysical" truths Nietzsche attributed to him; the Socratic life was not undermined, but rather defined, by the limits of Socratic knowledge. Despite his knowledge of ignorance, Socrates found the philosophic life best, because it was the happiest. In order for philosophers to be happy, they do not have to possess the truth; they merely need to see that they are making progress in their search for it.[6] As Socrates says in the *Apology* (38a), the unexamined life is not worth living, but conversing every day about virtue the way he does is a very great good for a human being.[7] In sum, Strauss's studies of the three original sources on Socrates convinced him that philosophy did not consist so much in the investigation of first principles and the articulation of cosmological doctrines, as Aristotle and his successors thought; philosophy was rather a way of life, the only truly satisfying and happy way of life. Its possibility did not depend upon the possession of absolute or certain knowledge. On the contrary, all we could ever expect to achieve would be imperfect knowledge, partial knowledge that we could hope to expand.

In *What Is Political Philosophy?* Strauss explained: "Socrates was so far from being committed to a specific cosmology that his knowledge was knowledge of ignorance. Knowledge of ignorance is not ignorance. It is knowledge of the elusive character of the truth, of the whole.... The whole eludes us but we know parts."[8] For Kant and Nietzsche the limits of knowledge are far more radical: strictly speaking, we cannot know anything at all. According to Socrates, we can know parts, but not the whole. Unless and until knowledge of the parts can be integrated into knowledge of the whole, our knowledge of the parts must remain tentative. A part of one whole is necessarily different from a part of another. Nonetheless, Strauss suggested that Pascal had captured the Socratic position perfectly when he said, "We know too much to be skeptics, but we know too little to be dogmatists."[9]

Nietzschean ignorance differed from Socratic ignorance because Nietzsche apprehended the problem of knowledge via the modern epistemological path pioneered by Descartes and brought to a peak or conclusion of sorts by Kant: *the* problem of knowledge is the problem of the subject and object. How can the subject ever penetrate to the known object (or the object sought to be known) when the subject always knows in and through its own subjectivity? Nietzsche followed the Cartesian-Kantian path, but, coming to the dead end of Kant's critical philosophy, he radicalized the modernist epistemology, by proclaiming that belief in the "real world," the world of truth or being as opposed to the apparent, sensible, deceptive world of becoming was merely a "prejudice" of the philosophers.[10] There was no other world; all such notions were merely human constructions. That "discovery" or proclamation opened the way for what we might crudely call Nietzsche's radical subjectivism, crudely because such terminology remains rooted in what Nietzsche seeks to dismiss as the old subject-object prejudice.[11]

Strauss agreed with Nietzsche's pessimism about the Nietzschean version of the Socratic promise, but he differed from Nietzsche quite drastically about wherein lay the problem of knowledge, or the limits of philosophy. The core difficulty that led Strauss to the Socratic conclusion that we know only that we do not know the most important things was far different from the Cartesian-Kantian problem, which formed the core of the challenge to philosophy for Nietzsche. Strauss observed:

> The knowledge which we possess is characterized by a fundamental dualism which has never been overcome. At one pole we find knowledge of homogeneity; above all in arithmetic. . . . At the opposite pole we find knowledge of heterogeneity, and in particular of heterogeneous ends; the highest form of this kind of knowledge is the art of the statesman. The latter kind of knowledge is superior to the former [because] . . . it is knowledge of what makes human life complete or whole. . . . But this knowledge—the political art in the highest sense— is not knowledge of the whole. It seems that knowledge of the whole would have to combine somehow political knowledge in the highest sense with knowledge of homogeneity. And this combination is not at our disposal.[12]

Like Socrates, Strauss thus concluded that the whole eludes us, but we know parts. We know parts of two sorts, or in two modes. We do not know how to combine knowledge of these two sorts into one comprehensive account of the whole. In language that Strauss often used, we can understand the fundamental alternatives, but not the one truth beyond the alternatives. The "structured ignorance" we attain by coming to understand why neither of the alternatives is satisfactory points away from both of the extreme positions sometimes attributed to Strauss. He does not think that philosophers can achieve knowledge of the whole. He himself surely never claimed to be a philosophic "know-it-all" (simply "wise") or that there are such "wise guys" who should rule, as Drury and the many others in the press who have charged him with elitism suggest. The philosopher, as Socrates understood him, is not marked by the arrogance of total knowing, but by the modesty promoted by his self-conscious recognition of the limits of his knowledge. The philosopher is prevented from being the most modest of humans only by virtue of the recognition that knowledge of ignorance is, when all is said and done, better than ignorance of ignorance. The philosopher can thus take some pride in his understanding of not merely the fact but also the causes of human ignorance, just as he can take pleasure in his own progress in learning. But the claims the philosopher can make are always limited.

Strauss's understanding of the nature of the philosopher's knowledge of ignorance also prevented him from falling into the opposite camp of the full-blown skeptics, the constructivists, or the historicists. We do know; the world is somehow, if incompletely, given to us to know. We may not know the whole, but human beings are aware of the whole and somehow open to it. "There is no surer protection against the understanding of anything than taking for granted or otherwise despising the obvious and the surface," Strauss was fond of saying. "The problem inherent in the surface of things, and only the surface of things, is the heart of things."[13] As Socrates showed, the problem is not "to discover the roots out of which the completed whole . . . has grown, or to discover the cause which has transformed the chaos into a *cosmos,* or to perceive the unity which is hidden behind the variety of things or appearances, but to understand the unity that is revealed in the manifest articulation of the completed whole." And this Socratic view of the whole as an order of essentially different kinds "makes possible the study of the human things as such."[14] There is no reason for a "subject" to stand completely naked in its lack of knowledge before the world, and even less basis for the dominating irruption of the subject into the world, aiming at the subjection of world or nature by man.[15] Strauss rejected, on the one side, the modern epistemological orientation, which denies the mind's access to the world and culminates in scientism, and the more radical Nietzschean constructivism, on the other. "By becoming aware of the dignity of the mind, we realize the true ground of the dignity of man, and therewith the goodness of the world, whether we understand it as created or as uncreated, which is the home of man because it is the home of the human mind."[16] Strauss thus resisted the movement within his own discipline of political science to transform itself into a science on the model of the natural sciences. Neither it, nor any other form of science, Strauss argued, tacitly following one of his philosophic mentors, Edmund Husserl, could escape reliance on "common sense," or on "pre-scientific awareness" of the world.[17] That awareness was sign and proof of the mind's "at-homeness" in the world.

Philosophy, as Strauss understood it, is not the constructivist activity made possible by the absence of a real world, or made necessary by our complete lack of access to such a world. It is rather the erotic activity made possible by the presence, if mystery, of the real world and our access to it. "Philosophy... could appear as Sisyphean or ugly," he admitted, "when one contrasts its achievement with its goal. Yet it is necessarily accompanied, sustained and elevated by *eros*. It is graced by nature's grace."[18]

One indication of the distance that separated Strauss and Nietzsche appears at the opening of the only writing Strauss devoted wholly to Nietzsche, an essay on *Beyond Good and Evil* that he wrote late in his life. There Strauss observed that Nietzsche is always pointing toward himself, to "Mr. Nietzsche." Plato, on the other hand, (and Strauss also, we might add) never points toward but always away from himself. Plato never speaks of "Mr. Plato."[19] This seemingly insignificant biographical or stylistic fact captures all the differences between Strauss, Socrates, and Plato, on the one side, and Nietzsche, on the other. For Nietzsche, philosophic activity represents a form of self-expression. According to Nietzsche, it is thus suitable for the philosopher as an individual to take center stage. For Strauss, Socrates, and Plato, philosophy results in a kind of wisdom that does not belong solely to a specific individual at a particular time or place.

In his analysis of Nietzsche's *Beyond Good and Evil*, Strauss suggested that Nietzsche's philosopher of the future shared something important with Socrates: Nietzsche's philosopher is also one who follows a certain way of life, not one who stands for certain doctrines. "No one has ever spoken so greatly and so nobly of what a philosopher is as Nietzsche," Strauss admitted in a lecture he delivered in February 1956 at the Hillel Foundation at the University of Chicago. But he also observed, "Philosophers of the future as Nietzsche described them remind one much more than Nietzsche himself seems to have thought of Plato's philosopher."[20] Nietzsche did not perceive the similarity, because he read the dialogues too much in terms of the standard views of both Socrates (the preaching and plebeian moralist) and Plato (the theorist of ideas) derived from Aristotle's *Metaphysics*.

Nonetheless, there are a number of important differences between Plato's Socrates and Nietzsche's philosophers of the future. When Nietzsche listed the virtues of his philosopher of the future, he added solitude and compassion to the Platonic virtues of wisdom and courage, but he dropped moderation and justice from Plato's list. The moral and political consequences of Nietzsche's philosophy of the future were thus very different from those of Socratic philosophy. And their differing lists of philosophical virtues reflected something much deeper in their differing conceptions of philosophy itself and therewith of human nature and nature altogether. Socrates' moderation was rooted in his knowledge of his ignorance and implicit in his knowledge of human nature or human being. The Nietzschean list of virtues rested on the very different conclusions about nature and humanity that he had drawn from his insight into the failure of previous philosophy. As Strauss pointed out, "for Nietzsche there cannot be a natural or rational morality because he denies that there is a nature of man: the denial of any cardinal difference between man and brute is a truth, if a deadly truth; hence there cannot be natural ends of man as man: all values are human creations."[21] The Nietzschean table of philosophical virtues reflects the daring required of a philosopher whose task is value-giving or value-making. Moderation and justice would not enable him to create a new meaning, justification, or goal for human existence.

Although, like Socrates, he did not claim that he or anyone else could give an adequate account of the whole, Strauss thought it was possible to identify something distinctively human. "Man is the only being which can be concerned with self-respect; man can respect himself because he can despise himself; he is 'the beast with red cheeks,' the only being possessing a sense of shame. . . .The presupposition of all this is that man is radically distinguished from non man, from brutes as well as from Gods, and this presupposition is ratified by common sense." As Nasser Behnegar rightly points out, Strauss's apparently frivolous, or at least nontraditional, definition actually implied within it the traditional (Aristotelian) notion of man as the rational and political animal: "Now, shame presupposes morality; an awareness of how one should live. But morality presupposes an awareness of how one ought to be, for we should live in such a way that we become what we ought to be. Now, this awareness cannot be clarified without the use of reason. Accordingly, the dignity of man is essentially connected with his capacity for morality, a capacity made possible because he is a rational being." Strauss saw that Nietzsche, in contrast, "taught that all human life and human thought ultimately rests on horizon-forming creations which are not susceptible of rational legitimatization. The creators are great individuals. . . . For Nature has ceased to appear as lawful and merciful."[22]

Nietzsche addressed his call "to individuals who should revolutionize their own lives, not to society or to his nation." Nevertheless, Strauss thought, Nietzsche expected to have a more general political effect. "He hoped that his call . . . would tempt the best men of the generations after him to become true selves and thus to form a new nobility which would be able to rule the planet. He opposed the possibility of a planetary aristocracy to the alleged necessity of a universal classless and stateless society. Being certain of the tameness of modern western man, he preached the sacred right of 'merciless extinction' of large masses of men." But, Strauss observed, "after having taken upon himself this great political responsibility, he could not show his readers a way toward political responsibility. He left them no choice except that between irresponsible indifference to politics and irresponsible political options." Nietzsche "thus prepared a regime which...made discredited democracy look like the golden age."[23] Strauss argued, however, that "liberal democracy, in contradistinction to communism and fascism, derives powerful support from a way of thinking which cannot be called modern at all: the premodern thought of our western tradition."[24]

It was not merely that the moral and political consequences of Nietzschean philosophy were vastly different from the moderation and justice of Socratic or Platonic political philosophy. According to Strauss, there was "one decisive difference between Nietzsche's philosophy of the future and Plato's philosophy" as philosophy. Unlike Socrates or Plato, Nietzsche's philosopher of the future was heir to the Bible.

> The philosopher of the future, as distinct from the classical philosopher, will be concerned with the holy. His philosophizing will be intrinsically religious. This does not mean that he believes in ... the Biblical God.

> He is an atheist, but an atheist who is waiting for a god who has not yet shown himself. He has broken with the Biblical faith...because the Biblical God as the creator of the world is outside the world.... The condition of the highest human excellence is that...there is nothing outside the world which could be of any concern to us—be it God or ideas or atoms of which we could be certain by knowledge or by faith.[25]

Following Nietzsche, Strauss observed that "modern thought reaches its culmination...in the most radical historicism, i.e., in explicitly condemning to oblivion the notion of eternity. For oblivion of eternity, or...estrangement from man's deepest desire and therewith from the primary issues, is the price which modern man had to pay, from the very beginning, for attempting to...become the master and owner of nature, to conquer chance."[26]

Rather than attempt to synthesize the two roots of Western civilization into a new "religious," if explicitly atheistic, philosophy, as Nietzsche did, Strauss attempted to revive the unresolved conflict between "reason" or philosophy and revelation that he thought was the "secret" source of the continued vitality of that civilization. Instead of declaring that "God is dead" and that "we have killed him," Strauss thus concluded his major book on ancient political philosophy by pointing out that "the all-important question which is coeval with philosophy although the philosophers do not frequently pronounce it [is] the question *quid sit deus* [what is (a) god?]." In a sense, he said in "Progress or Return?" both roots or poles of the Western tradition agreed, in opposition to modern thought, that what could be called "the divine law" was the most important thing to be learned. They differed radically, however, about what such learning entailed. For the ancient philosophers, the fact that human beings claimed to know a variety of divine laws meant that the question had to be raised, which was true. Positing one omnipotent and hence humanly unfathomable God, the authors of the Bible insisted that knowledge of the divine law as revealed mandated obedience, not impious questioning. Because revelation could not refute reason any more than reason was able to refute revelation, Strauss concluded, the question remained open. And so long as the question remained open (rather than being willfully closed, as it had been in modern political philosophy), both philosophy and faith continued to be real and vital possibilities. Unlike the modern synthesis, moreover, each of these poles mandated a strict morality. Indeed, Strauss went so far as to say: "The Bible and Greek philosophy agree in regard to what we may call, and we do call in fact, morality. They agree ... regarding the importance of morality, regarding the content of morality, and regarding its ultimate insufficiency. They differ as regards that 'x' which supplements or completes morality, [i.e.,] the basis of morality."[27] Unlike Nietzsche, Strauss did not think that he was "beyond good and evil." Nor did he call for other "philosophers of the future" to become so. There are thus other differences between Strauss and Nietzsche besides the one Laurence Lampert, Shadia Drury, and John Gunnell have all suggested, that Nietzsche was completely candid whereas Strauss was not. Strauss was not a hesitant Nietzsche so much as an admiring anti-Nietzsche.

Nietzsche's critique of modernity was, for Strauss, a possession of lasting value. Strauss refused to heed Nietzsche's call for a new "philosophy of the future," however. Instead, Strauss returned, almost alone in his generation, to the political philosophy of the ancients, even if to a novel version of it.

Strauss's deflection from Nietzsche's path was based on what he saw to be one of the chief difficulties in Nietzsche. Nietzsche's thought was marked by a "hesitation as to whether the doctrine of the will to power is his subjective project, to be superceded by other such projects in the future, or whether it is the final truth." Strauss thus discerned a "movement in Nietzsche's thought...from the supremacy of history towards the supremacy of nature." The movement of Strauss's thought back to the ancients may be understood as Strauss continuing on and completing that Nietzschean trajectory, so as to remove all the "hesitation" from Nietzsche's project and root it more solidly in nature.

Strauss's Postmodernism: After Heidegger

Strauss moved away from Nietzsche in one direction. He understood Heidegger's thought to be the most important effort to move in the other direction. "Existentialism is the attempt to free Nietzsche's alleged overcoming of relativism from the consequences of his relapse into metaphysics or of his recourse to nature."[28]

Heidegger also thought that a return to the ancients was required as a result of the failure of modern rationalism. But like Nietzsche, and unlike Strauss, Heidegger understood his own attempt to give a more original, explicitly untraditional reading of the ancients to be merely the first step toward making a "new beginning" or "leap" into an unknown future.[29] That difference has not prevented critics of Strauss, like Luc Ferry, from claiming that Strauss was both a Heideggerian and a Nazi. Even though he declared that "the only great thinker in our time is Heidegger," Strauss was, in fact, very critical of Heidegger's thought as well as of his politics.[30]

Strauss first encountered Heidegger in the early 1920s in Marburg, where Strauss had gone to study the neo-Kantian philosophy of Hermann Cohen. At that time, Strauss reports, Husserl had explained the difference between his own thought and that of the Marburg school of neo-Kantians by observing that the neo-Kantians began with the roof whereas he began with the foundations. "That meant that for the school of Marburg the sole task of the fundamental part of philosophy was...the analysis of scientific thought. Husserl however had realized more profoundly than anybody else that the scientific understanding of the world, far from being the perfection of our natural understanding, is derivative from the latter in such a way as to make us oblivious of the very foundations of the scientific understanding: all philosophic understanding must start from our common understanding of the world...as sensibly perceived prior to all theorizing."[31]

But, Strauss saw, Husserl's younger colleague Heidegger went much further in the same direction. "According to Heidegger Husserl *himself* began with the roof: the merely sensibly perceived thing is itself derivative; there are not first sensible perceived things and thereafter the same things in a state of being valued or in a state of affecting us. Our primary understanding of the world is not an understanding of things as objects but of what the Greeks indicated by *pragmata*, things which we handle and use."[32] In *Being and Time* Heidegger argued that the form of being traditionally called human finds and understands itself initially as "being-with-others" in a "world." We first come into contact with things as-ready-at-hand to use, and the use or other signal characteristic, such as holy or noble, depends upon the context or "world." Only when the "thing" does not work as expected do we stand back and ask, theoretically, what it ("taken by itself") is. Likewise, in everyday life we chatter to others in accepted terms without thinking much about what we are saying or our particular form of existence. Only when we are overwhelmed by an inexplicable sense of anxiety do we draw back into ourselves and ask why we continue to live as we do. At that point, we discover that there is no reason or cause; we continue to live only because we choose to do so. Our lives, our societies, and our thoughts do not have any fundamental ground or basis. They are products of our fundamental freedom. That freedom exists because we are mortal beings who live in time. Because we are mortal, moreover, the choices we face are severely restricted. We cannot and do not choose the time or place into which we are "thrown" at birth. We can choose only to persist resolutely into an unknown future—or not. Immortality is not an option. Any conception or belief about the eternal is posited and thus derivative from our temporality.

In *Being and Time* Heidegger had analyzed the only form of being, human being or *Dasein*, for which its own being was an issue. From that analysis he claimed to discover the essentially historical and so limited understanding of being as presence upon which Western philosophy had been founded. He had also proclaimed the need for a new kind of practical stance in the face of fundamental uncertainty—resolution. And in his notorious 1933 address as rector, as well as in the lectures he gave in 1936 as an "introduction to metaphysics," Heidegger found that resolution embodied politically in German National Socialism. As Heidegger saw it, two great, ideological superpowers, the Soviet Union and the United States, were competing for worldwide dominion. His own nation, Germany, was caught in the pincers.[33] Nietzsche had not been correct in thinking that everything at all times was fundamentally just an expression of the "will to power," but he was right about the twentieth century.[34] Individualism and collectivism were merely two sides or expressions of the same drive to reduce everything into material—Heidegger would later call it "standing reserve"—that had no inherent value, structure, or form of its own and that could, therefore, be transformed at will.

Unlike most other commentators, Strauss attributed the famous "turn" or change in Heidegger's thought partly to the defeat of Germany in World War II. Nietzsche had seen that "the twentieth century [was going] to be the age of world wars, leading up to planetary rule. If man were to have a future, this rule would have to be exercised by a united Europe." But, Strauss observed, "the failure of the Nazis [taught] Heidegger [that] ... Nietzsche's hope ... of a Europe not only united but revitalized by this new, transcendent responsibility of planetary rule" was "a delusion. A world society controlled either by Washington or Moscow" would mean, "as Marx had predicted, the victory of an ever more completely urbanized, ever more completely technological West over the whole planet—complete leveling and uniformity regardless of whether it is brought about by iron compulsion or by soapy advertisement of the output of mass production."[35]

Since "resolute" armed resistance had proved ineffective, Heidegger began to look for a different kind of "salvation" in the midst of the danger.[36] The task of what he now called "thought" in preparing for this salvation was twofold. The technology that threatened to make everything, including the human beings it was initially supposed to serve, into mere undifferentiated material or "standing reserve" to be transformed at will he now pronounced to be not merely rooted in, but a necessary outgrowth of, Western rationalism. Western rationalism was, in turn, a necessary outgrowth of Greek philosophy and its fundamental, if usually unrecognized, conception of Being as presence. To save humanity from the threat of technological extinction, it would be necessary to show that this old conception of Being was partial and therefore fallacious and so lay the grounds for the introduction of a new understanding of Being as ineluctable *Ereignis* (or "Event"). Like Nietzsche, Heidegger had observed that everything great or noble that human beings had achieved in the past was the result of their seeing something higher and better than themselves. Since the worldwide spread of technology was destroying all past ideals—or gods—Heidegger concluded, it would also be necessary for "thought" to prepare for the emergence of a new god.[37]

To counter the threat posed by the worldwide spread of technology, Strauss suggested, Heidegger's new god or religion would also have to be worldwide. Heidegger thus sought to initiate a dialogue between East and

West.[38] The East had an understanding of Being that did not lead to mastery, but despite its distinctive understanding of Being, the East was also threatened with extinction by the spread of technology. In order to have a dialogue—rather than a mere confrontation—between East and West of the kind Heidegger called for, Strauss suggested, it would be necessary to dig back into the roots of Western civilization to find a common ground. Because biblical religion was originally Middle Eastern, the West might find a common ground on the basis of which to begin a discussion by trying to understand the Bible not as the word of the universal god, but as a partial word, as Eastern, in the depths of our own Western tradition. (That would have provided a justification for Heidegger's use of biblical terms and categories in his purported secular, non-Christian analysis of human existence in *Being and Time*.)[39] Whether or not Heidegger himself saw the Bible as a potential basis for the dialogue he wished to initiate, it was clear that Heidegger's later poetizing "thought" had a distinctly religious character that left no place whatever for political philosophy.[40]

Although he often emphasized the connection between Heidegger's philosophy and his politics, Strauss insisted that *the* question, the only question, was whether what Heidegger claimed was true. The merits of the thought of an intellectual giant like Heidegger could not be determined merely by our gut reactions to his abhorrent politics. It was necessary, but not adequate, to point out the problematic political and moral effects of his thought. To respond to Heidegger adequately, one had to show where and how his analysis of human existence or *Dasein* was mistaken.

Heidegger himself had seen the difficulty Strauss pointed out in the analysis of human existence in *Being and Time*. To say that all thought is historically bounded without contradicting oneself by making a claim about all thought at all times and places, that is, a historically unlimited claim, it is necessary to argue that this insight arises at a special or "absolute moment" in history. Heidegger's later thought thus had the same structure as the thought of Hegel, Marx, and Nietzsche: he was led to claim that all past history led up to the discovery of a truth that was not available to people at other times and places. In contrast to Hegel, Marx, and Nietzsche, however, Heidegger also insisted that the truth of the history of Being or of the gradual forgetting and hence oblivion of Being that he himself put forward was limited. Neither he nor anyone else could know what would come in the future. Because they occurred at specific places and times, all views or understandings of "Being" or the world were partial. Neither he nor any other human being could choose or control the time and place at which he was born and from which he saw what he saw of the world. The particular, partial view any individual, people, or whole generation had was a dispensation of an ineluctable fate.

Heidegger thought he could perceive the limits of the understanding of Being as presence that had first been announced in ancient Greece, because he lived at the time at which the possibilities of that understanding could be seen to have been fully worked out by previous thinkers and thus exhausted. Heidegger had pointed out the limitations of the Greek understanding of Being as presence in *Being and Time*. Only later did he come to see that his own recognition of the limitations of the Greek understanding belonged to and resulted from a working out over time of the consequences of the "oblivion of Being," which he more or less equated with the history of Western philosophy. That history had come to its end and completion in the modern technological realization of the truth that there is no necessary, inherent, enduring, or intelligible order—or Being—in the world. Both in his infamous speech as rector (1933) and his posthumously published *Beiträge*, dating from the years 1936–38, Heidegger thus proclaimed the need for a new beginning. Because new understandings are "sent" or literally dis-covered, not made or created by human beings, the most Heidegger and his contemporaries could do to prepare for a new dispensation was to point out the limitations of the old. To say that all understandings of Being and the world are historically limited is to say that all such views are partial; in revealing some of the truth of Being, such views also necessarily cover over other aspects. Because all particular things are and must be understood in terms of their context, Heidegger insisted from the beginning of his career until its end, human beings cannot understand anything if their thought does not have a historical horizon that delimits and so defines a kind of whole, the whole of what they can see at their particular time and place.[41]

Even if Heidegger could justify his use of Christian categories in his first delineation of human existence and show that his claim to know that all thought is historically conditioned was not self-contradictory, Strauss pointed out, there was another fundamental problem with his new historically bounded and defined understanding of Being. Heidegger's insistence that Being could become known only in and through human beings meant, apparently, that there could be beings (e.g., the planets) without Being. In other words, Heidegger's account of human existence and understanding did not actually provide an account of the existence or intelligibility of the nonhuman cosmos. In his *Letter on Humanism*, Heidegger himself admitted that the analysis of human existence he had given in *Being and Time* was still too humanistic and hence traditional. In his later works

Heidegger thus dropped the references to Søren Kierkegaard and his understanding of angst, which had played a major role in *Being and Time*, "because Kierkegaard had spoken of existence within the traditional horizon, i.e., within the horizon of the traditional distinction between essence and existence."[42] But in trying to understand existence out of itself, Strauss charged, Heidegger's later thought remained fundamentally human in its scope or radius. It pointed out, correctly, that modern "natural science" is a human view and product, but it did not give an account of the existence of the nonhuman world or whole.

The reason Heidegger did not even try to present an account of the whole, Strauss indicated, was that Heidegger argued that "finitude" was the defining characteristic of human existence. He recognized, however, that finitude could be known and defined only in contrast to "infinity."[43] Heidegger thus said "ex nihil omne ens qua ens fit [out of nothing every being as being comes out]. This could remind one of the Biblical doctrine of creation [out of nothing]," Strauss commented. "But Heidegger has no place for the Creator-God."[44] Heidegger speaks of "Being" as "No-thing," because "Being is not a being," that is, Being has no limitations or definitions (although its "disclosure" or "truth" does).[45] In that sense, at least, in contrast to the finite beings, Being itself is in-finite. That is the reason Heidegger understands "Being" to be fundamentally unknowable and hence "mysterious." Human beings infer that there must be some cause for things as they are, but we define that cause or ground negatively, in terms of what it is not. According to Strauss, "*esse,* as Heidegger understands it, may be described crudely, superficially, and even misleadingly (but not altogether misleadingly) by saying that it is a synthesis of the Platonic ideas and the Biblical God: it is as impersonal as the Platonic ideas and as elusive as the Biblical God."[46] Like Hegel's philosophy of history and Nietzsche's conception of the philosopher-legislator, Strauss concluded, Heidegger's radically historicist understanding of Being thus seeks to combine the two basic elements or poles of Western civilization—the essentially mysterious but somehow personal biblical God with the impersonal, rational Cause of ancient Greek philosophy. But these two elements are, in fact, fundamentally contradictory, incommensurable, and incoherent.[47]

It was in *Natural Right and History* that Strauss responded most fully and emphatically to both Heidegger's analysis of human existence and the history of philosophy on which he later based his radical historicism.[48] The title of Strauss's book reflected both the parallel and the differences between his thought and Heidegger's. In *Being and Time* Heidegger wrote abstractly about "being"; in *Natural Right and History* Strauss referred more concretely to nature. Heidegger argued that human existence is essentially temporal and historical. Strauss contended that it is essentially moral and political. "The 'experience of history' and the less ambiguous experience of the complexity of human affairs may blur, but they cannot extinguish, the evidence of those simple experiences regarding right and wrong which are at the bottom of the philosophic contention that there is a natural right. Historicism either ignores or else distorts these experiences."[49]

According to Strauss, Heidegger had not correctly described or analyzed what he denoted first as human existence or *Dasein* and later as human being, but which Strauss would talk about in more traditional terms as human nature or the human soul. Heidegger had argued that the fundamental human experience is disclosed in a mood of anxiety that cannot, like fear, be attributed to any particular cause. By reflecting on the fact of this anxiety, however, human beings discover that it expresses the fundamental truth of their existence: it is not necessary. It is the result of a free choice. Strauss protested that the way human beings have actually experienced their freedom historically, that is, in the recorded past in many different times and places, has been by choosing between what they regard as good and bad. As Heidegger himself emphasized, human perceptions are not confined to the attractions of pleasure and aversion to pain. Human beings understand themselves, and choose what to do, in terms of a "world" that is defined by the gods, or what these particular human beings, living at that place and time, regard as holy, as well as by their animal needs and desires. Because human understandings of what is good and holy differ not only from place to place and time to time but also within any given society, Strauss pointed out, human beings are led to seek a universal standard of right, by nature as opposed to mere convention, that is, to engage in political philosophy. Philosophy or "theory" does not arise, as Heidegger had suggested, merely when a tool fails to function as expected. As Heidegger himself pointed out in describing what it means to live in a world with others, the functioning or nonfunctioning of any tool can be understood only in terms of the broader context of what is useful or important in a particular society at a specific time and place.

Strauss suggested that the experience Heidegger claimed was fundamental to human existence per se was, in fact, an experience peculiar to our time. As a result of the apparent success of modern natural science in providing people not merely with knowledge but with the ability to manipulate things, contemporary logical positivists had declared that anything that could not be studied with the techniques employed by modern natural scientists could not be known. Among the "things" that could not be studied or shown to be true by the collection and analysis of data were hu-man judgments concerning good and bad, right and wrong. Told that these judgments—which include the most basic as well as the most important decisions people make about their own lives—were merely irrational ex-pressions of feeling or arbitrary "values," people became uncertain about the rightness or wrongness, truth or falsity, of their judgments, and thus anxious.

Strauss concluded that "the uneasiness which today is felt but not faced can be expressed by a single word: relativism."[50] Contemporary liberals believe that our inability to know what is right or wrong compels us to be tolerant. But, Strauss observed, if there is no reason to prefer tolerance to intolerance, because both are equally "values," the choice between them appears to be an arbitrary decision that is more akin to intolerance than tolerance. "Once we realize that the principles of our actions have no other support than our blind choice, we really do not believe in them any more. We cannot wholeheartedly act upon them.... In order to live, we have to silence the easily silenced voice of reason, which tells us that our principles are in themselves as good or as bad as any other principles. The more we cultivate reason, the more we cultivate nihilism." Strauss thus thought that Heidegger understood the implications of the domination of modern scien-tific rationalism for human life much better than the more sanguine logical positivists or relativistic liberals.[51]

Strauss understood the character and effects of modern nihilism differ-ently from either Nietzsche or Heidegger, however. According to Strauss, the cause of nihilism is "the contemporary rejection of natural right," that is, the denial that there is "any standard with reference to which we can judge of the ideals of our own as well as of any other society."[52] Whereas Nietzsche and Heidegger both understood themselves to be responding to the nihilism of the past and the present by offering grounds of hope for a better future, Strauss thought their works not merely expressed but con-tributed to the loss of belief in any eternal truth and basis for moral order.

According to Nietzsche, modern nihilism consists in the denial that any thing, person, or way of life has any real or inherent value. This nihilism is the result of a historical development or "dialectic." Human beings had first tried to overcome the perceived limits on their own lives and power not only by enslaving others, but also by positing the existence of divine beings that lacked the primary and most fundamental limitation on human life—death. The people who were enslaved then took revenge on their mas-ters by comparing their masters unfavorably with these higher beings, and the masters, wishing to prove themselves the best, most superior human beings, gradually internalized the standards the slaves used to criticize them. As a result of the "spiritualization," which included both greater emotional depth and increased intellectual acuity, that developed as a result of the perpetual internal conflict between repressed desires and expressed beliefs, modern men discovered that the standard on the basis of which they found themselves lacking was a human projection. Having discovered themselves, rather than some independently existing god or nature, to be the source of value and valuation, Nietzsche concluded, human beings could now consciously and knowingly affirm themselves as such.[53]

Strauss agreed with Nietzsche, as opposed to Heidegger, in thinking that the modern crisis was primarily moral. But Strauss thought Heidegger had drawn out some of the implications of Nietzsche's analysis of the crisis of our time better than Nietzsche himself. In announcing that "God is dead" and arguing that everything is "will to power," Heidegger argued, Nietzsche had pronounced the truth of our times.[54] That nihilistic truth was made manifest in the worldwide spread of technology, which showed that nothing necessarily existed or had an inherent character and value in itself, because everything could be transformed. Human beings could not impress their own order or value upon things, because they, too, were essentially malleable.

Strauss agreed with Heidegger that unregulated technological development threatened to destroy the human race, if not the earth itself. Who would not agree in the age of nuclear war? But Strauss did not agree that the ever-increasing spread and power of technology was an inexorable historical result of the "oblivion of Being." Strauss saw technology, more traditionally, to be merely the practical application of modern natural science for the sake of relieving man's condition. And he argued that neither modern natural science itself nor its technological application necessarily results in the negation of all value or order in things. On the contrary, insofar as modern natural science claims that there can be infinite progress in our acquisition of knowledge, modern natural science suggests that we can never achieve knowledge of the whole. And if we cannot understand the whole, the universe is and always will remain fundamentally mysterious. In explicit opposition to Nietzsche, Strauss thus pointed out, modern natural science does not and cannot disprove the existence of the essentially mysterious biblical Creator-God. It is not modern natural science, but a certain interpretation or understanding of the implications of modern natural science for human life that has produced the current crisis of belief.[55]

If modern natural science can tell us only how things are and not how they should be, that is, if science can establish "facts" but not "values," science cannot answer the question, Why science? "If science or reason cannot answer the question of why science is good," Strauss reasoned, "science says in effect that the choice of science is not rational: one may choose with equal right pleasing and otherwise satisfying myths." Science no longer conceives of itself as the perfection of the human understanding, as it did in ancient philosophy; on the contrary, modern science "admits that it is based on fundamental hypotheses which will always remain hypotheses." We see that "the whole structure of science does not rest on evident necessities ... [and that] the choice of the scientific orientation is as groundless as the choice of any alternative orientation."[56] Reflection on the character of modern natural science thus seems to lead to the "existentialist" truth that Heidegger announced in *Being and Time.*

In his later work Heidegger admitted that the analysis of human existence he had presented in *Being and Time* was true only in and of our time. To show that all truth or knowledge was historically limited, he saw that he had to give a history—the history of Being, as he called it. In *Natural Right and History* Strauss thus criticized both Heidegger's claim that the truth of technology was available only in the twentieth century and the history of philosophy Heidegger proposed to support that claim.

A philosopher did not have to live in the twentieth century in order to perceive the dangers inherent in a technology emancipated from moral and political supervision, Strauss observed. "Aristotle did not conceive of a world state because he was absolutely certain that science is essentially theoretical and that the liberation of technology from moral and political control would lead to disastrous consequences." In the twentieth century we saw that "uncontrolled progress of technology has made universal and perpetual tyranny a serious possibility." Strauss thus thought that "only a rash man would say that Aristotle's view—that is, his answers to the questions of whether or not science is essentially theoretical and whether or not technological progress is in need of strict moral or political control—has been refuted."[57]

Nor did Strauss think that the spread of technology meant that the difference between the United States and the Soviet Union was negligible. On the contrary, he concluded his essay "The Three Waves of Modernity" by observing that "the superiority of liberal democracy to communism, Stalinist or post-Stalinist, is obvious enough." To bolster, if not establish, the conviction of citizens of contemporary liberal democracies that the principles of their governments and their way of life were superior to those of their enemies, Strauss saw that it would be necessary to meet and overturn the threat posed by the nihilist historicist argument that denies that human beings can have any access to a transcendent, eternal truth on the basis of which they can judge the goodness or badness of competing claims.[58]

Strauss observed that Heidegger's contention that all thought is historically limited was based on a history of philosophy, but that this history had never been submitted to critical analysis.[59] Nietzsche and Heidegger both claimed that there was an inexorable development from the emergence of rationalism in ancient Greece to modern nihilism. Strauss's studies of the works of early modern philosophers like Machiavelli and Hobbes convinced him, however, that these philosophers had knowingly and intentionally "lowered the sights." The change from ancient to modern philosophy was not the result of any necessity, but a product of human choice or decision. The modern reconceptualization of nature as the condition from which human beings should move as quickly and far as possible, rather than as the source of a general standard whereby all claims about what is good and right could be judged, had in the long run been the cause of the contemporary loss of faith in the capacity of reason to provide human beings with guidance. In both *Natural Right and History* and "The Three Waves of Modernity," Strauss argued that later modern philosophers corrected, but in doing so built on and extended, the modernist insights of their predecessors. By means of historical studies, Strauss thus tried to recover an understanding of classical philosophy "exactly as it understood itself" as an alternative to the ever-deepening crisis of modernity. He did not attempt to show that classical philosophy was simply superior to modern philosophy. "Who can dare to say that Plato's doctrine of ideas as he intimated it, or Aristotle's doctrine of the *nous* that does nothing but think itself and is essentially related to the eternal visible universe, is the true teaching?"[60] To respond to the claims of radical historicism, Strauss thought, it would be sufficient to show that ancient and modern philosophers addressed the same fundamental problems. In seeing that "problems, such as the problem of justice, persist or retain their identity in all historical change, however much they may be obscured by the temporary denial of their relevance and however variable or provisional all human solutions to these problems may be, . . . the human mind liberates itself from its historical limitations."[61]

Historicists assume, for example, that they have discovered "a dimension of reality that had escaped classical thought, namely, the historical dimension." But "the question becomes inevitable whether what was hailed in the nineteenth century as a discovery was not, in fact, an invention, that is, an arbitrary interpretation of phenomena which had always been known and which had been interpreted much more adequately prior to the emergence of 'the historical consciousness.'"[62] Ancient writers like Thucydides and Xenophon knew about something they called history. That history was preeminently a record of political events. It did not have a necessary order or logic. It merely recorded a series of thereafters. "What we call History would be the succession or simultaneity of [Platonic] caves," Strauss suggested. In Plato, "the [shadows reflected on the] ceilings [of the caves] are *nomoi* [by convention] which is understood in contradistinction to *phusei* [by nature]." In modernity, a new understanding of a kind of natural right emerged, "which was based on a devaluation of nature. Hobbes' state of nature is the best known example." This devaluation of nature was a necessary, but not a sufficient, condition for the emergence of a historical consciousness. "Nature" itself had to be reduced to a "conception" of nature or the world that varied from time to time as well as from place to place. From the earlier point of view, "history, the object of historical consciousness, [thus becomes] a sequence of *nomoi, phusis* being understood as one *nomos* among many."[63] Since neither modern natural science nor modern philosophy promises to provide human beings with knowledge of the whole, Strauss observed, we no longer talk about progress; we only talk about change. Under such circumstances, the older view of history might appear to be closer to the facts as we now see them than a philosophy that argues that these facts or Weltanschauungs have a necessary order. At the very least, by questioning the dominant understanding of our time, we can demonstrate in practice as well as in precept that human thought is not historically restricted in the way Heidegger maintained.

Derridean Postmodernism

Let us now compare Strauss's response to the problems—philosophical and political—bequeathed to us by Nietzsche and Heidegger with the response of a more obviously postmodern thinker, Jacques Derrida, to the same problems and philosophers. At first glance, no two thinkers would appear to have less in common. Strauss explicitly sought to revive the Western tradition in the face of the radical critique leveled by Nietzsche and Heidegger; Derrida just as explicitly attempted to carry the critique even further. Strauss's inclinations were politically conservative; Derrida's sympathies were with the radical left. The first and necessary step in reading any book, according to Strauss, is to understand it as its author did; Derrida is famous for arguing that the author's intention does not control the meaning of the text.[64] Strauss read Plato in terms of the "age-old quarrel between poetry and philosophy"; Derrida denied that there is a fundamental difference between mythos and logos.[65] Strauss argued that Plato's

Socrates represents a way of life, not a set of doctrines; following Heidegger, Derrida treated the history of philosophy from Socrates onward as the history of "metaphysics" or "onto-theology," that is, as doctrinal. Strauss emphasized the tension between politics and philosophy; Derrida thought all attempts to articulate and so establish order—poetic or rhetorical as well as scientific or philosophical—were essentially "political."[66]

In light of the apparently polar opposition, the similarities between Strauss and Derrida are both surprising and striking. Both men traced the origins of their own thought, at least in part, to their experiences as persecuted Jews.[67] Because both Strauss and Derrida argued that a careful reading shows that some—or perhaps in the case of Derrida, all—texts have multiple meanings; because they both insisted on "thick" interpretations or readings, both have been described as "Talmudic" commentators.[68] Both argued that what an author does not say is often as important as, if not more important than, what he does; it is necessary to read between the lines.[69] Both suggested in the case of Plato that careful reading of the dialogues shows that all the surface arguments and doctrines are undercut.[70] Both suggested that Plato shows that Socrates let the city of Athens kill him to prove in deed, as it were, that philosophy does not threaten to undermine the legal order.[71] Both suggested that the explicit teachings of the dialogues have a political function or purpose. But neither thought that Plato's philosophy—or that of anyone else—should be understood simply or solely in political terms. On the contrary, both Strauss and Derrida insisted that philosophers in general, and Nietzsche and Heidegger in particular, should not be judged solely in terms of their political associations or effects; but both also argued that Nietzsche and Heidegger *were implicated* in the rise of National Socialism.[72] Endorsing some aspects of the radical critique of the tradition by Nietzsche and Heidegger, both Strauss and Derrida sought to avoid the disastrous political results of that critique. Avoiding those results appeared, at least at times, to be the major purpose of both authors' works. Both concluded that everything is not and never will be wholly intelligible; on the contrary, both argued, in opposition to Hegel, that there are aspects of "things" that are not and never will be captured by or expressible in logos. Finally, in opposition to Nietzsche and Heidegger as well as to Hegel, both Strauss and Derrida insisted that there is no necessary direction or "end" to "history."

There is so much convergence in the midst of the divergence between Strauss and Derrida because, as Strauss says of himself and Gadamer, beginning at the same place, they subsequently marched in almost entirely different directions. Strauss followed Nietzsche and Heidegger in trying to get beyond modernity by returning to the ancients in order to make a new beginning; but Derrida took the modern critique of "metaphysics" and the "anti-theological ire" that fired it even further.

Like Heidegger and Strauss before him, Derrida's thought began with insights he gleaned from Edmund Husserl. It was, indeed, Husserl's failure to provide the foundation for science that he sought that sent Heidegger, Strauss, and Derrida back to the problem posed by Nietzsche concerning the limits of reason. But Derrida's studies of Husserl took him in a very different direction from that which Heidegger and Strauss pursued. If, as Husserl argued, science arises from and so depends upon prescientific experience, then, both Heidegger and Strauss concluded, it is necessary to engage in what Heidegger called the "de-struktion" of the philosophical tradition to clear away an accumulation of theoretical terms and conceptions that stand between us and the original experience we want to recapture. Because *consciousness* and *self-consciousness* are both terms that arise only in modern philosophy, Heidegger and Strauss jettisoned the phenomenological reductions, whereby Husserl himself attempted to reconstruct the basic elements of our consciousness, and proceeded directly to study the Greek origins of philosophy, philosophy that had not yet become encrusted by or with a tradition, and so philosophy that was closer to the prephilosophical or prescientific experience out of which it developed.

Derrida, in contrast, proceeded through Husserl's reductions. Early in his *Logical Investigations,* Husserl distinguished signs, which merely point to a meaning to be found elsewhere, from concepts, which contain their own meaning. We necessarily use signs in communicating with others, Husserl admitted. All language is essentially indicative. But, he suggested, we do not need to use signs in our own thinking or internal soliloquy. There we can proceed through or in terms of pure concepts, that is, nonspatial, nontemporal ideas, which have been the object of pure knowledge since Plato.

What reflection on the experience of internal soliloquy actually shows, Derrida argued, is that there is neither a unitary "self" nor any eternally present "ideas" for it to contemplate. Self-consciousness, that is, consciousness of oneself as a self, entails a certain division or doubling of itself within the self, so that a part separates in order to look back at itself. Likewise, the notion of atemporal, nonspatial ideas that can be infinitely recalled or recollected entails a certain deferral or reserve in the contents of the human mind. If they are subject to recall or recollection, these ideas are not always present to consciousness.[73] They do not, in other words, have Being in the traditional sense of presence that Heidegger had explicated. Derrida's study of Husserl's reduction of the basic objects or experience of consciousness thus led him to his famous notion of *differance*, the claim that all the contents of what used to be called consciousness—ideas, verbal signs for ideas, and the things to which these ideas and words refer—are characterized by an internal division that generates different things or meanings over time by deferring some of the meaning or effects of the division. Derrida combined this insight with another he took from Husserl's study of the *Origins of Geometry*, to formulate his signature contention that what we call "thinking" ought to be described, rather, as a kind of "writing."[74]

In the introduction he wrote to his translation of the *Origins*, Derrida pointed out that what is written down can always be erased. So if the transmission of knowledge over time entails writing, there cannot be any essentially eternal ideas; all are subject to being erased. As Plato's Socrates complains in the *Phaedrus*, moreover, anything that is written down becomes separated from its author or "father," who is no longer there to explain it. As a result of being written down, Derrida thus concluded, everything loses something of its original meaning, some aspects of what the author had in mind when she or he wrote. All we have, all that is left, are marks or "traces" of the intended meaning of an "author" or "source" who is no longer present, even if he or she is still alive, because we all change over time. In order to acquire a full meaning, to survive rather than gradually to fade away, these traces have to be reinscribed on the minds of readers in new writings. But in the books or minds of others, these marks or ideas will necessarily be put into a new context and thereby acquire a new meaning. The process is ongoing. And it is not limited to human productions or works of art. Following Heidegger, who described all the beings as "traces" of Being, Derrida regarded all "things" in the world as such traces or leavings from the past. Unlike Heidegger, however, Derrida insisted that there is no beginning or being (which cannot, therefore, be forgotten). The process of reinscription, in which some marks are erased by being crossed over by others, and others are deepened by repetition, goes on without origin or end, because it is impossible "to write on a blank slate." Writing presupposes something or someone already there to impress or inscribe.

In declaring that there is no eternal truth to be found, Derrida not only concurred with the critique of the Western philosophical tradition initiated by Nietzsche; he sought to carry that critique even further. Like Strauss, however, Derrida sought to avoid the totalitarian political consequences of Nietzsche's critique.[75] In response to Nietzsche's "totalizing" doctrines—the "eternal return of the same," "*amour fati*," and the "will to power"—Derrida argued on the basis of his analysis of everything as a trace (1) that nothing ever remains the same as itself, much less returns eternally, (2) that there is no necessity or fate, because all things are essentially and ineradicably "indeterminate" or "undecidable," and (3) that they are undecidable because we ourselves are not a unit or unity with a "will" that we can impose. If nothing ever remains the same, Derrida pointed out, the things we want to affect, we ourselves, and the circumstances under which we act are all constantly changing. And if all the factors are constantly changing, the direction or character of the changes and the conjunction of the various factors cannot be predicted or controlled. If we attempt merely to preserve or conserve, we will see things—ourselves, our bodies, our memories, our institutions, and our knowledge—all gradually decay, crumble, and fade away; they will be written over and erased. We cannot control the outcomes of our actions if the materials upon which we work, the circumstances, and we ourselves are in flux. Indeed, if we are internally divided, we ourselves are not of a single mind; we do not know, nor can we determine, what we really want to do. There is always something subconscious and unrecognized at work. Since we cannot preserve ourselves or control our fate, we have no option but to try to perpetuate our existence by opening ourselves and taking in new and different elements, if we are not simply and gradually to fade away, be covered or written over, and forgotten. What this means in political terms is that, rather than engaging in the "great politics" of imperial world conquest, Europeans must open themselves to the "Other," to the non-Western, and to the utterly unexpected.

Both Strauss and Derrida opposed Marxist as well as fascist totalitarianism, but the basis of their opposition and the alternative policies they suggested were radically different. To counter the threat of totalitarian tyranny, Strauss had argued, it was necessary to maintain a variety of regimes, especially liberal democracies. Although he criticized the Enlightenment political philosophy upon which Western liberal democracies were explicitly based, he thought there were premodern sources of support for these moderate forms of government. In contrast to the universal, purportedly rational principles of the Enlightenment, these "premodern" ancient and medieval sources suggested that political societies would always be particularistic and therefore somewhat closed. Defining themselves on the basis of affective ties, shared traditions, and beliefs, Plato and Aristotle pointed out, political societies tend to define themselves as a "we" in opposition to the strange or foreign "they."[76] Precisely because they are necessarily somewhat closed, Plato emphasized, political societies are likely to react negatively to critics, especially to philosophers like Socrates who question the justice of their particular laws on the basis of universal, rationally founded principles. Strauss thought contemporary students of political philosophy needed to recognize the tension between philosophy and politics in order to maintain the conditions under which both philosophy and a decent political order remained possible. Admitting that the particularistic ethnic basis and, even more, religious beliefs that had united polities in the past had led them to persecute free thinkers, Strauss nevertheless argued that the affective ties as well as the moral and religious beliefs characteristic of traditional societies had also prompted their citizens to fight and die in defending their communities. By criticizing the Christian roots of the dominant moral and political conceptions in the West, philosophers like Nietzsche had undermined the conviction that Western civilization was worth fighting and dying for. Living in the midst of a modern liberal democracy, Strauss did not think he had to promote intellectual and religious toleration so much as self-restraint on the part of intellectuals and philosophers, particularly in criticizing and opposing the religious beliefs of others.

Derrida also opposed "the frightening totalitarian dogmatism that some of us have known how to resist up until now," both in practice and in precept.[77] But, especially with the fall of the Berlin wall and the end of the cold war, he thought it was as necessary to oppose "the counter-dogmatism that is setting in today,... to the point of banning the word 'capital,' indeed even the critique of certain effects of...the 'market.'"[78] Derrida did not want to encourage or support "the great politics" of world-domination that Nietzsche had advocated any more than Strauss did. Perceiving the apparently inexorable spread of American culture and its equally, if more softly, homogenizing tendencies, Derrida, like Heidegger, sought to counter American technological and economic power by means of a reconstituted and reconceived "Europe." Unlike Heidegger, however, Derrida emphasized the pluralistic and democratic parts of the European "heritage."

Europe has not been and never will be perfectly united, Derrida pointed out. There had been an attempt to unify Europe in 1939, he reminded his listeners in a talk he gave in 1990. (Nietzsche had also called for such a unification of Europe in *Beyond Good and Evil,* we might recall.) The Nazi attempt had been blocked by the Western democratic nations in the name of another idea of Europe, and their victory had placed barriers or divisions that were just now coming down in 1990. But the fall of the Berlin Wall and the end of the cold war, which together had given rise to new hopes of reunification, had also revived the danger of the reemergence of old forms of religious fanaticism, nationalism, or racism (clearly seen first in Bosnia and then in Kosovo). And the danger was not limited to eastern Europe. In light of escalating discrimination and violence against non-Caucasian immigrants in virtually all western European nations, Derrida called for a policy not merely of toleration of racial and religious differences, but of open receptivity or "hospitality."[79]

"Europe" has always been composed of different nations speaking different languages under different governments, Derrida reminded his readers. He was not arguing in favor of political unification or even federation so much as cultural reinvigoration. The unity of "Europe" admittedly has a geographical foundation, but it is primarily cultural or spiritual. Especially since the nineteenth century, Europeans like Paul Valery, Husserl, and Heidegger have regarded "Europe" as the intellectual leader of the world. At the same time, they have feared that this intellect or its grounds were being eroded. In order for Europe to remain the intellectual and spiritual leader of the world, Derrida emphasized, Europeans could not merely and narrowly insist on their cultural superiority. On the contrary, it was the belief in their cultural and racial superiority that had almost destroyed Europe. Europe had become the leader or "head" of the world by innovating and exploring. In order to keep what was most worth preserving in the European heritage alive, Derrida thus suggested, it was necessary to see the European intellect looking forward into the unknown, so to speak, toward a "New World."

Europeans who come later thus have "a double, a contradictory, and hence a perhaps impossible responsibility." On the one hand, they need to recall what happened in the past and so preserve it, in order to avoid past excesses and evils. They need to remember that some of the worst abuses have been those undertaken under the banner of the completely "new," for example, attempts to wipe the slate clean and begin entirely anew—such as the terrors of the French Revolution and Stalin's new economic order. To preserve the core of their intellectual heritage, they must continue to experiment. They cannot, for example, turn their backs on technology; they must rather be attentive to the novel dangers it poses to their freedom. Rather than close themselves off from the new and strange, from foreigners, or from recent developments abroad, "the duty to recall what has been promised under the name Europe, to re-identify Europe" thus "also dictates opening Europe ... onto that which is not, never was, and never will be Europe." It "dictates welcoming foreigners in order not only to integrate them but to recognize and accept their alterity."[80]

Europe does not and should not constitute a cultural or a political hegemony. The political universalism for which it is and ought to be responsible is that of human rights and international law. By advocating the worldwide recognition and protection of human rights and the enforcement of international law, Derrida did not merely appear to be endorsing the political goals of the Enlightenment. He also seemed to want to impose uniform, universal standards. He admitted, in fact, that he was endorsing the goals of the Enlightenment. But he pointed out that he was not doing so in the same way or on the same grounds as early modern political philosophers did. He did not worry, therefore, as Strauss and Heidegger had, about a world government's becoming tyrannous if it enforced universal standards, even and perhaps even especially if these standards were egalitarian and hence "democratic." If, as Derrida is most famous for arguing, no single human being, much less a people or species, can ever remain the same, human beings will never be simply and completely equal or actually have the same rights. Nor, if everything is always changing, is it actually possible to formulate any law uniformly, much less enforce or impose it thus.

On the contrary, Derrida argued in an essay titled "Force of Law," a law necessarily loses its abstract generality each and every time it is applied. The limited, always somewhat partial, if not partisan character of the rule of law is demonstrated every time the law is applied to particular people and circumstances by a judge.[81] One party to the case necessarily loses, and that party is not likely to believe that it has been treated justly. If the rationality or justice of laws were universally and completely recognized, Derrida suggested, laws would not need to be enforced. The fact that force has to be threatened, if not used, in order to execute and enforce the rule of law indicates that laws never rest entirely on unanimous consent. But insofar as the law privileges one part of society over another, it is not perfectly or unambiguously just.

Strauss had also pointed out the gap between the generality of laws and the requirements of particular circumstances and had concluded, like Derrida, that the rule of law would never be perfectly just. That was the reason ancient political philosophers had argued that the only truly just form of government would be the rule of the wise "philosopher-kings." Unlike the laws, which must always be formulated as general rules, philosopher-kings would have the prudence to determine what was best to do under particular, changing circumstances. However, precisely because the ignorant do not possess wisdom and therefore cannot understand or recognize it in others, the ancients also saw that wise men would seldom if ever rule. The best outcome generally possible was, therefore, for a few relatively well-educated people to rule on the basis of laws to which the governed had consented.

Because he denied that there are any eternal, unchanging truths, Derrida also denied that there are any wise men who can say how these truths are manifested or can be applied in various circumstances. For Derrida, the gap between the generality of the law and the particularity of its application meant that there is always an occasion or "grounds" for a "deconstructive" critique. The role of an intellectual or a critic is to analyze and describe the injustice and irrationality inherent in any rule in order to prevent the development of a closed "totalitarian" system.[82] That is the only way human freedom can be preserved. If human rights and the rule of international law are posited as goals that admittedly can never be fully realized or achieved, Derrida thought, they become standards on the basis of which all contrary practice can be criticized. He thus urged his fellow Europeans to assume "the European, and *uniquely* European, heritage of an idea of democracy, while also recognizing that this idea, like that of international law, is never simply given, that its status is not even that of a regulative idea in the Kantian sense, but rather something that remains to be thought and to come; not something that is certain to happen tomorrow,... but a democracy that must have the structure of a promise."[83] Once they accept human rights and international law as the definition of right politics, Europeans will not merely be able to condemn their own past imperialism and colonialism. They will be able to strive for greater freedom, at home and abroad, at present and in the future, by pointing out the myriad threats to the securing of rights and the faults of all actual legal systems.

By urging Europeans to take "responsibility" for their "heritage," Derrida insisted, he did not mean taking "responsibility" in the old "juridical" or "ethical" sense. If, as he argued, there is no unified "self" and people cannot control the effects of their actions any more than they can be certain of their own motives, individuals cannot and should not be regarded as "agents" who should be blamed or held "responsible" for the evil effects of their deeds.[84] He thus emphasized the root of "responsibility" in "response." Because nothing exists "in itself," but everything, in fact, impinges upon everything else, he pointed out, human beings have no choice but to "respond." We can respond in a variety of ways, however. We can, fruitlessly and ineffectively, try to preserve past achievements by insulating them from present challenges. Or we can recognize the necessity of opening ourselves up to the challenge of the unknown and unfamiliar, and, remembering where and how we went wrong in the past, we can try to achieve more of what was good while avoiding what was bad. In particular, Derrida urged his fellow Europeans to remember all the bloodshed that racial prejudices, ethnic cleansing, and religious intolerance had caused in the past so that they would be more open in the future. One of the ways in which he hoped Europe would distinguish itself from both Islamic fundamentalism in the Middle East and American "theocracy" would be to represent and promote a nonreligious, a purely secular, form of modern democracy.

Contrasting the Two Forms of Postmodernism

Although they were both critical of the Enlightenment philosophy that underlies modern liberal democratic regimes, we thus see, both Strauss and Derrida nevertheless endorsed a version of modern democracy. The versions or visions of modern democracy and the reasons they embraced it were, however, rather different. Arguing that anything short of the rule of the wise will be unjust, Strauss urged his readers to moderate both their political expectations and their philosophical critiques of existing practice. In particular, he tried to pacify the "anti-theological ire" that gave rise to the modern Enlightenment by reminding his readers that the claims of revelation cannot be defeated by reason. He regarded modern liberal democracy not as the best kind of regime conceivable, but as the best, because the most moderate, regime possible under current circumstances. Denying that human life is or can ever be made entirely rational, Derrida, in contrast, explicitly reaffirmed the political goals of the modern Enlightenment, even though he admitted that these goals are and always will be impossible to achieve. By endorsing the Enlightenment goals, he sought to encourage his contemporaries to point out and fault existing institutions, wherever they fell short. Whereas Strauss urged his readers to recognize that all polities will be somewhat closed, Derrida argued that they should become ever more open. Instead of recognizing the role religion plays in supporting popular morality, Derrida explicitly hoped to see the "death of God" that Nietzsche had announced become even more pronounced.[85]

Strauss did not live into the period in which Derrida's work became popular, especially in the United States. We suspect, however, that he would have said some rather critical, if not negative, things about it. For example, Derrida has reiterated Heideggerian worries about technologically based homogenization, especially as a result of the power of the media, but Strauss would have observed that Derrida himself reduced or "redescribed" everything as a trace. Derrida himself thus contributed to the homogenizing tendency that Heidegger thought was inherent in modern philosophy and science. According to Derrida, everything is essentially different and therefore essentially the same, inasmuch as everything is always in flux. That is, of course, a very old position; it was the understanding of the world characteristic of all pre-Socratic poetry and philosophy, except for Parmenides.[86] Heidegger had given a new reading of pre-Socratic philosophy, but Derrida did not pay any attention to it, tied as it was to Heidegger's conception of Being as *Ereignis,* or event. Derrida presented his own version of a secularized conception of the Advent, in which the "coming" can only be anticipated, anxiously and receptively; it cannot be predicted or known. But, Strauss would probably have pointed out, Derrida had even less right to use or appropriate such Christian concepts than Heidegger did. Both Nietzsche and Heidegger at least wrote about the desirability of the emergence of new gods. Having shown the limits of reason, they were necessarily open not merely to the possibility, but even to the desirability, of a new inspiration or revelation. Derrida, however, shared the "anti-theological" ire with which modern political philosophy began.

Derrida would respond that he has not merely a "right," but a "responsibility," to reinterpret the concepts, beliefs, and practices we have received from the past. If we do not reinterpret our heritage in a manner that is open to the "other" (but not the Other, as divine or beyond, as in the writings of Emanuel Levinas),[87] our institutions, thoughts, and practices will not merely become rigid and be shown to be obviously partial and untrue; they will crumble, disintegrate, and disappear.

Strauss would answer Derrida by insisting that one cannot maintain or preserve differences without drawing distinctions. *The* problem with modern philosophy is that it denies Socrates' insight into the importance of recognizing that being is divided into essentially different kinds (or ideas). If there are no essential differences, Being, however it is conceived (materially or purely intellectually), is not intelligible. Derrida, on the contrary, argued that there are no essential differences precisely in order to show that there is no such "thing" as Being, anything in itself, or anything that is purely intelligible (as opposed to sensible). In particular, Derrida wanted to carry out Nietzsche's observation that there is nothing that fundamentally distinguishes human beings from other animals further and more successfully than either Nietzsche himself (with his teaching about the "Übermensch") or Heidegger (with his substitution of *Dasein* for human being) had. Like Heidegger, Derrida insisted that "ethics" is a subordinate part of the "metaphysical" understanding of the world that has been proved false and outdated by modern natural science and technology. He thus sought to substitute his own conception of "responsibility" as "response."

Strauss would point out that the practical problems that follow from a failure to distinguish between the human and the nonhuman show up in Derrida's politics. In the first place, Derrida did not and cannot give his readers any reason to prefer openness to closedness or secularism to theism. He claimed that openness is better and, in effect, truer, because it would be more effective in producing future history; but he argued, at the same time, that there is nothing good, true, or simply effective. If, as Derrida argued, it is impossible to begin completely "from scratch" and we cannot control what happens, "history" will go on with or without us. By reaffirming the goals of Enlightenment politics, Derrida posited a standard on the basis of which European religious and racial intolerance could be criticized. Precisely because that standard is historically based and geographically located, however, it would appear not to apply outside of Europe, unless non-Europeans like Nelson Mandela chose to embrace it on the basis of their own nations' histories. Although Derrida claimed to speak for the "margins" and on behalf of "the other," his definition of the promise of democracy appears to be very Eurocentric. Strauss, however, acknowledged that the great books of Asia are as worthy of study as those of the West; unfortunately, he confessed, he did not know the languages needed to study them.[88] Strauss did, at least, emphasize the difference between the status of philosophy and politics in religions of the law, such as Judaism and Islam, on the one hand, and a creed-based faith like Christianity, which has been dominant in the West, on the other hand.[89] He praised Heidegger for having attempted to initiate a conversation between the East and the West.[90] Whereas the truth philosophers seek is eternal and, in principle, universally accessible, Strauss would have said, the explicitly historical basis of Derrida's thought necessarily makes it time-bound if not place-bound and, consequently, parochial.

It may appear old-fashioned to write about human nature, but Strauss would probably have pointed out that Derrida's attempt to deconstruct and so to destroy the notion of anything distinctively human leaves the concept of human rights without any basis or effective meaning. Derrida sought to carry the modern critique of essences and the concept of a natural order even further than Nietzsche and Heidegger did, partly because, in the case of human beings, Derrida saw that the identification of any particular characteristic as distinctively human provides grounds for some to claim the right to rule others: they can say they have more of the characteristic in question. If there is nothing or no one distinctively human, however, it is difficult to see to whom human rights belong or in what they consist. Derrida's conception of "rights" would, indeed, appear quite close to the definition of "right" as liberty that Hobbes proposes in his *Leviathan*, that is, as unimpeded motion. By showing that everything is in process of being erased and rewritten, Derrida may have been able to show that no author or authority can impose his intended meaning or order completely or lastingly. But Derrida was not able to show why everything that has been written should not, cannot, or will not be erased. Why should history continue? Why should we respect human rights? If there is no such thing as a distinctively human form of existence, it is hard to argue that any form of existence has any particular value or "rights."

The advantage of Derridean deconstruction from a Straussian perspective is that Derrida shows the modern Enlightenment project for what it is and always was: neither rational nor necessary, it represents a choice. Derrida would have his readers embrace the political goals and antitheological ire of modern philosophy not as true, inevitable, or good, but merely as a possible and, in his eyes, desirable response. Embracing both the grounds and the ends of modern philosophy, however, Derrida would also show himself and his thought to be essentially modern, not postmodern. To go beyond the modern, Strauss agreed with Nietzsche and Heidegger, one must first return to the premodern in order, as it were, to begin anew. Strauss himself thus returned to both ancient Greek philosophy and Hebrew Scripture and gave both poles or conflicting "roots" of the Western tradition very untraditional readings.[91] In the literal sense, Strauss thus proved himself to be a much more postmodern thinker than Derrida, coming after and going beyond the modern, rather than merely intensifying or extending modern principles and tenets.

We are not sure that we would go so far as Emil Fackenheim, an early student and lifelong friend of Strauss, but his judgment may be worth quoting in this context. Whereas Derrida characterized himself as a French Heideggerian, Fackenheim predicted: "One day, because it is philosophically correct, and thus because it is just, the name Martin Heidegger will only be known because he made possible Leo Strauss."[92]

CHAPTER FOUR

The Man Who Gave Away the Secrets

ON ESOTERICISM

Strauss called for a return to the ancients, both for the sake of philosophy and for the sake of politics. The most vitriolic criticisms directed against him center on this call for return. Two themes stand out: first, his version of the ancients is held to justify "noble lies" or the shameless manipulation of "the masses" by political leaders. Thus Tim Robbins's play *Embedded* identifies Strauss, his face projected on the back of the stage, as the philosophic inspiration behind a lying cabal of policymakers who lead the United States into an unjust and foolish war in a distant middle-eastern nation. They recite Latin litanies to Strauss and punctuate their scheming with repeated shouts of "hail Leo Strauss." And of course the idea that Strauss taught them to tell "noble lies" about the war is featured prominently. The second questionable idea Strauss is said to have taken from the ancients is what Drury calls "the tyrannical teaching," the claim that the rationally right form of rule is lawless tyranny. The milder form of that claim asserts that Strauss and his ancients are deeply elitist and antidemocratic.

Both charges carry great emotional weight. The views attributed to Strauss do not merely appear to most Americans to be false, but worse, they appear to be insulting. Who are Strauss and his acolytes to think themselves so superior that they can lie to us at will—for our good or theirs, it hardly matters. Likewise, how can anyone endorse tyranny, lawlessness, and the unapologetic rule of elites?

In some form or other, both charges are widespread in the current spate of media attention to Strauss; although we have responded in passing to the first in chapter 1, a more direct consideration is due now, for these two charges carry much of the force of the animus against Strauss. If they are true as stated, his views seem sinister and dangerous indeed. Although both charges are widespread in the literature swirling about Strauss, many, if not all, versions of them are ultimately attributable to Shadia Drury. Hers is, moreover, the most intransigently formulated version of these charges; at the same time, given her undeniable efforts to study and understand Strauss, hers is the version most deserving of serious consideration. It is with Drury, therefore, that we may begin.

How Shadia Drury Read Leo Strauss

To her credit, Drury gives much thought to the question of how to read Strauss. She knows there is an issue because, she says in her opening paragraph, Strauss is an unusual scholar: he "insists that all great political philosophers conceal their true thoughts or leave them unsaid."[1] She takes Strauss's discovery of esoteric expression to be at or very near the center of his accomplishments. It is "the cornerstone of Strauss's thinking" (*PILS*, 14, 19). "It is the heart of the Straussian philosophy" (19). She recognizes, or takes for granted, that "a commentator . . . like Strauss . . . will also write esoterically" (6, 116).[2] She finds that "Strauss himself admits to being an esoteric writer" (*PILS*, 6). Yet she does not find Strauss's esoteric readings of the philosophic texts to be particularly persuasive. "I generally find his commentaries on the classic texts," she tells us, "arid, insipid, tedious and repetitive. I was sympathetic with those reviewers who were genuinely perplexed how such rubbish could have been published" (4). She also sympathizes completely with George Sabine's judgment that "Strauss's hermeneutic [is] an 'invitation to perverse ingenuity' " (11). Should one, thus, "apply Strauss's method of hermeneutic" (10) to his own work? In posing that question, she faces a dilemma: on the one hand, she is persuaded that he writes as he reads, that is, esoterically, which would imply that one must apply his methods to his works. On the other hand, doing so exposes one "to the sorts of objections to which Strauss's method is vulnerable." The main vulnerability, in her mind, is that "Strauss's method of interpretation is notoriously lacking in clarity and rigor" (11). There are, she concludes, "insurmountable difficulties" in applying the method.

In the light of her own observations, she adopts a surprising solution to her dilemma: she "will use only conventional methods in interpreting the work of Leo Strauss" (*PILS*, 13). She is of course aware that this decision leaves her with a problem: "is this . . . approach sufficient to unearth the esoteric philosophy of Leo Strauss?" (14). She assures us that it is, but her reasoning on behalf of this conclusion is elusive. She notes that despite the invitation to "perverse ingenuity" noted by Sabine, there is an "overwhelming unanimity readily observable among Straussian interpreters," by which term she means his students and followers. The "method," she concludes, is less that than "a philosophy in disguise." Or, as she also puts it, "what is important about Strauss's 'method' is not its form, but its *content*" (11–12 [emphasis in original]). She finds particularly revealing, and particularly supportive of her own methodological decision, a story Strauss retold from the pages of the Islamic philosopher al Farabi. In her version:

> [A] pious ascetic was well-known in his city for his abstinence, abasement, and devotion. But for some reason he aroused the hostility of the ruler of his city. The latter ordered his arrest, and to make sure he did not flee, he placed the guards of the city gates on alert. . . . Dressed as a drunk and singing a tune to cymbals, he approached the city gates. When the guard asked him who he was, he replied that he was the pious ascetic that everyone was looking for. The guard did not believe him, and let him go. (x–xi)

Strauss is esoteric, Drury believes, but in the sense of the pious ascetic: he speaks the truth as he understands it but clothes it in such a way that the reader is disinclined to notice or believe what she or he is reading. Strauss, like the ascetic, "does not lie." His esoteric message reveals itself to a careful and literal reading.[3] "Strauss is esoteric, not devious" (*PILS*, 9). "Strauss is a political philosopher. That is not the same as being a liar. Political philosophy is not a bundle of lies. Like Farabi's pious ascetic, it tells the truth and nothing but the truth" (24).

Her decision to "use only conventional methods" on Strauss leads to the promulgation of a number of rules of method. The first set is self-denying: she will not do unto Strauss what he did unto others. "I will not under any circumstance maintain that he believes the opposite of what he says explicitly" (*PILS*, 24). She eschews all arithmological modes of interpretation, all emphasis on central chapters and central items in lists (favorite devices of Strauss in reading others). She refuses to "look behind the surface" or "between the lines," as Strauss did (ix). What she finds in Strauss must be clearly there, and she refuses to credit the idea that he meant the opposite of anything he explicitly said. If Strauss practiced a hermeneutic of absence (what was "between the lines" was often taken to be more important or revealing than what was on the lines), then Drury practices a hermeneutic of presence (what is on the lines [or very clearly implied by what is on the lines] is all that is to be credited, and all that is on the lines is to be credited).[4]

But this first set of rules is difficult to apply to a thinker like Strauss, because he comes before us in the guise of a scholar, a historian of political philosophy. Most of the time he gives us an interpretation of one or another historical thinker—Plato or Xenophon, al Farabi or Maimonides, Machiavelli or Nietzsche. Drury cannily notices Strauss's comment about Farabi, an earlier commentator on the texts of others: he "avails himself of the specific immunity of the commentator or the historian in order to speak his mind concerning grave matters in his 'historical' works, rather than in the works in which he speaks in his own name."[5] Noting how well this description fits Strauss himself, Drury needs a way to discern which, if any, of the various historical figures Strauss dealt with provide him with that "specific immunity of the commentator." Unlike Farabi, Strauss commented on a wide range of philosophic authors. Drury thinks she knows which figures speak for Strauss: he "almost never refrains from passing judgments on the philosophers whose work he seeks to understand. . . . Strauss's narrative . . . leaves little doubt that his preference is for the ancients" (*PILS*, 9). Therefore, she concludes, "we cannot hope to understand Strauss unless we understand the ideas he attributes to the ancient philosophers" (10). Her second large rule for reading Strauss, then, is "to attribute to Strauss the ideas he attributes to the wise ancients" (15).

To her discredit, Drury neither consistently follows her own rules nor succeeds in making a persuasive case for those rules. One would think that her second rule would be particularly easy to abide by, but she violates this one almost from start to finish when she announces that "Strauss used Machiavelli as his mouthpiece" (*PILS*, 117; also see 26, 120). What does Strauss say via his use of Machiavelli as spokesman? "What Machiavelli hides," but Strauss brings out in his interpretation of the Florentine, "is the extent to which he is opposed to the pagan tradition of Greek philosophy. Machiavelli is not the admirer of the ancients that he pretends to be" (118). Drury not only uses a nonancient as guide to Strauss's real thoughts, but she uses the thinker who, Strauss insisted, made the break with and opposed the ancients. Her use of Machiavelli leads into an inverted world in which she not only violates her rule, but in doing so undermines or contradicts the rule completely: her Strauss speaks through Machiavelli to deny that he admires or agrees with the ancients. We must wonder who is engaging in esotericism here, who is accepting "the invitation to perverse ingenuity."

In breaking her second rule in such a decisive way as to overturn it, she is also violating her first rule: not ever, under no circumstances, to attribute to Strauss any views contrary to his explicit statements. But Strauss is quite explicit, as she herself notes, in preferring the ancients to Machiavelli, no matter how much he may be charmed by Machiavelli.

Drury violates both rules repeatedly, because that is the only way she can make her case against Strauss. Since she claims Machiavelli to be

Strauss's spokesman, she can then surge to the assertion that the philosopher as understood or trained by Strauss "will give advice that is not unlike the sort that Machiavelli gives his prince," that is, advice marked by "moral ruthlessness" (*PILS*, 29–30). Along the same line, again in open violation of her first rule, she tells us that "Strauss may have paid lip service to the rule of law" (that is to say, he defended it explicitly in nearly everything he ever said or wrote), but, according to Drury, "in reality his esoteric philosophy subverts it" (200).

In all fairness to Drury, we must entertain the possibility that her primary error is not in breaking her rules, but in promulgating them. They surely do not seem well conceived or responsive to the features of Strauss's texts to which she herself calls attention. Consider her use of the Farabian story about the pious ascetic. It is meant to support a certain conception of esoteric communication: truthful speech in what may be misleading contexts. Both her rules follow in a sense from this conception of the nature of Straussian esotericism.

Yet consider what Strauss himself makes of Farabi's story. It is about a man known habitually to tell the truth, Strauss points out. In a sense the man remained true to his character, for he spoke with veracity. But, Strauss emphasizes, "the pious ascetic lied in deed." Indeed, "his not lying in speech was part of his lying in deed. Only because he lied in deed could he afford not to lie in speech." As Strauss reads the story, and Farabi's use of it, "unqualified veracity" was "essential to a pious ascetic" and made his "lie in deed" palatable to the public or decent in their eyes when it was discovered. But Strauss insists that "the public is mistaken as regards the reason why the pious ascetic's seemingly indecent action is not indecent: that action is justified by compulsion or persecution."[6] That last conclusion is presented by Strauss as Farabi's own gloss or lesson from the story. Telling the unqualified truth is not always a requirement of decency, for compulsion or persecution can excuse some exceptions. Strauss's Farabi does not therefore conclude from the story what Drury's Strauss does—that esotericism involves telling the whole truth, albeit in misleading or distracting contexts. Strauss's Farabi does not believe that the ascetic, lying in deed, in fact told the truth.

Strauss believes that this particular strategy suited the pious ascetic, but he does not generalize to the Drurian claim that it suits all manner of esoteric writers. Strauss applies the story to Plato as he thought Farabi meant it to apply: "Plato was not a pious ascetic. Whereas the pious ascetic almost always says explicitly and unambiguously what he thinks, Plato almost never says explicitly and unambiguously what he thinks." Platonic (and thus perhaps Farabian) esotericism thus differs from pious ascetic es- otericism in quite decisive ways, sharing with it only a certain concealment justified by the kind of necessities contained in the story.[7]

Drury's reading of the story of the pious ascetic was, to put it generously, casual. She leaped too quickly from it to her conclusions about the nature of esotericism as understood by Strauss and from there to her rules, so often broken in her book. The kind of esotericism explained or justified by that story is not the kind of esotericism practiced by the pious ascetic and, therefore, not the kind of hidden communication Drury's rules were fashioned to bring into the open.

Before we leave the pious ascetic, we must take more care in interpret- ing his behavior than Drury did. Not only did she draw the wrong infer- ences from the story as to the universal character of esoteric communi- cation, but she leaped to the unwarranted conclusion that the story was meant to explain Strauss's way of writing. Strauss explicates the Farabian story in order to grasp the Farabian understanding of Platonic esotericism, and perhaps Farabian esotericism as well. One cannot move on from these points, without much more evidence, to draw the conclusions Drury does about Strauss himself. It is not merely that she mistakes the substantive conclusions to be drawn, but she too hastily applies the story to Strauss. To say nothing of other matters to be explored later, Strauss proceeds in his essay very differently from the way Farabi himself did. Farabi, we might say, esoterically communicates about Plato's esotericism. Farabi stands in continuity with Plato in a way that Strauss does not. Rather than being a second Farabi or a third Plato, Strauss appears here as an anti-Farabi.[8]

On Esotericism and Noble Lies

It is difficult not to be struck by the ironies involved in Strauss's identifica- tion with the thesis of esoteric communication. As he presents it, esoteri- cism was first and foremost a device whereby thinkers of the past concealed some part of their thought for the sake of guarding themselves against per- secution. It was a device to give them safety in a world not made safe for philosophy. Yet in Strauss's case, the esotericism thesis has been the means by which great opprobrium, if not exactly persecution, has been called down upon him.[9] Moreover, in the past what was controversial or dan- gerous about esotericism was what was hidden—the doctrines that went counter to reigning authorities, the doctrines that exposed their advocates to personal danger and their societies to the disruption and scandal that may occur from challenges to deeply held and widespread convictions. But today what is controversial about Strauss's esotericism thesis is the very idea of esotericism—not what is hidden, but that something is hidden. We moderns not only believe that we can (or must) face any substantive ideas thinkers choose to throw at us in "the marketplace of ideas" that is the best test of truth, but we take the very notion that there might be some justification for lying to us as patronizing at best, insulting and dangerous at worst. It is an affront to our dignity as rational and equal moral beings; it is an affront to our inherent freedom.[10]

Given the fact that esotericism had much the opposite effect from what it had or was intended to have in its historical uses, one wonders why Strauss made so much of it in a climate of opinion he knew to be in the significant respects different from the past. As he emphasizes in his most programmatic statements on the subject: "this [esoteric] literature is . . . essentially related to a society which is not liberal." The possibility, to say nothing of the plausibility, of esoteric communication has faded from public awareness precisely because scholars in the West live in societies which "have enjoyed a practically complete freedom of discussion."[11] The fact that he and his main audience live in liberal societies would seem to disqualify esotericism as an authorial strategy, for, Strauss tells us, "writing between the lines" makes sense "in an era of persecution, that is, at a time when some political or other orthodoxy was enforced by law or custom."[12] Precisely because of this new liberal climate, Strauss's esotericism thesis has met with great resistance, even anger.

In the recent discussions of Strauss, in the accusations that he justifies, even advocates, the use of "lies" and manipulation, the most significant fact about the esotericism thesis has been lost to view: it is first and foremost a method for historically understanding writers in the past who incontestably lived in nonliberal societies, and not a prescription for writers living today.[13] It tells scholars how to read past writers, not how to write or what to say. Originally, Strauss's argument was taken in just that way; and it was resisted by scholars—as he predicted it would be—even in that apolitical form.[14] The mandate to read past authors for their esoteric views encountered resistance because it does not meet, or has difficulty meeting, criteria of historical exactness or scientific truth. As Strauss puts it, when reading an author who writes esoterically, one must accept the fact that "the real opinion of an author is not necessarily identical with that which he expresses in the largest number of passages"; it requires discounting what the author says openly and loudly in many passages. How can one reach a scientifically satisfying reading of an author, then, if the normal rules of evidence must be waived so? Strauss concedes that "reading between the lines will not lead to complete agreement among all scholars." This may be a drawback to the method, but the opposite procedure imposes "an arbitrary standard of exactness which might exclude a priori the most important facts of the past for human knowledge." The key phrase here is "a priori": it cannot be ruled out in advance by a merely methodological demand that writers facing a climate of opinion hostile or resistant to their true thoughts would conceal their thought or accommodate to the climate of opinion in which they found themselves. Strauss himself, in putting forward the many controversial readings of past thinkers that he did, accepted the burden that he clearly recognized followed from adopting his method. He thought the controversy and sometimes hostile rejection worth it: "the truly exact historian will reconcile himself to the fact that there is a difference between winning an argument, or proving to practically everyone that he is right, and understanding the thought of the great writers of the past."[15]

Whether Strauss's esotericism thesis is valid as an insight into the character of past thinkers, or whether it can provide reasonably valid readings of those past thinkers is not at issue here, however. Many fruitful debates have occurred on this topic, and we do not mean to rehearse them now.[16] The more significant questions in the present context are two: given the resistance the thesis raises, resistance Strauss anticipated, why did he persist in making it so central to his work?[17] Second, and perhaps most germane today, what are the implications of the thesis for his own writings, or for politicians and other writers of our day who came under his influence? Does the esotericism argument provide a justification for political leaders to manipulate the masses with lies, noble or otherwise, as is so often said in the media, and even on Broadway?

Strauss's most systematic presentation of his thesis is found in his book *Persecution and the Art of Writing*, a volume that appeared in 1952 but which collected essays he had written in the decade of the 1940s. In the introduction to that book, Strauss appears in the guise of a "sociologist of knowledge," that is, in the form of a certain kind of scientific historical inquirer. Much of Strauss's work was indeed undertaken as a historian, but it is clear that there is a philosophic dimension as well to his advocacy of "reading between the lines."

In *Persecution and the Art of Writing* Strauss identifies changes in the climate of intellectual opinions that have led scholars away from crediting esotericism, whereas in earlier ages it was regarded as most plausible. Recent research has been carried out under the thought that "each period of the past . . . must be understood by itself, and must not be judged by standards alien to it. Each author must, as far as possible, be interpreted by himself; no term of any consequence must be used in the interpretation of another which cannot be literally translated into his language, and which was not used by him or was not in fairly common use in his time."[18] Such views form part of the criteria of scholarly objectivity that Strauss himself endorsed and applied (e.g., in insisting that a Greek polis was not a state). But Strauss saw in the first of these seemingly innocent methodological strictures a more significant and more philosophical thought that he called historicism. In *Persecution* he refers to ours as an "age of historicism" and identifies that historicism as a barrier to acceptance of the esotericism thesis.

Strauss defines historicism as the idea that "all human thought is historical and hence unable ever to grasp anything eternal."[19] Thought necessarily reflects or is limited by its historical setting. "Historicism rejects the question of the good society, that is to say, of *the* good society," the question of political philosophy per se, "because of the essentially historical character of society and of human thought."[20] Historicism is the enemy-in-chief of political philosophy, or of philosophy per se. In part, historicism is supported by evidence meant to show that "all human thought belongs to specific historical situations." The most common historical or empirical evidence for these propositions consists in showing that the philosophers in point of fact shared the dominant or authoritative opinions of their times and places and were bounded in their thinking by those thoughts. "Most historicists," says Strauss, "consider decisive the fact, which can be established by historical studies, that a close relation exists between each political philosophy and the historical situation in which it emerged.... The history of political philosophy ... shows," think the historicists, "that no political philosophy can reasonably claim to be valid beyond the historical situation to which it is essentially related."[21]

Here the esotericism thesis comes into its own. It is Strauss's way of undermining the alleged empirical evidence in favor of historicism and of establishing his counterclaim that philosophy and political philosophy are and always have been meaningful possibilities, because human thought is not historically limited as the historicists claim: the so-called evidence of agreement between all previous thinkers and their times, or of the domination of thought by history, is an artifact of the conscious accommodation thinkers made to dominant opinion in their times.[22] These accommodations testify to the power of authority, but not to the limits of the possibilities of human thought. It is not enough for Strauss to affirm that it is possible to think outside the historical box, so to speak: he must show that it has indeed happened, and thus that it may continue to happen. "The historical form" of his work is a "not inappropriate" response, Strauss once said, to the "spread of the teaching that . . . all human thought is historical. There seems to be no more appropriate way of combating this teaching than the study of history."[23] The esotericism thesis is a central part not only of Strauss's agenda as a scholar of the history of political philosophy, but also of his larger agenda to revive and reinstate political philosophy itself by challenging its enemies, the chief among which is historicism. Strauss put himself in the way of certain kinds of danger—the contempt of the scholars (e.g., Burnyeat) and the drivelings of a Tim Robbins—for the sake of his larger philosophic agenda.[24]

Strauss not only described a practice that he believed older writers had engaged in, but he defended and justified it. Scholars have objected to the first on scientific or scholarly grounds; many average citizens, journalists, and others object to the latter on moral and political grounds. The defense of lying violates one of the deepest and widely held—if not always honored—moral norms; it also arouses our resentment insofar as Strauss seems to be authorizing the superior few to lie to the inferior many. In 2003–4, as we have seen, Strauss's defense of esotericism or "noble lies" was widely cited as the philosophic rationale for a group of Strauss-influenced policymakers to lie about weapons of mass destruction and any number of other matters concerning Iraq. Does Strauss's justification of the "writing between the lines" practiced by a Farabi or a Plato justify the knowing purveyance of falsehoods by political leaders, such as allegedly occurred before the Iraq war?

Let us say, first off, that we are not convinced that the Bush administration in fact engaged in the deceptions of which it has been accused. The debate about the Iraq war is not our topic, but nothing we have seen thus far (as of November 2005) convinces us that the administration knew that Saddam Hussein did not have those weapons. Recall that nearly everyone else in the world suspected that he had them, and they held that suspicion with good reason. He had definitely had them and had used them. He had no good documentation or other evidence that he had destroyed them, and only a few years prior to the war, he had expelled weapons inspectors. He surely acted like somebody who had the weapons or wanted to build or acquire them. Perhaps, as some surmise, he did not have them but wanted to engage in a bluff to make the United States, or his neighbors, or the Israelis believe he had them. The real issue in the months before the war was not whether he had such weapons, but whether the UN inspection system was to be allowed the time to find his weapons or to satisfy the world that he did not have them. Many believe that would have been the wiser and more just policy. Nonetheless, prior to the war it was not unreasonable to believe, or very strongly suspect, that Iraq had such weapons.

Even if it turns out on fuller information that members of the administration did lie about the WMD, this does not itself prove that Strauss had anything to do with it. Unless we are mistaken greatly, political leaders have lied innumerable times, without the aid or justifying arguments of Leo Strauss. Indeed, it would not be too far off to say that political leaders frequently lied well before Leo Strauss wrote *Persecution and the Art of Writing*. We would guess that such practices may even have existed before he was born.

Nonetheless, we must ask, does Strauss's defense of esoteric philosophic communication justify lying by political leaders and contemptuous manipulation of the American people as allegedly occurred before the Iraq war? Let us consider the kinds of rationales Strauss puts forward. He begins with the straightforward phenomenon of persecution. There are some individuals who live in societies where free expression is not allowed and tyrannous rulers attempt to dominate all means of communication. We are very familiar with such situations from the post-Straussian writings and reflections of men like Alexander Solzhenitsyn and Vaclav Havel, by the circulation of samizdat literature in the former Soviet empire, and so on. Do we believe that a Havel was morally wrong to forbear from saying what would land him in prison? Even though we may admire in a certain way the completely candid writer, who will speak the whole truth whatever the expense, we normally consider this heroic (or foolish), not morally mandatory, behavior. As Robert Howse observed, "only people who believe that intellectuals are (or should be) martyrs to the truth would be terribly surprised or find it controversial that thoughtful people use secret communication for self-protection under conditions of ruthless oppression."[25] Do we believe that Farabi's pious ascetic was wrong to lie in deed about his identity in the circumstances in which he found himself? Do we think that Farabi, assuming he doubted some of the core tenets of the accepted religion of his society, was wrong to cover over or even deny that doubt, in order to survive and write in his cautious way the truth as he saw it? Was he wrong to supply professions of allegiance perhaps warmer than he felt in order to satisfy the watchful that he was a loyal son of Islam, or was it wrong for the Communist dissident to be similarly less than forthright? (Even if one contests Strauss's reading of Farabi, it is surely possible that some individual arose within Islam, or Christianity, or Judaism, or Hinduism, who doubted, as Strauss claims Farabi did, and was tempted to camouflage himself, as Strauss said Farabi did.)

Does the pious ascetic, or Farabi, or the Communist dissident provide justification for political leaders to lie to their publics, to engage their nations in wars for illicit purposes, to shamelessly manipulate the facts? The clear answer is no. As Strauss recounted, the lesson of the pious ascetic was that his "action was justified by compulsion or persecution." Such "compulsion or persecution" cannot be brought to testify for the alleged lies now blamed on Strauss.[26]

Yet there is, at the same time, a broader conception of the purpose of esoteric writing, not related immediately and directly to persecution. Thinkers who wrote "cautiously," to use a favorite Straussian phrase, believed "that there are basic truths which would not be pronounced in public by any decent man, because they would do harm to many people." There are "popular views which are indispensable for all practical purposes," but which are not, strictly speaking, true. How far these popular views deviate from the truth will vary, of course, depending on what the views are. How obliged to these views any thinker may believe himself to be will depend on a variety of factors that cannot be stated in general terms. It may be the case, for example, that the popular beliefs in question are vicious and lead to much avoidable injustice.[27] A philosopher may well attempt to counter such falsehoods. But it is possible that popularly accepted falsehoods may be very beneficial to many people, and the philosopher may hesitate to upset the consensus around them. An example Strauss may have had in mind is the common view among premodern peoples that their legal codes derived from gods. It does not require an atheistic philosophy to doubt that all legal codes have divine origins. The Athenian Stranger, the central philosophic spokesman in Plato's *Laws*, seems to have his doubts about the claim of the Spartans and the Cretans that their laws derived from Apollo and Zeus, respectively. But he does not find himself obliged to question that opinion: it lends authority to laws by associating them with the divine, and in the Stranger's view (and Plato's as well), law can always use authority.[28] Even in modern times, James Madison spoke of the need to clothe law with the authority and veneration that age and habituation provide. He therefore rejected Thomas Jefferson's proposal that constitutional questions be reopened among the people periodically, even though he knew that not everything about this or any constitution was as good as it could imaginably be. The harm of disrupting habitual attachment to the legal order outweighed, in Madison's judgment, the potential gain from the public reconsideration of the constitution. Madison's point is very close to Strauss's and Plato's, and it demonstrates that Strauss's notion is not hostile or alien to liberal democratic commitments.

Strauss willingly accepts the label "noble lie" for this philosophic reticence, although he also says it can properly be called "considering one's social responsibilities."[29] Strauss's emphasis was always quite different from that of contemporary commentators on his doctrine: they emphasize the "lie"; he emphasized "noble."[30] They think he means to justify all lying to the masses by elites, but that is far from his point. The lie (if it is really that) is justified not because elites are superior to the masses and have a right to do whatever it takes for them to rule or maintain themselves; insofar as philosophic reticence or accommodation is justified, it is justified by the public good, that is, by the fact that some opinions held by the public do great good and, disturbing them, even if and when they are not strictly true, may do harm. The moral rule with regard to philosophic speaking is much the same as the rule covering most other public acts in which one may engage: does it serve the common good? When Strauss speaks of the common good, it is not at the level of policy proposals either, but rather concerns what we might call the background public opinion at the level of principle.

Does the Platonic/Straussian doctrine of the noble lie serve to justify the kind of alleged lies critics of Strauss like Drury, LaRouche, and Robbins lay at his doorstep? Does it justify knowingly misrepresenting the weaponry of Iraq in order to begin a war, the main intent of which is to focus attention away from a sluggish economy and thus help the reelection chances of the ruling party, as Robbins claims was the case with the Iraq war? The answer is a plain and resounding no. This is not to say that political leaders do not on occasion do such things. But again, they did not learn to do this from Strauss, and had they looked to him for guidance on the acceptability of such behavior, he would not have given them succor.

We have proceeded to this point on the tacit assumption that the defense or justification Strauss gives of esotericism would apply here and now and that it would, among other things, serve as justification for esotericism by him or his followers. This is the assumption of Drury as well. She sees Strauss's discussion of esotericism not as a thesis about writers of the past—she refuses to investigate and tends not to credit his historical studies—but as a manifesto or program for himself in the present. We can no longer take that assumption for granted, however, but must subject it to critical scrutiny.

Does Strauss's discovery and defense of the use of esotericism in the past serve as a justification or announcement of an esoteric agenda for him in the present? This notion too is filled with many ironies. Esoteric writing is a way, Strauss tells us, to convey secrets. The way to write esoterically is not to call attention to esotericism. One must announce one's esotericism esoterically. Strauss, however, surely does not speak of esotericism sotto voce: he uses a megaphone, he shouts from the rooftops, and he never lets us forget it. As Laurence Lampert said of one of the devices Strauss found characteristic of writers who write between the lines, the central item in a list or the central part of a text may be particularly well suited for conveying a thought one wishes to keep out of view, for the center is where readers' (or listeners') attention tends to flag. Both the beginning and the end are more prominent, more noticeable, and more likely to be noticed. But that is no longer true after Strauss trumpets the significance of the center: it is no longer the least but now the most obtrusive place.[31] Lampert's point holds more generally for the issue of esotericism altogether.[32] As Stanley Rosen rightly said, Strauss writes with a "peculiar candor."[33] Can it be that he then intends to practice what he has so thoroughly exposed? Can a forensic scientist who exposes the use of heretofore undetected illegal steroids be planning to use such steroids in the future? On the face of it, Strauss would seem the anti-esoteric, not the devotee of esotericism in his own writings, despite his dictum that a man writes as he reads.[34] This dictum applied to writers in the past who did not make esotericism centrally thematic to their writing and thereby preserved it as an option for themselves.

Strauss's most explicit statement on the relation between exposing esotericism and practicing it is in his posthumously published essay "Exoteric Teaching." That essay discusses the doctrine of esoteric/exoteric writing in the eighteenth-century thinker Gotthold Lessing, who "discussed it as clearly and as fully as could be done by someone who still accepted exotericism not merely as a strange fact of the past, but rather as an intelligible necessity for all times and, therefore, as a principle guiding his own literary activity. In short, Lessing was the last writer who revealed, while hiding, the reasons compelling wise men to hide the truth: *he wrote between the lines about the art of writing between the lines.*"[35]

This is a beautiful statement for throwing into high relief the problem of conceiving of Strauss as an esoteric writer. He shows that he clearly understands that esotericism only remains a live option for a writer who treats esotericism esoterically. Strauss not only reveals what Lessing has written between the lines about esotericism, but he puts the whole doctrine in boldface. By his own testimony, this is not what a writer looking to write esoterically can do.

Strauss did more than expose the fact and practice of esotericism; he brought into the open, often to the loud dissent of fellow scholars, the unorthodox views of the thinkers whose works he was interpreting.[36] To take a particularly important example from Strauss's first major study of a classical text, his book *On Tyranny* does exactly the reverse of what Xenophon, the author he is interpreting, did. Xenophon came to a certain understanding (explored in chapter 5) of the problem of tyranny, which Strauss called "the tyrannical teaching." This was, he insisted, a "theoretical thesis" and not at all a practical proposal. Nonetheless, he also insisted, "it is one thing to accept the theoretical thesis concerning tyranny; it is another thing to expound it publicly." Xenophon, Strauss affirms, "does not expound the 'tyrannical' teaching." It can only be pieced out by a careful study of Xenophon's dialogue, *Hiero*, together with a subtle grasp of "the relevant passages of Xenophon's other writings."[37] What Xenophon did not expound but presented esoterically, Strauss in his book expounds quite openly. Strauss proceeds in exactly the opposite way from the ancients he is explicating.

Strauss also, therefore, made explicit Machiavellian blasphemies that even the Florentine had left partially concealed; he insisted that Locke was far more like that bad boy Hobbes and much less Christian than previous interpreters had suspected; he emphasized the difference between Jerusalem and Athens, faith and reason, religion and philosophy, when nearly every historical thinker he discussed labored strenuously to deny or cover over the differences. He went out of his way to deny or question doctrines, such as immortality of the soul and reward and punishment in the afterlife, that most later philosophers and scholars have attributed to Plato, by suggesting that they were poetically presented in an attempt to reconcile philosophy and the city.

Let us be more precise. The phrase "noble lie" derives from a specific place in Plato's *Republic*. The "noble lie" that Socrates proposes to tell the citizens of the city he and his fellow participants in the conversation are "building" in speech has two parts: first, he will attempt to persuade them that they were born of the land where their city stands. This is the "myth of autochthony." Then he will tell them the "myth of the metals," that in their making, "the god, in fashioning those of you who are competent to rule, mixed gold in at their birth; this is why they are the most honored; in auxiliaries, silver; and iron and bronze in the farmers and the other craftsmen."[38] The point of the "noble lie" is to persuade the citizens that their civic arrangements are more completely natural and just than they really are. They are children of the land they possess, and thus belong to it as it belongs to them. There is thus no question about the justice of their possessing their land. Likewise, their civic friendship as fellow citizens, their common devotion to each other and their city, is to be seen as natural, for they are all brothers and sisters, descendants of the same parent (the land of their city), in effect, children of the city itself. Their civic duties are thus as natural and intense as their duties to kin. Finally, since this city has a hierarchy, or class structure, within it, according to which some serve higher functions and derive greater honor than others, the second part of the lie grounds this hierarchy in purely natural differences. The lie is a lie—if indeed one unlikely to be believed—but it is in the service of justice and the truth. Every city requires a place to be and an attachment of the citizens to each other and to it. No city has such natural origins as the "lie" presents, and therefore no city has such a completely natural claim to justice, but it cannot be entirely unjust for cities to possess exclusive claim to their sites, or for citizens to feel joined to each other. Nature points toward political life, but not as completely as the lie depicts. Of course, since Socrates tells his interlocutors, and Plato tells all of us his readers, that the lie is a lie, the point of the lie is not to fool us into believing it. It is rather to make clear the ways in which nature falls short in supplying a perfectly just foundation for political life.

The second part of the lie is similar. Every effort is made by Socrates to engineer a convergence between natural merit and class position within the city, but again nature does not cooperate sufficiently to make this possible. There are at least three ways in which nature falls short. First, qualities of a person that make for merit are not always (to say the least) visible to the naked eye. Second, merit of character is a matter of education as much as of nature. In the context in the *Republic*, Socrates introduces the noble lie to "persuade" the citizens that "the reasoning and education we gave them were like dreams." Finally, even if we could identify natural merit and equalize education, merit does not pass on from generation to generation with certainty. Good parents can have weak children; individuals of great natural ability can spring from modest backgrounds. Socrates attempts to sort the generations by merit by having the guardians observe and test the group, but this can never be done completely correctly. And it is a fact about human societies that those in the upper strata tend to structure matters so that the advantages of their higher position are passed on to their offspring, whether deserved or not. Nature points to a class structure for society—so Socrates argues in the *Republic*, and human experience so far confirms—but nature does not provide completely that even in the best cases, the class structures correspond with the natural order of desert. The noble lie pretends that nature supplies justice to a higher degree than it does, and along the way the lie implies that every actual political community necessarily participates to a greater or lesser degree in injustice.[39]

Even in Plato, then, the noble lie is misread if it is taken as a warrant for lying to the people. It is an expository device for revealing an important set of truths about political life and also revealing, perhaps even exposing, the mythical character of the ideological supports that actual political communities tend to generate for themselves. Thus a reader educated by Plato's *Republic* is likely to doubt the theory of the divine right of kings, or, should he or she accept it, it would not be on the basis of anything learned in Plato.

Let us also see what Strauss says and does in his own name. In his *Thoughts on Machiavelli*, Strauss refers to the modern American equivalent of the myth of the first origin in autochthony: "If we can believe Thomas Paine, all governments of the Old World have an origin...laid in crime....But...the foundation of the United States was laid in freedom and justice." Strauss points out, however, that "the problem is more complex than it appears in the presentation by Paine." He goes on to cite some facts from American history (about the treatment of the native inhabitants, for example) that speak against Paine's view. That is to say, Strauss does not tell the noble lie of their origins to the Americans, but he does what Socrates does in the *Republic*—he questions the noble lie the society tells itself and reminds of the limits of the justice underlying any political society.[40]

Likewise, Strauss is far from being a purveyor of the second part of the noble lie. "It is," he insists, "a demand of justice that there should be a reasonable correspondence between the social hierarchy and the natural hierarchy. The lack of such a correspondence [in premodern times] was defended by the fundamental fact of scarcity." But today, things are sufficiently different because of "increasing abundance," that it is "possible to see and to admit the element of hypocrisy which had entered into the traditional notion of aristocracy...thus it became possible to abolish many injustices or at least many things which had become injustices." Strauss exposes rather than tells the noble lie about natural inequality. He does not deny that there are natural inequalities, but he does not identify these in any way with the existing class system.[41]

One of the most revealing indications of the difference Strauss announces between himself and the older esoteric writers about whom he writes is contained in the title of his book devoted to a writer he considered particularly adept at esoteric expression. Strauss called his book *Thoughts on Machiavelli*, a title meant to be a clear echo of the title of one the two chief works of Machiavelli discussed in that book, *Discourses on...Livy*. Strauss invited his readers to reflect on titles, particularly juxtapositions of titles of works by the same author or of books clearly relevant to each other.[42] The two titles here contrast "discourses" with "thoughts." Discourses are what one says aloud. They may conceal what one believes, as Strauss insists is the case with Machiavelli's *Discourses*.[43] Thoughts are what one says to oneself; in presenting his interpretation of Machiavelli as his "thoughts," Strauss is announcing the character of his book to be exactly the opposite of the character of Machiavelli's. It is not an esoteric book. Strauss differs from Machiavelli in form and method of exposition as much as in substance. This, of course, is not to say that Strauss's Machiavelli book is an easy book: non-esoteric is not equivalent to easy.

Contrary to what appears obvious to Drury and many others,[44] we are maintaining, then, that Strauss does not write as he reads, that he is not presenting esoteric expression as necessary or desirable for himself or his followers. Peter Levine says, "Strauss asks us to apply his own method to his own works."[45] But does he? Where? Levine can cite no texts. But how can this be? Is not Strauss famous, or notorious, for his claim that philosophy and the city stand in inexorable tension with each other, that opinion is the element of society and that philosophy represents an intransigent commitment to examine opinion, to challenge what is taken for granted in society?[46] Does he not attribute the birth of political philosophy to the experience of that tension by Socrates, and does he not see the emergence of esotericism as the philosophers' response to that tension? Does he not blame the moderns, Machiavelli and his Enlightenment followers, for failing to understand that tension and seeking to replace (necessarily partial and false) opinion with knowledge? Yes to all of these questions. But does it follow that someone who accepts all these points returns to the advocacy and practice of esotericism?[47] Here the answer appears to be no, for, as we have seen, Strauss exposes esotericism and thus undermines the further practice of it.[48]

How can Strauss be both the rediscoverer and the destroyer of esoteric writing? Esotericism was intended to protect or insulate philosophy and politics from each other. It protects the philosopher from persecution; it protects the city, to use Strauss's term, from the dissolving and irresponsible action of philosophy, which questions and challenges received opinion. Philosophy must learn a sort of political responsibility, a kind of moderation, and it must put on a public face in order to preserve the possibility for its own pursuit, as well as to act benevolently in society. These rules of philosophic action and philosophic politics were foundations for and have their primary validity in preliberal, pre-Enlightenment societies. As we have seen, Strauss admits, even insists, that thinkers in liberal societies do not face the same threat of persecution as thinkers did in preliberal societies.[49]

For a person writing in a post-Enlightenment environment, the reasons favoring esoteric philosophy no longer had the force they once had, and stronger reasons emerged, which led Strauss to reveal and thus undermine esotericism.[50] Strauss wrote in a situation he regularly and dramatically called a "crisis." The crisis had two sides: the two things he cared most about, philosophy and politics, were both in danger and were both endangered by the same cause, the corrupting and corrosive effect of Enlightenment modernity, which had turned into its opposite during the twentieth century. Philosophy, as practiced by the greatest philosophers of the age, had "progressed" to the point where it declared philosophy impossible and unworthy. Postmodernism has advanced this thesis much further since Strauss's death. At the same time, the spread of Enlightenment or post-Enlightenment thought has had the kind of corrosive effect on political opinion and thus on political life that the original political philosophers worried about.

Although it gave him little satisfaction, Strauss saw the course of modern philosophy and politics as vindication of the Platonic analysis underlying the original version of political philosophy. The post-Enlightenment, in Strauss's view, proved what Platonic political philosophers knew all along—the Enlightenment was a foolish, even dangerous enterprise. Had Strauss lived on the verge of the Enlightenment, and seen the world then as he did in the twentieth century, he would no doubt have attempted to prevent the Enlightenment project from taking off. He would have acted to preserve political (i.e., esoteric) philosophy as it was.

But Strauss did not live at the time of the emergence of the Enlightenment. The occurrence of the Enlightenment and the post-Enlightenment meant that one could not simply return (pace Lampert), or could not restore the pre-Enlightenment esoteric philosophy. As the saying goes, the genies were out of the bottle. Strauss would be a foolish thinker indeed if he did not realize that the unprecedented situation required an unprecedented kind of response.

Rather than reinstating esotericism, Strauss exposed it. Given his view that the tension between philosophy and politics is coeval with society, and given his view of the disproportion between philosophy and society, this was a problematic strategy indeed, but it rested on his conviction that the current crisis required a more radical and open response than ever was necessary in the past. For the sake of both politics and philosophy, Strauss had to bring into the open the character of Platonic political philosophy.[51] Although the truth about philosophy might, under pre-Enlightenment conditions, be dangerous for both philosophy and the city, in the post-Enlightenment condition the absence of truth was much more dangerous. The only possible cure for the ills of Enlightenment was a new kind of enlightenment, a kind of enlightenment that could save the possibility of philosophy by showing its true nature, its real worth, and its content freed from its exoteric accoutrements. At the same time, the true account of philosophy could supply new grounding for "values," for it could supply a doctrine of natural right to hold against the extreme relativism and loss of confidence in the good, the true, and the just characteristic of Western modernity in our post-Enlightenment age.

So, Strauss openly taught, philosophy is in its nature different from religion or theology. It was a truth he believed to be eternal, but one that previous philosophy had very often done its best to disguise. Strauss did not disguise this truth, though; he paraded it, because in the post-Enlightenment context, the truth about the relation between philosophy and religion was more salutary, more socially responsible, more preservative of philosophy than the false theories circulating in society under the most charismatic philosophic sponsorship, for example, that of Nietzsche or Heidegger. "Advanced thinking" proclaimed that "God is dead." Strauss insisted on the inability of philosophy to make that claim.[52] Philosophy may not be as unambiguously supportive of theological claims as certain forms of earlier philosophy—exoteric philosophy—had claimed, but true philosophy was nowhere nearly as hostile or unsettling of religion as the overreaching postmodern philosophy of Strauss's day was. Strauss's philosophy, far from being the dogmatic atheism Drury thinks it is, accepts the limits of philosophy, which prevent it from dogmatic atheism along with any other form of dogmatism. In another age, philosophy's distance from theology would have been unsettling; today it is, in its way, supportive of religion, not as mere public teaching for the masses, but as an alternative answer to the question of how human beings should orient themselves in life.

It is a regular criticism of Strauss, leveled by such as Burnyeat, that he is a "sphinx without a secret," that is, that the "hidden truths" are not so amazing but quite commonplace.[53] This is not a surprising charge, but it completely misses Strauss's point. Machiavelli, Hobbes, Nietzsche, and other Enlighteners said all (and more) that the premodern thinkers feared would be unsettling for common life. Of course, the hidden truths that Strauss finds in Plato or Farabi sound familiar—later writers have blared them from the rooftops. For Strauss to expose the practice and content of esoteric writing is not really to tell the intellectually sophisticated among us things we have never heard, although we may not have thought that ancient or medieval or early modern thinkers had these thoughts. Strauss can and must expose what has become familiar so that the unfamiliar and surprising core of the older philosophy can become visible to us. Thus Strauss shucks off Platonic Ideas and Platonic immortality of the soul as mere exotericism in order to reveal the truer and still valid inner character of Platonic philosophizing. Acceptance of the Platonic exotericism has long since faded, so it does no harm for Strauss to reveal its exoteric nature. It does the potential good of making available to us a version of Plato (or Farabi, or many other ancient philosophers) that he thought could withstand the acidic effects of postmodernity.

The Straussian philosophic activity did not represent a continuation of the esoteric tradition so much as the uprooting of that tradition by exposing it to the light of day. Martin Heidegger had famously said, "Only a God can save us." Strauss, the rediscoverer of the role of untruth in philosophy, said, in effect, that only the truth, the real stripped-down truth about philosophy, can save us.

Readers who have struggled with the obscurity of Strauss's texts, with the intentional withholding of conclusions, who have noted or been frustrated by his failure to express himself with the degree of explicitness taken for granted as a proper part of contemporary academic writing, may doubt the main lines of our argument thus far. We have, it must be said again, treated Strauss's problem of philosophic expression as a problem governed by two principles: the fear of persecution and the need for social responsibility. But there is a third reason for inexplicitness in philosophic expression: the needs of philosophic education. The situation of post-Enlightenment societies changes the imperatives deriving from the danger of persecution and the moral need for social responsibility, but it affects much less the requisites of education. The last words of Strauss's most thematic discussion of esotericism affirm the educational purposes behind "writing between the lines" for books of the past, but it is clear from his context that these reasons retain their force even in a liberal or post-Enlightenment age: "The works of the great writers of the past are very beautiful even from without. And yet their visible beauty is sheer ugliness, compared with the beauty of those hidden treasures which disclose themselves only after long, never easy, but always pleasant work. This always difficult but always pleasant work is, I believe, what the philosophers had in mind when they recommended education."[54] That sense that Strauss withholds, that he wants his readers to work hard to piece out his conclusion, follows, we believe, from this purely educational side of his enterprise. By writing what appear to be mere summaries, Strauss forces his readers to study the original texts, on their own and thoroughly, in order to ferret out his interpretative moves.[55] The peculiar mode of writing that Strauss adopted in his later works no longer concerns persecution or noble lies, but only the leading up of the young that Strauss called education. Strauss says in one of his earliest forays into the interpretation of a classical text: "I believe that I have not dotted all the i's." But failing to dot the i's is not to tell noble lies. Strauss, we are tempted to say, practiced a "noble reticence," or a "pedagogical reserve," rather than noble lying. "Socratic rhetoric," he said in one of his most thematic statements on the subject, "is meant to be an indispensable instrument." It is not indispensable because of the danger of persecution or the political need for "noble lies"; "its purpose is to lead potential philosophers to philosophy by training them and liberating them from the charms which obstruct the philosophic effort."[56] The exoteric revelation by Strauss of the nature of esotericism is, in connection with the enterprise of philosophic education, not self-defeating, for the young of the post-Enlightenment age require an indication of the path.[57] But this is a very different sort of esotericism, far removed from the bustle of politics, aiming only at theoretic insight and connected in no way to Broadway.[58]

Looking for Secrets in All the Wrong Places

Strauss writes with "pedagogical reserve." He does not, as he said in *On Tyranny*, "dot all the i's." Nor, we might add, does he cross all the t's. Is there any significant difference between the practices of esotericism and pedagogical reserve? We believe there is. In practicing pedagogical reserve, Strauss fails to say all that he thinks, or, better put perhaps, he fails to flesh out (as we poor readers often wish he would) the full scope of his reasoning. The difference between this sort of writing and esotericism is relatively clear-cut in our context. Esoteric writers like Maimonides give the impression that they agree with the religious orthodoxies of their day, and the true understanding of such writers involves bringing out the esoteric doctrine, which stands at a distance from the dominant impression left by the surface of their texts. As we have commented earlier, the esoteric writers use their esotericism to blend in better with their surroundings than they would if they spoke bluntly. In order to do so, esoteric writers, among other things, say things they do not believe. Michael Kochin expresses it well when he says that "in exoteric writing, the philosopher's hidden or esoteric teaching is expounded through the careful arrangement and selection in his presentation of the opinions that comport with convention. . . . The esoteric teaching is written between the lines, in that the lines themselves present to the reader, or at least to the careless reader, only what can safely be known to any reader."[59]

The practice of pedagogical reserve, however, may find the author saying less than he thinks, but not other than what he thinks, except as he may tentatively adopt or consider one or another view as a step in his developing argument, a practice characteristic of completely non-esoteric writing. But the point is not systematically to suggest the contrary of what he thinks, or even to withhold the main conclusions to which he has come. Thus Strauss, unlike the esoteric writer Maimonides, does not leave his readers with the impression that he is a spokesman or partisan of Judaism or of the revelatory perspective, or of the harmony between faith and reason. Unlike the esoteric writer Plato, Strauss does not leave his readers with the impression that he is an advocate of the theory of Ideas, or of the doctrine of immortality of the soul.[60]

There is an obvious, but not therefore obviously correct, retort to the argument we have thus far made. Strauss is the "man who gave away the secrets," but his unusual, nay, unprecedented candor is a blind, a decoy meant to distract from yet more secret things that remain hidden. In the abstract, this is, of course, possible. There is no way to disprove it as a possibility. The best one can do is examine candidate esoteric doctrines that have been put forward by those who think they are there. Although many have tried, we are not persuaded that anybody has come up with an esoteric doctrine in Strauss. If there is one, it is buried so deep as to be irrelevant for all practical purposes.

Many of the attempts to read Strauss as an esoteric writer amply testify to the potential abuses many critics of Strauss have pointed to when they have criticized his hypothesis as a method of reading authors of the past. A particularly clumsy and unpersuasive effort to treat Strauss as an esoteric writer is Peter Levine's *Nietzsche and the Modern Crisis of the Humanities*. He maintains that Strauss is an "esoteric Nietzschean." For evidence of Strauss's Nietzscheanism he quotes passages from Strauss's essay on Nietzsche's *Beyond Good and Evil*, an essay intended to give an account of the German's thought. Since Strauss frequently distanced himself from Nietzsche,[61] it is quite unacceptable to cite Strauss's presentation of Nietzsche's thoughts as though they were his own. By this method, one could identify Strauss with Thucydides, Hobbes, Rousseau, Weber, and a large number of others as well as with Nietzsche. It really will not do to argue, in effect, that (a) Strauss is (obviously) an esoteric writer, that is, he doesn't say openly what he believes; (b) Strauss frequently rejects Nietzsche, Heidegger, historicism, and nihilism in his texts; (c) therefore,

Strauss must be a Nietzschean, a Heideggerian, a historicist, or a nihilist. To prove that Strauss is a nihilist, Levine brings to bear such other "evidence" as Strauss's expressed doubts about Plato's theory of Ideas. In rejecting that theory, Strauss is trying "to show that Plato was a secret nihilist."[62] Since Aristotle also rejected the Platonic Ideas, Levine no doubt considers him a nihilist as well.

There are, however, several much better attempts to claim Strauss as one of the clan of writers between the lines. One practice of Strauss's that sometimes leads clever readers to conclude that he must be an esoteric writer is his occasional deployment of devices he finds in or attributes to the writers he identities as esoteric. For example, in his study of Machiavelli, he finds that the Florentine plays with numerological significances, especially with the number thirteen and its multiples. *The Prince* has twenty-six chapters, a fact to which Strauss attributes much significance. He also calls attention to the chapters in Machiavelli's *Discourses on . . . Livy* that are multiples of thirteen. Some readers of Strauss notice that his chapter on *The Prince* in his *Thoughts on Machiavelli* has twenty-six paragraphs, surely no mere coincidence.[63]

Readers who notice such things often wish to conclude that Strauss is "writing as he reads," that is, using these devices for the presentation of his esoteric teaching. If so, it is a remarkably ham-handed device: since he has just called so much attention to these numbers, the deployment of them would seem a very poor way to hide something. It is hardly different from the new obtrusiveness of the center in the wake of Strauss's hermeneutics of the center. Larry Peterman unwittingly captures the paradox when he remarks on *Thoughts on Machiavelli* that it "provides an especially good opportunity for investigating Strauss's teaching because its esotericism is so obvious."[64] But "obvious esotericism" is not esotericism.

Nonetheless, it is true that Strauss employs such devices. What can it mean? The proper context for understanding Strauss's practice is the reaction his announcement of esoteric writing evoked in the scholarly world. Although there were some who were undeniably intrigued, many others were undeniably repelled, either by moral objections or by a sense of the sheer implausibility of it. That writers would or could pay attention to the kinds of details Strauss claimed they did seemed highly unlikely. Thus Strauss's ways of reading (and counting) often earned him good-natured and not-so-good-natured ridicule. As we indicated earlier, he expected that this might happen, yet persisted in his advocacy of the esotericism thesis and in presenting esoteric readings based thereon, because he thought the future of philosophy depended on an accurate grasp of its past and was convinced that was possible only on the basis of the esotericism thesis.[65] He knew many contemporary readers would or did find the whole theory implausible. Could anybody really write like that? Yes, Strauss set out to show—he himself could. And if he could, then Plato, Xenophon, Farabi, Maimonides, Machiavelli, and Locke could do so as well. To borrow a phrase of which Strauss was fond: he sought to demonstrate *ad occulos* that writers could write as he said they did by writing in that way himself. But his purpose in doing so was not the same as theirs. Writing like that was Strauss's playful way of demonstrating his serious thesis about esotericism. It was not his way of hiding or falsely insinuating "noble lies," but of revealing the possibility of the "forgotten kind of writing."

One of the most detailed and, in its way, stimulating attempts to read Strauss as he read others is Peterman's application to *Thoughts on Machiavelli* of the devices Strauss applied to Machiavelli's *Discourses on . . . Livy*. Peterman pulls out most if not all the stops: he tells us in one place of something said in the second-to-last paragraph of one chapter, which he then relates to something said in the next-to-last paragraph of another chapter, with the theme raised by the two paragraphs resolved in the second-to-last paragraph of yet another chapter, which it turns out is dead in the center between the first two paragraphs mentioned. He out-Strausses Strauss in method, but, it must be said, not in clarity of exposition. Nonetheless, Peterman displays great ingenuity and patience in giving his partial reading of Strauss as Strauss read Machiavelli.

He arrives at such conclusions as these: "Strauss's treatment of Machiavelli on religion and belief, then, suggests the existence of a tension in modern thought between hopefulness and fearfulness. . . . [This] suggests the possibility that Machiavellianism rests on fragile foundations and must eventually fail." Any reader even slightly familiar with Strauss's writings on Machiavelli is not likely to find the lines of this conclusion any too surprising. Strauss is open both about his view of the defectiveness of Machiavelli's position and about his view that Machiavelli's modern successors will subject the Florentine's thought to transformative pressure. As Peterman conjectures, Strauss's idea of what will replace Machiavelli can most likely be gleaned from "Strauss's comments on the second wave of modernity." That is almost certainly correct, but the chief significance of Peterman's analysis lies in the fact that treating Strauss as an esoteric writer yielded up what was more or less evident to most readers of Strauss, few of whom have engaged in the strenuous enumerations and calculations undertaken by Peterman. This is not to say that Peterman's analysis yields nothing of value. Far from it. He presents a plausible interpretation of a line of criticism that does not leap off the page. This is not to say that Peterman's account is accurate, however, for the theme of the combination of hope and fear in the religious life is one that Strauss regularly emphasized.[66] In any case, the results of Peterman's esoteric reading do not lead away from what Strauss seems (exoterically) to be saying about Machiavelli. Let us be generous: Peterman has dotted an *i* that Strauss left undotted.

Peterman's closing paragraph provides unwitting testimony, we think, to our main argument about Strauss: summing up his essay, he says, "this may stand as our final comment on Strauss's achievement as a teacher." This conclusion echoes nicely with Peterman's opening discussion of the general issue of esotericism. He quickly passes over, almost dismisses, persecution, and altogether fails to mention the "disproportion" between philosophy and the city as a ground for esotericism. He fastens instead on the third, quite different impetus to philosophic writing: "Thus the hidden or difficult to attain teaching becomes a vehicle for attracting and tantalizing the best students, for drawing them to the higher teaching as it were."[67] To translate into our language: Peterman is actually dealing with Strauss's pedagogical reserve. Without taking a stand on what he claims to have found, we find his inquiry guided by and issuing in the same understanding of Strauss's mode of communication that we have been putting forward here.

Another well done but ultimately unpersuasive effort to read Strauss esoterically is Kenneth Hart Green's thoughtful analysis of Strauss's essay on Judah Halevi's *Kuzari*, an essay to be found in *Persecution and the Art of Writing*. Green argues that Strauss appears on the surface to accept Halevi's self-presentation as a Jewish thinker hostile to philosophy, but that he esoterically reveals Halevi to be a philosopher warning his fellow philosophers of the need for a greater esotericism than they have been practicing. Strauss paints Halevi not as a son of Abraham, but as a son of Socrates. But Green's analysis, despite its attention to detail, does not bring out anything that actually undermines the already subtle and somewhat esoteric position Strauss openly attributes to Halevi: the latter is a Jew who was once a philosopher and understands the philosophic position perfectly well but presents it in a muted way, because he does not want to give any aid to the possibly subversive effects of philosophy within Judaism. Halevi, on Strauss's account, attempts to refute or at least expose the defects of the philosophic stance at the level of philosophy, and along the way to bring out the genuine ground for revelation. Halevi exposes the nature of morality as morality, that is, as binding in itself, or as nonconsequential, and shows that under the glare of philosophy, morality loses its specific character as morality and becomes instrumental. Strauss's point is

not that Halevi accepts this philosophic challenge to morality, but that he
rejects philosophy because of it. Revelation, or the theological worldview,
is embraced by Halevi as the worldview consistent with and grounding the
priority of the moral. Strauss's analysis of Halevi exposes the deep connection between morality and the claims of Jerusalem, a theme that pervades
much of Strauss's work.[68] It also gives a better and deeper understanding
of his notion of "the fundamental alternatives" and sets one on the path
to understanding the choice Strauss himself made with regard to those alternatives. Of course, there is an easy way to reconcile Green's reading of
this text with ours: if our reading is correct, and Halevi is exposing the true
character of philosophy and its deep differences from the law and revelation, then to a philosopher reading his text the point might be just what
Green says it is—to warn the philosophers to better conceal their heterodoxy. But as the primary point of Halevi's text (or of Strauss's "secret" version thereof), that seems dubious, for in order to make it, Halevi is led to
expose the heterodoxy of philosophy to a greater degree than may already
be visible to the ordinary or even thoughtful believer. To warn the philosophers, on Green's reading, the philosopher would be further endangering
philosophy.

The most serious, the most persuasive of the efforts to read Strauss esoterically come, however, not from the word processors of Tim Robbins or
Shadia Drury, nor even from those of Larry Peterman and Kenneth Green,
but from Laurence Lampert and Stanley Rosen. Part of what makes these
two especially noteworthy is that both give full weight—perhaps not full
weight, but real weight—to the consideration that has dominated our reasoning about Strauss: Strauss reveals rather than conceals the esoteric tradition, both that it exists and what it is. Rosen and Lampert call attention
to Strauss's "peculiar candor."[69] Rosen goes so far as to pose as "the crucial question: "Why did Strauss devote so much effort to publicizing the
existence of an esoteric teaching in the western tradition?" And he raises
exactly the right considerations for seeing that as a "crucial question," if
not the primary one. "On the one hand," Rosen observes, "these efforts
brought him and his disciples an almost unmitigated ridicule, not to say persecution, at least in the English-speaking academy." These words, we note,
are even truer today than when Rosen first published them in 1987. "On the
other hand," Rosen continues, making the really crucial point, "such pub-
licity seems to violate the moral and prudential principles of the practice of
esotericism itself."[70]

Rosen, and Lampert to a lesser degree, nonetheless persist in the view
that Strauss does have a secret or esoteric doctrine. Drastically simplifying

Lampert's intelligent, textually detailed, and sophisticated reading, one can say that he argues that Strauss is "really" a Nietzschean, no matter how much the surface of his work points away from Nietzsche. Unlike some others who have made the same claim, Lampert demonstrates real knowledge of both of the relevant authors: he makes a powerful, but not, in our opinion, a compelling case. As we have argued in chapter 3, we do not find the various efforts to assimilate Strauss to Nietzsche, including Lampert's attempt, to be accurate; and so we cannot follow Lampert in thinking Strauss's anti-Nietzscheanism to be merely an exoteric teaching. He admired much in Nietzsche and he admittedly learned much from him, but his opposition to Nietzsche is the genuine article.

Rosen requires more attention at this point; for one, he has returned to the theme of Strauss's esotericism with a persistence bordering on obsession. He seems to have taken his cue from Lewis Carroll's "Hunting of the Snark," for he has addressed three separate essays to the topic. Not only the frequency of his turn to the esotericism issue, but also the range of his learning, the passion of his engagement with and against Strauss, and the sheer radicalness and daring of his conclusions compel further discussion.

Rosen is convinced that Strauss writes esoterically—that claim remains constant across his three essays—but the identification of what is esoteric in Strauss shifts over time. The leading elements in his treatment of Strauss remain fairly constant, but in his most recent essay he achieves greater clarity and focus.

In the first two essays, written very near to each other in time, two themes vie for Rosen's candidate for Strauss's esoteric teaching. One is a claim he shares, or almost shares, with Lampert: "Strauss," says Rosen, "is himself almost a Nietzschean, but not quite." We reply to this just as we did to the similar claim raised by Lampert. No matter, however, for by the time Rosen comes to write on Strauss again, more than a decade later, he himself emphatically rejects the idea that Strauss is a "secret Nietzschean."[71]

In both of the earlier essays on Strauss, Rosen points out another example of a doctrine he believes to be merely exoteric, namely Strauss's identification of the rural aristocracy as the preferred ruling group in the eyes of the classical Greek thinkers, both because of their moderation and virtue and because they are most likely to be open to and protective and supportive of philosophy. Rosen doubts the last claim: "However much gentlemen may look down upon the rulers, they do not look up to philosophic theory, as Strauss perfectly well knew."[72] As Rosen has it, this doctrine is "manifestly based on an act of will" and is Strauss's exoteric effort to appeal to conservative political forces in his own day. It is not so clear that

Rosen is correct, however. In his sketch of the best regime at the end of his *Politics,* Aristotle emphasizes the educated or cultured nature of his ruling aristocratic gentlemen. We in the postclassical world have much experience of gentlemen open to intellectual pursuit and culture, if not to philosophy per se. One might consider Henry Fielding's Squire Allworthy as a case in point. Allworthy's neighbor and contrasting model of a gentleman, Squire Weston, stands as a case in Rosen's favor, for he is indeed indifferent if not quite hostile to all intellectual pursuits: he would far rather pursue a fox than the truth. Like Callicles in Plato's *Gorgias,* he would not see the philosophic life as a fully "manly" life. But there is no reason to say that Strauss's discussion of the ancients on the educated aristocracy is "exoteric" or that his appeal to a liberally educated "natural aristocracy" in our day is mere exotericism either.[73]

In his essay on Wittgenstein and Strauss—admittedly a bit of an odd couple—Rosen radicalizes his position by bringing to the fore a claim that had rattled through the previous two essays: "the truly secret teaching is the impossibility of philosophy, an impossibility that must be concealed from the human race for its own salvation."[74] Rosen best explains the last part of his thesis in one of his earlier essays on Strauss. "Strauss (rightly) attributes to Nietzsche the view that the theoretical analysis of the relativity of all comprehensive views, if publicly disseminated, would make human life itself impossible."[75] Rosen opines that Strauss shares this Nietzschean view and, moreover, that Strauss agrees with Nietzsche that the "relativity of all comprehensive views" is the conclusion to which "theoretical analysis" leads. That is to say, philosophy as discovery of natural right, as the overcoming of this relativity, is impossible.[76] But the world of ordinary mortals cannot proceed well without the belief that a true "comprehensive view" is available, and Strauss's political philosophy, that is, his political rhetoric, is the willful purveying of the myth that philosophy is possible and can discover natural right. Rosen thus concludes that "Strauss believes philosophy to be a noble lie."[77]

Since Strauss's central thought is or seems to be the possibility and goodness of philosophy, Rosen's claim is radical indeed. It goes further than his earlier assertion and Lampert's recurrent claim that Strauss is a closet Nietzschean, for Nietzsche believed that despite the radically critical character of philosophic analysis, philosophy is possible. Indeed, his work is a protracted call for a new philosophy, a "philosophy of the future." Rosen's insistence that Strauss is no "secret Nietzschean" is the result of his conclusion that Strauss does not accept Nietzsche's new grounding of philosophy in will to power. Strauss "grasped the defects of the Enlightenment as these were delineated by Nietzsche, [but] he never drew Nietzsche's conclusions. . . . It is a complete misunderstanding of Strauss's views to associate him with Nietzsche's positive program."[78] (Take that, Lampert!) Rosen's thesis may also make one think of Drury and some of the more semipopular media presentations of Strauss, but it is importantly different from these claims. It shares nothing with Drury's attribution of vulgar and narrowly self-interested motives to Strauss. Rosen's Strauss is not seeking the Hugh Hefner life, not seeking the glory and satisfaction of rule for himself or his followers, but is attempting to help humans continue to find their lives possible and meaningful.

Given the place of the philosophic life in Strauss's thought, Rosen's arresting claim begs for serious attention. On examination it turns out to be based on many misunderstandings and, at best, a very partial and very selective grasp of Strauss's position. To be more precise: Rosen's presentation of Strauss is marred by one major incoherence and three large misunderstandings. The incoherence arises when Rosen returns to the question he had cagily pressed in one of his earlier essays. How can we account for Strauss's candid exposure of the tradition of philosophic esotericism? Rosen, it should be noted, has no doubts that as a historical matter, Strauss is absolutely correct that such a tradition did exist and that understanding it is key to grasping the Western philosophical tradition.[79] What puzzles Rosen is that, as he sees it, Strauss both wants to continue the tradition (himself) and to expose it, thus making its continuance problematical in the extreme. Rosen explains Strauss's position as a "dilemma," as a self-defeating halfway house, for he has to combine frankness with concealment in a way that Rosen judges cannot be successful. The combination is necessary, Rosen surmises, because Strauss has two competing aims in his handling of the esotericism theme. Strauss has both a "political program" (a "political politics") and a "philosophic politics," and esotericism plays a role in both. The political politics aims at "contributing to the modification of contemporary liberalism by the moderate tendencies of the classical political thinkers as well as of the liberal rationalists of the seventeenth and eighteenth centuries."[80] This is the side of Strauss we have already noticed Rosen critiquing when he objected to Strauss's apparent advocacy of the role of aristocratic gentlemen in politics.

The "philosophic politics" has another goal, however, a goal Rosen presents as closer to Strauss's heart: "the highest political goal of the philosopher [i]s the preservation of philosophy." The coexistence of Strauss's two political goals accounts for the paradoxes of Strauss's stance toward esotericism. That coexistence "complicated Strauss's rhetorical

task." The political goal proper requires moderation and a conformist surface, conformist to those aspects of the ongoing regime and those moderating aspects of the tradition that support the moderating aims of his "political program." His "political politics" thus requires continuation of the esoteric tradition. Strauss's revelation of the esoteric tradition is related to his
philosophic politics. "Strauss frequently stated that thought should be daring, even mad, whereas action should be moderate."[81] However, the revelation of the "mad" or "daring" practice of esotericism, together with some
of the "mad" conclusions of the philosophers, namely, their reservations
and critical questions about the moderate political and moral views contained in social and religious orthodoxies and in Strauss's exoteric teaching, undermined esotericism. So Rosen explains, Strauss "shifts back and
forth from the subtle flirtation of Jane Austen to the relative frankness of
Nietzsche."[82] "Philosophy," he announces, "is by nature immoderate," but
Straussian politics is nothing but moderation.[83]

Rosen sees the competing aims and necessities of Strauss's two politics as producing an incoherence in Strauss's theory—or between his theory and practice. The more interesting incoherence, however, is in Rosen's
view of Strauss. On the one hand, he asserts that Strauss's "secret" is that
philosophy is impossible, nothing but a noble lie. But on the other hand he
affirms that the goal of Strauss's philosophic politics is to preserve philosophy, an activity Strauss believes, on Rosen's account, to be impossible. It
should be clear from this aporia in Rosen's account of Strauss that something has gone wrong somewhere. We believe he has lost his way because
of his misunderstandings of three critical ideas in Strauss.

One of the misunderstandings lurking somewhere inside Rosen's incoherence is a view that he, and perhaps others, hold about Strauss on the
very meaning of political philosophy. In Rosen's case, it is a claim tendered
most forcefully in his earlier *Hermeneutics as Politics*, but the lingering effects of it are still present in his later book *The Elusiveness of the Ordinary*.
The claim is this: "political philosophy is the public appearance of philosophy." Rosen means that, for Strauss, political philosophy is nothing but
the form in which philosophy presents itself to the city; political philosophy
is merely the rhetorical face of philosophy, the exoteric version of philosophy. Rosen then considers it perfectly appropriate to conclude that political
philosophy for Strauss is only a kind of "propaganda."[84]

Rosen rests his case most solidly on a passage in which Strauss says "political philosophy consists . . . in convincing the city that the philosophers
are not atheists, that they do not profane all that the city regards as sacred,
that they respect that which the city respects, that they are not subversive,

and finally that they are not irresponsible adventurers but good citizens and even the best of citizens."[85] This conception of political philosophy is intimately linked to Rosen's view of the aim of the philosopher's philosophic politics: "the preservation of philosophy." Political philosophy for Strauss is, indeed, the "public face" of philosophy and the action by philosophers on behalf of philosophy, but it is much more than that too. In addition to this aspect of political philosophy, there are at least three others that Rosen altogether misses. As we indicated in chapter 1, political philosophy for Strauss is also a branch of philosophy per se: "Philosophy, as quest for wisdom, is quest for universal knowledge, for knowledge of the whole. . . . It is . . . the attempt to replace opinions about the whole by knowledge of the whole."[86] Political life is part of the whole, and political philosophy is that part of philosophy which seeks knowledge of that part of the whole. It is in principle not different from the knowledge philosophy seeks of other parts of the world.

Yet, for another but related sense of political philosophy, political life is not only an element of the whole that philosophers seek to understand, but an especially privileged part of it. In accord with the Socratic idea of "the second sailing," the ingress to knowledge is not via direct access to the phenomena ("looking at the sun"), but via opinion. Thus we arrive at Socratic dialectical or conversational philosophizing. The opinions human beings hold are not merely individual matters, Strauss observes. The political community is the source and locus of the "authoritative opinions," and, beginning in opinion, philosophy must self-consciously clarify the source, the setting, and the nature of the opinions it takes as its point of departure. Thus the notion of Socratic philosophizing requires a theorization of politics, requires that it be political philosophy, more than it requires it to be, say, an aesthetic philosophy or even a philosophy of mind.[87]

Finally, as we indicated in chapter 1, the philosopher as Strauss understands him acts benevolently toward his fellow citizens and human beings. Since so much of the felicity of human life depends on political arrangements, the philosopher as a just, or benevolent, person attempts to contribute what he can to the well-being of his fellows. Thus, Strauss emphasized, Aristotle took the part of "the umpire" of claims to political justice, helping citizens and statesmen to see justice more comprehensively than they were otherwise inclined to do and offering advice on how to improve political practice within the limits of possibility or probability.[88]

Strauss's conception of political philosophy has far more to it than Rosen (or Drury) seems to suspect. It is not one-sidedly interested in politics from the perspective of the good of the philosophers or philosophy; it is richer and more complex. Although the esotericism issue is relevant to it, political philosophy is far from being identical with and limited to the exoteric communication of the philosopher with the city. So far as Rosen fails to see more to political philosophy than the one-sided activity he discusses, he is destined to miss much of Strauss.

A second misunderstanding vitiating Rosen's daring thesis that Strauss's secret is the impossibility of philosophy is his failure to grasp the nature and locus of philosophic inquiry in Strauss. One of Rosen's major concerns in his essay in *The Elusiveness of the Ordinary* is the problem of surface and depth in Strauss, or the problem of where Strauss looks to find philosophic truth. Strauss once famously said: "There is no surer protection against the understanding of anything than taking for granted or otherwise despising the obvious and surface. The problem inherent in the surface of things, and only in the surface of things, is the heart of things."[89] This passage is a good warning by Strauss himself against the tendency of many of his readers to assume he despises the surface and is a devotee entirely of the hidden or secret depths.

Rosen attempts to take this maxim to heart and concludes that Strauss must mean by "the surface of things" the ordinary or prephilosophic view of things. He thus connects Strauss's maxim to Strauss's historical studies, especially his effort to discover the Greek prephilosophic grasp of politics and other matters.

Rosen has little confidence in this procedure, which is part of his reason for including his essay on Strauss in a book on "the elusiveness of the ordinary." In this essay he uses his doubts about this philosophic method as part of the evidence that Strauss thinks philosophy to be impossible. He has two related points. First, the recapturing of Greek prephilosophic opinion either gives us something universal, in which case it is superfluous as Greek and Strauss's inquiries are misguided, or it gives us something peculiarly Greek and thus is limited as to what it can tell us universally. Rosen seems to lean to the latter alternative as Strauss's view of the matter (as based on Strauss's practice). But if Strauss gets back to, or looks for, philosophic truth in Greek prephilosophic opinion, he is in fact taking a historicist course, a course that accepts the historicity of thought that he himself considers contrary and inimical to philosophy. Alternatively, Rosen claims that every "deconstruction" of philosophy "is itself philosophical" and thus that there is never any getting back to the pretheoretical ground of truth that Strauss seems to be seeking. The knowledgeable reader might notice that, in effect, Rosen is arguing that Strauss is caught within a Heideggerian cage and must ultimately agree with Heidegger.

Rosen is not very attentive to what Strauss actually says, but there seems to be an association of ideas based on Strauss's language that leads Rosen to his view of what Strauss is saying. As we have seen, Strauss insists that philosophy never can achieve its aims—a complete or comprehensive account of the whole. But he does believe philosophy can achieve insight and clarity about "the fundamental problems." Rosen seems to think that the "problem inherent in the surface of things" is the same as "the fundamental problems" Strauss seeks. Thus he frequently or almost always rephrases (rather than quotes) Strauss's "maxim" to read: "the depth is contained in the surface." As a thinker himself, Rosen does not believe that the "surface" can be recovered, or even that it exists as Strauss seems to think of it. As an interpreter of Strauss, he comes to think that Strauss agrees. Hence his conclusion that Strauss thinks philosophy impossible.

It is, first of all, interesting to note that Rosen's preferred reformulation is in fact quite different from Strauss's original saying. Strauss does not speak of "depth" at all, but "surface" and "heart."[90] Moreover, Strauss does not say that the depth or "heart" is "contained in" the surface. Strauss's "maxim" contains two emphases quite different from Rosen's restatement. First he emphasizes the *problem . . .* in the surface of things," not the surface per se. He is not saying that the surface maps onto the heart, but that the problem in the surface is the heart.

But what, according to Strauss, is "the problem inherent in the surface of things?" "Philosophy, as quest for wisdom, is quest for knowledge of the whole. The quest would not be necessary if such knowledge were immediately available. The absence of such knowledge of the whole does not mean, however, that men do not have thoughts about the whole: philosophy is necessarily preceded by opinions about the whole. It is, therefore, the attempt to replace opinion about the whole by knowledge of the whole."[91] The surface, what we see first, are opinions. The opinion-in-chief, which defines the surface for Strauss, is the one Socrates took as thematic: "Socrates discovered the paradoxical fact that, in a way, the most important truth is the most obvious truth, or the truth of the surface."[92] Philosophy is motivated by the recognition both of the fact of opinions and the manifest inadequacy of the opinions. The opinions are multiple, internally inconsistent, and incomplete. The problem in the surface is the duality of human opinion—open to the whole and yet falling short of giving us knowledge of the whole. That recognition sets in motion the task of philosophy, which is the examination and transcendence of opinion. The method is Socratic dialectic; the goal sought is knowledge of the whole; the end (at best) achieved is knowledge of the "fundamental problems," and that knowledge among other things, reflects the beginning point, the incompleteness and clash of opinion, the problem of the surface. Strauss does not, as Rosen seems to believe, look to the surface, that is, the recovered pretheoretical understanding, to give us philosophic truth, but only to get us out of the "cave beneath the cave" that the overlay of a nearly three-millennia-long tradition of thought has dug for us. To ascend from the "cave beneath the cave" does not get us to the philosophic truth, but it does get us to a starting point for the Socratic philosophical dialectic.[93] Strauss's maxim about "surface" and "heart" and Strauss's practice of engaging in historical inquiry are not, then, signals of the impossibility of philosophy, but rather tokens of his understanding of what philosophy is and what one must do today to recapture political philosophy in its original or primordial sense.

Rosen's third and, in the context, most important misunderstanding of Strauss centers on the famous Athens-Jerusalem dualism in Strauss. At bottom it is Strauss's treatment of this theme that leads Rosen to his "conjecture" that Strauss believes philosophy to be but a noble lie. Rosen begins this part of his argument with a quotation from Strauss's chapter on Max Weber in *Natural Right and History*. Strauss, trying "to state in more precise terms" what Weber had in mind, says that philosophy must concede that revelation is possible, for it is unable to prove it impossible. This is a conclusion we have seen Strauss himself draw in his early book on Spinoza, and (to our knowledge) we never see him deny it. Nonetheless one cannot, with no more ado, attribute to Strauss the entire chain of thought Strauss attributes to Weber. Strauss, still speaking for Weber, goes on to say that if philosophy cannot refute revelation, if it must concede that revelation is possible, then philosophy cannot show itself to be "the one thing needful." In the absence of that demonstration, a rational grounding of philosophy cannot occur; the life of philosophy would then "rest merely on an unevident, arbitrary, or blind decision." But if that is so, then revelation or faith has in effect won: the consistent, rationally grounded life of rationality is itself only an arbitrary choice. "The mere fact that philosophy and revelation cannot refute each other would constitute the refutation of [the life of] philosophy by revelation." In the sequel, as in the preface to this passage, Strauss makes it ultra-clear that he is here explicating Weber's, not his own considered views.[94] This does not hinder Rosen from attributing to Strauss the whole argument, making the singularly odd claim that part of it is stated in the subjunctive, and the use of the subjunctive is a way Strauss has of signaling his own views. This is an odd argument, for Strauss is using the subjunctive to indicate that the latter part of the argument is a conditional, dependent on premises he is thereby distancing himself from affirming. The conclusion is in the subjunctive because Strauss pointedly failed to put it in the indicative.

Nonetheless, Rosen moves quickly to the conclusion that stands as the premise for the daring surmise of his essay: "It must follow on Straussian grounds that philosophy has been refuted, that it was impossible from the outset."[95] The Athens-Jerusalem issue is thus the clearest basis on which Rosen premises Strauss's esoteric commitment to the impossibility of philosophy. Rosen's provocative pressing of the Jerusalem-Athens issue provides an opportunity for us to clarify Strauss's position on the implications of the reason-revelation impasse for his doctrine of natural right.

We may begin by noting that Rosen draws an inference from the impasse between reason and revelation that is quite different from what Strauss actually said. Strauss said that the impasse "would constitute the refutation of [the life of] philosophy." This is not the same as claiming that the possibility of philosophy is refuted. Indeed the reasoning Strauss attributes to Weber does not in any way depend on a denial of the possibility of philosophy, that is, of the quest to replace opinions about the whole with knowledge of the whole. It says instead that rational validation of that life as the best life, or as "the one thing needful" is not (or would not be) possible. This is an important claim, if true, but it does not entail the impossibility of philosophy. It may not be possible rationally to show that the life of, say, a professional baseball player is the best human life, but it does not follow from that that playing baseball is impossible.

Moreover, as we have noted more than once, the argument Rosen is relying on is not presented by Strauss as his own view, but as the view of Weber. That it is not Strauss's view is evident from the facts that he developed the argument in his own name in a different direction from Weber's and that he drew a completely different conclusion from his own argument.

On many different occasions Strauss responded to the Weberian conclusion that the impasse leads to a merely arbitrary decision in favor of philosophy, a decision that proves not the impossibility of philosophy but the impossibility of rational proof that the life of philosophy is best, is the life in accord with natural right. Perhaps the most direct reply is Strauss's affirmation that "revelation cannot refute philosophy.... All theological arguments directed against philosophy are defective because they are circular: they are conclusive only on the basis of faith." If the theologian cannot refute philosophy, or prove the fact and content of revelation, then, Strauss concludes, "the philosopher can say there is no shred of evidence against the view that the right way of life is the philosophic life: revelation is nothing but a *factum brutum*, and in addition an uncertain one."[96] Since revelation cannot refute philosophy, it is not irrational in any strong sense for a human being to pursue the philosophic life, for revelation cannot show that it is irrational for an individual to inquire into, among other things, the *brutum factum* of revelation, or alleged revelation. The fact is, moreover, that revelation is not just one *brutum factum* but a series of *bruta facta*; that is, the philosopher discerns a variety of divine laws or alleged revelations of God or gods. So the philosopher has all the less of a reason to surrender to any one of them and all the more reasons to ask, which of them, if any, is the true revelation of the true God?

Strauss insists that ultimately the philosopher's inquiries will produce only the knowledge that he does not know, understanding that formula in the special way Strauss does: that highest philosophic knowledge is equivalent to the awareness that the search for wisdom is and will remain incomplete. It will never give the complete account of the whole it seeks. It cannot rule out the possibility that a mysterious God who reveals Himself is a part and cause of that whole.[97] It is not that the philosopher concludes that such a God exists, but, it seems, he cannot apodictically rule him out. The revealing God is a possibility, for all the philosopher can prove, and thus the life in obedience to the revealed word of the revealing God may indeed be the right life. The philosopher may have been mistaken to follow the path of philosophy. The philosopher cannot have known that prior to setting out in a life of philosophic inquiry, however, so the knowledge cannot invalidate his quest. But does the Socratic culmination of the philosophic quest retrospectively invalidate the path, or demand that the philosopher turn away from philosophy to the "life of loving obedience"?

On this last question, Strauss's position is complex. On the one hand, the answer would seem to be no. The philosopher, for good and sufficient, that is, nonarbitrary and rational, reasons, has set off on the life of philosophy, and the discoveries that greet him along the way suggest the bare possibility that there may be something that can trump his quest for knowledge. But it is not irrational to persist in one's way just because one knows that there may be a trump that could be played.[98] And even if it were, the philosopher would still face the problem of deciding which of the alleged revelations was the true one. It may be said that through grace or the direct action of God he will know, but still the philosopher, if lacking that grace, rightly persists.

However, Strauss also saw that philosophy must remain incomplete and in a sense "hypothetical" so long as the philosopher cannot disprove the possibility of God and revelation. That is, as Strauss says at the end of his lecture series "Progress or Return," probably his most extended examination of the reason-revelation problem, "philosophy or science, however you might call it, is incapable of giving an account of its own necessity."[99] This is the same idea that Rosen picks up from Strauss's Weber chapter in *Natural Right and History*. If philosophy cannot prove its own necessity, then "philosophy itself is possibly not the right way of life, ... not evidently the right way of life, because this possibility of revelation exists." Strauss draws a radical conclusion, which runs in a different direction from our discussion above: "But what then does the choice of philosophy mean under these conditions? In this case, the choice of philosophy is based on faith." In other words, the quest for evident knowledge rests on "inevident premises."[100]

From this perspective, the Socratic character of philosophy appears to be quite damning to philosophy: "the philosopher, when confronted with revelation, seems to be compelled to contradict the very idea of philosophy by rejecting [revelation] without sufficient grounds." Rosen's more serious, or more defensible, point arises from this part of Strauss's argument. It is not that philosophy or the philosophic life is impossible, but that the choice for it would seem to rest on a mere act of will. And, as Strauss points out in his autobiographical preface to *Spinoza's Critique of Religion*, "an act of will ..., being based on belief, is fatal to any philosophy."[101] Believing that the choice of the life of philosophy for Strauss is ultimately willful, Rosen is at times tempted to draw Strauss close to that other philosopher of will, Nietzsche. But Rosen knows that there is yet more at stake: if the life of inquiry is a matter of will, then the "nature" discovered in that life is a matter of will, not of nature, and a man who fully understood this would have to know that he was acquiring not knowledge, not even knowledge of the parts, but only some function of his will. That is to say, a man who understands philosophy as Rosen thinks Strauss does would conclude that philosophy as quest for knowledge is impossible. Such a man would teach philosophy as the highest human possibility only as a noble lie. Such, we believe, is the thought underlying Rosen's extrapolation from what Strauss said about the impasse of reason and revelation.

But Rosen has radically misinterpreted Strauss's point. A full appreciation of Strauss on the implications of the unfulfillable character of philosophy requires a brief analysis of "Progress or Return." In those lectures Strauss twice raises the question whether the inability of philosophy to complete its task means that philosophy is a mere matter of faith, whether philosophy fails to ground itself adequately. On one occasion he seems to conclude in the affirmative. These are the passages at the end of the lectures that remain in readers' minds. The other time, in the second of the three lectures, Strauss emphatically concludes in the negative. There he gives "the philosophic reply" to the surmise that the reason-revelation impasse makes philosophy an arbitrary and irrational commitment.

> The question of utmost urgency, the question which does not permit suspense, is the question of how one should live. Now, this question is settled for Socrates by the fact that he is a philosopher. As a philosopher he knows he is ignorant of the most important things. The ignorance, the evident fact of this ignorance evidently proves that quest for knowledge of the most important things is the most important thing for us. This is, in addition, according to him, confirmed by the fact that he finds his happiness in acquiring the highest possible degree of clarity which he can acquire. He sees no necessity whatever to assent to something which is not evident to him.... At any rate, philosophy is meant, and that is the decisive point, not as a set of propositions, a teaching, or even a system, but as a way of life, a life animated by a peculiar passion, the philosophic desire, or eros.[102]

The philosophic life as life, Strauss is arguing, is both reasonable, a rational response to the evident need to answer the question of how one should live, and natural, a manifestation of the manifestly natural eros for understanding, which Strauss interprets as an eros for the eternal. The choice for philosophy is then not an arbitrary decision. Strauss does not believe that philosophy as a life is a "noble lie.

Yet, Strauss returns to the impasse and at the end of the essay draws conclusions apparently less favorable to philosophy. We must be careful and precise in approaching that return and in appreciating the conclusions Strauss draws there. The third lecture is a return to the reason-revelation issue on the basis not of the Socratic understanding of philosophy, but on the basis of "the present-day argument in favor of philosophy."[103] The relevant parts of "the present day argument" occur at "a more elementary stratum of the conflict," which involves a "use of the term philosophy ... in the common and vague sense of the term where it includes any rational orientation in the world, including science and what-have-you, common sense."[104] Strauss makes clear in this context that he includes Weber and "the value problem ... in the social sciences." That is to say, the conclusion he draws here is the same as the conclusion he drew in the Weber chapter of *Natural Right and History* and with regard to the philosophy of Spinoza in his preface; in both cases he is speaking of the modern, not the Socratic, conception of philosophy. The latter culminates in a natural and rational affirmation of philosophy; the former in the notion that the choice for philosophy is an arbitrary one, based on mere decision. Somewhat paradoxically, then, Strauss argues that it is the Socratic position, formulated without knowledge of the biblical God, which supplies a reliable and rational answer to the problem posed most emphatically by the biblical God.

Nonetheless, Strauss never retreats from his conclusion that philosophy, Socratic or otherwise, can never complete the circle of knowledge. That does not mean that the choice for philosophy is arbitrary or indefensible, but it does mean that the two lives stand as fundamental alternatives. It is the unresolved and irresolvable tension between them that forms "the core, the nerve, of western intellectual history.... This unresolved conflict," he concludes, "is the secret of the vitality of Western civilization."[105] The exposure of the tension, of the difference between reason and revelation, is a hallmark of Strauss's philosophic activity. It marks him off very notably from most others in the Western tradition, many of whom, he says, understood the conflict, but most of whom attempted to convince their readers that there was a fundamental harmony of some sort between reason and revelation. Thinkers as diverse as Maimonides and John Locke taught this harmony exoterically, Strauss argued. What they taught as an esoteric doctrine, the difference and conflict of reason and revelation, Strauss taught openly. We have explored his reasons for doing this already, but we must note now that he affirms the open knowledge of the tension to be a good, perhaps a blessing. But why is it good now, when it was apparently not good in the past? Let us close with one suggestion on this multilayered problem. The tension is the reverse side of the Socratic character of philosophy. If philosophy could become a completed system of the kind many modern philosophers hoped to produce, then the tension between reason and revelation would disappear. This end of philosophy has not been achieved, however. The belief or hope that philosophy could culminate in complete knowledge of the whole was based on a falsification of the true character of philosophy. It also led to the deleterious effects modern philosophy had on politics, as well as to the various abuses and now uncertainty about philosophy itself. The tension—neither a surrender nor a triumph of philosophy—helps remind us of the limits (but the reality) of philosophy and of its genuinely Socratic character.

CHAPTER FIVE

Leo Strauss — Teacher of Evil?

Strauss earned the bemused, if not irate, contempt of many in the scholarly world (as he foretold he might) when he opened his book on Machiavelli by pronouncing the old verdict on the Florentine as a "teacher of evil" to be, in his judgment, more sound than the newer, intellectually sophisticated characterizations that absolve Machiavelli of that opprobrium. In one of the supreme ironies of intellectual history, that charge, considered by many scholars to be too harsh for Machiavelli, too reflective of a moralistic outlook on the part of Strauss, is now being turned on Strauss himself. Strauss is now called a Machiavellian, or a Nietzschean, or a follower of the Nazi apologist Carl Schmitt. This is the conception of Strauss that has captured the imagination, informing such analyses as Earl Shorris's essay subtitled "Leo Strauss, George Bush, and the Philosophy of Mass Deception."[1] It would surely be a matter of interest for a psychologist to explain why so many intellectuals, journalists, and others, like Tim Robbins, find the story of Strauss the puppeteer behind the Bush administration to be so attractive. That is not our brief, however. We wish rather to examine Strauss's thought for the ground on which those claims are made and then to assess what in them, if anything, is sound.

Like most of what is said of Strauss in the popular press, this notion of Strauss as Machiavellian also traces back ultimately to Shadia Drury. Once again, therefore, we begin with her. Drury captured the imagination of the scholarly world with her first book, *The Political Ideas of Leo Strauss*. The reasons for the relative success of her book are not difficult to state. Although Strauss was a major figure in the small world of those who devote themselves to the study of political philosophy, nobody had previously attempted anything like a comprehensive statement of his overall position. Recall that most readers were likely to find Strauss's thinking elusive, in part because it was so allusive and in part because his writing was almost entirely devoted to elucidating the thought of historically important political philosophers. Drury found a vacuum, and filled it.

Moreover, she filled it in an undeniably intriguing way. As reflected in the early reactions to Strauss's characterization of Machiavelli, he was for the most part seen as a rather old-fashioned, moralistic fellow.[2] Strauss was known for attacking, not endorsing, Machiavelli, Nietzsche, and all moderns who smacked of historicism and moral relativism. He was very well known in the political science profession for attacking the behavioral science of politics, particularly its distinction between facts and values, which led, he argued, to a kind of "moral obtuseness" on the part of the new science, if not on the part of its practitioners. In the mind of his public (both friends and foes), he stood for the reverse of moral obtuseness—for moral engagement, for the cognitive viability of moral judgments, for an essentially conservative moral outlook. Imagine the astonishment when Drury not only presented a seemingly connected, coherent, comprehensive account of his thought, but one that reversed nearly everything nearly everybody thought about Strauss.[3]

One cannot always persuasively do what Drury attempted to do. Strauss himself was resisted when he argued for such reversals, as in his claims that Plato did not seriously mean to advocate the rule of philosophers but to show the impossibility or deep unlikelihood of that rule, or that Machiavelli did not aim at a restoration of ancient politics but at the initiation of an altogether new understanding of politics, what Strauss called modernity. Drury, however, was able to take advantage of the phenomenon discussed in the previous chapter: Strauss did not write esoterically about esotericism. He wrote openly of it and gave readings of older philosophers based on the premise that if they read others "between the lines," they must have "written between the lines" themselves. Even though she explicitly eschewed such a way of reading Strauss, Drury in effect capitalized on Strauss's explicit engagement with esotericism. It was plausible to many that Strauss himself meant something different from what he said. That, we have argued, is a mistaken but not completely implausible inference to draw from his historical studies.

Drury and many others following her lead find the following message between Strauss's lines or even in them: Strauss follows the ancients, but his ancients are a very different lot from the ancients as understood by most other writers. They are Machiavellian, in the sense of being committed to a politics of "moral ruthlessness" and moral cynicism; and Nietzschean, in the sense of being committed to atheism and the moral silence of the universe. They differ from Machiavelli and Nietzsche in one way only: they believe that harsh truths are not fit for general consumption but are to be limited to philosophers alone. For Drury all the chief elements of Straussian political thinking follow from this core claim. The philosophers must not voice their truths openly but must practice esoteric communication—harsh truths for each other, socially salutary myths for everyone else. The philosophers are the only ones who see the truth; they are the intellectually and morally strong (the "real men," who can endure the deadly truths), and they deserve to rule, if not directly then indirectly. They manipulate the many, or the few "gentlemen," who in turn manipulate the many. The rule of the philosophers is justified by their intellectual and moral superiority; it is thus tyrannous rule, in the sense of standing above the claims of law, consent, or any other principle that would limit them. The moral truth, insofar as there is one, is that pleasure is the good; but political society cannot sustain itself on the basis of this truth, so the philosophers exoterically preach virtue, justice, self-sacrifice, and so on, while they secretly know that pleasure is the good or true aim of life. Their rule is therefore directed to their good, that is, their pleasure. The notion of the common good is thus merely one of the moral myths the philosophers purvey, for the good of the rulers is the goal of their rule, not the good of all. The nonphilosophers are enlisted in the enterprise of moral and political life for the sake of sustaining the life or way of life of the philosophers.

Some of the modern philosophers, like Kant, were taken in by the exoteric doctrines of the ancients, but the more common error of the modern philosophers, according to Drury's Strauss, was the belief that political life could somehow be planted anew on the basis of these truths. They thus initiated the Enlightenment to spread the truths. This was doubly a mistake, for political life cannot stand on these foundations; moreover, the new dispensation of modernity undercuts the elitism of the old philosophy; the clear line between the few, who live in the truth and rightly rule the others on that basis, and the many, who do not know the truth, is erased, or at least greatly blurred. The natural order of hierarchy is thus lost, and society is in danger of collapsing in the moral cynicism unleashed by the Enlightenment: only the few can take the truth and live healthily and happily with it.

Such is the core of Drury's indictment of Strauss; such is the story—or pieces thereof—that have been picked up by the media in their eagerness to explain aspects of Bush administration policy. Our interest is not to attack or defend the Bush administration or neoconservative or conservative policy, but to explore the various dimensions of the thesis that Strauss is a teacher of evil. Although we argued earlier that Drury is far from satisfactory in living up to her own rules for reading Strauss (chapter 4), and far from living up to Strauss's rules for reading an esoteric writer (chapter 1), nonetheless she does have a number of specific pieces of evidence in her bill of particulars, to which we now turn. We are all the more eager to consider these matters, for they not only give us an opportunity to consider the bases for the view of Strauss now becoming so widespread in the intellectual and political culture, but they also allow us further opportunity to explicate some of the more important features of Strauss's thought.

Strauss and the "Tyrannical Teaching"

Strauss opened his reply to two of the more thoughtful reviews of *On Tyranny* with the following punchy assertion: "A social science that cannot speak of tyranny with the same confidence with which medicine speaks, for example, of cancer, cannot understand social phenomena as what they are." Strauss complained, in effect, that contemporary social science, in thrall to the fact-value distinction, cannot recognize tyranny as what it is—the opposite of political health.[4] His point was clear and his stance toward tyranny even clearer: tyranny is a political pathology. Yet Drury argues that contrary to what he so clearly said, Strauss was not an enemy to tyranny, but a partisan of what she calls the "tyrannical teaching." According to Drury, Strauss's "tyrannical teaching" holds there is "only one natural right, the right of the superior to rule over the inferior, the master over the slave, the husband over the wife, and the wise over the vulgar many." This "teaching" is "tyrannical in the classic sense of . . . rule in the absence of law, or rule by those who were above the law."[5] Tyranny of the wise, that is, the absolute rule of the wise without law, is, she believes, Strauss's idea of "natural right" or "the best regime."[6] It makes no difference, she argues, whether the "wise" come to power legitimately or via crime; nor even whether they commit "innumerable crimes" while in power. Tyranny of the wise is not identical with ordinary garden-variety tyranny, of course, and Drury concedes that Strauss objects to the latter. But his objections are different from those of ordinary people: "What they [the wise, i.e., Strauss] despise about tyranny is what they despise about every form of government—namely its failure to listen to the counsel of the wise."[7] The lawless (and presumably criminal) rule of the wise is best, but unlikely and dependent on chance. "In practice, only an approximation of the best regime can be hoped for." What this best practical regime is, however, is quite anticlimactic after Drury's dramatic brandishing of Strauss's partisanship of tyranny: "the practically best regime is the rule under law of 'gentlemen,'" the latter being men of good moral character and education.

Strauss finds that modern liberal democracy has much in common with this desirable form of rule.[8]

The last bit about the lawful and law-bound rule of gentlemen as the most desirable political regime is the only part of Drury's explication of the "tyrannical teaching" that is not inaccurate or misleading. Her account goes astray in several important places and makes Strauss both incoherent and demonic-sounding. She makes Strauss incoherent in moving between the claim that natural right points to the "absolute rule of the wise" (i.e., the tyranny of the wise) as best, and then the rule of gentlemen under law as best. She nowhere makes intelligible how these two quite different ideas fit together.

She makes Strauss sound demonic as well as incoherent when she attributes to him the view that "tyranny, or rule in the absence of law, comes closest to the best regime, which is absolute tyranny of the wise." According to Drury, Strauss's "way of speaking allows one to do injustice with a clear conscience."[9] It is difficult to imagine a less insightful or more confused reading of Strauss's *On Tyranny*. She almost completely misses or suppresses Strauss's explanation of Xenophon's point in his dialogue *Hiero*, and of Strauss's own point in his interpretative study of that dialogue.

Let us recall Strauss's description of his aim in his study of tyranny: to show the way toward a social science that can diagnose and understand tyranny as a pathology with the same confidence that medicine can diagnose and understand cancer as a pathology. Drury's construal of Strauss makes his position on tyranny even more incapable of telling the difference between political health and the political pathology of tyranny than the fact-value–dominated social science Strauss is attempting to correct. The failure of our social science to grasp tyranny is not merely an abstract or academic danger, according to Strauss: "When we were brought face to face with tyranny—with a kind of tyranny that surpassed the boldest imagination of the most powerful thinkers of the past—our political science failed to recognize it."[10] Instead our political science spoke of "authoritarianism," or "post-constitutional" rule, or even of "totalitarianism"; the last was a form of opprobrium that the stricter-minded social scientists attempted to avoid as too judgmental, but a term that nonetheless lacks the descriptive or normative clarity of the term *tyranny*.

Strauss agrees that contemporary tyranny is an "unprecedented" phenomenon, combining technology and ideology with those elements that it shares with the tyranny that "is a danger coeval with political life."[11] The ultimate aim of Strauss's book is to recapture the original understanding of the original and universal character of tyranny, so that we in our time can build on that base toward an understanding of the peculiarly modern and peculiarly dangerous forms of tyranny that we face. Drury's reading of Strauss on tyranny has the consequence of making that set of goals unattainable, for, as we have seen, it makes Strauss not a pathologist seeking to diagnose an old disease in its new and more virulent form, but someone who thinks the disease in question is health itself. Or, insofar as Drury's Strauss objects to tyranny, it is solely for the reason that it fails to listen "to the counsel of the wise," that is, a failure it shares in common with "every form of government." If that is his point, then obviously it is not possible to speak with clarity of the difference between, say, the Soviet Union under Stalin or Germany under Hitler and the United States under Franklin D. Roosevelt or Britain under Churchill. Surely this cannot be the conclusion to which Strauss's analysis is tending: "Don't worry, Mr. Jones, your cancerous lung is no different really from a healthy lung."

The classic analysis of tyranny, as Strauss presents it, concludes that "tyranny is essentially rule without laws, or more precisely, monarchic rule without laws."[12] Monarchic, or what contemporary analysts would be inclined to call authoritarian, rule is but half the story: rule without law is the other. Modern tyranny, accordingly, would be monarchic or authoritarian rule without law, supported by modern technology and ideology. We speak in chapter 2 of how technology and ideology, especially in conjunction with each other, relate to the modern project of actualization. In *On Tyranny* Strauss adds to that analysis two insights of great importance: first, he makes clear that rule without law is the core defining element of tyranny, and he leads us to consider how modern technology and ideology contribute to lawless rule. On the one hand, if traditional tyrants, attempting to impose their will rather than rule via the traditional or collective and formal will of the community (law), require a "body guard" or "mercenaries," that is, armed forces loyal to them and able to impose themselves on an unwilling community, then the development of technology is a particular danger, for it makes available to tyrants more formidable and effective means of imposing their will than tyrants like Hiero ever possessed.[13] The modern tyrant has, among other things, the ability to kill much larger numbers of people more quickly and efficiently than any Nero or Caligula. On the other hand, ideologies contribute to the pathology by supplying justifying rationales for "trumping" rule of law and for not entrusting governance to "gentlemen" as defined above. Ideologies supply utopian or quasi-utopian goals for political life and scientific or quasi-scientific analysis of the means to achieve those goals. Ideologies justify or prompt to extreme actions in order to achieve their goals. Law—formal and conservative as it always appears in the light of ideology—impedes the movement toward these goals and thus is one of the first victims of modern ideological movements.

In his analysis of *Hiero,* Strauss also attempts to clarify the source in the human soul of the tyrannical impulse. He finds that source to be universal, or nearly so, and readily confused with motives that are good and laudable. The tyrant, or at least the most interesting and revealing kind of tyrant, seeks to be loved by all human beings, a goal he has great difficulty achieving through his tyranny but one that interacts in a potentially vicious way with modern ideologies and technology. Ideologies, with their aspiration to "relieve man's estate" in ever deeper and more thoroughgoing ways, add to tyrants' own tendency (as well as that of their coerced people) to pretend that they are acting for the good of the people, or of humankind, no matter how lawless or criminal they become.

Strauss's presentation of the classic doctrine of tyranny is fully accessible only if we juxtapose to it the most famous shorthand account of tyranny produced in antiquity—that of Aristotle. Tyranny, according to the Aristotle's analysis, is a "deviation" from monarchy—it is "monarchy with a view to the advantage of the monarch," rather than "that which looks toward the common advantage."[14] This definition highlights the common good or benefit rather than the rule of law. Aristotle helps clarify the particular emphases of Strauss's discussion: the latter means to establish the necessity for rule of law and at the same time to reveal the necessary limitations of law, thereby revealing the necessary limits of politics as such. Strauss's real point is more or less the opposite of what Drury attributes to him. His point is to show that despite the limits of law, and in the face of any temptation there may be to waive the rule of law, the regime of law is best. In order to show that, he must explore both the limits of law and the temptations to rule without law, temptations accentuated or institutionalized in modern ideologies. It is those moments of exploration that Drury pounces on, but she completely misses Strauss's point.

Strauss explicitly states that "the 'tyrannical' teaching . . . serves the purpose, not of solving the problem of the best political order, but of bringing to light the nature of political things." Strauss's Xenophon does not leave things where Drury sometimes claims he does, with the assertion that tyranny is best in theory, but rule of law best in practice. Xenophon, as a "pupil of Socrates must be presumed to have believed . . . that nothing which is practically false can be theoretically true."[15] The "tyrannical teaching" is not true even as a theoretical proposition. It reveals something about political life that is true, however.

The "tyrannical teaching" is a step along the way toward the affirmation of the necessity for rule of law. It emerges in Xenophon's *Hiero* as part of a conversation between Simonides, a "wise man," and Hiero, a tyrant. They are discussing which is best, the private life or the life of a tyrant. Strangely enough, Hiero the tyrant condemns the life of tyranny, and Simonides the private man praises it. It is not a mere matter of "the grass is greener"; according to Strauss's subtle analysis of the action of the dialogue, Hiero is led to say what he does partly out of fear that the clever Simonides may seek to "contrive something" that might allow him to replace Hiero.[16] Simonides, for his part, seeks to bring Hiero to reform or improve his rule, which requires a complex two-stage process. He must first encourage Hiero to explore what is unsatisfactory about his situation and to voice his sense of the profound failures of the tyrannous life to satisfy his desires. Having disheartened Hiero, Simonides must, in effect, rehearten him, by holding out the promise that political life could be far more satisfying to him than he professes it to be. The life of the tyrant can be greatly improved, Simonides maintains, if the tyrant becomes beneficent, if he seeks the good or benefit of his people. Simonides, in accordance with the necessities of his dramatic situation, does not propose that the tyrant give up tyranny altogether, but that he become a great benefactor. As benefactor he could retain his position as tyrant, the one who rules according to his will rather than law, and at the same time win the love of his people.

This is the moment in the dialogue when Xenophon, or rather, his Simonides, puts forward the "tyrannical teaching." A tyranny that is wise and beneficent could be not only acceptable, but good, perhaps best. A Hiero who became perfectly wise and good, who knew what to do, sought to do it, and had untrammeled power to do so, could be an acceptable or good ruler independently of how he came to power; his "reformation" could make good his earlier misdeeds. A Hiero who became perfectly wise and good would be superior to the laws. He would accomplish more good for his city than laws, which are in their nature less wise because inflexible, formal, fixed, and most often formulated by the less-than-wise. The laws necessarily have a "one-size-fits-all" quality, whereas the rule of the wise man is like custom tailoring: every person and situation gets the provision most suited to her, him, or it. The rule of the wise would fulfill the requirements of natural justice to a much higher degree than any regime of rule of law, for everyone would get his or her due. Such a ruler could be called a tyrant in the sense of Strauss's definition, but not in the sense of Aristotle's. Compared to the rule of the good and wise individual, Strauss concedes, the rule of law is a limited thing indeed. But the benefits of the lawless rule of the wise and the just never justify the lawless rule of the unwise and the unjust. Drury systematically ignores the terms of the hypothesis of the "tyrannical teaching": the reformed tyrant is wise and just. Her statement that "so understood, *natural right places no restrictions on wisdom*" is quite misleading; the rule of the wise is right by nature because it is best and just for all.[17]

Strauss insists that the "tyrannical teaching," whatever its attractiveness, is not intended as even a theoretical (much less a practical) answer to the question, What is the best regime? It is meant to bring out the reasons why rule of law is best, but limited. Strauss points out that the "tyrannical teaching" is put forward by a character in a Xenophontic dialogue named Simonides. That is in itself striking, for, as in Plato, the more common lead speaker in Xenophon's dialogues is Socrates. Simonides was a poet, an actual historical figure who had a reputation for flattering tyrants. Socrates was a philosopher, and the distinction between poetry and philosophy had abiding significance for all the Socratics, including Strauss. Most significantly, however, Simonides is referred to within the dialogue as "wise," which is how Strauss constantly speaks of him. Socrates, as we have already seen, was not wise. He was a philosopher, a lover and seeker of wisdom, whose pursuit led him to the conclusion that he was not wise. Simonides is not referred to within the dialogue or by Strauss as a philosopher. The Socratic conclusion, which is also Strauss's conclusion, is that "no man can be simply wise."[18] If "wisdom is inaccessible to man," as Strauss often affirms, then "virtue and happiness," the fruits of wisdom, "will always be imperfect."[19]

In Xenophon's dialogue the "tyrannical teaching" is put forward on the basis of two premises Strauss argued were false: first, that there could be a "wise man," and, second, that a ruler can be both fully wise and wholly virtuous. Strauss thus concluded that *Hiero* and its "tyrannical teaching" was a thought experiment, very like that he found in Plato's *Republic*, where the difference between wisdom and philosophy is abstracted away. Strauss made it clear that according to himself and Xenophon, Simonides is not "a truly wise man." He pointed out that "the form in which [the 'tyrannical' teaching] is presented characterizes it as a philosophic teaching of the sort that a truly wise man would not care to present in his own name."[20] Simonides does present it in his own name and thereby reveals his lack of true wisdom. Strangely, perhaps, his lack of wisdom is his failure to appreciate the limits, or more strikingly, "the inaccessibility" of wisdom.

Even if we were for the moment to accept Simonides and the wise ruler of the "tyrannical teaching" as genuinely wise, we would have to take note of another abiding theme of Strauss's: the wise, or the philosophic, do not desire to rule. In contrast to political individuals, who seek honor or love, the philosopher seeks wisdom. The philosopher's quest can be stated in terms of pleasure. "No man can be simply wise [according to Socrates and Strauss]; therefore, not wisdom, but progress towards wisdom is the highest good for man. Wisdom cannot be separated from self-knowledge; therefore, progress toward wisdom will be accompanied by awareness of that progress. And that awareness is necessarily pleasant. This whole—the progress and the awareness of it—is both the best and the most pleasant thing for man. It is in this sense that the highest good is intrinsically pleasant."[21] The philosopher seeks the highest good, which is at the same time the most pleasant thing. The philosopher is not much tempted by the specific pleasures and goods associated with the political, or the tyrannical, life. As Socrates' life well evidences, politics is a distraction for the philosopher, for the quest for wisdom is a full-time job, in the sense that it is never finished. If wisdom per se were attainable, then perhaps the philosopher could choose to move on to other things, like politics; but it is not.[22]

Strauss's thought here is completed in his interpretation of Plato's *Republic*, where the theme of the relation between philosophy and political rule returns. There Strauss announces his conviction that the Platonic/Socratic view is that the "philosophers are unwilling to rule."[23] They are unwilling to rule because, "dominated by the desire, the *eros*, for knowledge as the one thing needful, or knowing that philosophy is the most pleasant and blessed possession, the philosophers have no leisure for looking down at human affairs, let alone for taking care of them" (*CM*, 124–25). The philosophers would rule only if compelled to do so, but the nonphilosophers, especially the Hieros of the world, are not about to compel them. Therefore, even granting the first hypothesis of the "tyrannical teaching," that there are wise individuals, the second hypothesis, that those wise individuals will rule, is false.

The failure of the first two hypotheses also negates the third, that the wise rulers are virtuous or just enough to rule with perfect benevolence, or public spiritedness, or full dedication to the public good. The very qualities of the wise or the philosophers that fit them for rule, their detachment from the normal satisfactions of life, the satisfactions that attach men to their own good at the expense of the common good, are the qualities that drive the wise or the philosophers away from political life. The good that they seek weans them from greed, excess love of honor, desire for power, and all the other desires that dominate individuals who do devote themselves to public life (*CM*, 125). "Since the wise man does not need human beings in the way in which, and the extent to which, the ruler does, his attitude toward them is free, not passionate, and hence not susceptible of turning into malevolence or hatred. In other words, the wise man alone is capable of justice in the highest sense." The Straussian wise thus possess high moral qualities, including justice to the highest degree, not the self-seeking desire for power as Drury and many in the media have claimed as a result of not having read Strauss with even minimal care, if they have read him at all. These moral qualities are part of the "tyrannical teaching," but the sad truth is that these moral qualities are not available for practical life in the way the "tyrannical teaching" postulates. Either they exist and lead their possessor away from public power, or they, along with the claims about wisdom in the "tyrannical teaching," are overstated. As Strauss says, "each man loves what is somehow his own, his private possession." The philosopher too has a "private possession," his quest for wisdom and the peculiar satisfaction he derives from it. Thus Socrates, an otherwise exceedingly law-abiding individual, states that he will not give up philosophizing, even if the laws demand it of him.[24] There are limits to the public-spiritedness of the philosopher.

According to the "tyrannical teaching," the rule by the wise and the just without law would be superior to the rule of the gentlemen or anybody else with law. However, the rule of the wise and the just is a mere subjunctive: if such individuals exist, they will not rule. Those who claim a right to rule in the name of wisdom prove by the very fact of raising that claim that they are not among the wise, and therefore they cannot raise a claim to rule on that basis. That is what Strauss stood for, and not the view we find in Drury and much of the media, that Strauss claimed for the wise, himself or his followers, the right to rule on the basis of their alleged wisdom.

The tyrannical teaching reveals what would have to be true and effective in order for there to be a form of rule higher than rule under law. The hypothetical or counterfactual character of the tyrannical teaching, however, shows why rule of law is the necessary, if not sufficient, condition for good rule. It shows why the definition of tyranny as rule without law suffices to capture the essence or core of tyranny, for rule without law is necessarily bad rule. Just as the tyrannical teaching shows the necessity for rule of law by showing what the conditions would have to be for a better kind of rule, so it reveals the limits of all regimes of rule of law and thus reveals the grounds for the temptation to transcend the imperfections of even the best existing political orders. Law is limited, and since it is necessary, the possibilities for politics are limited also. The aspiration to escape those limits, often expressive of what is transcendent and best in humanity, nonetheless leads under modern conditions to gulags, death camps, and killing fields. To absorb the lesson of the "tyrannical teaching" is not to lust after philosopher-kings but to become cautious about the possibilities of political life. It is in this sense that Strauss is a political moderate; he is moderate in advocating the rule of law and constitutionalism, despite the known limitations, as the best possible form of politics. He most definitely does not say that "if man is to be moderately happy, wisdom must replace law."[25]

The Thrasymachean Thesis

Thrasymachus is one of the eleven persons identified as present at the discussion recorded in Plato's *Republic*. Socrates' confrontation with Thrasymachus constitutes the culmination and by far the largest part of book 1 of the *Republic*. He puts forward the last and most radical of the three definitions of justice that Socrates attempts to refute before the conversation moves, beginning in book 2, to Socrates' attempt to build a just city. Thrasymachus provides the most cynical or hard-boiled answer to the question they are pursuing: he says, "justice is nothing other than the advantage of the stronger."[26] His position is equivalent to the notion that might makes right. Socrates reacts forcefully to Thrasymachus's cynical view and appears to refute him, or at least to silence him, in the remainder of book 1.

In another of Drury's startling reversals of the ordinary view of things, she argues that although "in Plato's dialogues everyone assumes that Socrates is Plato's mouthpiece, . . . Strauss argues in his book *The City and Man* that Thrasymachus is Plato's real mouthpiece."[27] Using her principle that Strauss agrees with the ancients, Drury concludes that "Strauss shares the insights of the wise Plato (alias Thrasymachus) that justice is merely the interest of the stronger, that those in power make the rules in their own interests and call it justice."[28]

Strauss agrees with Thrasymachus, she believes, "in thinking that the just man is a fool, or a man duped by convention."[29] In sum, "Strauss learns from Plato [Thrasymachus] . . . that there is nothing sacred about the rules of justice." Thrasymachus, "the embodiment of the 'unjust speech' of Aristophanes' play *The Clouds*," is thus another teacher of evil in whose school Drury finds Strauss enrolled. Strauss is such a good pupil that he "makes the case for Thrasymachus more eloquently than it has ever been made before."[30] How this "Thrasymachean Thesis" comports with the "tyrannical teaching" she also attributes to Strauss is hard to say. Right as the absolute rule of the wise is a very different matter from right or justice as the interest of the stronger, for, in Strauss's view, the wise are surely not the stronger.

Drury argues that for Strauss, Thrasymachus, not Socrates, is Plato's spokesman and that to follow Plato, as Strauss professes to do, is therefore to follow Thrasymachus. She reasons this way: Thrasymachus puts forward a definition of justice that, according to Strauss, Socrates only appears to refute. It "remains victorious" because Socrates does not really refute Thrasymachus, and both he and Plato know that he does not.[31] Indeed, the action of the dialogue as explained by Strauss shows that Socrates agrees at bottom with Thrasymachus, even though on the surface (i.e., in speech) he may appear to disagree with him. Thrasymachus knows Socrates is not telling the truth.[32] The Thrasymachean view of justice is "enlarged and deepened" in the *Republic* but essentially "substantiated."[33]

As with much in her book, Drury's reconstruction of the Thrasymachean themes in Strauss's account of the *Republic* combines shrewd insight with outright error and misleading interpretation. Let us begin by noting Strauss's statements about the role of Thrasymachus in the *Republic*. To give Drury her due, she is correct to notice that Strauss pays more attention to Thrasymachus than is common in readings of the *Republic*. Thrasymachus "in a sense . . . forms the center of the *Republic* as a whole."[34] But she ignores several other statements by Strauss that run quite contrary to her views: Thrasymachus, Strauss says, is "the antagonist of Socrates in the *Republic*."[35] So far is Strauss from endorsing Thrasymachus's position that he says that "we ought to loathe people who act and speak like Thrasymachus and never to imitate their deeds and never to act according to their speeches" (*CM*, 74). All statements of this sort are suppressed by Drury and those who echo her views in the current discussions of Strauss. Strauss does not believe the dialogue displays the correctness of Thrasymachus's position, but rather the reverse. "Classical political philosophy," Strauss tells us in one of his statements on the *Republic*, "is opposed, not to another political philosophy, but to rhetoric," the profession of Thrasymachus. Strauss's most general statement on the overall place of Thrasymachus identifies "the action of the *Republic* in Socrates' first bringing into the open his latent conflict with Thrasymachus, then in his silencing Thrasymachus, and finally in reconciling Thrasymachus by assigning him an important, if subordinate, place in the best city."[36] "It would seem," Strauss says, that the foundation of the good city requires that Thrasymachus be converted into one of the citizens" (*CM* 116).[37] To be converted into a citizen is not the same, we must note, as having his thesis vindicated. Strauss connects the appearance of Thrasymachus in the *Republic* with the Aristophanic comedy *The Clouds*, a comedy in which Socrates is a central character. In that play a personified "Unjust Speech" not merely debates but decisively defeats his counterpart, "Just Speech." Strauss finds Plato's *Republic* "to be the reply *par excellence* to Aristophanes."[38] Part of the reply consists in Plato's restaging of the debate between Justice and Injustice. In Plato's version, as Strauss understands it, "Thrasymachus represents the Unjust Speech, and Socrates takes the place of the Just Speech." Contrary to what Drury says is Strauss's opinion about Socrates and Thrasymachus, he is very clear in pronouncing his actual judgment: "the Just Speech in Plato, is, of course, victorious." Socrates' "primary function" is to show "the strength of the Just Speech."[39]

Drury's references to the places where Strauss finds Thrasymachus's views to be unrefuted or carried forward in the *Republic* are also quite misleading. In book 1 of the *Republic*, according to Strauss, "Socrates refutes a number of false opinions about justice. Yet this negative or destructive work contains within itself the positive or edifying assertions of the bulk of the work." This is the "point of view" from which Strauss discusses Thrasymachus's view of justice, along with the other views put forward by the old father Cephalos and his son Polemarchus (*CM*, 68). All three definitions are "false" and rejected, but all three are carried forward, in some form, into the final positive doctrine of justice that emerges in the course of the dialogue. That is to say, the Cephalean notion of justice as paying one's debts, though incorrect as stated, and the Polemarchean notion of justice as helping one's friends and harming one's enemies, also incorrect as stated, are, when reformulated and better understood, carried forward positively just as Thrasymachus's view, reformed, is carried forward. Indeed, Strauss makes clear, it is not Thrasymachus but Polemarchus who comes closest to the ultimate Socratic understanding of justice. "It is the only view of justice which is Socrates' own" (70). "Polemarchus's opinion, properly understood is the only one among the generally known views of justice discussed in the first book of the *Republic* which is entirely preserved in the positive or constructive part of the work" (73). One could with more justice say, then, that Strauss finds Polemarchus, not Thrasymachus, to be Plato's spokesman (after Socrates) in the *Republic*. But that would be inaccurate as well. Strauss's point about the Platonic dialogue is that nobody is *the* Platonic spokesman: what Plato has to say comes out only when what is said by the characters is interpreted in light of the action of the dialogue, including the action of the reader, who must read actively and critically.[40] When Strauss finds that all three of the false doctrines voiced in book 1 are reformed and refined and in some sense affirmed in the end, he is merely applying a conviction common in Plato studies: the Platonic dialogue reflects the Platonic view that common opinions contain some intimation of truth but require dialectical clarification and refinement.[41]

A particularly telling example of the way in which Drury distorts Strauss and Strauss's substantive understanding of both the Thrasymachean thesis and justice is Drury's claim that according to Strauss, Thrasymachus's view of justice is "highly respectable."[42] What Strauss actually says is that the Thrasymachean thesis "proves to be only *the consequence* of an opinion which is . . . highly respectable." The "highly respectable" opinion of which Thrasymachus's doctrine is a consequence is that "justice consists in obeying the law or that the just is identical with the lawful or legal." This is "the most obvious, the most natural thesis regarding justice" (*CM*, 75 [emphasis added]). That "highly respectable" view, we should note, is identical to, or at least a very close corollary to, the conclusion Strauss found in Xenophon's *Hiero*: tyranny is lawless rule.

Yet, Strauss has said Thrasymachus's thesis proper—justice is the interest of the stronger—is not identical to the proposition that "justice is the lawful." It is a "consequence" of that thesis. But in what sense, or on the basis of what reasoning is it a consequence? The connecting link is the idea that the laws are made by the ruling element or party in any city. As rulers, they are "the stronger." Only two more steps are needed to transform the "highly respectable" thesis into Thrasymachus's much less reputable claim. If the rulers rule in their own interest, then justice, that is, obeying the laws, is serving the interests of those who make and enforce the laws. That does not yet get us to Thrasymachus; the further premise that there is no common benefit, no common good, is also needed (*CM*, 76). With that premise justice becomes bad, serving the interest of others at one's own expense; it also becomes unnatural, if one adds the simple additional premise that nature mandates (at least) that one seek one's own benefit or good. Thrasymachus thus poses a radical challenge to the conclusions of the *Hiero*: lawful rule, too, is tyranny.

Drury correctly notices that Strauss pronounces Thrasymachus unrefuted after the long exchange between him and Socrates in book 1 of the *Republic*. Strauss's point is not, however, to affirm the Thrasymachean thesis as identical to the Socratic or Platonic or his own thesis on justice. Rather, it is to recapitulate what is accomplished in the first book in the *Republic*: it has made clear "not perhaps what justice is, but what the problem of justice is" (*CM*, 83). Since the *Republic* goes on for another nine books, it is not surprising that its opening book should not settle the question of justice, but should set up the issue to be addressed in the remainder of the text.

Strauss concisely states "the problem of justice" as it comes to light in book 1: "Justice has proved to be the art which on the one hand assigns to every citizen what is good for his soul and which on the other hand determines the common good of the city" (*CM*, 83). We have two notions about justice that are potentially in conflict with each other: justice as the common good, as when we say that rulers rule well and justly when they serve the common good, not their own good. But it is also commonly said that justice is giving to each his due. The Socratic/Straussian formulation represents an interpretation of that idea: what one is due in the emphatic sense is what is beneficial, what is good for one.[43] It is not just to return to a madman the revolver he has left in your keeping if he will use it to harm himself or others.

Neither of the two notions of justice is identical with the Thrasymachean thesis, but the tension between them provides an opening for it. "There would be no difficulty if one could be certain that the common good were identical or at least in harmony with the good of all individuals" (*CM*, 83). Without that certainty, something like Thrasymachus's thesis could be true: justice (law-abidingness) is to serve the good of others. The real issue that emerges, which was already dimly visible in Thrasymachus's first intervention, concerns the existence or possibility of a true common good, which can provide a basis for law and a standard for rule that would indeed refute Thrasymachus.

The conversation in the *Republic* does not proceed in a straightforward way to examine that question, because the two brothers of Plato, Glaucon and Adeimantus, intervene. Picking up on the notion that justice is benefit or good, they insist that Socrates prove that justice is inherently good for the doer (not recipient) of justice, apart from any consequence or external reward. They introduce further the idea that the good or benefit of justice be understood in terms of happiness: justice must be shown of itself to produce happiness, not only independent of external rewards and benefits, but despite external sufferings and penalties. Socrates admits that this is a formidable challenge and denies his ability to meet it (*CM*, 91). The gauntlet thrown by the two brothers differs from that of Thrasymachus but is related to it. Strauss indeed claims that Socrates' manifestly insufficient argument against Thrasymachus has no purpose other than to provoke Glaucon to pose this most serious, and therefore most revealing, formulation of the problem of justice (85). Glaucon's challenge both builds on Thrasymachus's and goes beyond it. "The view which Glaucon maintains in common with Thrasymachus implies that there is an insoluble conflict between the good of the individual and the common good" (88). He goes beyond in the "demand on Socrates that he praise justice as choice worthy for its own sake, or pleasant, or even by itself sufficient to make a man perfectly happy in the midst of what is ordinarily believed to be the most extreme misery" (91). Thrasymachus had not demanded that justice *be* the sufficient good, merely that it be in harmony with the good. The brothers go beyond even Kant in demanding that justice, or doing one's duty, also satisfy one's natural inclinations, that is, that doing justice be not only one's duty but also one's pleasure.[44] No wonder Socrates finds this a daunting challenge.

Strauss points out that with the intervention of the two brothers, "the discussion changes its character profoundly." The most important change resides in the fact that "while Socrates is responsible for the fact that justice is the theme of the conversation, Glaucon is responsible for the manner in which it is treated" (*CM*, 85). Among other things, the "manner of treatment" and the particular charge Socrates is attempting to meet deflect attention from Thrasymachus's thesis and render less visible the answer ultimately provided to it. Thrasymachus focuses attention on the conflict or potential conflict between the individual good and the common good, with individual good understood in an ordinary and everyday way. Glaucon focuses attention more firmly on the question of what is truly good for a human being, for in his demand that Socrates praise justice as good, even when the just man suffers as much as Job for his justice, Glaucon has broken with ordinary and everyday ways of thinking about the good. In any case, that is the path Strauss finds the *Republic* traversing.

Strauss's analysis of the *Republic* is rich beyond our capacity to summarize here, but the conclusion he reaches can be simply put. If justice is doing good, or benefiting, then what is most urgent to be known is the human good. That good is philosophy: "the work with which the philosopher is concerned above everything else is intrinsically attractive and in fact the most pleasant work, regardless of what consequences it may entail" (*CM*, 127). The philosopher is not only the one who achieves the human good, so far as that is attainable, but he also turns out to be the "only ... truly just" person. "The just man," according to the *Republic*, "is the man in whom each part of the soul does its work well. But only in the philosopher does the best part of the soul, reason, do its work well, and this is not possible if the two other parts of the soul do not do their work well also: the philosopher is necessarily by nature both courageous and moderate."[45] The philosopher satisfies the conditions for justice in the special sense in which that virtue is understood in the *Republic*, but he also satisfies more ordinary notions of justice. Driven by his eros, his intense desire to know the truth, he is not driven to the things that lead other men toward injustice: desire for wealth, power, and sensual pleasure. Not only does the philosopher lack the incentive to do injustice so common in other men, but he also understands the way general good order and decency are prerequisites for the activity in which he willingly engages. "That is to say, the philosopher is just also in the sense in which all members of the just city, and in a way all just members of any city, regardless of whether they are philosophers or not, are just . . . he obeys the law." Or, as Strauss puts it, "according to a notion of justice which is more common than the one referred to in Socrates' definition, justice consists in not harming others; justice thus understood proves to be in the highest case merely a concomitant of the philosopher's greatness of soul" (*CM*, 128). Philosophers' "very justice—their abstaining from wronging their fellow human beings—flows from contempt for the things for which the non-philosophers hotly contest" (*CM*, 125).

Glaucon had demanded that Socrates display justice as *the* human good, sufficient to produce happiness no matter what. We now see that Socrates has only partly complied with this demand. He has not shown that justice is the good, except in the formal sense, that it is the rational part of the soul doing its work properly. He has, however, shown that the good understood as philosophy is in harmony with justice as obedience to the law and forbearing from harming others, denying oneself the pleasures of tyranny, and so on, the sorts of things Glaucon had in mind when he wanted Socrates to show that justice is the good. Socrates goes far enough, apparently, to satisfy Glaucon, but we do need to notice that he does not meet the more extravagant elements of Glaucon's charge. He does not prove that the just man, the philosopher, would be happy even when tortured, contemned, or otherwise made miserable. The life of Socrates itself proves that wealth and bodily comforts are not necessary for a good and happy life, but Socrates, for all his poverty, does not live the life of, say, the man in the iron mask.

More serious are two other as yet unaddressed questions: given Socrates' partial success in showing that justice is harmonious with the good, at least in the case of the philosopher, what about nonphilosophic individuals? In particular, does Strauss's position on justice amount to an endorsement of Drury's rendition of Strauss's Thrasymacheanism? Thrasymachus thinks, says Drury, "that the just man is a fool, or man duped by convention." The just man is a fool, as she puts it, because "acting justly consists in benefiting others, in acting contrary to the natural human inclination to prefer one's own good."[46] This question is closely linked to the second: what about Thrasymachus's denial of a common good? The Thrasymachean thesis differs from that of, say, liberal social contract theorists just on the point of the common good: contract theorists like Hobbes argue that the good of all is found in constituting government and maintaining order through law. Law may be the interest of the rulers or lawmakers, but it is the interest of the ruled as well.

The Thrasymachean thesis differs from the Hobbesian thesis in presuming that the true good, the natural good, is mastery, a proposition that Hobbes goes out of his way to reject. Only on the basis of that premise does Thrasymachus's a priori rejection of a common good make sense; mastery is a zero-sum affair—if some have it, the others necessarily do not. Those who rule achieve their natural good; those who are ruled are "dupes" or at least too weak to pursue their own good. Such is the inner nerve of the Thrasymachean thesis.

Strauss has in fact responded quite adequately to this core Thrasymachean argument. Thrasymachus is mistaken in what he takes to be the good, or benefit, or advantage of human beings—not mastery but philosophy is the human good. Thus Strauss cannot agree with the position Drury attributes to him, that the masterful achieve their good and the obedient eschew theirs. Yet Strauss, following Plato, admits that there is a problem: mastery, wealth, and sensual pleasures may not be the true human good, but most individuals act as if they were and seek them. Their inclinations run against the grain of justice. Thus, Strauss points out, "Plato states towards the end of the *Republic* (619b–d) . . . that a man who . . . [participates] in virtue by habituation and not by philosophy chooses the greatest tyranny for his next life."[47] What then is the status of justice for the nonphilosopher, for the individual of ordinary morality?

Strauss's answer to this question consists in his theory of the two sources of morality; the title of his chief book on ancient philosophy, *The City and Man*, captures this theory in shorthand. One source of the moral rules that govern life is "man," that is, the true human good, the human being operating in his peak way: philosophy. Morality as practiced by the philosopher is cause, concomitant, and consequence of the philosophic life itself. But there is another source of morality: the city. Successful social and political life has normative prerequisites that constitute the rules of justice. Although there is some flexibility in the range of such rules, depending on circumstances, there is no ground for the wide-ranging relativism that Nietzsche or modern positivists and historicists proclaim. In particular, justice and dedication to the common good are required. As we have already seen, Strauss has solid ground for rejecting the challenge to the common good as an illusion posed by Thrasymachus. The "rationale or root" of morality in this sense, Strauss says, "is the need of the city."[48]

In one of his most striking passages, Strauss explicitly raises the question of the relation between the two sorts of morality (philosophic and political): "Yet if morality has two radically different roots, how can there be a unity of morality, how can there be a unity of man, and how is it possible that the moral requirements of society on the one hand and the moral requirements of the life of the mind on the other agree completely, or at any rate to a considerable extent?"[49] The chief questions that follow from his doctrine of the two roots are two: one is the problem of integrity. Is there a unity to the moral phenomena and to the human person such that the two roots of morality harmonize in some way? Or, differently put, is there a connection or bearing of the two roots on each other? The Drurian charge against Strauss is that there is not. The second major issue Strauss raises is what we might call the problem of fortuity: how can it be that two such radically different roots produce more or less the same moral code? Is this not so coincidental as to call into question the validity of the two-roots theory?

Strauss addresses the problem of integrity as follows: "The unity of man consists in the fact that he is that part of the whole which is open to the whole, or, in Platonic language, that part of the whole which has seen the ideas of all things. Man's concern with his openness to the whole is the life of the mind. The dualism of being a part while being open to the whole, and therefore in a sense being the whole itself, is man."[50] The problem of integrity posed by the two roots reflects a larger problem of integrity, the way in which man is both part and, via his intellect, also whole. Man is unique within the whole in being both divided and integral in this manner. Although Strauss does not make the good explicit here, the two roots ultimately reflect the integral duality of man as part and whole, or as part open to and sharing in the whole. Man is embodied, not pure intellect. As embodied intellect he shares in all the needs of living bodies, as well as in the individualized character of the body. Each embodied intellect is embedded in its own body, mortal, needy, vulnerable, marked by love of its own. Yet, the duality that is man masks a wholeness. Strauss, like Hegel, sees that all parts point beyond themselves to that of which they are a part, but man does so to a degree and in a way that other parts do not. Man is self-consciously or manifestly open to the whole and erotically driven toward that whole. The most significant or revealing factors of human life are manifestations of this erotic impulse toward the whole: philosophy, religion, morality.

Strauss connects morality, the ordinary morality of the nonphilosopher, with the specific duality-integrity of humankind via the observation that "society and the whole simply have this in common, that they are both wholes which transcend the individual, inducing the individual to rise above and beyond himself. All nobility consists in such rising above and beyond oneself to something greater than oneself."[51] The two roots, in other words, are not altogether different: society is both a means to bodily existence and a manifestation of the whole that transcends the individual. Joining in that transcendence is to share in the noble, that is, the fair or the beautiful, as in the Greek word *kalos*. Understanding the two roots of morality as sharing the openness to the whole "makes...clear the difference between the gang of robbers and the good city: these kinds of society differ essentially because [moral men are] animated by the *eros* for everything beautiful and graceful" (*CM*, 100).

The two roots thus remain two, but they share something that points to an ultimate common good uniting the philosophers and the men of ordinary morality. The parallels between the moral codes deriving from the two roots are not merely fortuitous. They reflect the common impulse to transcend the mere partiality of the part at work throughout human existence. As Strauss said at the conclusion to his *Natural Right and History*, the ancients and the moderns differ most deeply on the status of the individual. The ancients understood the individual as part of the true whole or of the city; the moderns understand the individual to be fundamental and the whole constructed. The modern doctrine about society sees society as an artifact, a made thing, that is, not a true whole; the modern doctrine about the whole per se sees it, too, to be a construct, also a made thing. Thus it is no accident that the fate of modern philosophy is historicism: the affirmation that the historically constructed is superior to anything natural or merely given.[52]

Philosophy and morality share the concern with the noble, that is, with transcendence toward the whole; but in the light of philosophy, morality appears as a deficient or lower form of transcendence, a reflection of the philosophic transcendence. Human nature points toward philosophy as its completion, but it is a rare completion: not only do most human beings not achieve it, but they fail even to seek it. In embodied intellects the entanglements with body and the realm of need are too potent to allow or produce the universal triumph of the philosophic eros. The individual embodiment, from which derives love of one's own, is a force that restrains all forms of transcendence, not only philosophy. Thus, Strauss points out, the opinion of the sophists or the rhetoricians about the sovereignty of speech or persuasion is mistaken. "It is against nature that rhetoric should have the power ascribed to it [by Thrasymachus, by the rhetoricians in general, and hypothetically, by the action and argument of the *Republic*]: that it should be able to overcome the resistance rooted in men's love of their own and ultimately in the body" (*CM*, 127).

Morality is a form of transcendence toward the whole, but, paradoxically, human beings are not directed by nature toward this whole as they are toward the whole to which their minds are open. The paradox lies in the fact that morality, the less natural manifestation of this form of transcendence, is a much more common phenomenon than philosophy. Nonetheless, the way transcendence is operative in morality produces certain limitations on it: morality, especially justice, requires compulsion, even if sometimes self-compulsion (*CM*, 128). There is no simple harmony or congruence between the morality of the philosopher and the morality of common life. The incongruity is precisely the reverse, however, of what Drury, Lampert, and many who speak about Strauss today believe: the philosopher is the most just; the ordinary man requires compulsion and moral training despite the natural roots of morality. The incongruity in question leads to some paradoxical phenomena. For instance, Strauss once pointed out that "philosophy is as such transpolitical, transreligious, and transmoral, but the city ought to be moral and religious," a result of the difference between the two roots of morality. Strauss went on to illustrate one of the consequences of this incongruity: "moral man . . . in the common meaning of the term, is not simply closer to the philosopher than a man of the dubious morality of Alcibiades," a fact that helps explain the greater interest Socrates had in Alcibiades in the Platonic dialogues than in many more upstanding young men like Polemarchus. It is easy to misinterpret Strauss's point, however. Strauss does not say that Alcibiades, the man of "dubious morality," is "closer" to the philosopher, much less just like the philosopher. The moral man is "not *simply* closer"; that is, he is closer, but in a complex way. He is closer because, as we have seen, the philosopher and the moral man share a commitment to virtue. The closeness is not simple, however, because a gifted and searching soul like Alcibiades reveals, even in the dubiousness of his morality, something of the eros for wisdom. More than some, or perhaps even many, of the ordinary moral men, Alcibiades has a potential for philosophy—this, according to Alcibiades' testimony in Plato's *Symposium*, is what brought Socrates to him (not bodily eros). As a potential philosopher, Alcibiades is in this sense closer to the philosopher. But he is not on the whole and on balance closer, for his eros did not lead him either to philosophy or morality. In the end, that which was best in him, failing to achieve its proper goal, led him to be the worst, a potential or aspiring tyrant, furthest from the philosopher.

Another limitation resulting from the nature of morality is that the institutions proposed for the just city constructed by Socrates in the *Republic* are also "against nature." "The equality of the sexes and the absolute communism are against nature" (*CM*, 127), for both depend on ignoring the embodied partiality that is humanity, and both overstate the impulsive force toward the social whole that underlies the urge to justice. The *Republic*, as Strauss reads it, is thus a demonstration of both the naturalness of justice and the nature of justice, especially the limited nature of justice. His account of the *Republic* does indeed make clear why he had such limited political hopes and expectations, but it does not underwrite the claim that he is a teacher of evil or an adherent of the Thrasymachean thesis. Quite the contrary. As Drury rightly says, he finds Thrasymachus unrefuted in book 1; but as she fails to notice, he finds the entirety of the *Republic* to be the just speech, which does indeed refute Thrasymachus.

The Machiavellian Moment

The name probably most frequently associated with Strauss in the recent discussions is Machiavelli. Strauss's politics or his influence on politics is regularly described as Machiavellian in character, as we document in the introduction. The identification of Strauss as Machiavellian is fairly new, dating so far as we can tell (once again) to Drury, who, it will be recalled, went so far as to claim that "Strauss used Machiavelli as his mouthpiece in order to avoid pronouncing unpleasant, unsalutary and dangerous truths in his own name."[53] The pre-Drury view was mainly the reverse—that Strauss had been far too harsh on "old Nick," that the Florentine was not so bad as Strauss made him out to be. Nobody thought that Strauss himself adhered to the position he attributed to the Florentine.

The charge of Machiavellianism exists in two forms—a looser and more popular version, and a more precise and more scholarly version. The latter belongs especially to Drury; the former informs the media discussions of Strauss. We believe we have already made very clear the basis for dismissing the looser, more popular notion of Strauss as Machiavellian. The looser notion identifies Machiavelli with moral cynicism and amorality. The most sweeping and loosest version sees as Machiavellianism the commission of sly, duplicitous, immoral, or criminal acts for the sake of personal advancement or even ordinary malice. In this sense, Shakespeare's Richard III is seen as a classic Machiavellian character. This crude Machiavellianism surely has nothing to do with Strauss. As we have shown, his theory of esotericism does not supply warrant for lying and deception for the sake of personal gain, except in the fairly narrow circumstances of philosophers in nonliberal societies who conceal something of themselves for the sake of avoiding persecution. The use of exoteric or deceptive communication, insofar as Strauss defends the practice, is strictly governed by considerations of justice and the common good. So, even if the justification for esotericism holds in our day, it does not justify "Machiavellian" deception in the sense we are now considering. As to the immorality of crude Machiavellianism, we have shown Strauss's distance from any such thing. He defends morality, both for philosophers (or "the elite" as the media writers put it) and for everyone else. He defends the rule of law as the right political order, and obedience to law and the morality contained in the law as justice for all individuals.

A slightly less crude version of Machiavellianism justifies amorality and aggrandizement for political leaders and states, if not just anybody, whether acting for their own benefit or for the common good. But when Strauss rejects the tyrannical teaching, he rejects this version of Machiavellianism as well. As a political matter, he favors governance not by the sly, the deceptive, or the manipulative, but by individuals of merit and moral character, by persons who are devoted to the whole that is their society and the common good that serves that society as a certain sort of whole. He favors governance by individuals who love the fair and noble, which leads them to contemn low Machiavellian acts and even lower Machiavellian goals. If anything, Strauss's position might be faulted for being too high-minded; that is probably what Machiavelli himself would say of him, as he said of Plato and Aristotle. In particular, Strauss is not attached to that crude Machiavellianism (or even a sophisticated version) which justifies or advocates imperialism. The right political order aims at the highest degree of self-sufficiency and independence that is possible for it. Imperialism as a way of life does not comport with the conditions for a community's seeking the best way of life possible for its citizens. Strauss's philosophic heroes—Plato and Aristotle—are quite clear in rejecting the imperial ways of Athens and the martial life of Sparta as models for the good society.[54] Strauss never slighted the requirements of defense or the need for "preparedness," but he insisted that war was always for the sake of peace, and peaceful life for the sake of the good life—the life of virtue, understood first and foremost as the life of philosophy and secondarily as the life reflecting the life of philosophy, the life devoted to virtue, the life that serves to distinguish the good political community from a gang of thieves. Strauss was realist enough, of course, to see that many, perhaps most political communities failed to live up to these standards, but he always resisted the

Machiavellian desire to "lower his sights" in order to bring the norms more in accord with how men live, rather than how they ought to live. Strauss, we think we have shown, was, in fact, the anti-Machiavellian he presented himself to be.

Drury stands behind the now-common claim that Strauss is a Machiavellian, but she raises this claim in a specific and more precise way; and, unlike most of the media writers, she actually brings forward some evidence and argument to support her charge. Drury takes as her point of departure three observations about Strauss's treatment of Machiavelli, one of which is sound, the other two not. She correctly points out "the deep and apparently genuine admiration that Strauss seems to have for the man he has so unconditionally castigated." "What," she asks, "is the meaning of such superlative praise" as Strauss lavishes on Machiavelli? Her second observation is to the effect that Strauss brings to bear on Machiavelli his full arsenal of tools for reading esoteric books, but she, along with unnamed other commentators, "wonder[s] if Strauss's ingenuity is not wasted in the lengths to which he goes to uncover in the strangest places what Machiavelli says so boldly elsewhere. How much more boldly could Machiavelli have expressed himself?" Machiavelli says right on the lines all and more than Strauss digs for between the lines. Finally, she insists, careful attention to what Strauss says shows that he does not blame Machiavelli for his anti-Christian doctrine, but he rather blames him "for having been ultimately seduced by Christianity."[55]

Drury puts these various observations together to arrive at two conclusions of particular importance. First, the esotericism involved is Strauss's, not Machiavelli's. Machiavelli writes straightforwardly, but Strauss conceals himself as a commentator behind Machiavelli. Strauss uses Machiavelli as his spokesman, just as, according to Drury, Plato (or Strauss) used Thrasymachus as his spokesman.[56] Strauss hides behind Machiavelli to pronounce the truth that the ancients understood politics substantively just as Machiavelli did. Strauss, she believes, "thinks . . . Machiavelli's conception of the relationship between politics and morality" to be "shocking, repugnant, evil, irreligious, diabolical and dangerous"—but not false. "On the contrary he thinks it a true account of the real nature of politics."[57] That truth about politics is just the same truth Strauss's ancients taught, but they, like Strauss, taught it esoterically, not openly and in their own name as did Machiavelli.[58] Machiavelli, in a word, breaks with the esoteric tradition that Drury's Strauss finds so necessary. He begins the Enlightenment.

Machiavelli's differences from the ancients stem, she thinks Strauss thinks, from what Machiavelli took over from Christianity, the attempt to effect a moral revolution through "preaching the truth." That is, Machiavelli's break with the esoteric tradition and his setting off on an Enlightenment path were inspired by the success Christianity had in propagating itself via "propaganda." Christianity led Machiavelli to conceive and practice a new mode of interaction between philosophy and politics; it thus led him to break with the substantive principles of ancient philosophy. In addition to the rejection of esotericism, Machiavelli "breaks with the aristocratic tradition and exalts the multitude."[59] In doing so, Machiavelli "accelerates the Christian revolt against the aristocratic tradition of Greek philosophy." Finally, Machiavelli also "rejects [elitist] contemplation as the end beyond politics for which the latter exists."[60]

Drury is correct to notice that after having tentatively endorsed the old view that Machiavelli is a "teacher of evil," Strauss does praise Machiavelli; he does, as she says, seem to have a "deep admiration for his genius."[61] Strauss finds Machiavelli to be a philosopher, and he admires philosophers, even those with whom he disagrees. He said on one occasion:

> Philosophy as such is nothing but genuine awareness of the problems, i.e., of the fundamental and comprehensive problems. It is impossible to think about these problems without becoming inclined toward a solution, toward one or another of the very typical solutions. Yet as long as there is no wisdom, the evidence of all solutions is necessarily smaller than the evidence of the problems, therefore the philosopher ceases to be a philosopher at the moment at which the "subjective certainty" of a solution becomes stronger than his awareness of the problematic character of that solution. At that moment the sectarian is born.[62]

It is perfectly in accord with Strauss's conception of the philosophic vocation to admire Machiavelli as a philosopher even if he inclines—strongly inclines—to another of the "typical solutions" to the "fundamental and comprehensive problems."

We ought to notice, moreover, that Drury is rather misleading in her report of Strauss's admiration for the Florentine. It is true enough that Strauss expresses admiration, but his admiration is balanced—more than balanced—by blame. Machiavelli may have been very intelligent and thoughtful, he may even have been moved by a desire to do good; yet, Strauss is quite insistent, he did not do good. Strauss reports, for example, Machiavelli's claim "to have discovered a new moral continent," a claim he finds "well founded." Yet, Strauss retorts, "the only question is whether the new continent is fit for human habitation."[63] Strauss goes out of his way to show that despite its "revolutionary character," Machiavelli's new moral continent is not as unfit for human habitation as it might appear.[64] Nonetheless, Strauss pronounces his comprehensive judgment on the author of *The Prince*: "An amazing contraction of the horizon presents itself as an amazing enlargement of the horizon."[65] Drury leaves us with the misleading impression that Strauss, at bottom, praises more than he blames Machiavelli and in that way tries to render credible her thesis that Strauss uses Machiavelli as his mouthpiece.

Not only does Strauss balance his praise of Machiavelli with devastating criticism, but that praise is rather carefully focused. In the passage to which Drury seems to direct our attention, Strauss singles out one aspect of Machiavelli's text for signal admiration. "Time and again we have become bewildered by the fact that the man who is more responsible than any other man for the break with the Great Tradition should in the very act of breaking prove to be the heir, the by no means unworthy heir, to that supreme art of writing which that tradition manifested at its peaks."[66]

Perhaps Strauss's expression of bewilderment can be taken as support for Drury's second observation, to the effect that Strauss deploys a strenuous effort to read as if he were an esoteric writer a man who wears his heterodoxy on his sleeve. We incline to think otherwise. Strauss's bewilderment is sufficiently explained by noticing that Machiavelli, on Strauss's reading, sets in motion the break with the tradition that ultimately makes esoteric writing superfluous. All the more remarkable that he should be a master of the practice he is doing his best to consign to the dustbin of history. No need to have recourse to the hypothesis that Machiavelli's alleged esotericism is actually a surrogate for Strauss's own.

Drury nonetheless raises an important issue when she notes, in effect, that Machiavelli is no Xenophon—he seems to say loudly what he has on his mind, whether it shocks or not. In fact, he seems to go out of his way to shock: the "R" rating character of his book contributes to its appeal, at least for some readers. Machiavelli is bold, but does his boldness imply that Strauss's attribution of esotericism is merely an esoteric way for Strauss to announce his own esoteric use of Machiavelli as a spokesman? We think not.

Our concern here is a limited one; we do not wish to enter into the many interesting debates over whether Machiavelli really wrote as Strauss says he did. We merely wish to assess whether Strauss deploys his esotericism thesis and accompanying techniques of reading to produce an interpretation of Machiavelli that goes beyond "what Machiavelli says so boldly elsewhere."[67] The answer to that question must be yes. A great controversy persists to this day, almost fifty years later, over Strauss's reading of Machiavelli. Many readers reject the chief claims Strauss makes. They are not obvious on the surface of the Florentine's text. To take a very straightforward issue: Strauss argues that Machiavelli is thoroughly anti-Christian, but many other interpreters reject this conclusion and argue instead that Machiavelli was more an enemy of the church, or a certain interpretation of Christianity, than of the religion itself.

Strauss also uses his technique of reading to make the case that Machiavelli's aim is to break completely with the tradition and invent a wholly new kind of political philosophy, a break that required a critique of all prevalent systems of opinion. Although there are places where Machiavelli suggests a project of this sort, as when he claims to be a "new Columbus" or when he announces his deviation from all previous writers,[68] there are many other places where he suggests much more modest goals, for example, to recapture an ancient notion of politics, as Renaissance artists had recaptured ancient art. Strauss reads Machiavelli as an esoteric writer with a hugely ambitious project that outstrips anything lying about on the surface. Again, evidence that Strauss was going beyond what Machiavelli boldly said on the surface abounds in the scholarly literature. The best known of the post-Strauss interpreters of Machiavelli strongly rejects his "founder of modernity" thesis and sees Machiavelli instead as a restorer of Greek or Roman political conceptions.[69] In the face of such evidence, we do not believe Drury's case for the superfluity of esoteric techniques applied to Machiavelli has been made.

Her observations about Christianity are even more misleading. Strauss does not blame Machiavelli for falling prey to rather than trashing Christianity. Contrary to what Drury says, Strauss is very clear that Machiavelli is a root-and-branch enemy of Christianity: the "profound changes" wrought in the world by Christianity are identified as the driving forces behind what Strauss considers Machiavelli's unfortunate break with the ancients. Strauss is quite insistent that "the only element of Christianity which Machiavelli took over was the idea of propaganda."[70] This is admittedly a very significant borrowing, but Drury quite misses the tenor of Strauss's interpretation of Machiavelli when she attributes Machiavelli's embrace of the "many" and his rejection of the "few" to a democratic impulse that Strauss finds him adapting from Christianity. Both of those significant modifications of the tradition derive, in Strauss's view, not from Christianity but from Machiavelli's project of "actualization."

The reasons Drury invokes to attach Strauss to Machiavelli are not, in sum, at all persuasive. Even Drury does not go so far as to conclude that

Strauss agrees simply with the Machiavelli he lays out for us in the nearly 350 densely argued pages of *Thoughts on Machiavelli*. Although, as we have seen, she affirms that Strauss's Machiavelli gives what Strauss considers "a true account of the real nature of politics," and especially of "the relationship between politics and morality," she nonetheless concedes that Machiavelli deviates on two points from Strauss. The first is the openness Machiavelli practices in speaking aloud and in his own name harsh truths that the classical writers would conceal or put in the mouths of disreputable characters like Thrasymachus, or Callicles, or Hiero. She considers this the Machiavellian deviation that particularly turns Strauss against him.[71] The second deviation is more important, however. Machiavelli "rejects contemplation as the end of politics for which the latter exists."[72] As should be clear from our earlier discussions, we do not agree with Drury's way of putting this point, but she is onto something important. It is not quite accurate to say that for Strauss "contemplation" is "the end of politics," for he insists that the polis cannot contemplate or philosophize, and he recognizes that the city does not have as its aim the production of philosophers. But "contemplation," or, better put in the Straussian idiom, philosophy, as the pursuit of wisdom, is the true and natural end of human life and the key to understanding and grounding morality in nature. As we believe should be clear from our discussion of the Thrasymachean thesis, Drury has put together two claims that are simply incompatible. It is not possible for Strauss to accept Machiavelli's doctrine on the nature of politics and the relation between morality and politics as true while disagreeing with Machiavelli's failure to take account of philosophy: Strauss's understanding of the nature of politics and of the relation between morality and politics depends entirely on his understanding of philosophy. You cannot have one without the other. Strauss's point is that Machiavelli enters completely new moral waters when he cuts philosophy out of the picture. Without a mooring in man's natural end, the moral universe comes to look entirely different.

Not the good or the best, but the necessary came to hold sway in Machiavelli's world. Strauss was open-minded enough to concede that Machiavelli hit a correct chord when he emphasized the necessary; it is not always possible, Strauss admitted, to achieve the good or the best. In extreme circumstances the normal rules of morality or justice may not hold. Strauss, in his most quasi-Machiavellian moments, noted how even the Bible recognizes the sway of necessity. Strauss cited in this context the story of Lot and his daughters: laboring under the presumption that there were no other humans left alive, Lot, a pious man, lay with his daughters so that the race could be propagated. Machiavelli's emphasis on necessity and the

amoral foundation and prerequisites of morality in the extreme case converges with Aristotle's doctrine as interpreted by Strauss that there are no
ineluctably valid moral rules.[73] Strauss, therefore, always took care to insist
that the doctrine of the ancients was one of natural right, not natural law.
The naturally right is unchangeable but does not have the character of law,
an always and under all conditions valid rule of action.

The doctrine of natural right recognizes that at times political life or the
common good requires actions that fall beneath or outside the standards
of normal morality; for example, violating people's privacy is not right, but
sometimes in dealing with enemies of the public, one must engage in practices like wiretaps. Strauss thought that a sound doctrine of natural right
made room for necessities of this sort. Such practices and necessities were
not the rule, however, nor did the rule derive from them. The rule derived
from the nature of virtue and the noble. One of Strauss's most common
formulas for characterizing Machiavelli is to the point here. Machiavelli,
Strauss said, took his bearings by the extreme case.[74] Every community, for
example, faces other communities, which are actual or potential enemies.
From that fact, from the potential for enmity and vulnerability, Machiavelli
moved to the conclusion that the best or only electable kind of polity was
like Rome, rather than Sparta, Venice, or Florence. To be like Rome meant
to be organized around war and expansion. In terms of contemporary international relations theory, Machiavelli concluded first for preemption and
then for prevention. The proper polity must be indefinitely expansive. This
is a conclusion Strauss rejected as based on the extreme case; the extreme
case, Strauss thought, should be confined to the extreme situation. Since
Machiavelli had cut himself off from the end or perfection of human beings, he had no bearings but necessity. Strauss instead attempted to take
his bearings in the Socratic manner, from the natural human good of philosophy and from the noble. Strauss and Machiavelli thus touch at some
points, but their positions are otherwise entirely at odds with each other.[75]
Strauss takes his bearing by philosophy, and therewith justice and virtue,
and makes room for the pinch of necessity. Machiavelli takes his bearing by
necessity and allows that to swallow up the entire moral universe. Strauss,
in a word, is no Machiavellian.[76]

Strauss and Schmitt

Carl Schmitt is one of an unholy triumvirate with which Strauss has been
increasingly identified.[77] The other two are Nietzsche and Heidegger. Their
unholiness derives from their links with Nazism: in the case of Schmitt and

Heidegger, actual party membership, and in the case of Nietzsche, the perception of an intellectual affinity by some Nazi party ideologues. (It should be noted that Nietzsche also said a great deal that was not in any way supportive of Nazi ideologies and politics, including a rejection of anti-Semitism.) The alleged connection between these three and Strauss is then used to suggest (and it is even at times said outright) that Strauss, despite being Jewish, was also a Nazi or a Nazi sympathizer. In our opinion this is the greatest misinterpretation of Strauss of the many that have recently been promulgated.

We have already spoken at some length of Strauss's view of and differences from Nietzsche and Heidegger. We see no need to return to these figures now, other than to point out some specific comments he made on their politics or political leanings and influence. Nietzsche, according to Strauss, "used much of his unsurpassable and inexhaustible power of passionate and fascinating speech for making his readers loathe, not only socialism and communism, but conservatism, nationalism, and democracy as well." He was not, however, able to lay before his readers a positive alternative to the ones he had attempted to discredit. "He left [readers] with no choice except that between irresponsible indifference to politics and irresponsible political options."[78] Because Nietzsche was so "indefinite and vague" about the desirable political future, Strauss concludes, "in a sense all political use of Nietzsche is a perversion of his teaching."[79] Strauss most definitely did not believe that "Nietzsche understood the cure as well as the disease" of modern politics.[80] Yet he did have a political effect: "what he said was read by political men and inspired them." And what it inspired them to was fascism.[81] That regime, Strauss says, "made discredited democracy look again like a golden age."[82]

Of Heidegger Strauss spoke explicitly much less often, and of Heidegger's politics even less. But his most clear-cut comments leave no doubt as to how Strauss stood with regard to those politics: Heidegger, referred to by Strauss as "the most radical historicist" of the day, in accord with his philosophic orientation, "welcome[d] as a dispensation of fate, the verdict of the least wise and least moderate part of his nation while it was in its least wise and least moderate mood."[83] So far from having sympathies with the fascist leanings or influence of Nietzsche and Heidegger, Strauss sought a philosophic path completely different from their version of late modernity, in part because of the political consequences of their thought. Those who claim that Strauss sympathizes with fascism commit the very elementary but, we believe, irresponsible error of concluding that because Strauss is critical of some of the theoretical premises of liberal democracy, he is a critic of liberal democracy tout court, and that therefore he (being a conservative and not a leftist critic) must be sympathetic to fascism. None of this chain of reasoning is grounded in what Strauss actually said or thought.

Despite his philosophical and political disagreements with Nietzsche and Heidegger, Strauss considered them great philosophers. There is no evidence that he had as high regard for Schmitt. When he was in his early thirties, Strauss did write an article-length review of Schmitt's best-known book, *The Concept of the Political.* He indicated the essay was of some importance, moreover, by reprinting it as an addendum to the 1965 English translation of his early (1930) book on Spinoza's *Critique of Religion.* In the preface Strauss explained why he had reprinted the essay: Published two years before the Schmitt essay, the Spinoza book "was based on the premise...that a return to pre-modern philosophy is impossible." The Schmitt essay was significant because in it Strauss's "change of orientation," that is, his conviction that a return to premodern philosophy is both desirable and possible "found its first expression."[84] He did not, it should be noted, republish the essay to announce his allegiance or even agreement with Schmitt's philosophy.

Let us begin with Schmitt. He was about a decade older than Strauss and was well established as a professor of law at the University of Cologne at the time Strauss wrote his essay. Strauss had no teaching position and was just finishing up his period as an editor of the works of Moses Mendelssohn. Schmitt joined the Nazi Party in 1933 (after Strauss's essay) and quickly became a leading Nazi jurist and legal theorist. He was, in the words of Mark Lilla, "a committed, official advocate of the Nazi regime." His involvement and outright support for the Nazis appear to have been much greater than that of, say, Heidegger. In his writings he attempted to supply theoretical support for the legality of apparently illegal acts; he joined his voice to the chorus of official anti-Semitism.[85] By the end of the war, he had lost most of his influence and prestige in the regime, but he did keep his prize professorship at the University of Berlin. Despite the fall from favor, there were few prominent intellectuals as much entangled with the Nazis as Schmitt was. After the war, he was also, by some accounts, "aggressively unrepentant about his collaboration."[86]

Strauss's essay on Schmitt has been important in the recent literature on Strauss, because it is alleged to be a place where he adopts Schmitt's antiliberal (and by extension in the minds of some, pro-Nazi) agenda, or where Strauss goes even further than Schmitt in an antiliberal direction. That Strauss is not a "follower" of Schmitt, as is sometimes claimed, is clear from Schmitt's own comments on Strauss's essay. Schmitt referred to the latter as "a very good essay about my book—very critical of course."[87] Strauss's critics respond that to the extent that Strauss was critical, he was critical from the right.[88] The basis for this reading is Strauss's concluding summary of his exposition of Schmitt. According to Strauss, Schmitt intended not merely to present a critique of liberalism but to go beyond it. In appealing to a Hobbesian philosophic position, Schmitt had remained inside the orbit of liberalism, however; at the most, he had negated it, and thus remained in thrall to it. On the basis of that observation, Strauss proposed that "the critique introduced by Schmitt against liberalism can therefore be completed only if one succeeds in gaining a horizon beyond liberalism."[89]

It should be clear what that pronouncement means from the perspective of today, but it was not likely to be clear to Schmitt or his contemporaries. This was Strauss's way of announcing his "return to the ancients," or at least the premoderns, a project he meant to conduct via a confrontation with the philosophy of Hobbes, in which, he believed at the time, modernity first reared its head. Partly with Schmitt's aid, Strauss received a grant from the Rockefeller Foundation to go to Paris and then to England, where he pursued his project in a two-pronged study. First he continued work on the form of premodern philosophy that most attracted him at the time, the thought of the medieval Jewish philosopher Moses Maimonides, whom he saw as a premodern and superior parallel to Spinoza. The result of this work was his next book, *Philosophy and Law* (1935). He was also pursuing, apparently simultaneously, his studies of Hobbes, which bore fruit in *The Political Philosophy of Hobbes: Its Basis and Its Genesis* (1936), his first book to appear in English. This was also the book that called the attention of the scholarly world to him. Strauss believed he had won a superior vantage point for a critique of modernity by getting behind Hobbes, the modern, so to speak, rather than by returning to Hobbes, as Schmitt had done.

It is important to be clear that Strauss's agreement with Schmitt that critique of liberalism was in order does not mean that Strauss agreed with Schmitt on the substance of that critique. Strauss's charge that Schmitt remained within the orbit of modernity constituted a very substantive critique of Schmitt's thought. To go beyond the horizon of liberalism would mean for Strauss to produce an alternative to liberalism that was not a mere negation of it, as he thought Schmitt's critique was. To go further or deeper than Schmitt did not mean in this context going further in the same direction Schmitt had gone.

Strauss made much, from the very outset of his essay, of Schmitt's view that "all political concepts, ideas, and words [have] a polemical meaning;

they have a concrete opposition in view, they are tied to a concrete situation."[90] In a sense the entire difference between Strauss and Schmitt turns on Strauss's rejection of that claim as a universal truth. Yet Strauss took it as descriptive of Schmitt's own thinking. The jurist saw the defining character of liberalism to be "negation of the political," that is, the attempt to be neutral, pacific or even pacifist, humanitarian, cosmopolitan. His *Concept of the Political* was intended to be the negation of this liberal negation of the political; it made sense as stated by Schmitt only in the context of liberal negation.

Schmitt's affirmation of the political contained a certain ambiguity, which Strauss worked hard in his essay to expose. Schmitt perhaps meant to say that the political is an inevitable and inescapable part of the human condition, and thus that liberalism is deluding itself in attempting to negate it. But, Strauss suggested, the deeper level of Schmitt's argument lay elsewhere. The liberals were correct in thinking the political could be escaped, but they were quite mistaken in thinking this would be good or desirable. The political, as Schmitt understood it, is the tendency of the human world to divide into groups of friends and enemies. One group exists and its identity is defined only against the backdrop of "the other"—the enemy. That every human group has enemies means that actual or potential struggle and war are pervasive and determining forces of human existence. The political, as the situs of the friend-enemy distinction, has priority over every other realm of culture: war disrupts commerce and demands of citizens that they put their lives on the line.

Schmitt objected most, in the prospect of the triumph of liberalism, to the robbing of life of all *real* seriousness. The possibility of a life-and-death struggle with the enemy makes life serious, not just an arena for entertainment. In Schmitt, Strauss thus detected a strong Nietzschean strain: like Nietzsche, Schmitt was most repelled by the triumph of "the last man," the man who sees life as nothing more than entertainment.[91] In objecting to Schmitt's way of negating liberal modernity, Strauss was thus also signaling his own move away from his early infatuation with Nietzsche. That move had already occurred, and it had been subtly announced in his Spinoza book, but he now added new dimensions (moral, not just theological) to the earlier break with Nietzsche; he also added the promise of a horizon beyond liberal modernity and of a positive task beyond negation of a negation.

The alleged connection of Strauss to Schmitt is important in the present-day context of anti-Straussian polemics because Schmitt's friend-enemy distinction grants primacy to foreign policy and supports a martial stance toward other nations. The imagined picture of Strauss as a Schmittian helps make the case that Strauss has somehow inspired what his critics see as an overly bellicose foreign policy.

It is thus imperative to be clear on just where Strauss agrees with Schmitt and the limits of that agreement. To facilitate comparison with Strauss, we can reduce Schmitt's complex position to three simple propositions:

1. Liberalism has failed. Writing in late Weimar Germany, Schmitt could almost take this thesis for granted.
2. Liberalism's failure can be traced to its "negation" of the political. The political is a pervasive and formative part of society and thus of human life. In a sense, it trumps the other spheres of culture and is superior to them. Schmitt reaffirms the sovereign state, supreme over and directive (in principle) of all other parts of society.
3. The core or essence of the political is the distinction between friends and enemies. The political carries with it the threat of war and the range of necessities that go with the actual or potential threat to group survival. Given the fact that the core of the political is the actual or potential conflict (internal as well as external) that follows from the friend-enemy distinction, Schmitt was skeptical about liberal attempts to contain political power within the bounds of law and the norms of compromise and deliberation. Decision and decisiveness are needed, and the days of peace, which allow the vision of rule of law to grow up, are illusory: the core of the political remains conflict, and political societies in principle regularly face the situation of emergency. Emergency requires untrammeled authority, authority outside the bounds of law. Like Machiavelli, Schmitt is convinced that the extreme situation is more revealing of the truth of politics and sets the terms around which political life must be lived. Thus Schmitt favors (in the extreme) dictatorship, militarism, and imperialism.

Strauss agrees to a large extent with Schmitt's first point. Liberal democracy had certainly failed in Weimar Germany. The failure of liberal democracy in Germany was not solely the product of factors unique to German political history and culture. Strauss believed it was an episode in what he came to call "the crisis of our times," a crisis compounded of extremist ideologies on the one hand, and a congenital weakness of liberal (modern) theory, which made the moderate, centrist, liberal order particularly vulnerable to attack from the extremes, on the other hand.

Unlike Schmitt and Heidegger and others of that sort, who had given up on liberal democracy, Strauss took a different way. He did not seek to overturn liberal orders and replace them with something illiberal; rather, he sought, and thought he had found in premodern political philosophy, a better way to defend constitutional orders. He believed, in particular, that the return to the ancients would allow the partisans of liberal democracy to meet "the crisis of our time" better than the classic versions of liberalism, which had decayed, apparently irrevocably, into positivism, historicism, and forms of relativism that robbed partisans of liberal democracy of grounds on which to stand firm. Thus Strauss sought a stronger defense of liberal democracy than one finds in its postmodern defenders like Richard Rorty, who has nothing more to say for it than that it (or some version of it) is ours. Rorty even undercuts his own rationale when he affirms, on the basis of his antifoundationalist philosophy, that it is not even clear that liberal democracy is "ours." There is as little truth about history, political culture, and political opinion as there is about anything else. What is "ours" is subject to "redescription" by any interpreter. Rorty has his version of what is "ours," but so do the members of the Michigan militia. The difference between Rorty and earlier defenders of liberal orders against illiberal challengers, defenders like Thomas Jefferson, is that Rorty believes he actually has nothing true to say to those who choose to "describe" our order differently. Rorty embodies the crisis of belief in liberal democracy that Strauss attempted to head off with his return to the ancients.

Strauss thus agrees, in a sense—but only in a sense—with Schmitt's first point. Liberalism is in crisis, but it is a different crisis from the one Schmitt sees. The appropriate response to that crisis is also quite different from Schmitt's. It is both more and less radical. Strauss goes further than Schmitt in orienting his thinking by premodern thought rather than by earlier modern thinkers like Hobbes or Machiavelli, whose doctrines ultimately led to the very real crisis that made a reorientation in thought necessary. At the same time that Strauss is much more radical in thought, he is much less radical in his conclusions about politics. Politically he is conservative in a double sense. He proposes a reorientation in thinking for the sake of the defense and support of constitutional democracy. It is a conservative but not a reactionary version of liberal democracy, as we have shown in chapter 2. (In the contemporary political sense, Strauss's politics are probably closest to those of the communitarians.)[92] Above all, Strauss affirms the rule of law and moderate politics.

Strauss also accepts much of Schmitt's second point. One of the major points in his reconstruction of classical political science is his affirmation of the ancient notion of regime, and therewith of the primacy of the political.

> *Politeia* is ordinarily translated by "constitution" ... [by which modern men] almost inevitably mean a legal phenomenon ... yet ... the classics used *politeia* in contradistinction to "laws." ... The *politeia* is rather the factual distribution of power within the community than what constitutional law stipulates in regard to political power.... *Politeia* means the way of life of a society rather than its constitution.... When speaking of *politeia*, the classics thought of the way of life of a community as essentially determined by its "form of government." ... The character, or tone, of a society depends on what the society regards as most respectable or most worthy of admiration.... When the classics were chiefly concerned with the different regimes ... they implied the paramount social phenomenon ... is the regime.[93]

The regime, then, is the form of government, or rather the ruling element within any given form or the ruling norms embodied in the ruling element. All societies are constituted by a variety of different types of human beings, and the notion of regime holds that one or some of them achieve an authoritative place in every community. The liberal effort to affirm rule of all by all, or of all by none, is illusory. It is necessary to recognize the partial character of all rule or regimes in order to create a mixed regime that has results most like the liberal goal of regimeless rule. It is worth noting that the analysis of political societies in terms of regime does not amount to a warrant to foster regime change. It certainly does not justify the overthrow and imposition of regimes in other countries by force.

Strauss sees the political in the form of the regime as supreme— pervasive and architectonic. He thus agrees with Schmitt on the centrality of the political, but he understands that centrality differently.[94] Schmitt's theory of the political harks back to Hobbes, with his absolute sovereign, whose word is law and against whose word there is no law. Hobbes's sovereign is the locus for all necessity-dealing authority. It embodies the "emergency" that is the Hobbesian state of nature dwelling always just a little offstage. Strauss looks back instead to Aristotle for his notion of regime and the priority of the political. Although regime is more fundamental than law (for laws are made by the ruling elements in any society), the notion of regime is thoroughly compatible with rule of law in the Aristotelian rendition that Strauss follows.[95] The political is supreme for Strauss and

Aristotle because it gives society as a whole its overall character, a very different matter from the supremacy Schmitt and Hobbes affirm.

Strauss agrees in part with Schmitt's first two points, but he disagrees entirely with Schmitt's third and most important point: according to Strauss, the political is not defined or constituted by the friend-enemy distinction.[96] The attentive reader might have concluded that Strauss also agrees with Schmitt's formula for the political, for that formula reminds more than a little of the position taken by Polemarchus in the *Republic,* and Polemarchus seems to keep the friend-enemy distinction as constitutive of the political. Polemarchus's position, in turn, seems to be the Socratic (Straussian) view, because, according to Strauss, Socrates most agrees with Polemarchus: Strauss points out that "the opinion of Polemarchus properly understood is the only one among the generally known views of justice discussed in the first book of the Republic which is entirely preserved in the positive or constructive part of the Republic" (*CM*, 70). But Strauss's statement contains an important qualification: "properly understood," it is carried forward. Not every possible version of "friends and enemies" is a proper understanding. "Properly understood," in this case, means understanding Polemarchus's definition in the sense of "public-spiritedness" or "full dedication to the common good." Polemarchus's notion of justice is identical to "patriotism, and consists indeed of helping one's friends, i.e., one's fellow citizens, and harming one's enemies, i.e., foreigners. Justice thus understood cannot be entirely dispensed with in any city however just, for even the most just city is a city, a particular or closed or exclusive society" (73). The political is not constituted by the friend-enemy distinction. That distinction is a necessary derivative of the fact that every political society is a particularistic entity, separate in identity from every other political society and potentially at war with other societies. The classic view of the nature of the political is presented by Strauss as the result of two central human qualities: human sociability and human rationality: "man is by nature a social being." Human life and, even more, the good human life cannot be maintained or achieved without human society. Human beings are "social in a more radical sense than any other social animal; humanity itself is sociality."[97] Sociality by itself does not make man the political animal, however. Man is also the rational animal, and "by virtue of his rationality, man has a latitude of alternatives such as no other earthly being has." As rational beings, human beings are reflexive beings: they are guided in their actions by their understandings of what they wish or ought to do. Along with this freedom comes "a sense that the full and unrestrained exercise of that freedom is not right. Man's freedom is accompanied by a sacred awe, by a divination that not everything is permitted."[98] Human beings require (and merit) both rational guidance and restraint. "Man is so built that he cannot achieve the perfection of humanity except by keeping down his lower impulses." The lower impulses are potent; the force of reason, which ought to govern them, is limited. Individual self-rule needs to be supplemented by the coercive rule of law. But law must or ought to apply to men in a way that is consistent with their dignity, that is, with their social and rational nature. In any case, the city or civil society is that human association which comes into existence on the bases of human sociality and rationality and which, in the best cases, seeks to perfect human nature as social and rational. The political association, and thus the political per se, is not constituted by the friend-enemy distinction.[99] Strauss accounts for the political within an altogether different horizon from the one Schmitt employs.

The political society, according to the classics, is "a closed society," "a small society." "A society meant to make man's perfection possible must be kept together by mutual trust, and trust presupposes acquaintance." Because trust, as well as "man's natural power of love or active concern, is by nature limited," a good city will have to be small.[100] There is no possibility that all human beings could belong to one political society, at least not a society that honors human freedom. In order for freedom to thrive, there must be many political societies, and thus the particular attachment to one's own and potential hostility to others.

Unlike Schmitt, Strauss does not consider the cosmopolitan ideal simply false. Like the ancients, he begins from a conception of a common, universal human nature: man is the rational animal. The human beings in whom that rational capacity is fully developed are, in effect, fellow citizens of a universal human society. Knowledge is one good that can be shared without being diminished. But Strauss was also convinced that no political society as political society could be founded on philosophic truth per se or on the philosophic life. Every political society rests on a set of more or less true (and therefore more or less false) opinions, which serve as the common basis and bond for the members of that society. These opinions differ from political society to political society, producing a uniqueness to each and a certain closedness as each rallies around its own version of truth. Thus the division of the world into a variety of different political communities (friends and enemies) follows from the Straussian theme of the rule of opinion and the construction of political societies. Strauss agrees with Schmitt that it is necessary to recapture an awareness of the significance and even primacy of the political, but the meaning of "the return to the ancients" lies in his rejection of Schmitt's modernist mode of doing so. Schmitt's rejection of liberal democracy produced an illiberal toleration, or even advocacy, of indecency. Strauss sought for a higher, not a lower, understanding of the significance and priority of the political. Strauss came to understand the political in relation to the highest in humanity, and that led him to emphasize the dignity, not the viciousness, of political life.

PART II

Straussians

CHAPTER SIX

The Emergence of the Straussian Study of America

In the present discussions of Strauss it is, of course, not Strauss who is said to have gone to Washington, but his students and the students of his students. Strauss himself remained distant from practical politics and scanty in his pronouncements on the American regime, but many of his students have been much more engaged with the study (and practice) of American politics. Although the media tallies of Straussians in George W. Bush's Washington are grossly overstated, it is nonetheless a fact that more than a few Strauss-influenced individuals have played a role in American politics. To mention a few: Harry V. Jaffa, one of Strauss's earliest students, was heavily involved in the Barry Goldwater campaign and is credited with (or blamed for) penning the very un-Straussian sentiment that Goldwater delivered in his 1964 nomination acceptance speech: "Extremism in defense of liberty is no vice; moderation in pursuit of justice is no virtue." Robert A. Goldwin was in the White House under Gerald Ford as a liaison to the academic community and before that was campaign manager for moderate Republican Senator Charles Percy of Illinois. William Galston was a senior adviser to Independent candidate John Anderson and to Democratic nominee Walter Mondale and then served in the Clinton White House as deputy assistant for domestic policy.

More significant, certainly more widespread, than their political participation, however, has been the turn by many of Strauss's students and students of his students to the serious study of the American regime. Strauss's students have obviously invested much in their American studies, for they have split into factions, often bitterly divided factions, over their differing interpretations of America. Just as one finds so-called Straussians at many different places on the spectrum of practical politics, so one finds the Straussians in the academy far from united. Contrary to what is frequently claimed by outside critics, those influenced by Strauss do not form a unified movement or stand for a single dogma.

On reflection, it is not surprising that Strauss's students have made systematic study of America one of their chief foci, even though Strauss himself did not do so. He was not an American, but they are, and concern for one's own is a powerful force. Strauss had observed that in the quest for scholarly knowledge of politics, the "center of reference is the given political situation, and even in most cases the given political situation in the individual's own country. It is true that a botanist in Israel pays special attention to the flora of Israel, whereas the botanist in Canada pays special attention to the flora of Canada. But this difference, which is not more than the outcome of a convenient and even indispensable division of labor, has an entirely different character than the only apparent similar difference between the preoccupation of the Israeli political scientist and the Canadian political scientist."[1] Both the "given political situation" and the natural concern for their own led Strauss's American students to study their own country, because America is, in obvious ways, at the center of the present "political situation." Strauss had set down as one of the guiding principles of an adequate political science that it "view political things in the perspective of the citizen" and the statesman. Given the place of the United States in the world, and the necessary concern with the United States by all citizens and statesmen, the turn by Strauss's students to the study of the United States was in accord with his mandates for political studies.[2]

This turn was both facilitated and complicated by Strauss's own somewhat fragmentary reflections on America. As we have seen, he bequeathed to his students a puzzling legacy of thought on the subject. Recall the three propositions that together make up Strauss's thesis about America:

1. America is modern
2. Modernity is bad
3. America is good

When stated as starkly as this, Strauss's position seems to contain an outright contradiction; but, as we have also seen (in chapter 2), a more nuanced approach makes better sense of these three claims. Strauss reconciled his three propositions by arguing, in effect (1) that the judgment about America's goodness was a comparative judgment: relative to the main alternatives within modernity, America is good; (2) that modernity is not wholly bad, or not all parts of it are equally bad; and (3) that America is not wholly modern.

Strauss endorsed America, and that endorsement is genuine, credible, and serious. Yet the endorsement is also and always qualified in various ways: it is relative and contextual, it tends to the lukewarm, and it is shot through with long-term pessimism. We can appreciate the limitations of his endorsement of American liberal democracy by reviewing the grounds on which he made it.

1. *America in the Context of the Cold War.* Strauss never equivocated or wavered in his judgment of the superiority of America to communist (or fascist) regimes, but in itself this commits him only to a very relative and contextual judgment.

2. *America in the Context of His "Three Wave" Theory.* As we pointed out in chapter 2, Strauss considers America a "first-wave" regime.[3] Two issues stand out in relation to Strauss's emphasis on that theme. Although America is superior to regimes informed by the later waves, it is also rightly subject to the criticisms raised by second-wave theorists. Strauss always found Rousseau's and Nietzsche's critiques of the thinkers and philosophic positions previous to themselves to be compelling. This consideration implies Strauss's acceptance of some grave criticisms of America.

Strauss has a strong sense of the vulnerability of first-wave thinking. It is no accident, he thinks, that the earlier thought gets supplanted. He very strikingly says that the defects of second- and third-wave practice do "not permit us to return to the earlier forms of modern thought: the critique of modern rationalism or of the modern belief in reason by Nietzsche cannot be dismissed or forgotten." That Nietzschean critique is, he says, the ultimate ground of the "crisis of our time."[4] The broader culture—not only Strauss—finds itself unable to overcome that critique and remain committed to the modern rationalism of first-wave theory and practice. America may be a first-wave regime, but that in itself will not, Strauss fears, prevent it from being swamped by the failures of the first wave. Thus positivism and historicism undermine American faith in its own first-wave commitments.

3. *America Redescribed in Classical Terms.* No matter how much Strauss rehabilitated American liberal democracy by redescribing it in Aristotelian terms, Strauss's view of the truer and better political principles remained at some distance from the American regime. In his major work *Natural Right and History*, for example, he indicated some of that distance: "Since men are then unequal in regard to human perfection, i.e., in the decisive respect, equal rights for all appeared to the classics as most unjust. They contended that some men are by nature superior to others, and, therefore, according to natural right, the rulers of others." America is founded in the conviction that "all men are created equal" and that government exists to

secure the equal rights possessed by all men. America is thus an order that is, according to the ancients whose views Strauss endorses, "most unjust."[5] Moreover, to the degree that America as a first-wave regime is vulnerable to second- and third-wave onslaughts, it tends to lose its character as a mixed regime. Thus Strauss saw a tendency toward democratization in American politics and culture, a tendency he understood to be the result of later thought. It was a tendency he feared was robbing America of its mixed character.

Leaving that important reservation against America aside, at its best Strauss's effort at redescription leaves an important disparity between American self-understanding and Strauss's redescription. He leaves us in a position of having to disregard, to depreciate as misguided and unhelpful finally, the political principles explicitly articulated and adopted by American statesmen and founders. To take one important example: although Strauss often seems to defend the American Declaration of Independence, in point of fact he disagrees with it. In opting for an Aristotelian grasp of the American polity, he depreciates the Madisonian political science that informed the construction of the constitutional order. In effect, Strauss is counseling us that it is best not to understand America as it has understood itself.

4. *America and Premodern Residues.* Strauss is especially pessimistic about the classical and religious residues in America. In his essay on liberal education, he makes clear his belief that these residues are vanishing from American life, diminishing in their presence and impact over time. "We must disregard here the older traditions which fortunately still retain some of their former power; we must disregard them because their power is more and more corroded as time goes on."[6] If these residues are crucial for the (relative) health and goodness of America, then America is indeed in deep trouble, according to Strauss's pessimistic analysis. It is no accident that Strauss regularly spoke the language of crisis—America is in a real sense good, but the inherent dynamic of modernity is robbing it of that goodness.

Strauss's students took this continuing tension and long-term pessimism in his thought as their point of departure, developing at least three alternative approaches to the study of America. The tensions among Strauss's three propositions turn out to demarcate the fault lines along which the divisions among Strauss's students emerged. The three factions formed according to which of Strauss's three propositions his students rejected, or, perhaps more accurately put, the one they deemphasized or ignored. The East Coast Straussians tended to address far more explicitly and openly than Strauss himself had done the limitations and defects of America. In a word, they no longer quite adhered to Strauss's third proposition, "America is good." The West Coast Straussians, to some degree emerging as a reaction to the East Coast school, took a different tack. They affirmed more strongly and unequivocally the third proposition but came to reject the first, "America is modern." The Midwest Straussians, in the largest departure from the original Strauss position, rejected (or at least challenged) the second proposition, "Modernity is bad." Now it must be said of all three of these positions that their rejection of (or serious reservations about) one of Strauss's three propositions does not commit them to the extreme alternative view. To reject "America is good" does not commit the East Coasters to the obverse, "America is bad." Among the East Coast Straussians are great patriots and lovers of their country. To reject the third proposition, "Modernity is bad," does not commit the Midwest Straussians to an unequivocal and indiscriminate endorsement of everything modern.

We have deployed a geographically based terminology to describe the three schools of Straussians, but these names are more metaphors than accurate descriptions, for membership in one or another of these factions is a matter of understanding, not literally of the geographical region in which a scholar happens to reside. We had hoped to scrap these somewhat traditional but now misleading geographic names. They no longer accurately capture the location of the various members of the different schools, if they ever did, and they fail to give any substantive insight into what is at issue between the schools. Nonetheless, the names have become common enough that it is difficult to jettison them entirely.

Strauss's students did not set out to found different schools. They hoped rather to provide samples of a political science rooted in political philosophy as informed by Strauss's scholarship. Strauss had made the deficiencies of the reigning political science one of the chief themes of his own work, and his early students quite self-consciously were attempting to develop the kind of political science he called for in place of the dominant approaches. It took quite a long while for the different schools to realize they had developed in such different directions as to foment often acrimonious hostility and bitter conflict among themselves.

The first sign of factionalization was the split that emerged between Harry Jaffa and Martin Diamond in the mid-1970s. They had been friends and colleagues but then for a variety of reasons grew apart. It has been wrongly thought that this and other divisions that soon appeared were prompted by personal causes. The splits were genuinely intellectual in origin and reflected the varying approaches Strauss's students had taken in trying to think through and cope with Strauss's tense legacy.

The three earliest of Strauss's students to produce significant work on the American political order were Walter Berns, Harry Jaffa, and Martin Diamond. All three have had an impact on American studies reaching well beyond the Strauss circle. Berns has for many years been a leading student of the U.S. Supreme Court. He recently received a lifetime achievement award from the Public Law section of the American Political Science Association, an award rarely given and amounting to plain recognition of his prominence in the study of public law.

Harry Jaffa has published two wide-ranging and philosophic studies of Abraham Lincoln and the American regime, studies that have been hailed as among the very best work ever done on that much-worked-over figure. As Allen Guelzo, a much honored Lincoln scholar himself, and a man with no connections to the Strauss circle, testifies on behalf of Jaffa's second book: "Forty years ago, Harry Jaffa wrote the greatest book on Abraham Lincoln's politics for a generation; now, Jaffa has written the greatest book on Lincoln's politics for another generation." Martin Diamond focused his scholarly attention on the American founders, and most especially on James Madison. He was among the scholars who helped reorient founding studies from the paths, increasingly seen to be dead ends, which had been cut by Charles Beard and the Progressive historians. Diamond's work has achieved wide recognition for its importance. The late Senator Patrick Moynihan commented, for example, that "Martin Diamond almost single-handedly established the relevance of the thought and doings of the Founding Fathers for his generation."[7]

Berns's *Freedom, Virtue, and the First Amendment* appeared in 1957; Jaffa's *Crisis of the House Divided* and Diamond's seminal essay "Democracy and the Federalist" both appeared in 1959. Both Berns and Jaffa acknowledge Diamond's aid in their volumes, and all three show the obvious influence of Strauss. The three works are important not only because they are the first sustained efforts to apply a Straussian approach to the understanding of America, but also because in them we see the beginnings of the three main Straussian schools, peeping out from under the more noticeable common themes that Berns, Jaffa, and Diamond have taken over from Strauss and applied to American materials.

Walter Berns: The Virtuous Republic

Freedom, Virtue, and the First Amendment is a consistently bold, even daring, sometimes brilliant book that initiated the Straussian study of America with an in-depth examination of the way the Supreme Court was dealing with First Amendment speech and press issues in the 1940s and '50s. Berns proudly announced his Straussian-inspired effort to reorient the study of American politics. He took issue with every one of the then leading approaches to free speech on the Court, with the approach to constitutional studies among the legal professoriate, and with the dominant approaches to the American tradition as a whole among historians and political scientists. A book so unorthodox was not met with approbation in all—or hardly any—circles. As Berns says of the book's reception, "Most of the reviewers . . . disagreed with it, some of them rather vigorously."[8] Nonetheless, like many an unorthodox statement, it was a fresh perspective on what had become by the mid-1950s a stale discussion.

Freedom, Virtue, and the First Amendment is not much read these days. Berns has importantly modified his position and in this sense has superseded his own work.[9] The argument of the early book, challenging liberal shibboleths about freedom of speech, was sufficiently out of the mainstream to raise hackles. Probably the chief reason it is seldom consulted today, however, is the consequence of one of its great strengths when it was first published. Berns treats his readers to an in-depth survey of the Supreme Court's free speech and press jurisprudence, with lengthy and detailed discussion of cases and issues that at the time engrossed the attention of all, but which have today receded from the center of interest, even for specialists in the field.

Berns analyzed the Court at a time when it was dominated by one of the great factional battles of the century, the colossal conflict between the civil-libertarian, activist wing led by (and for some of the period, composed exclusively of) Justices Hugo Black and William O. Douglas, and the more "restraintist" bloc, led by Justice Felix Frankfurter (*FVFA*, 178). The leaders of the two blocs had been appointed to the Court by Franklin Roosevelt, and their split over what to make of the Court's chastened position after the New Deal Court crisis of 1937 surprised most Court-watchers when it first emerged in the 1940s.

Berns brought a fresh perspective to this now familiar topic by applying Strauss-honed tools of analysis to the issue. His thesis was both novel and radical. Rather than taking sides with one or the other bloc, as most in the legal and political community did; rather than being neutrally analytical, as many of the social-science-oriented academics were, Berns argued that both sides (and the somewhat uncommitted center, too) were approaching the issues of speech and press in a manifestly inadequate and inappropriate manner. The inadequacy was due in all cases, he argued, to the liberal horizon, which encompassed all parties to the "great debate":

the "great debate" was not so great after all (*FVFA*, 46). Most off-putting to the orthodox was Berns's insistence that to approach freedom-of-speech questions as a matter of maximizing freedom (as the so-called liberal bloc did), or as a matter of maximizing control by majoritarian political decision makers (as the so-called conservative bloc did) was a mistake (197): the real goal of politics is virtue, not freedom or majority rule per se (229, 251). Particularly grating to establishment sensibilities must have been Berns's pronouncement that liberal jurisprudence proceeds on the assumption that there is "a basic right or even a natural right" to freedom of speech, to which Berns countered: "No citizen has a right to free speech." He urged on his readers the proposition that the "only reasonable" way to read the First Amendment's apparently absolutist language is in quite other terms: "Congress shall extend freedom to all good speech" (250–51).

Whether or not Berns's conclusions are precisely what Strauss's would have been, it is easy to see the ways in which Berns's work represents an effort to practice the kind of political science Strauss called for: it is a public-spirited intervention, based on knowledge of political philosophy, intended not only to provide insight into our political life, but also to supply guidance for the improvement of political practice. It is a call for a return to "ancient wisdom" (*FVFA*, 252, 255). Berns's book brims over with the confidence and the enthusiasm derived from an inner sense of new and deeper insight, of a new wisdom of transformative power. It is a book, moreover, that self-confidently challenges all conservative orthodoxy just as much as the liberal orthodoxies it makes its more obvious targets (6, 229).

It is not difficult to detect the presence of Strauss's syllogism on America in *Freedom, Virtue, and the First Amendment*. Indeed one of the virtues of the book is its effort—and large degree of success—in putting real flesh on Strauss's sketchily presented views on America. The intellectual scaffolding of the book is Strauss's distinction between ancient and modern political philosophy (*FVFA*, 228, 240). America, Berns had no doubts, was a society founded on the modern philosophy, on the liberal theory of law originated by Hobbes and slightly modified by Locke (245). This Lockean political philosophy "finds expression within . . . the American Constitution"; the Declaration of Independence endorses Lockean-liberal conceptions of politics (246). The entire Lockean-liberal tradition conceives of freedom as the highest good of political life, and government appears largely in the guise of a threat to freedom or, at best, as a "necessary evil" to maintain the peace (157, 164, 228). The Declaration of Independence is noteworthy for expressing "the [liberal] attitude of distrust of government" (157).

Berns broadened the discourse about freedom of speech and press by setting the concern for free speech clearly within the context of his larger Strauss-derived theories on the nature of modernity. American liberal "judicial practice . . . is . . . based on" these modern theories (*FVFA*, 248). "Liberalism . . . has its origin in the natural rights philosophies of the seventeenth century" (45). The libertarians, in particular, have adapted basic Lockean theory to entail the proposition "that freedom of speech is a basic right, or even a natural right, which is everyman's birthright simply because he is born into the world" (248). The libertarians consistently approach issues of regulation of speech with the broader liberal mind-set that freedom is always good, government always a danger. From such an attitude derive the favored libertarian constitutional doctrines for settling First Amendment questions: the clear and present danger test, the "preferred position doctrine," and the absolutist "no law means no law" mantra of Justice Black (67).

Moreover, Berns endorses Strauss's second proposition: modernity is bad. For example, he speaks of "the modern and vulgar tradition of the political philosophy of John Locke," a much more dismissive turn of phrase than Strauss ever used (*FVFA*, 96). The Lockean philosophy of the Declaration of Independence, "by concentrating attention on one political problem, . . . tends to conceal others of equal importance and, so far as the United States is concerned, of greater relevance" (156). The liberal philosophy wrongly elevates freedom to the top of the list of political goods and obscures the central question: "how man becomes civilized, or what is the role of government in the civilizing process" (159). The modern theory underlying the American regime is based on "precepts [which] would not conflict with man's passions." The resulting theory of law and government is "amoral"; this deep-going amorality is the real but perhaps concealed basis for the bias toward freedom within modern philosophy and politics (245).

The liberal theory is doubly defective. It fails normatively, for freedom, as an amoral good connected to the passions, cannot be the highest human good (*FVFA*, 28, 244). It is "alien to civilization" (245). It fails as the highest political virtue, because freedom is not equivalent to justice, or is not the totality of the common good (46–48, 125, 127, 129, 161–63). The liberal theory underlying the American regime, American law, and the activities of the Supreme Court is vulgar and false. It depends on "untenable principles" (166).

Liberal theory fails descriptively as well. The liberal aim to maximize freedom and treat government simply as a threat to freedom "failed because of the demands of social life, the demands of justice. They failed because American law-makers recognize, however dimly, the role of law in the civilizing process; because they recognize the necessary relation between law and custom; because they recognize that man is not a being who is naturally good, a being who needs no guidance, or who may be left free to live as he will" (*FVFA*, 247). The truths about humanity and the needs of social and political life obtrude themselves, willy-nilly, into the awareness of political leaders (242). That is in accord with Strauss's view that human beings have an awareness of their natural end and do not require theory to find their way in the world of practice. Berns, like Strauss, sees that in modern times false theories interpose, distorting and occluding sound intimations of practical principles of action. His intervention is meant to counter false theory and thereby arm and guide the natural awareness that pokes through even in a regime as doggedly modern in its foundations as America. Berns attempts to show his readers that the liberal theories, which loom so large for them, are "erroneous" and that they—his readers—should look to "the wisdom of the ancients," especially the wisdom of Aristotle in place of Locke, and behind Locke, of Hobbes (154, 155, 159, 164). Contrary to what the Declaration of Independence says, "man is by nature not an individual with inalienable rights, but a political being, who can achieve his nature, his end, only in the *polis* [political community], if at all" (247).

Berns adds to Strauss's analyses the demonstration that the Supreme Court, in its attempts to construe the First Amendment, illustrates anew the dual failings of liberal theory. The judicial libertarians, according to Berns, are particularly disappointing on the normative side of their task; they cannot give an account of why freedom, or freedom of speech, is such a great good or the highest good. They tend to fall back on selective quotations from libertarian authorities—Jefferson or Milton or Mill—or on literal readings of the constitutional text. They prove unable, also, to maintain their libertarian commitments in practice. At the time of his writing, Berns was of the opinion that the profreedom position was definitively on the wane, because it was untenable in the face of the real needs of governing. This, like several other of his prognostications, proved to be false, for the Warren Court's expansion of speech and press freedom was just around the corner (*FVFA*, 127, 129).

Berns stands as the first formulation of what evolved into East Coast Straussianism, because he hesitates to endorse Strauss's third proposition, "America is good." Berns took Strauss's first two propositions too seriously to do that. In his book we find echoes of many of the Straussian caveats regarding the first two propositions that allowed Strauss himself to be more positive about America. Berns endorses the comparative judgment that "not only is the American regime more just than the Soviet regime, but the latter is unjust—it is a tyranny" (*FVFA*, 219). Berns also recognizes the "residues" on which Strauss had put substantial weight, but he seems even more pessimistic about them than Strauss was (234–35n5). Moreover, Berns has an even stronger notion than Strauss himself that the non-modern truth about politics imposes itself on persons in political life who are attempting to govern. Thus the Supreme Court, at some distance from the day-to-day business of governance, is more vulnerable to the deleterious effects of bad theory than are mayors and police chiefs. For this reason, Berns has some sympathy with the Frankfurter judicial-restraintist wing of the Court; this bloc is more likely to give governors the space to do what they see they need to do. Yet Berns has surprisingly strong reservations about the Frankfurter bloc as well. The American regime is not set up to produce the good character and prudence in citizens that a good Aristotelian regime would. Even when they operate relatively freely (emphasis on "relatively," in America) from the liberal-regime theory, American governors tend to fall short of justice and the common good in ways that a Supreme Court could set straight if it was more intelligently guided by a better political philosophy. In light of his later sympathies with originalism and judicial restraint, Berns is surprisingly eager in the mid-1950s to see the Court play an activist role beyond the Constitution. Contrary to Frankfurter, who insisted that wisdom and constitutionality are not necessarily the same and that the Court is properly concerned only with the latter, Berns looks to the court to "unite constitutionality and wisdom" (189). Since the Constitution itself is (mainly) based on defective modern philosophy, this task seems to open up a great sphere of judicial action beyond the positive law. He cites approvingly the example of Abraham Lincoln, who "would ask that the Constitution be interpreted by the Court so that wisdom and constitutionality merge on the level of wisdom" (190). That is to say, wisdom trumps the Constitution when they are not identical. "Lincoln was right," Berns holds, "when he interpreted the Constitution according to natural justice" (191).

In other words, Berns sees the Supreme Court, if properly instructed, to be a vehicle for greatly improving the regime by bringing to bear the wisdom and natural justice it tends to lack. Without interventions by the Court, and the prior intervention of Berns and before him of Strauss, the American regime is doomed to be very defective. It shares in, even if it transcends in some ways, the defectiveness of the modern political philosophy it imbibed so deeply. For Berns the only real hope seems to be a large-scale shift in opinions and law from its grounding in early modern political philosophy to Aristotle, who, Berns insists, provides very different guidance on politics than Americans are used to.

As powerful a statement as *Freedom, Virtue, and the First Amendment* is, it is difficult not to see flaws in it as an adumbration of the Straussian perspective. Although Berns's book is unthinkable without Strauss's work as background, Berns's work nonetheless seems to miss some of the important themes in Strauss's work. The difference is first visible in the shift in Berns's book toward a less affirmative view of America. What, we are wondering, produces this difference? Perhaps the answer lying closest to the surface, which nonetheless is an answer that goes quite deep, is the relative role of Plato and Aristotle in Strauss and Berns. A glance at the index to his book shows Plato hardly to be a presence for Berns, whereas Aristotle is appealed to as *the* ancient alternative to the moderns. In one sense, this is in accord with Strauss's own work, for he emphasizes Aristotle as the appropriate guide for political scientists; yet it also misses the way in which Plato is of greater authority for Strauss and the way Strauss tends to read Aristotle in light of Plato.[10] Berns's appeal to Aristotle over Plato (surprisingly) accounts for the less moderate character of his argument, for the higher hopes for an intervention and reorientation of political life, and for a willingness to appeal to the Court to go beyond the law in the name of wisdom and justice. For Strauss, Plato taught, above all, the limits of politics. Those limits derived more than anything else from the unlikelihood of the rule of wisdom or the wise in politics. Because the legitimate transcendence of law toward wisdom is not in the cards, Strauss very firmly settles on rule of law and constitutionalism as the sine qua non of healthy politics. Strauss would be unlikely to call for the Supreme Court to transform itself into aspiring philosopher-kings, transcending the decent if not morally inspiring American constitutional order. Strauss would emphasize the positive side of the American order and the relative strengths of first-wave modern philosophy, as Berns does not.

Berns, we think, goes beyond Strauss in ways that are questionable from a Straussian perspective, but in doing so he is responding to an ambiguity in Strauss's own thought. On the one side, Strauss emphasized the need to reconceive the history of philosophy with an eye to a "return to the ancients." He sees this return as "the last best hope" for the best kind of regime of modern times, liberal democracy. At the same time, he emphasizes the limits of politics and, unlike Berns, emphasizes the flexible character of classical political philosophy. The best regime is an object to be prayed for, but not one to be expected or, in most concrete circumstances, to be expressly sought. Strauss's notion of a "return to the ancients" is meant to supply the basis for an intervention in political life, but the character of that intervention remains in the shadows. Berns took the leap toward a full-scale attempt at reorientation. That is certainly true to something in Strauss, but it both misses the countervailing limits Strauss saw to such interventions and downplays many of the considerations Strauss had raised that allowed him to conclude, in a spirit of sobriety and caution, that America, despite its modernity, is good.

Martin Diamond: Finding the Founding

Martin Diamond was the first student of Strauss to publish extensively on the American founding, a topic that afterward became a frequent one for other Strauss-influenced scholars. So substantial did the Straussian writing on the founding become that in 1987 Gordon Wood could title a review of a number of books on the topic "A Straussian Bicentennial." In 1959 Diamond published an essay, "Democracy and *The Federalist*," that proved to be quite influential in the field. He followed that up with a large number of studies on the *Federalist*, including the essay on that work in the *History of Political Philosophy* coedited by Strauss and his colleague Joseph Cropsey.[11] Although Diamond's work on the founders has proved to be controversial, it has also had a large impact on the field.

Diamond was among the earliest of Strauss's students to turn his attention away from the heady topics in the history of political philosophy on which the group had largely focused earlier; he very self-consciously saw his turn to the noncanonic founding materials as in line with, if not perhaps strictly mandated by, Strauss's own approach to political science. Two lines of thought at or near the core of Strauss's recovered Socratism pushed Diamond in this direction. He took seriously Strauss's emphasis on *political* philosophy, that is, on the thesis that philosophical inquiry always occurs as a politically situated activity. As Strauss put it, political philosophy is philosophy that takes seriously the *problem* of political philosophy and the city. The political community is not and can never be philosophical; philosophy by its nature is at least potentially in conflict with the city. Political philosophy is philosophy that comports itself both prudently and justly in the face of that conflict. Both necessity (the vulnerability and dependence of philosophy on the city) and justice (the duty to return good for good, or at least to do no harm) require that philosophy self-consciously accommodate itself to the city. Diamond spoke of this accommodation as a kind of "coming to terms" with the polity. "The way to come to respectable terms . . . is to give the decent polity and its constitutive opinions a central and respected place in the teaching of political things." At the least, philosophical inquiry and the education built on or leading to it gives due honor and respect to the "constitutive opinions" of the community, in the case of America to "the founding documents of this political order, the Declaration of Independence and the Constitution."[12]

This kind of accommodation is not merely a matter of prudence and justice, however. "To come to such terms is also in principle the dialectically sound way to begin the educational ascent."[13] Diamond clearly means to evoke Socrates' account of the ascent from the cave. Strauss taught that the beginning point for political philosophical inquiry is neither the Cartesian cogito nor the modern social scientist's equivalent, "raw behavior." Political inquiry begins with opinion and attempts to ascend to the truth to which the opinion points, or which it confusedly contains, for political opinion contains "a rational intimation of what is really just."[14] The model is Socrates, who began by examining the opinions of the Athenians. Diamond was famous for a quip to the effect that certain of his contemporaries who misunderstand the Socratic method do the same—study politics via an examination of the opinions of the Athenians. To follow Socrates and Strauss today requires not beginning with the Athenians, but with the opinions of the Americans, and subjecting them to Socratic scrutiny. One must begin with what is one's own, with what is naturally familiar, and move toward the philosophic universal from there.

Just as with Berns's *Freedom, Virtue, and the First Amendment*, the tracks of Strauss's three propositions are evident throughout Diamond's early work. Diamond emphatically identified America with modernity: "The American regime is a paradigm of modernity. It is in a way *the* modern regime. The American things are particularly instinct with the virtues and vices that modern men must understand." The American founders, Diamond concluded, were "thoughtful partisans of modernity."[15] Diamond consistently and without hesitation attributed to the founders a commitment to a "new 'science of politics,'" which he identified unequivocally with modern political philosophy.[16] The founders, or the leading ones among that generation, were "men learned in the new science of politics." With regard to the "new science," Diamond always emphasized how "deeply indebted" he was "to the late Professor Leo Strauss, whose instructive account of the 'battle of the books,' ancient and modern, has done so much to restore to our understanding the meaning of the modern enterprise." "The American Founding," Diamond insisted, must be understood "in the context of . . . this new science of politics."[17] He saw the Americans' adherence to the new science of politics as an integral part of the modern break with earlier theory and practice. He followed Strauss in understanding modernity as a "lowering of the aims and expectations of politics" in favor of the greater likelihood of achieving the end in view. The new science took its bearing not "from the highest possibilities of human nature," but rather took an "aggressively more 'realistic'" idea of human nature. The new science would take human beings as they actually are, accepting the self-interestedness and passion displayed by all people everywhere as primary in their nature, and, on that basis, work out decent political solutions.[18]

The identification of the founders as practitioners of the "new science of politics" provided Diamond with his chief thread through the maze of the founding. His first essay on the *Federalist* had as its dominant goal the overturning of the then popular view that the Constitution represented a "Thermidorean" reaction against the democratic aspirations and achievements of the Revolution. One piece of evidence often cited in favor of that view was an alleged retreat from a commitment to democracy in the Declaration of Independence to an antidemocratic bias in the Constitution and in the theoretical document explaining the Constitution, the *Federalist*. Diamond contested both sides of that claim, and used insights derived from Strauss's studies of modern political philosophy to do so. Thus, whereas the Progressive historians took it for granted that the Declaration was a democratic document, Diamond used his knowledge of the political philosophy of John Locke to help attain a more adequate understanding of the Declaration: "The Declaration, although it is now seen as the very embodiment of the democratic spirit, was in fact neutral with regard to the democratic form of government." The authors of the Declaration were "following John Locke's social contract theory, which taught the right of the people to establish any form of government they chose."[19]

Diamond reversed the reigning judgment of the historians. The constitution was actually more, not less, democratic, more firmly committed to democracy than the Declaration of Independence was.[20] Diamond picked up on and took seriously the many statements in the *Federalist* and other sources about the necessity to found a "wholly republican" or "popular" constitutional order, which would achieve the substantive ends governments are to achieve (e.g., secure rights) and at the same time overcome the deficiencies that theory and practice had identified as typical of popular regimes (e.g., majority tyranny). Indeed, Diamond saw the commitment to popular government and modern political philosophy to be intimately connected. Premodern politics had "traditionally considered . . . a wide range of non-economic tasks [to be among] the decisive business of government." Modern political philosophy of the Lockean variety, however, had reduced the proper tasks to "security" and "happiness," with the latter understood "to consist primarily in physical preservation from external and internal danger *and* in the comforts afforded by a commercial society; which comforts are at once the dividends of security and the means to a republican rather than repressive security."[21] Diamond took the reduction of the ends ("the lowering of the sights") to be the means of reconciliation to democracy: "the traditional criticism of popular government was that it gave over the art of government into the hands of the many, which is to say the unwise. It would be a formidable reply to reduce the complexity of the governmental art to dimensions more commensurate with the capacity of the many."[22] That is indeed the "reply" Diamond thought the founders gave, the reply that allowed them to be much friendlier to democracy than previous generations of wise and prudent statesmen and political thinkers had been.

Diamond found tracks of modern realism all through the *Federalist*. For example, in *Federalist* 43 "the great principle of self-preservation" is pronounced the basis for the objects and aims of "all political institutions." Diamond takes this to be "perhaps the most explicitly fundamental utterance of *The Federalist*."[23] He finds the founders to have revised their notion of the means to successful politics in the modern direction, along with their revision of the ends. Instead of relying on a strenuous moral education aimed at "bringing toward completeness or perfection the relative few who were actually capable of fulfilling their humanness," the American founders followed the modern political philosophers in building on the far more universal and reliable passions and interests of humanity. "Employing the 'new science of politics,'" Madison had discovered in "'interest'" its latent possibility."[24] Diamond summed up the general character of the Americans' "new science of politics" in a quip by Strauss: "From the point of view of modern thought, [Strauss] says, 'what you need is not so much formation of character and moral appeal as the right kind of institutions, institutions with teeth in them.' The Americans followed [the moderns] in their reliance on institutions, and not the ancients regarding the necessity of character formation."[25] That is to say, the most pervasive presence of "the new science of politics" in the American regime is not this or that particular institution, but the thorough reliance on institutions as such, institutions of a sort which, as Diamond once put it, "smacked much of 'private vice public good.'" As Diamond emphasized, Madison rejected a reliance on "moral or religious motives."[26]

Madison's famous argument in *Federalist* 10 for an extended republic was always taken by Diamond to be the high point of the founders' political wisdom, and it was a "solution" that breathed the spirit of the new science of politics through and through. It was the classic instance of the eschewal of moral and religious qualities and the reliance instead on self-interest as properly structured in institutions. The same could be said for the separation of powers.

In his early work Diamond also strongly endorsed Strauss's reservations about modernity, and thus, having identified the founders so definitively with the modern political project, he expressed grave reservations about the American foundations. In his 1959 essay "Democracy and *The Federalist*," Diamond emphasized the lowered ends of politics sought within modern political philosophy. "Other political theorists had ranked highly among the legitimate objects of government, the nurturing of a particular religion, education, military courage, civic spiritedness, moderation, individual excellence in the virtues, etc. On all of these *The Federalist* is either silent or has in mind only pallid versions of the original, or even seems to speak with contempt." Perhaps because of his own background in socialist politics, Diamond was very impressed with the way in which Madison's version of "the new science" represents "a beforehand answer to Marx": "Madison's solution to his problem worked astonishingly well. The danger he wished to avert has been averted and largely for the reasons he gave."[27] Yet Diamond hardly paused to dwell on Madison's successes; he may have succeeded in solving the problem of majority tyranny (and class warfare), but "it is possible to question now whether he did not take too narrow a view of what the dangers were.... We may yet wonder whether he failed to contemplate other equally grave problems of democracy." Although Diamond does not specify what these other "grave problems" are, we can note here strong echoes of Strauss's own reservations about the modern democratic venture. Diamond also wonders "whether his remedy for the one disease had not some unfortunate collateral consequences."[28] Diamond had in mind here "the reliance on ceaseless striving after immediate interest," a striving which, as Tocqueville pointed out, robs society of "that calm ... which is necessary for the deeper combinations of the intellect." Again, the evidence of Strauss's concerns with the very highest human possibility, the pursuit of philosophy, is very visible here. Diamond, in a word, joined Strauss in decrying the lowering of sights, the loss of moral dignity that is the price for social peace in the modern order. The founders' "liberalism and republicanism are not the means by which men may ascend to a nobler life; rather they are simply instrumentalities which solve Hobbesean problems in a more moderate manner."[29]

Diamond even doubted the merits of the Madisonian solution as a means to its own political ends. The founders, he thought, made "a powerful distinction . . . between the qualities necessary for founders and the qualities necessary for the men who came after." The founders required great virtues—dedication to the public good and immense political wisdom—but those who came after them, they seemed to think, could get by with much less—that self-interest on which Madison so heavily relied and a "veneration" for the system within which they acted. "The reason of the founders constructs the system within which the passions of the men who come after may be relied on." Diamond, however, did not believe this to be sufficient provision for the "perpetuation" of the regime. "Does not the intensity and kind of our modern problems seem to require of us a greater degree of reflection and public-spiritedness than the founders thought sufficient for the men who came after them?"[30] Diamond thus seems headed toward recognition of a need to transcend or supplement the founders in the direction of the ancients. In any case, Diamond in the late 1950s and early '60s endorsed the view that America, because modern, falls short of the politically best.

Nonetheless, the overall impression left by Diamond's early works, and of his corpus as a whole, for that matter, is not a negative judgment on America. Equally or perhaps more strongly present were echoes of Strauss's third proposition: America is good. That impression of a positive assessment of American foundations derives in large part from Diamond's point of departure. Like Berns before him, Diamond took reigning liberal orthodoxy in his sphere of inquiry as his polemical starting point. Thus, just as Berns started with the intraliberal battle on the Supreme Court over speech and press freedom, so Diamond started with the views about the American founding sponsored by the Progressive historians. By the mid-fifties the study of the founding had securely belonged to historians of the Progressive persuasion, Charles Beard and his heirs, for roughly a half century. "Beard's influence was immense and . . . his argument came to be treated as having settled the fundamental question," concluded Diamond. Beard's was "the conventional wisdom on the subject."[31]

Diamond objected frequently and strenuously to the chief substantive conclusions of the Beardians—that the Constitution was an aristocratic or oligarchic reaction against the democratic forces and ideas that made the Revolution, that the Constitution was the product of the personal and class interests of the wealthy, designed to protect their own property from troublesome democratic majorities. Indeed it would not be too much of an exaggeration to say that Diamond's chief conclusions were meant above all to place a negative sign to all that the Progressives had said.

Diamond was quite explicit in identifying his goals in countering the Progressive views of America. As their name suggests, the Progressives were committed to progress, which in the context of their study of the founding meant an effort to free the United States from the authority of the founding so it would be freer to progress, to change. The Progressives thus emphasized the "surpassability" of the founders. Their position was moderately complex in that they had two rather different kinds of critiques of the authority of the founders. First, they argued that whatever the merits of Washington, Jefferson, Madison, and the others, circumstances in the United States were so drastically different in the twentieth century that what might have been a suitable set of institutions and a suitable philosophy in the eighteenth century no longer were so. The founders' Constitution was tied to political practices no longer viable—for example, extreme decentralization through federalism, fragmentation of authority through separation of powers, and the narrow-minded protection of property through an old-fashioned doctrine of natural rights. The development of a national, industrial economy, replete with dislocations and injustices, required effective exercise of national political power.

The founders' Constitution was not only outdated, they argued further, but also had been designed to achieve improper ends. It was not mere coincidence that the Constitution thwarted national action and protected property, empowered the wealthy and set barriers against democratic majorities—these were the very qualities it was meant to have. As Beard so famously put it, the framers' Constitution was designed to protect and enrich themselves and men like themselves against threats posed by a democratically empowered majority. Worship of the founders as "our fathers," benevolent and wise, stood in the way of progress, and Beard's exposé was meant to help the country overcome its own past.

The Progressives taught anything but a usable past. Although by the time Diamond wrote, others had contested one or another element of the Beardian past (e.g., there had been studies contesting Beard's construal of the economic interests of the founders), Diamond was probably the first to challenge Beard at the comprehensive level of Beard's own argument. Diamond quite explicitly rejected Beard's chief conclusion: according to Diamond the past was eminently usable, or in his term, "available to us for the study of modern problems."[32] The founders remain available and, in a way, necessary, for they carry both the authority of the founding and a wisdom that has not been surpassed within the American tradition. The usable past, the recapturing of the founding, is for Diamond a rough equivalent to Strauss's rediscovery of the ancients. In both cases, the beginning is seen as the reservoir for a wisdom superior to any available in the present, but a beginning that must be rewon in the face of progressivist prejudices that steadfastly reject the beginning as superseded.

Diamond differed from Berns, then, in not seeing the contemporary liberal orthodoxy he was opposing as a version or direct descendant of the founding modern political philosophic principles. It was a misunderstanding, a falling away, a diminished theory of politics. Thus Diamond attempted to recover the founders and the American foundation as superior and available to us, whereas Berns aimed to uncover the foundations as the unrecognized source of modern error.

So it was no accident that Diamond opened his piece "Democracy and *The Federalist*" with a concise typology of ways in which the founders might, or might not, be relevant to us: (1) They can be more or less completely adequate and relevant; (2) their principles can be basically sound, but modern developments require some modifications in their position; (3) modern developments may have made them completely "obsolete"; or (4) "they may have been wrong or radically inadequate even for their own time." The Progressives had, in effect, taken the third and fourth positions. Berns had, in the main, taken the fourth. In setting up his essay in this way, Diamond clearly signals his concerns with the abiding relevance of the founders, but it is not clear that he endorses any of the four alternatives he lays out. It is clear that his substantive findings about the founding do lead to the rejection of some of his propositions, for what is most striking about his conclusions is how they make the founders rather like New Deal Democrats. In the essay on democracy, he established their bona fides as democrats, committed to popular government and majority rule but wisely aware of some of the dangers of democracy, as the Progressives were not. Likewise, in his early works, he forwarded the remarkable and very influential claim that the leading founders were not committed to federalism but were solid nationalists, who settled for the federal features of the Constitution only because they had to and who firmly expected and hoped that the system would evolve in a more purely national direction. The Progressive story of American history as movement toward greater democracy and centralization against the wishes of the founders and against the original constitutional order was thus incorrect.[33] The modern democratic, centralized polity was perfectly in accord with the best founders' intents. They were enough like us that insofar as they were an authority—and Diamond saw them as such—they lent authority to our contemporary politics; and insofar as they were like us but wiser, we could be improved by listening to them.[34]

More than Strauss himself, Diamond was willing to connect the good-ness of American foundations with the grounding in modern political phi-losophy. He clearly was impressed—more than impressed—by the institu-tional solution Madison found to the most pressing and difficult problem of popular government, the theory of the extended commercial republic. Thus far we can see in Diamond's early works the seeds from which grew the position we are calling Midwest Straussianism. Nonetheless, the affir-mative judgment of American foundations and of the approach to poli-tics taken within modern political philosophy was matched and perhaps trumped in Diamond's early work by his simultaneous endorsement of the Strauss-identified defects of modern political philosophy and therewith of the American regime founded upon it.

In his early work, Diamond's mode of reconciling these various threads was best captured in a programmatic statement in his essay "Democ-racy and *The Federalist.*" The "political thought of the Founding Fa-thers...remains the finest American thought on political matters." That is to say, it is better than the reigning liberal orthodoxies, such as Pro-gressivism. "In studying [the founding fathers] we may raise ourselves to their level, for achieving their level we may free ourselves from limitations that, ironically, they tended to impose on us, that is, in so far as we tend to be creatures of the society they founded. And in so freeing ourselves we may be enabled, if it is necessary, to go beyond their wisdom."[35] From Strauss Diamond took the idea that it was indeed "necessary to go beyond their wisdom," but Diamond never had a clear statement of what going be-yond the founders would mean concretely, or at least he never presented it. That was a task at which Harry Jaffa proved far more successful than Diamond in his 1959 study *Crisis of the House Divided.* In Diamond's case, it is difficult not to sense that although he repeated the words about the limitations of modernity, there was always a bit of a mismatch between the words and the music. In any event, his views about America continued to be marked by a certain tension that he came close to resolving only late in his life.

Harry Jaffa: Aristotelianizing America

Harry Jaffa's *Crisis of the House Divided* appeared in the same year as Di-amond's essay on the *Federalist.* His focus of attention was not the found-ing, but what Herbert Storing, another of Strauss's students, called "the refounding," the political thought and statesmanship of Abraham Lincoln in the context of the Civil War crisis.

Jaffa was one of Strauss's first students, receiving his PhD at the New School for Social Research in New York, the institution where Strauss taught from 1938 to 1948 before he moved to the University of Chicago. Before publishing his book on Lincoln, Jaffa had written a highly regarded study, *Thomism and Aristotelianism*, which was an effort to show that Thomas Aquinas's Christian commitments led him to modify Aristotle a good deal more than he admitted to doing. Jaffa's *Crisis of the House Divided* was a study of the famous Lincoln-Douglas debates on the eve of the American Civil War. During the 1850s the conflict over slavery, especially over the spread of slavery into new territories and from there into new states of the Union to be constructed from these territories, became the major feature of American politics. Every effort to admit a new state to the Union led to a renewed battle in Congress and throughout the country about slavery and its extension. Stephen A. Douglas, the Democratic senator from Illinois, a very powerful member of Congress, attempted to deflect this increasingly political conflict by promulgating a new doctrine and a policy to deal with it. In place of the previous policy, the so-called Missouri Compromise approach, which banned slavery outright in certain of the territories of the United States, Douglas proposed his doctrine of popular sovereignty. Under this doctrine Congress was not to settle such questions; the local inhabitants of the territories or new states themselves were to do so.

Douglas justified his policy on the grounds not only that it would pacify national politics, but also that it rested on the true principles of political right underlying the American political system, the doctrine of popular sovereignty. In America, the people rule; they should make fundamental decisions for themselves and not be subject to a distant majority in Washington. In the Kansas-Nebraska Act of 1854, Douglas managed to win repeal of the Missouri Compromise principle and replace it with his popular-sovereignty doctrine.

The repeal of the Missouri Compromise moved Abraham Lincoln, retired from public life after several terms in the Illinois State Legislature and one term in the U.S. Congress, to return to politics. He "hated" the new Douglas principle of popular sovereignty, for he saw it as nothing other than the old doctrine that might makes right: the legislative majority, the strongest force in the community, may rightfully enact whatever it desires, even if at the expense of the rights of others.[36] Lincoln spoke out loudly and often against the Douglas position all during the 1850s. In 1858 Lincoln and Douglas became rival candidates for the U.S. Senate. This election provided the occasion for the formal debates between them.

These debates have long been held to be among the high points of American political history, a judgment with which Jaffa very definitely concurred. He added philosophic depth to the analyses the debates had already attracted. Lincoln and Douglas not only debated the merits of their respective immediate policies; the debates rose to the level of examining and advocating competing theories of the overall meaning of American political life, with Douglas championing popular will as the core and Lincoln championing equality and universal rights.

Jaffa's book was far more ambitious, however, than a mere description of its subject matter conveys. He aimed at nothing less than bringing to bear on America the methods and substance of the Straussian revival of the Socratic tradition of political philosophy. Jaffa's book is arguably very close to what Strauss implied for the study of America. It contains the main elements of Strauss's position: the modernity of the American founders; the tendency of that modernity to degenerate into politically and morally unhealthy (and theoretically inadequate) doctrines, such as Douglas's doctrine of popular sovereignty; and the need to recognize the limitations and liabilities of the modernity of the founding and to replace that with a more Aristotelian or more classical political philosophy, as supplied by Jaffa's Lincoln.

Crisis of the House Divided is a celebration of Lincolnian statesmanship, which Jaffa presents in large part as the effort by Lincoln to fix American public opinion on the proposition to which the nation in 1776 became dedicated: "that all men are created equal."[37] Lincoln's effort was required because Stephen Douglas, among others, was attempting to replace that dedication with commitment to the principle of popular sovereignty, that is, the principle that a community may rightly do whatever its majority wishes to do, including the claim that it may rightly enslave some, that it may deny the proposition that all men are created equal, and, at bottom, that it may deny all natural substantive standards of right (*CHD*, 317). Jaffa's Lincoln calls Americans to resist the Little Giant's siren song and urges instead a restoration of the "ancient faith of our fathers."

Given that strong emphasis on restoration, it is striking how prominent a feature of *Crisis* is the critique of the founders attributed by Jaffa to Lincoln. Jaffa's Lincoln is no antiquarian: while apparently calling the nation back to its "ancient faith," he is in fact rejecting the old and putting forward a new faith. Jaffa's critique and reformulation of the founders' views is complex, for he presents, in effect, two different critiques and reformulations, one far more radical than the other, one inspired, one might say, by Kant, the other by Aristotle. The more radical one appears first in

Crisis, in a section significantly titled "The Political Philosophy of a Young Whig." Jaffa, as a student of Leo Strauss, does not throw the title of "political philosopher" around lightly; Jaffa includes Lincoln in the narrow and select circle of true philosophers. The less radical version of the critique of the founders occurs later in the book, in the context of the presentation of "The Case for Lincoln," that is, Lincoln's position in the Lincoln-Douglas debates. As a participant in these debates, and in political action as such, Lincoln acts more the part of the statesman than that of the philosopher. It is perhaps not surprising that the less radical critique of the founders occurs in the context of Lincoln the statesman, and the more radical in the context of Lincoln the political philosopher. It is, in any case, noteworthy, again in the context of Jaffa's relation to Strauss, that he in effect casts Lincoln as a "philosopher-statesman," if not quite as a philosopher-king. Reversing the order of Jaffa's presentation, we propose to consider first the less and then the more radical version of the critique of the founders. That order will best bring out the tension between the two critiques and the distinction Jaffa sees between the task of the philosopher and that of the statesman, a distinction that has important implications for his own work.

The point of departure for both critiques is the same Strauss-inspired move we have seen at the foundation of Berns's and Diamond's work, the identification of the founders as Lockeans, all of whom "read the Declaration [of Independence] as an expression of the sentiments of Locke's *Second Treatise of Civil Government*" (*CHD*, 314). As Lockeans, the founders affirmed two doctrines that Jaffa claims Lincoln did not accept: they understood the proposition that "all men are created equal" as equivalent to the Lockean doctrine of the state of nature, and they understood natural rights in the Hobbesian-Lockean manner as "an indefeasible desire or passion" (319, 329). In Lockean theory the state of nature is a state of equality because it is a condition in which no person rightly can claim authority over any other.[38] "The equality, which all men are in, [is] in respect of jurisdiction or dominion one over another . . . being that equal right that every man hath to his natural freedom, without being subjected to the will or authority of any other man."[39] Lockean-Jeffersonian equality is thus the beginning point; the movement into civil society is a movement away from it, indeed is an abrogation of it, for the coming of government is the coming of legitimate authority of some over others. For Lincoln, however, according to Jaffa, equality is not that *from which* we move but that *to which* a just society moves. As Lincoln said in the Gettysburg Address, the nation is "*dedicated* to the proposition that all men are created equal." That dedication is forward-looking, not merely a status to be left behind. Jaffa relies heavily on Lincoln's theory about what the founders meant to achieve regarding equality. "They meant to set up a standard maxim for free society, which should be familiar to all, and revered by all; constantly looked to, constantly laboured for, and even though never perfectly attained, constantly approximated."[40] For Lincoln, equality is an attainment, or what Jaffa often calls "a transcendental goal."[41] Equality is "a condition *toward* which men have a *duty* ever to strive, not a condition *from* which they have a *right* to escape." It is a condition in which "every man [has] an equal right to be treated justly" (320).

The early Jaffa's Lincoln modifies the founders' Hobbesian-Lockean theory of rights in much the same directions. As Jaffa sees it, the rights affirmed in the Declaration do not carry with them any genuine corresponding or correlative duties. The rights, as indefeasible passions, are merely the recognition that human beings are constituted in such a way that the strongest moving forces in them, their passions, drive them to preserve themselves. They cannot be blamed for doing what they cannot help doing. It is right, at least in the sense that it is not wrong, that they do what they must. Rights of this sort impose no obligations on others, however, for they merely pronounce morally blameless the agent who pursues his preservation (*CHD*, 323, 324).

So far as there are quasi-obligations entailed by this theory of rights, they derive from "enlightened self-interest"; they are rules or limitations one should follow in dealing with others, rules that will make one's own preservation more secure (*CHD*, 324–25). "No man," says Jaffa, "from the strictly Lockean standpoint, is under an obligation to respect any other man's unalienable rights until that other man is necessary to the security of his own rights" (325). At best, the "duty" to respect the rights of others is a "hypothetical imperative"; that is, if you wish your rights to be secure, respect the rights of others as the most likely means to that end, under some circumstances at least (327).

Morality thus understood leaves, of course, a large opening for oppressing and even enslaving others. If one can get away with enslaving others without endangering one's own security, then there seems to be no serious moral objection to it (*CHD*, 327). "The widespread lack of moral concern over the moral challenge of Negro slavery to the doctrine of universal rights in the Declaration in the Revolutionary generation can be traced to the egoistic quality of these rights in their Lockean formulation" (*CHD*, 324). Jaffa, it seems, is willing to impugn Lincoln's credentials as an historian, in order to elevate him as a moralist. Lincoln's "rendering of the . . . Founders' meaning . . . cannot be endorsed on historical grounds" (318). But in playing the bad historian, Lincoln "gave a greater consistency and dignity to the position of the signers than was theirs originally" (324).

The core of Lincoln's reformulation, according to Jaffa of the *Crisis*, was contained in the way Lincoln went beyond the Lockean-Jeffersonian hypothetical imperative. "He . . . said, in substance: he who wills freedom for himself must simultaneously will freedom for others. Lincoln's imperative was not only hypothetical; it was categorical as well" (*CHD*, 327). Let us call this Jaffa's (or Lincoln's) "Kantian Moment." According to this Kantian interpretation, duty is coconstituted with rights. It is a genuinely moral doctrine, establishing a duty to respect the rights or recognize the equality of others. This reinterpretation of the founders' rights doctrine seems to be the foundation for the reinterpretation of their equality doctrine: treating others as equal remains a task, ever before us. The Lockean-Jeffersonian theory of equality and rights can accommodate slavery to a remarkable degree, Jaffa has argued, but not so the Kantian-Lincolnian theory of equality and rights.

Yet beneath (or above) the Kantian Lincoln is an Aristotelian Lincoln. That Jaffa is not quite serious about his Kantian Lincoln is indicated by his later outright contradiction of key elements of the critique on which the Kantian Lincoln was built. A prominent part of Jaffa's critique of the founders was the claim that, according to Lockean doctrine, in the state of nature men "have no real duties. . . . Only men bound to each other by the social contract are, in a strict sense, bound to respect each other's unalienable rights" (*CHD*, 323, 325). But later on Jaffa argues quite the contrary point: according to "the conception of the origin of civil society implicit in the Declaration . . . the duty not to injure others and to repay benefits, etc., are duties which men have toward each other irrespective of the bond of civil society. They exist in the state of nature" (378). Now Jaffa is either very confused about what the doctrine of the Declaration is, or he is not quite leveling with us about wherein he thinks Lincoln's critique and modification of the founders lie.

The evidence supports the latter supposition, for Jaffa presents another critique of the founders' political thinking, which goes much further than his Kantian Lincoln. According to the first critique, Lincoln gives a richer, fuller, more morally satisfying interpretation of the defining claim of America: "all men are created equal." In the second critique, Jaffa's Lincoln denies the truth of that proposition—men are not created equal. In his youthful address, "The Perpetuation of Our Political Institutions," Lincoln described men who "belong to the family of the lion, or the tribe of the eagle," Lincoln is "denying, in a wholly relevant sense, that all men are created equal" (*CHD*, 211). Indeed, Jaffa goes so far as to affirm that Lincoln appears to accept the thesis of Callicles, a character in the Platonic dialogue *Gorgias*. Jaffa summarizes a long Platonic passage as follows: "According to Callicles, a government founded upon a doctrine of equal human rights is a lie, a myth imposed upon the stronger by the weaker, in order to deprive them of the just share to which they would be entitled by their strength" (212–13). The implications of this natural inequality are very great: "The Declaration of Independence affirms the natural equality of men and conceives political obligation in light of that equality. But by equal reason obligation must correspond to inequality if men are as naturally unequal as they are here asserted to be" (213).

Of course, Jaffa's Lincoln comes round to reaffirming equality, but he does so neither on the Hobbesian basis of rights grounded in indefeasible passion, nor on the Kantian ground of universal equal obligation. This version of Lincoln transcends the founders by recapturing the Aristotelian moral horizon, according to which human beings are genuinely unequal and differential political rights justly follow from that fact. This version of Lincoln, then, does not depend on the dubious claim Jaffa made, and later retracted, about rights and duties in the state of nature. Jaffa's contradiction of that theme is his way of subtly indicating the proper grounds (as he sees it) of Lincoln's transcendence and reformation of the founding: not Kant but Aristotle.

Jaffa uses Aristotle (and Plato's Callicles) to transcend the founders' moral and political orientation, but he uses Aristotle then to restore, although on a different plane and with a different meaning, the founders' perspective, or rather Lincoln's commitment to their equality proposition. The truly superior man, the man who embodies human inequality in the highest degree, is the magnanimous man, who does not, like the Caesars, Napoleons, and other lions and eagles, "thirst for distinction," that is, for honor bestowed by his community in the recognition of his right to rule. "Like Aristotle's great-souled man . . . he alone is worthy of the highest honor who holds honor itself in contempt" (*CHD*, 218). The Caesars and Napoleons, in thrall to honor and fame, and thus to the judgment of their putative inferiors, prove themselves thereby not to be superior. The truly superior man does not seek the honor that is rightly his: "For [him] to claim superior rights would be absurd, because such a claim would imply an appetite for those political goods for which [he has] no desire" (222). In a daring move, Jaffa then concludes that "'all men are created equal' remains the decisive *political* truth, because those who with justice might deny it have no motive to deny it, while those who do deny it can only do so because of an unjust motive."[42] It is a "political truth," but not strictly speaking *the* truth. As a political truth, it is rightly affirmed by a statesman; as less than the truth, it is subjected to doubts by the philosopher.

And what would a philosophic writer addressing the political life around him do? He must, it would seem, combine the two roles: he would second the statesman's commitments, knowing all along that in so doing he was saying less than the truth. He would explore the philosopher's doubts, disturbing as little as possible the statesman's commitments. For the most part, this describes Jaffa's manner of speaking in *Crisis*. He introduces, but then in the main passes over in silence, the Aristotelian perspective. But it is only in the main, because he is deeply concerned also to show that the Aristotelian perspective remains relevant to modern political analysis and indeed supplies a basis for the affirmation of liberal republicanism superior to philosophers like Locke and Kant. Therefore Jaffa from time to time not only openly appeals to his Aristotelian perspective but even flaunts it: "The heart of Lincoln's case for popular government is the vindication of the people's cause on the highest grounds which had hitherto been claimed for aristocratic forms" (*CHD*, 306).

Jaffa in *Crisis* set himself an extraordinarily complex task, which produced an attractive, but in many respects historically implausible and philosophically problematical, account of Lincoln in the 1850s. One aspect of his intention required him to expose, even emphasize, the Aristotelian aspect of his enterprise; another required him to conceal it. The result was his Lincoln's vacillating and momentary Lockeanism, Kantianism, and Aristotelianism. One of the deep historical implausibilities of *Crisis* developed out of the corner into which Jaffa's Aristotelian analysis painted him. He was forced to conclude that Lincoln, the truly superior magnanimous man, who thus could save rather than overturn the republic, was not ambitious for honor. But this portrayal of Lincoln hardly fits the man; even Jaffa quotes the famous description by Lincoln's law partner, William Herndon: "That man who thinks Lincoln calmly gathered his robes about him, waiting for the people to call him, has a very erroneous knowledge of Lincoln. He was always calculating and planning ahead. His ambition was a little engine that knew no rest." This does not sound like the man who has "no desire" for the "political goods" of honor, fame, and so on (*CHD*, 222).

Although it would take more space than we have at our disposal to explore the philosophically problematical aspects of *Crisis*, let us mention a few in the Lockean, Kantian, and Aristotelian moments in *Crisis*. One does not know how seriously to take Jaffa's version of Locke or the Lockean founders. In his later work, as we shall see in chapter 7, Jaffa decisively rejects the version contained in *Crisis*, and we have pointed to at least one passage in *Crisis* that contradicts the main line of his argument. Whatever his view of Lockeanism in *Crisis* may be, the presentation he gives is for the most part quite mistaken. He suggests that the notion of equality as the condition of the state of nature is completely different from Lincoln's notion of equality as transcendent goal. This is to miss the notion strongly present in Locke and the American founders that the original equality, indeed to be moved away from, has great and continuing significance in civil society. It requires, the Americans thought, republicanism as the only legitimate government and public policies such as a ban on monopolies, the abolition of primogeniture and entail, the institution of public education, a nonimperialist foreign policy, and so on. Admittedly, not all adherents of the Lockean philosophy saw the same implications of the original equality, but it was certainly a widespread view that there were such. That is, equality for the founders (and Locke) was never merely a condition to be escaped with no lasting significance or implications for civil society.

The Jaffan version of Lockean rights theory is also mistaken. Neither Locke nor the Americans understood rights as Jaffa says they did, namely, as implying no correlative duties. They did suspect that the duty in itself, unless backed up by law, would not suffice to render rights secure, but the question of the efficaciousness of duty is quite different from the question of the existence of duty. Jaffa's "Kantian moment" requires more fleshing out to be philosophically coherent. We suspect he does not expand upon it because this is merely a way station on the road to his Aristotelianism. The Kantian, or Kantlike, elements in Lincoln's thought do, however, deserve more attention.[43]

Finally, there is the Aristotelian argument. The least that one can say here is that Jaffa has developed some Aristotelian themes in a very un-Aristotelian way. Aristotle never drew the conclusions Jaffa does about magnanimity and honor. The man of surpassing virtue deserves surpassing honor, including rule.[44] The magnanimous man is not a man who despises honor; magnanimity is a virtue respecting honor; that is, it is the right way to orient to honor. The magnanimous man is the man of great virtue, who recognizes and accepts his great desert—of honor. He is, indeed, caught in a dilemma, because honor, almost by definition, must come from those who are his inferiors, and therefore it cannot be of full value—as though one were to be paid one's debts in depreciated currency. Nonetheless, the magnanimous man does not turn his back on honor or on his claim of desert of superior position.[45] Of course, Jaffa is not obliged to follow Aristotle precisely, but his claims in *Crisis* to do so are not viable. As Charles Kesler pointed out in an excellent study of Jaffa, the magnanimous man of *Crisis* is not the magnanimous man of Aristotle; Jaffa has transformed Aristotle by adding in Christianity, an addition that works an important transformation indeed.[46] But in *Crisis*, as Kesler suggests, Jaffa does not make this Christian addition thematic.

There are also significant reasons to question Jaffa's interpretation of Lincoln himself. Let us mention one point only: Jaffa's all-important chapter on the Perpetuation Address has as its central theme the "political savior," the hypermagnanimous man who saves republics from Caesars, but the speech it is explicating contains not one word about such a figure. Indeed Jaffa's entire discussion of the political savior per se contains not one citation to or quotation from the speech it is purportedly explicating.[47]

The difficulties Jaffa ran into in *Crisis* were in large part related to his attempt to remain true to the heritage of Strauss. Jaffa of *Crisis* was working within the dualities for which Strauss has become famous: ancients and moderns, Jerusalem and Athens, the city and man. In all three of these cases, Strauss had insisted on emphasizing the differences between the elements in each pair. He was interested not only in the difference between ancients and moderns, for example, but also in making or remaking the case for the ancients, for modern philosophy, in its best forms, was low and ignoble and in its worst forms degenerated into positivism and historicism, thereby undercutting altogether the possibility for philosophy and sound political life. But Strauss had also emphasized, as Jaffa pointed out, that America was modern (Lockean) in its original philosophic inspiration. For whatever reason, perhaps his deep and passionate patriotism, Jaffa was not content with Strauss's lukewarm and hesitant endorsement of America. The project of *Crisis* was defined by Jaffa's attempt to remain true to the deep themes of Strauss's political science but at the same time to arrive at a more elevated view of America. Lincoln, the Aristotelian-philosopher-statesman-refounder, was the solution on which Jaffa hit. The founders were, as Strauss had said, Lockean moderns. Their Lockeanism was highly problematical, even defective. Lincoln transformed the regime in accord with Aristotelian (ancient) principle and himself stood as the highest point therein, the man of consummate virtue whose life and deeds served to vindicate and ennoble what had started out as "solid but low."[48] More than the others, Jaffa was alive to the large tensions in Strauss's project, or at least more deeply responsive to them. The original version of the Straussian project involved locating American origins within the "enlightenment project" and thus implied a limited appreciation for that project. It also contained an open critique and rejection of that project. It involved, therefore, a critique and consequent partial delegitimation of the American origins and therewith of the American regime. The American regime was to be built up and made stronger by pummeling at one of its chief supports. This is particularly a problem in America, for Lincoln only accentuated an ongoing trait of American political culture—the degree to which the political founding stands as a source of common focus, national union, and political legitimacy. But in his effort to enlist Lincoln in a Strauss-inspired reformulation or refounding of America, Jaffa unwittingly fell into a serious self-contradiction. A central part of Lincoln's "refounding" or reformation of the regime is the effort to instill a reverence for the laws and the source of the laws, "the fathers," and the principles on which they based their legislation. One cannot carry out the Lincolnian project by, in effect, discrediting the founders, as Jaffa does. *Crisis of the House Divided* is itself a book divided, a book caught up in a self-contradiction. It tells us: follow Lincoln, the higher path, because the founding was modern and therefore imperfect and inadequate. Yet Lincoln tells us: follow the founders. We are to follow the imperfect founders as a solution to the imperfection of the founders. That self-contradiction led Jaffa to modify his position over time; these modifications led to the creation of West Coast Straussianism.

CHAPTER SEVEN

Straussian Geography

The early Straussian efforts to study America armed with the tools of political philosophy derived from Strauss produced a set of works that, in our judgment, are of considerable merit and lasting importance. All three of those we have discussed—and others of Strauss's first generation of students could be mentioned as well—have contributed in significant ways to the reshaping of their fields of inquiry. Berns, Diamond, and Jaffa all show the power of Strauss's work to open new questions and to provide new tools of inquiry, which contributed to the impact these scholars continue to have. All three also show the marks of attempting to come to grips with the tense legacy of Strauss's teaching on America. We have observed different emphases in the three efforts to do so, but in retrospect their common approach seems more striking than their differences. Later on the differences become far more striking than they were in the 1950s.

The different schools of Straussian Americanists developed primarily as a result of the internal dialectic set in motion by the difficulties we have identified in these early statements. We will treat the later works of Allan Bloom, Harry Jaffa, and Martin Diamond as paradigmatic of the three approaches to the study of American political principles and institutions that gradually developed, each emphasizing two of Strauss's theses more than the other one. We do not attempt to give a comprehensive survey of the many studies of American public policy and institutions undertaken by students of Strauss or their students. We hope to show, among other things, that the Straussians do not form a unitary "sect" with a party line. On the contrary, the attempt to apply Strauss's principles to American politics has stimulated a lively debate among the Straussians.

Although the different "schools" that developed out of the tension among Strauss's three theses are our central focus in this chapter, it must be noted that external events also contributed to the evolution of later

Straussian approaches to American politics. Between the late 1950s, when the Straussian study of America emerged, and the late 1970s and beyond, when the three geographically named schools formed, two events or sets of events occurred which had a very large impact on the development of the Straussian schools. One was the death of Strauss in 1973, after which there was nobody with the authority to say one or the other approaches taken was *the* authoritative or truly valid version of Straussian thought— although there is little evidence that Strauss had intervened in any way before his death to judge among the different lines of thought pursued by his students. Nonetheless, with Strauss himself no longer on the scene, his students felt less need to restrain the expression of disagreement with one another and, we sense, felt freer to follow out their lines of thought wherever they might lead.

The other event, or rather large set of events, is that circus we have come to know as "the sixties." Strauss's students were no more immune from the effects of those large upheavals than the rest of politically literate America. Insofar as Straussians are more aligned with conservatism than liberalism, that alignment mostly occurred in the wake of the sixties.[1] Earlier, Straussians were politically quite divided, with some, like Jaffa, having deep and long-standing conservative roots (he speaks in one place of the effects of reading Hayek's *The Road to Serfdom* and once said that he agreed with Milton Friedman so far as he goes); others, like Berns, Diamond, and Bloom, had liberal roots, were much less market-oriented (indeed some of them were quite hostile to market capitalism), and had been New Deal Democrats for the most part.

The late sixties did have an aligning effect on the Straussians. Even those who remained liberals and Democrats, such as George Anastaplo and William Galston, were to be found in the moderate or conservative wing of the American left. The sixties put great pressure on American political culture, pushing some into a position of intense opposition to the established political order and raising extraordinary hopes for political transformation. One need only recall such manifestations of the "Spirit of the Sixties" as Yale law professor Charles Reich's description of the "Greening of America" and the emergence of a wholly new "Consciousness III," which was supposed to produce a transformation of the human soul in ways that would render the whole previous history of mankind irrelevant. Likewise, there were Bob Dylan, telling us that "the times, they are a-changin'," and John Lennon encouraging us to "imagine" a world without war, greed, private property, or religion. These utopian ideas were not the property of fringe groups—the popularity of Dylan and Lennon speaks for itself;

Reich's reflections on "Consciousness III" originally appeared in the *New Yorker*, not a journal we usually think of as the mouthpiece of chiliastic sects. With the capture of the Democratic party by the George McGovernites in 1972, these sixties ideas proved themselves to have real power in the political arena itself.

Strauss's political doctrines had not appeared to have clear partisan implications; in the presixties era some of his students supported John Kennedy; others, Barry Goldwater. But the sixties circus turned all of them onto more conservative paths. Many Straussians who had formerly been Democrats became Republicans. The hopes and theories of the sixties, unlike earlier political disagreements, aroused almost uniform opposition among Straussians on the basis of Straussian principles. Sixties ideas were utopian through and through, and the main theme of Straussian political philosophy was anti-utopian. Strauss taught that the preeminent political virtue was moderation and the most desirable political arrangement was constitutionalism and the rule of law. The inordinate hopes of the sixties certainly had no room for moderation as the chief political virtue, and life under the aegis of "Consciousness III" had no need for such old-fashioned and constrained things as constitutionalism and the rule of law.

The inordinate hopes of the sixties utopians combined with the inordinate hopes of the social engineers who brought us the Great Society to produce an important intellectual backlash known as neoconservatism. Contrary to much mythology in the press and elsewhere, neoconservatism was not (nor ever has been) dominated by Straussians; but when it emerged, many Straussians sympathized with it, and more than a few became publicly associated with it. Irving Kristol's definition of a neoconservative as "a liberal who had been mugged by reality" could not be applied to Strauss, however. Leading neoconservatives like Daniel Patrick Moynihan or Nathan Glazer had had nothing to do with Strauss, although they tended to share Strauss's deep sense that humanity was unlikely to change as much as the New Left believed and his sense that political life should not be conducted on the basis of unfounded hopes. The most characteristic initial outgrowth of neoconservatism was the journal *The Public Interest*, a journal devoted to the encouragement and promulgation of social science research that soberly assessed the possibilities and limitations of public policies. Although Irving Kristol, one of the founders of *Public Interest*, identified Strauss among the chief influences on him, he said the liberal thinker Lionel Trilling had an equally major influence on him, and he oriented his own political intervention toward social science research. Those who know of Strauss's doubts, even hostility, to social science, should be able to see that the original new conservatism was definitely not a Straussian venture, even if many Straussians could be and were sympathetic to some parts of it.

For the Straussians, then, as for much of the rest of America, the late sixties proved formative and transformative experiences. The three schools of Straussian Americanists were all shaped to some degree by the attempt to come to terms with the charged political culture, as well as by the ongoing effort to grapple with Strauss's legacy.

East Coast

Without any doubt, the best-known student of Strauss is Allan Bloom, and the most widely read (or owned) book produced by anybody influenced by Strauss (including Strauss himself) has been *The Closing of the American Mind*. It certainly bears the marks of the late sixties and seventies. A very prominent part of the book was a chapter called "The Sixties," which was devoted to his very disparaging account of events at Cornell, at the time his home university, when a group of armed students seized the student union building on campus. Much of the rest of the book presents an "idiosyncratic history of the university" aimed at making clear how things could have gotten so bad that Cornell could act so abysmally when faced with a group of armed students.[2] More than that, the moral sensibility that found expression in the sixties is just the frame of mind to which Bloom devotes the most substantive segment of his book, under the title "Nihilism, American Style." It would be fair to say, in fact, that *Closing of the American Mind* is largely a polemic against the sixties, and it is hardly conceivable that Bloom or any other individual influenced by Strauss would or could have written a book like this independently of that experience.[3]

However, to take *Closing of the American Mind* primarily as a critique of the sixties is also to court serious misunderstanding of the book. Much of the considerable criticism the book aroused—and it was considerable—derived from various misunderstandings of Bloom's intentions in it. This book was often taken to be a member of the jeremiad genre, that is, comprehensive culture-critique. It certainly had some qualities in common with such writings, but that is not the proper context or setting for reading *Closing*. Read in that setting, it was usually found wanting as not comprehensive enough, not supplying an adequate analysis of the causes, character, and consequences of the state of American culture. Since he did not set out to do such a task, it is no wonder Bloom did not succeed at finding what these critics were looking for.

Bloom's intentions were far narrower and far more carefully focused than those found in the "culture-criticism" genre. As he announces in the very first pages of his book, he writes of "the young and their education, from the perspective of a teacher" (*CAM*, 19). It is not a comprehensive account of American life, but an account of our life as it bears on education. His focus is thus broader than that of many other books on education, which limit themselves to the standard topics of curriculum, dorm facilities, training of faculty, and so on, but it is not so broad as a jeremiad.

Bloom says he writes from the perspective of a teacher, the teacher that he is. He wrote, that is, a very personal book. This is another source of misunderstanding. Critics frequently called on him for statistics, for some comprehensive evidence to back up his empirical claims. Such calls are not irrelevant to a final judgment of the book's argument, but they mistake the character of his enterprise. He wrote what he called a "meditation" on education, a meditation that took off from his personal observations, experiences, and ponderings.

Thus, when Bloom wrote, for example, of students in a part of the book that attracted a great deal of attention, his concern was with them as students, as individuals on whom he and other teachers might or might not have an effect as teachers. Bloom was not attempting a general sketch of the state of students and student life (and still less of American society in general). He looked at students instead from the point of view of their educability; he concluded that the formative experiences contemporary students undergo at home, in school, and elsewhere in American society, are not conducive to learning.

Bloom famously discussed rock music; this was not meant to be a foray into music criticism, but an attempt to diagnose the state of student preparedness (in the broad sense) for real education. Bloom's discussion of rock music was consequent on his observation that young people today put music in the place that books held (for some at least) in earlier generations. He concluded that the formative education young people receive today does not serve as well as other forms did in preparing students for the rigors and beauty of a proper liberal education.

When Bloom spoke of teaching and education, he knew of what he spoke, for he was a masterful teacher, perhaps the student of Strauss who had the most success himself as a teacher. He produced wave after wave of students who went on to work with Strauss, or who received their PhD's under his own direction. He was clearly a pied piper, an extraordinarily gifted teacher.

Unlike Berns, Diamond, and Jaffa, Bloom did not make America the center of his intellectual focus. He was greatly interested in literature and wrote a book on Shakespeare. He was also much concerned with education and produced translations, complete with commentaries, of the two books he considered the best ever written on education, Plato's *Republic* and Rousseau's *Emile*. Nonetheless, America was constantly in his sights in his earlier work, and *The Closing of the American Mind* moved it to center stage.

He began *The Closing of the American Mind* with a description of "our virtue," a quality he called "openness." This "virtue" to which modern Americans (especially the young) declare allegiance and on which they particularly pride themselves, is so far from being good that our adherence to it will produce nothing less than the "collapse" of the West, and an equally grave deformation of individuals as well (*CAM*, 39). Bloom's chapter on "our virtue" is clearly meant to echo and revise Nietzsche's similarly titled chapter in his *Beyond Good and Evil*. "Our virtue . . . the one from which we cannot get away," according to Nietzsche, is *Redlichkeit*, probity or honesty. It is, in Nietzsche's presentation, a heroic virtue: it is the hard virtue that prevents conscientious modern individuals from accepting consolatory or comfortable truths. It is, Nietzsche shows in *Genealogy of Morals*, an ascetic, that is, self-denying virtue, which condemns modern humanity to live without the solace of God or God's "shadows."[4]

Bloom quite intentionally evokes Nietzsche in his opening chapter, for "openness," "our virtue," is almost the opposite of Nietzschean *Redlichkeit*.[5] It is self-indulgent where Nietzsche's virtue is self-denying; it is soft where Nietzsche is tough. The "openness" of which Bloom speaks is the easygoing tolerance of all views, indistinguishable in practice from simple relativism, which, Bloom thinks, characterizes American young people and the culture of educated Americans in general. It affirms tolerance (or rather, equality of all views) as both an epistemological claim and, more decisively, as a moral claim (*CAM*, 25–26, 29). The commitment to openness shows a widespread skepticism about the possibility of moral knowledge, but it derives more powerfully from the alleged moral and political mandate that democracy requires all views to be treated equally. In place of the Declaration of Independence's claim that all men are created equal is the commitment to the view that all moral views are created equal. Bloom's emphasis on the evil of "openness" is clearly descended from Strauss's emphasis on the evils of positivism and historicism.

At first glance it appears that Bloom is contrasting America as it is today with America as it was. Openness, Bloom tells us, "is the modern replacement for the inalienable natural rights that used to be the traditional American grounds for a free society" (*CAM*, 25). The old American "public philosophy" was conveyed in "the letter and spirit of the Declaration of Independence." That philosophy gave Americans "a fundamental basis of unity and sameness," allowing Americans to transcend differences of "class, race, religion, national origin, or culture" (27). It provided a basis for social unity and for "uniting the good with one's own" (39). "The United States," Bloom insists, "has one of the longest uninterrupted political traditions of any nation in the world." The "meaning" of that tradition "is articulated in simple, rational speech that is immediately comprehensible and powerfully persuasive to all *normal human beings*" (55 [emphasis added]). "But the unity [and] grandeur . . . of the founding heritage was attacked from so many directions in the last half-century that it gradually disappeared from daily life." Behind the attacks is the demon "openness" (56, 58).

Bloom appears to be telling a tale of degeneration—from the good American origins to the bad present. He appears, then, to be a counter-Jaffa: not the bad origins improved by the good classicizing Lincoln, but the good origins decayed over the course of the twentieth century. That impression is quite mistaken, however—doubly so, in fact. The American origins, as it turns out, were not good; and the present decline into "openness," renamed by Bloom later in the book as "nihilism—American style," is a direct and apparently inevitable development out of the defective origin.

The American origin—the American Revolution—"had been thought out beforehand in the writing of Locke," as the French Revolution had been in the writings of Rousseau (*CAM*, 162). To an even greater degree than Strauss, Bloom has an "idealist" view of history—"ideas have consequences" as one American writer put it.[6] Not merely the Revolution, but the character of the society that followed from the Revolution can apparently be read out of the texts of Locke. As Bloom says, "Americans are Lockeans." What Bloom reads in Locke's texts is "low but solid," as he quotes Strauss on Locke in the single quotation from Strauss in the book (*CAM*, 167). Bloom has a fairly standard Straussian reading of Locke: the Englishman who inspired the Declaration of Independence is, contrary to first impressions, a close follower of Hobbes. That means that human beings are affirmed to be free and equal by nature. This natural status paves the way for revolutions, because it robs kings and aristocrats of all claim to rule by divine or natural right (162). But the equality and freedom Locke accepts are very limited and impoverished things. Humanity is free in the first instance, because either there is no God, or he does not concern himself much with earthly life. He neither provides for human beings nor punishes them. Humans must therefore provide for themselves. They are free to do so, and they must do so: freedom and necessity in this sense are one (163).

Locke affirms men to be equal in that all have an "animal nature," that is, all are moved by passion, pleasure, and pain. Reason is demoted to an instrument of the passions. As with Hobbes, all human beings are driven by the desire for preservation above all. This is the truth nature reveals; the "moral heights" often sought in the premodern world are said to be illusory (*CAM*, 158). Natural rights arise from the equal and indefeasible desire for preservation; these rights are the expression of and means toward the satisfaction of that desire. Locke modifies Hobbes in revealing that the greatest enemy is not so much other human beings but scarcity. Men are not noble enough to want to fight each other for the sake of glory, domination, or merely out of high spirits, as Hobbes had emphasized. They are driven apart more by their desire for comfortable preservation in a world of scarcity, where the production of comfort requires hard and painful labor and the temptation to violate each other's labor is great. Locke shows that the most needful thing is a strong economy, and the human qualities most needed are moneymaking and productive skills. Lockean man, pacific and commercial, is in many ways more debased than Hobbesian man, and surely more than Machiavellian man (165, 263).

Locke, following Hobbes, leads to "a new kind of morality, solidly grounded in self-interest" (*CAM*, 166). Locke breaks with past visions of man by asserting that "no part of man is naturally directed to the common good" (167). Locke also rejects the old way of providing for the common good, moral education in "austere virtue." "Self-interest is hostile to the common good, but *enlightened* self-interest is not." Locke and his America are not opponents of the common good, but it is understood to be entirely artificial and a product of "enlightened," that is, calculating, self-interest.

Locke promotes what Bloom points out is called bourgeois morality in Europe, a term Americans do not apply to themselves, but one that Bloom believes fits them well. A member of the bourgeoisie is a "diminished, egotistical, materialist being without grandeur or beauty of soul" (*CAM*, 167). Thus Europeans (and Bloom) see Americans as "superficial," or, in Bloom's term, "flat" (157). They have no place for tragedy in their view of life; they are "at home" in the world (158). Locke, and the Americans after him, believe that "self-interest ... is in ... automatic harmony with what civil society needs and demands" (168). There are no tensions or insuperable conflicts, the kind of conflicts that deepen souls and give a tragic dimension to existence. Americans of the late twentieth century may have jettisoned much of the moral orientation present at the origin of the nation, but much of the moral orientation Bloom finds in the era of "openness" is already visible in the era of the founding. The flatness, the lack of yearning, the "niceness"—all these stand in remarkable continuity with American origins.

Bloom attempts to trace the transition from the original American founding to "openness" via a discussion of "the German Connection." The story he tells here is a version of Strauss's "three waves theory." Most of Bloom's version of the story occurs on the continent of Europe, for there Rousseau, not Locke, had the formative influence. Rousseau denied the easy harmony between natural man and society that Bloom finds in Locke and his America. Rousseau denies the natural or spontaneous or easily attained wholeness or integrity of man that Locke and his Americans believed to exist. Rousseau introduced a deeper and broader moral horizon than Locke did. Rousseauian Europeans were less "flat"—more interesting, if less satisfied—than Locke's Americans. They probed (invented?) things like the self and culture in the quest for the real wholeness of man (*CAM*, 170, 185, 188).

The path from Locke to Rousseau to Nietzsche to "Nihilism—American Style" is long in the making and rather winding. Like Strauss, Bloom argues that the successive modern philosophers successfully critique their predecessors. According to Bloom, the driving force behind the dynamic of modern philosophy is the effort "to break out of nature's narrow bonds, and hence out of the degrading interpretation of man in modern [i.e., Lockean or Enlightenment] natural and political science" (*CAM*, 187–88). "The idea of culture was established in an attempt to find the dignity of man within the context of modern science. That science was materialistic, hence reductionist, and deterministic. Man can have no dignity if his status is not special, if he is not different from the beasts" (193). That last is the point that Bloom's Locke, with his endorsement of modern natural science and harmonization of mankind with it, and thus with his animalic concepts of humanity, did not see.

The effort to escape the ill consequences of modernity proceeds on the basis of the continuing acceptance of fundamentally modern premises. "No influential thinker," Bloom observes, "has tried to return to the pre-Enlightenment understanding of nature, the so-called teleological view, in which nature is the fullness in its own kind that being strives to attain" (*CAM*, 181). Eschewing a return to a premodern understanding of nature,

Rousseau and his successors were driven to move further and further away from nature—to posit reason or freedom, creativity, culture, or "will to power"—in order to find a space for human dignity. Finally, Nietzsche attempts to lay to rest all the dualisms of modernity, not by returning to the older teleological nature, but by using the discovery of human creativity ("value making") to overcome science and with it the nature it discovered.

The whole Nietzschean enterprise is for the sake of resting human dignity on creativity understood as value-creation. To create and have "values" is to reach out beyond oneself. It is to yearn for some unpossessed wholeness, to strive for some not-yet-achieved state. In this Nietzsche was merely accentuating the chief quality of European thought and culture in contradistinction to American thought and culture. The Europeans felt longing, yearning, the need for effort, the necessity of inequality, and the seriousness of existence and of the tasks all these imposed on human beings.

All the while that these philosophic, artistic, and cultural efforts were going on in Europe, Americans were fairly unaware of them, or of the seeming problems to which they attested. Only in the twentieth century did the message cross the ocean. The relation of this European line of thought to America was complicated, however. In Bloom's rendition, it is clear that Rousseau and his successors were far superior to Locke and the Americans. One was deep where the other was shallow. The critique of the Enlightenment raised by the nineteenth- and twentieth-century Europeans was essentially sound, even if America proceeded more or less in blithe unawareness of it (*CAM*, 207). Whether the Americans knew it or not, Nietzsche had a (not unambiguously) superior moral and philosophic position. American life and culture were vulnerable to European thought and were refuted by it in absentia.

During the twentieth century this late European thought reached America. Bloom sees Max Weber as the main vehicle of transmission, but Freud is also very important. Nonetheless, to paraphrase the title of an American musical, "a funny thing happened on the way to New York." "Nihilism—Nietzsche style" was transformed into "nihilism—American style," that is, openness and its attendant ills. American nihilism is easygoing; instead of the life-and-death struggle between cultures that Nietzsche posited, we find the easy acceptance of all cultural expressions, indeed the reduction of all goods and evils to "values." The "open" youth of America lose all yearnings, all transcendence. They are thus ineducable and lacking in real relationships. They find it difficult to be serious about life when they are so detached from all that they are supposedly attached to. The vulgar American spirit managed to vulgarize and co-opt the Rousseauian- and Nietzschean-inspired challenges to it.

American Lockeanism, what Strauss sees as the first-wave regime in America, is vulnerable to the critique leveled by third-wave German thought—witness the dominance of the moral vocabulary of third-wave thinking (culture, authenticity, etc.) that Bloom traces in contemporary American discourse. The Nietzschean wave of modernity can dissolve the old attachments and "values," robbing Americans finally of belief in themselves and their traditional bearings. Thus American youth are now embarrassed about patriotism and find the "self-evident truths" of the Declaration of Independence to be far from that. They are, like all such things, "values." Thomas Jefferson and the founders sink to the same level as Santa Claus. The Nietzschean impulse has its negative effect but is transformed in such a way that any positive effect it might have had is lost, because the Nietzschean striving for greatness and true creativity is diluted and democratized when it enters the American atmosphere.

So, to conclude, although Bloom makes occasional concessions to Strauss's third proposition ("American is good"), on analysis these seem to be mainly rhetorical. The very strong impression one comes away from the book with is that "Bloom doesn't seem actually to *like* America."[7] The issue, of course, is not merely one of liking or not. Bloom resolves the tensions within Strauss's three principles by strongly retreating from the third while adhering particularly strongly to the first two ("America is modern"; "Modernity is bad"). Writing fifteen years after Strauss's death, in the decades following the traumatic sixties, Bloom is less impressed than Strauss was with the premodern residues in America. Religion, in particular, is presented by Bloom as a dying and ineffective force. Moreover, although he does notice the ways in which first-wave (i.e., Lockean) political philosophy is superior to second- and third-wave philosophy, he is far more impressed with the power of the latter's critique of first-wave thinking, with the moral and broadly human deficiencies of first-wave thought and practices. He believes in the vulnerability of American first-wave culture to third-wave invasions. He would no doubt defend his deviation from Strauss here by claiming that by the time of his own writing, the third-wave invasion had proceeded much further than it had in the early 1960s when Strauss did his main writing on the subject.

The general thrust of Bloom's position was visible in Berns's ur–East Coast position, but Bloom is much weaker on Strauss's third proposition than even Berns was. Berns was writing, of course, before the sixties, a period that in Bloom's opinion heralded the triumph of the "German connection," that is, of second- and third-wave thinking. Thus, Berns sought to overcome America's bad modernism and allow the sounder natural imperatives of practice, supplemented by a recaptured Aristotelianism, to triumph. America could be good. Bloom is far more romantic and far more pessimistic. His story of the history of the West as applied to America is different from Strauss's own version in one important respect. Strauss feared the triumph of more advanced modernity with the attendant triumph of positivism and historicism. Bloom thinks advanced modernity superior to earlier, more vulgar modernity, and he decries not so much the triumph of advanced modernity as the transformation that it undergoes upon entering American air space.

Bloom's views are perhaps the most extreme example of the East Coast position, for nearly all other adherents of this tendency make a stronger effort to reaffirm Strauss's third proposition as well as his first two. In the work of Thomas Pangle or Harvey Mansfield, to mention two prominent East Coast Straussians, the East Coast position remains truest to the original Strauss doctrine; but in their work, as in his, the tension between the three Straussian propositions remains potent. Given Bloom's relatively extreme version of East Coast Straussianism, it is not surprising that the West Coast position emerged in some large part as a dialectical reaction to it.

West Coast

There was a general consensus, we believe, that Jaffa's *Crisis of the House Divided* was the preeminent achievement of the first generation of Strauss's Americanist students. Yet Berns, the ur–East Coast Straussian, could later write of Jaffa: "Who will rid us of this pest of a priest?"[8] The context of Berns's frustrated comment was a running battle between himself and Jaffa. That conflict was but one of a series of such instigated by Jaffa against other students of Strauss and, more broadly, against other political conservatives. West Coast Straussianism emerged in a kind of act of secession, accompanied by much artillery fire and not a few casualties. Unlike East Coast Straussianism, which has no one dominant voice, nor even one dominant founder, West Coast Straussianism has in Jaffa both its Saint Peter and its Saint Paul. Not even Bloom, who achieved a certain *public* preeminence, ever achieved among East Coasters the unrivaled preeminence that Jaffa did in the West—there were always Berns, Mansfield, Pangle, Bruell, and Benardete, to mention a few.

Although Jaffa provoked arguments with nearly every other well-known student of Strauss by the turn of the century, the first published battle occurred with his one-time close friend Martin Diamond in the mid-1970s. Jaffa's attack on Diamond was remarkable, not only because the two had been friends, but especially because Jaffa attacked Diamond for adhering to views Jaffa himself had voiced a mere three years earlier. That fact, together with the personal break that preceded the public intellectual break, led many to conclude that Jaffa was pursuing a private vendetta of some sort. Such an explanation misses what is most significant about the path Jaffa set off on in the mid-1970s. The break with Diamond was but a step along the way toward the development of the West Coast doctrine, which, as we have suggested, breaks with the then-prevailing Straussian view, including the view of Jaffa himself in *Crisis of the House Divided*, that America is modern. Jaffa did not arrive there all at once, however; his reaction to Bloom's *The Closing of the American Mind* represented a more advanced phase of the West Coast position. It reached a kind of peak expression in Jaffa's long-awaited *A New Birth of Freedom*, published in 2000, more than forty years after *Crisis of the House Divided*, to which it was the sequel. Nonetheless, the West Coast position was worked out well before *New Birth* appeared.

Jaffa's "turn" was provoked, we believe, at least in part by a response to *Crisis*. In 1970 Willmoore Kendall and George Carey published *The Basic Symbols of the American Political Tradition*, a work that challenged Lincoln, the Jaffan construal of the Declaration of Independence, and the Straussian approach to American politics. That work expanded upon an earlier review of *Crisis of the House Divided* that Kendall had written in the *National Review*. *Basic Symbols* led Jaffa to reconsider the earlier Kendall critique, and it is that event more than any other, we believe, that set Jaffa off on his new path. Kendall's review made Jaffa aware of the real implications and meaning of the strategy he had followed in *Crisis*.

Jaffa thought Kendall's insight into *Crisis* was so keen that he quotes the relevant passage several times in his response to *Basic Symbols*: "Jaffa's Lincoln [said Kendall in his review] sees the great task of the nineteenth century as that of affirming the cherished accomplishment of the Fathers by *transcending* it. [Jaffa thus prepares] a political future the very thought of which is hair-raising: a future made up of an endless series of Abraham Lincolns, each persuaded that he is superior in wisdom and virtue to the Fathers, each prepared to insist that those who oppose this or that new application of the equality standard are denying the possibility of self-government."[9] Kendall saw very clearly the odd and ultimately problematical strategy of *Crisis*: Jaffa's Lincoln apparently endorses the founders and their work but in fact overcomes and transcends them. Kendall saw what Jaffa did not: this characterization and justification of Lincoln is an open-ended warrant for "transcending" the founding in, Kendall feared, undefined and endlessly "progressive" ways. In the context of *National Review* and the explicitly stated conservatism of Kendall and Jaffa, this was a problematic implication indeed, for it showed Jaffa's Lincoln to be the sponsor not of a conservative but of a historically "unfolding" liberalism, or even historicism.

Kendall appreciated the importance of Jaffa's transformation or transcendence thesis and promptly identified it as illegitimate. In *Basic Symbols* the transcending Lincoln thus appears not as the savior but as the villain of the American political tradition. Lincoln "derailed" the tradition, Kendall and Carey say. Jaffa, of course, had not intended or understood his Lincoln to have done any such thing. His Lincoln "transcended" the founders, all right, but on the basis of Aristotelianism. One response to Kendall would have been to say just that. But at the same time Jaffa was reconsidering Strauss and his legacy for a political science of America. That reconsideration helped shape the direction of the response Jaffa actually made to Kendall.

The eulogy of Strauss that Jaffa gave in 1973 nearly begins with a quotation from Willmoore Kendall: Kendall was at the top of his mind as Jaffa turned to address (among other things) the relation of his own work to Strauss. Kendall had proclaimed Strauss the greatest teacher of politics since Machiavelli, a judgment Jaffa persistently demurred from endorsing; apparently he did not doubt its truth so much as his own competence to render it. (He seems to have doubted Kendall's competence to pronounce such a judgment as well.)

Jaffa's discussion of Strauss himself moved from Machiavelli to Socrates, from the lower to the higher. Socrates was "the preoccupation of [Strauss's] last years." Socrates was so central to him because Strauss's topic was political philosophy and "Socrates was the man who seemed to have discovered, or have invented, political philosophy." The recognition of Strauss's "preoccupation" with Socrates is the occasion for Jaffa's reflections on Socrates' practice of political philosophy. Those reflections are not in every respect positive. "The Socratic way of life was a continual demonstration that the rulers of Athens—and, of course, of every political regime anywhere—did not really know the things they thought they knew, knowledge of which was implied in every action they took." The demonstration had real political implications: "By implying that statesmen should know what they needed to know, Socrates intimated that every existing regime was defective, and that it had a duty to transform itself into something better—ultimately into the best regime." At this point Jaffa quietly draws a remarkable conclusion: "That of course implied a disloyalty to Athens sufficient to justify Socrates' execution."[10] The practice of Socratic political philosophy and perforce of all political philosophy in the Socratic mode, for example the political philosophic practice of Strauss himself, implies disloyalty to Athens—"and, of course, [to] every political regime everywhere." The disloyalty contained within Socratic political philosophy is of sufficient severity as "to justify Socrates' execution"—and that of any similar political philosopher.

Jaffa had earlier spoken of Strauss's "practice," or of his "career" on "the practical level"; that practical side of his career "was constituted by the articulation of the differences between the ancients and the moderns." Strauss had demonstrated, Jaffa went out of his way to emphasize, that the moderns were, to a man, Machiavellians, who violated the rule that one should understand the low in light of the high (the ancient stance) rather than the reverse. At the same time, the most obvious connection of Strauss to America was his "many expositions of Locke, and Locke's massive influence on America." Strauss had been "careful to emphasize Locke's ultimate, if concealed insobriety," that is, his bad modernism.[11] Strauss was disloyal to America, Jaffa is implying, to at least as great a degree as Socrates was to Athens.

Nonetheless, "no one appreciated better than [Strauss]—nor was anyone more grateful than he—for the strength no less than the decency of Anglo-American democracy."[12] Yet Strauss's practice was in some tension with this "appreciation" and "gratitude"—as Socrates was a disloyal son of Athens, so Strauss was a disloyal stepson of America. Jaffa's eulogy, while full of praise and sincere admiration for Strauss, raises questions about Strauss's philosophic practice and indeed about political philosophy altogether. Aristotle had asked whether the good man and the good citizen were or could be the same. Jaffa thought that Socrates and Strauss answered definitely not: the good man, or at least the political philosopher, is ipso facto a bad citizen, of this or any other regime.

Strauss's career and his recovery of the Socratic perspective led Jaffa to ask again the hard question of theory and practice: must the philosopher be a bad citizen? His path to West Coast Straussianism represents his attempt to find a way to answer that question in the negative. Jaffa saw the need for a more practice-friendly approach to theory than Strauss had cultivated, for the Strauss approach so transcended all practice that it undercut even strong and decent regimes like "Anglo-American democracy."[13] Thus Jaffa cultivated a kind of theory that not only was compatible with decent practice, but could allow him to pronounce, as he later did, that America *is* the *best* regime. Unlike Strauss, who insisted that the best regime was a regime in speech, Jaffa found the best regime to be actual. If one did not know better, one would think Jaffa had been reading Hegel.

The most direct way to state Jaffa's new path is to say that he reinterpreted the Declaration of Independence so that Lincoln would no longer have to reinterpret or transcend it in order to make it the legitimate guide to the "best regime." Jaffa's reinterpretation was at once a response to Kendall's reservations about Lincoln and to Jaffa's reservation about Strauss's Socratism.

The earliest public appearance of the new interpretation was in a 1972 lecture on the Declaration by Jaffa. In "revisiting" the Declaration, Jaffa refused the path taken by Kendall himself, who, as Jaffa put it, "devoted the last years of his life to an extraordinary effort to read John Locke out of the American political tradition." Jaffa stuck to the standard Straussian version: he "would never contend that there are no non-Lockean elements in the founding"; in other words, he accepted the Strauss "residues" theory. Nor would he contend "that the Founding Fathers always interpreted the Lockean elements in a Lockean manner"; but that meant, of course, that they sometimes did interpret them "in a Lockean manner." After these provisos, Jaffa affirms: "Locke is nonetheless there. The primary appeals to principles in the Revolution are Lockean. The principle of limited, constitutional government, by which the Fathers rejected despotism and by which they constructed their own governments, were fundamentally Lockean. Without understanding this, no other aspects of the Revolution, or of the American political tradition, are intelligible."[14]

Despite this affirmation of continuity with Strauss and with *Crisis*, there are many surprising but unremarked reinterpretations within the lecture. Perhaps most striking is the reinterpretation of rights. No longer finding in the Declaration a rights theory that is essentially Hobbesian in character, Jaffa now explains: "The unalienable *rights* mentioned in the Declaration are those from which *obligations* can be inferred or deduced." Lincoln had not "moralized" the Declaration's rights doctrine; that doctrine was already moral. Rather than deriving rights from indefeasible passions, as Jaffa, following Strauss, had done in *Crisis*, Jaffa now derived rights from equality. As he put it in a later essay, "the rights themselves form a continuum of inferences from man's natural equality."[15]

Equality in turn is interpreted quite differently from the state-of-nature construal in *Crisis*. Although Jaffa reiterates the Lockean provenance of the ideas in the Declaration, he explicates the Declaration's affirmation of "self-evident truths" by reference to Thomas Aquinas rather than to Locke's non- or even anti-Thomist version of self-evidence. The equality that is more fundamental than, and the source of, the rights and the principles of constitutionalism is now presented in terms of "otherness": men are the same or equal to each other in rights because they are other than and unequal to other sorts of beings in something like "the great chain of Being." "We understand" human equality and rights only by understanding that "man is not either beast or God." Although Jaffa later speaks often in heavily theistic language, in 1972 he is certain that "whether the God whom the Signers assume to exist can be proved to exist is not necessary to the argument of the Declaration." This "God" that man is not could just as well be an idea of pure reason as a reality, in order for it to serve its purpose in the argument. "Men form the idea of such a perfect being as much to understand the limits of their own humanity as to decide objectively on that superior being's existence." God thus represents the idea of a being so superior to humans that he could rightly rule them without their consent and, moreover, could rightly combine all powers—legislative, executive, and judicial—in his hands. The God-idea reveals the nature of man as less than this sort of being and from the idea derives rights (in a somewhat unclear manner) and also the main demands of constitutionalism: separation of powers and rule of law. "The equality of mankind is an equality of defect, as well as an equality of rights."[16]

However, "if man is not God, neither is he a beast." The relation between humans and lower animals helps round out the natural mandate for the relations between humans. "If man cannot justly rule man, except by law, nevertheless, he can, indeed must, rule beasts despotically. We do not expect a man to ask his dog's consent to be governed. In fact, the dog is incapable of giving that consent, for consent implies a rationality lacking in the dog's nature." From all this Jaffa draws his general conclusion: "In short, as men are neither beasts nor gods, they ought not to play God to other men, nor ought they to treat other men as beasts. Here is the elementary ground, not only of political, but of moral obligation. Thus it is that the starting point for the comprehension of the source of the just powers of government lies in the proposition that all men are created equal."[17]

Although Jaffa has over the years added bells and whistles to this argument, it has remained the core of his teaching from 1972 through the great restatement of his doctrine in *New Birth*. It is the core of West Coast Straussianism when suitably broadened to address the modernity issue.

Let us see how it responds to the various crises left over from *Crisis*. One of the problems of *Crisis* is the odd doctrine with which it ended:

Lincoln improved on or transcended the founders by calling for a return to the founders. Jaffa's reformulation of the doctrine of the Declaration allowed him to make Lincoln less paradoxical and more consistent. Lincoln need not be seen as improving or transforming the doctrines of the founders, but merely as restoring them, as he always claimed to be doing.

The revision of Lincoln's stance toward the founders also responds to Kendall's misgivings about Jaffa's (or Lincoln's) transformative lesson for American political life. The justification for Lincoln now lies not in going beyond the founders but in living up to them. And what is to be lived up to is not an open-ended, potentially radical commitment to ever new meanings of equality, but the (somewhat) carefully tailored—and limited—doctrine of the equality of men within the tripartite chain of being. Lincoln is thus not to be mistaken for the "spiritual father of the New Deal, of the expanded Presidency of the twentieth century, and of the welfare state," as Kendall and other conservatives suspected.[18] On the basis of their misinterpretation, Jaffa even accuses Kendall and Carey of having charged Lincoln with "somehow transform[ing] the *ethos* of American life" with respect to equality, without giving a "demonstration" of such a transformation.[19] That accusation would have had a better foundation if Jaffa himself had not made the original claim in *Crisis* that Lincoln had worked a transformation in the understanding of equality!

Jaffa's reinterpretation of rights and equality in the early 1970s also responded, in a more subtle and perhaps ultimately in a more important way, to his concerns about Strauss. "Leo Strauss is the man who in our time has made possible the serious study of political philosophy. He is therefore the one who made possible the serious study of the Declaration of Independence and of the regime founded upon its teaching."[20] Strauss's Socratic political philosophy with its depreciation of moderns is not at all "disloyal" to the Declaration and its regime. On the contrary, Strauss's loyalty to political philosophy is identical to loyalty to the Declaration, for "the conviction that there is a permanent order in the universe by which human beings ought ... to be guided [is] the heart of the Declaration [and] is also the one upon which the idea of natural right—the idea of political philosophy—stands or falls." According to Jaffa, "the commitment to Equality in the American political tradition is synonymous with the commitment to ... permanent standards." (Thus Kendall need not worry about the open-endedness of the commitment.) "Whoever rejects the one [equality], of necessity rejects the other [permanent standards], and in that rejection opens the way to ... relativism and historicism." That is to say, the alternative to the relativism and historicism that Strauss spent his life opposing in the name of political philosophy is the Declaration of Independence's doctrine of equality. Commitment to the Declaration's equality doctrine is the same as commitment to morality, constitutionalism, the "ought" rather than the "is," and "the higher law tradition which is the heart of . . . civility."[21] The equality doctrine "meant nothing more [or less] than the equal right of all men to be treated justly."[22]

Jaffa's new orientation toward the Declaration governed his confrontation with Diamond and stood behind this first open and bitter break between students of Strauss. Somewhat like Kendall and Carey, Diamond had defended a position many of the elements of which had been endorsed earlier by Jaffa himself. Jaffa did not mention that fact, as he had not mentioned it in his response to Kendall and Carey.

Diamond's essay had been one of a series of special lectures commissioned by the American Enterprise Institute to commemorate the then upcoming bicentennial of the American Revolution. Delivered in 1973, it bore the marks of the late sixties and the difficult events of the seventies: Watergate, the collapse of the American effort in Vietnam, urban riots. He evoked "the grave contemporary issues that tear at us and surfeit us with apparently endless crisis." In the background of his reflections was his ongoing crusade against the Beardian construal of the founding. In 1973 this crusade was given an extra boost of contemporary relevance; it had become commonplace in the discourse of the day for "the Declaration's heady rhetoric of revolution and freedom [to be] foolishly cited as authority for populistic passions."[23] Among other things, Diamond meant to counter that sort of rhetoric by holding up "the Constitution as the necessary, forming, constraining, and sustaining system of government that made our revolution a blessing to mankind and not a curse." The argument of the essay was familiar to those who were acquainted with Diamond's earlier writing on the founding: the Declaration was not the source of America's commitments to democracy (it was open on form of government), but the Constitution was. The Constitution committed the nation to democracy, but a "sober" and sane version of democracy. In the context of his polemic against the lingering voices of the sixties, Diamond made his usual points with extraordinarily strong rhetoric. His key note—at least the note that caught Jaffa's attention—was the strong claim that "the Declaration . . . can offer *no guidance whatsoever . . .* for the American democratic institutions. That guidance is to be found in the thought that shaped the Constitution and is to be found in the Constitution itself, which formed the institutions under which we live."[24] That is the central claim in Diamond's fourteen-page essay, to which Jaffa devoted a sixty-five-page rebuttal.

Diamond no doubt overstated his point, but he did have real textual support in the Declaration and behind the Declaration in Locke. Jaffa had endorsed key elements of Diamond's position in *Crisis* and as late as his 1972 revisit to the Declaration. Nonetheless, his reconstrual of the Declaration, especially its doctrine of equality, committed him, he now realized, both to full-blown doctrines of separation of powers, constitutionalism, and rule of law, and to a "more radically democratic" theory of politics "than has hitherto been understood."[25] Jaffa's new rendition of equality points unequivocally to democracy; democracy, indeed democracy American style, is the very fulfillment of political philosophy per se. In light of that conclusion, Diamond's "no guidance whatsoever" thesis had to be pummeled into submission. In drawing his very strong conclusions about America, Jaffa was clearly driven by his devotion to Strauss's third proposition ("America is good") and his gathering doubts that Strauss's other students had developed an adequate approach to the defense of that proposition.

Jaffa's statements of the mid-1970s did not yet comprise the full West Coast position, however, for Jaffa had not yet worked out his full response to Strauss's first proposition: "America is modern." In a recent statement, Jaffa dates to 1988 the beginning of the turn of thought that became West Coast Straussianism, but in truth the West Coast reorientation had been in development for more than a decade before that.[26] Jaffa's turn against Diamond was not the only milestone; another was his attack on Pangle's introduction to Strauss's posthumously published *Studies in Platonic Political Philosophy* in the mid-1980s. It was the reaction to Bloom's *Closing of the American Mind* by Jaffa and his students in the late 1980s, however, that crystallized the major themes of West Coast Straussianism.

Crisis, it will be recalled, presented Lincoln as Aristotelian critic and corrector of the modernist Lockean American founders and founding. The much later *A New Birth of Freedom* presents Lincoln differently: he scrupulously follows the founders and neither criticizes nor corrects them. This version of Lincoln accords much better with the historical Lincoln's self-presentation and avoids the grave incoherence at the heart of *Crisis*. This shift is made possible by and is subordinate to a much more significant shift: the founders are no longer presented as moderns. Jaffa thus reiterates and extends his earlier retraction of his previous critique of the founders. Whereas in *Crisis* he attributed to them a defective view of rights, he now endorses their rights doctrines; whereas he earlier criticized them for embracing the notion of a state of nature and attempted to distance his Lincoln from any such idea, he now concedes that Lincoln accepts the state of nature, and he himself has no problem with it or the social compact, which puts an end to it. Whereas he accused the founders of an openness, or even a moral indifference, to slavery, he now forcibly denies there was anything but unmitigated opposition to "the peculiar institution" among the leading founders.

The founders do not require correcting in nonmodernist terms because, Jaffa now concludes, in the decisive respects they were already not modern. They were, indeed, Aristotelian, or what Aristotle would have been in a post-Christian context. When West Coast Straussians affirm that America is good and that America is not modern, they have in mind a fairly restricted set of claims. The West Coast Straussian response to Bloom's book is especially revealing of the nuances of their position. At least three substantial West Coasters (Jaffa himself, Thomas West, and Charles Kesler) wrote in response to Bloom. The West Coast assessment of Bloom's achievement was quite mixed. West put it most succinctly when he declared "the book most sound . . . in its description of current pathologies, . . . partly sound and partly unsound in its account of their origins . . .[and] least sound in its prescriptions for their healing."[27]

The West Coasters share with Bloom a sense of the pathologies and vulnerabilities of contemporary American life. They differ most on the analysis of the source and cure of these pathologies. Bloom sees them resulting in part from the nature of American origins themselves and in part from American vulnerability to European nihilism, a vulnerability itself related to American origins in modernity. West Coasters deny that the origins are any part of the problem; rather, West insists, "instead of debunking the founding . . . Bloom should be celebrating it as a fund of wisdom to be recovered for the sake of the very enterprise he wishes to foster." The American origins are part of the solution, not part of the problem. Thus, when West Coasters affirm that America is good, they do not so much mean the America of today; they mean America as it was and as it could be if it fully lived up to its originating principles.

When Jaffa and other West Coasters deny that America is modern, they do not mean to deny one of the critical claims of *Crisis* and of Jaffa's mid-seventies writing: they continue to affirm the Lockeanism of the American founding. Locke is "America's philosopher."[28] But they now read Locke differently than Jaffa did at first and differently than Strauss did. The chain of modification that has transformed Jaffa's original Straussianism into West Coast Straussianism thus proceeds from Lincoln to the American founders to Locke.

Jaffa's revision of Locke has three elements. He begins by conceding the error of his earlier ways. "I took for granted," he says, "that the account of the Hobbesean Locke in Leo Strauss's *Natural Right and History* represented the Locke that informed the American founding." But, he observed, the founders do not sound much like Strauss's Locke when they explain themselves. As West points out in one place, they renounce Hobbes whenever they take notice of him.[29] They unselfconsciously speak of virtue and vice, the common good, God, and other matters that Strauss's Locke has left behind. The founders are Lockeans, but they do not read Locke as Strauss did. This would seem to suggest either that the founders were not very astute readers of Locke, or that Strauss was quite mistaken in his reading of Locke. Jaffa attempts to say both and neither, and therein lies a continuing incoherence in his position.

He does note that "Strauss himself never said that this Locke was the Founders' Locke, but the spell cast by his book led many of us to apply it to the Founders." Strauss's Locke, Jaffa points out, was the "esoteric Locke," the deep-down Locke but not the surface Locke. According to Jaffa, Strauss saw "the exoteric Locke," the surface of Locke, to be "far more conventional, and far more consistent with both traditional morality and traditional (albeit more tolerant) Christianity."[30] Jaffa differs from Bloom, then, by maintaining that Bloom mistakenly attributed to the founders a philosophic grasp of the esoteric, when in fact they only understood the exoteric Locke. As Jaffa sees it, the exoteric Locke is morally and politically superior to the esoteric Locke; the founders' failure as philosophic readers was a fortunate thing.

This line of argument remains problematic in several ways, however. First of all, it seems to derogate from the honor due the founders and Lincoln: they were not intelligent enough to grasp the real Locke and were saved from falling into dark modernity only by their stupidity (to put it harshly). More significant, it misses the point of Strauss's reading of Locke: Locke seems to have ties to traditional morality and religion, but in fact he has broken with both, argues Strauss. Locke retains the appearance of orthodoxy, but in fact his positions are not orthodox. To follow the exoteric Locke, according to Strauss, is to follow him a long way (if not quite all the way) to the conclusions of the esoteric Locke. It is not that there is a surface that is nearly the same as, say, Thomas Aquinas or Richard Hooker and a wholly different depth that is Hobbes. No, Strauss's Locke has a surface that makes concessions to and builds bridges to Aquinas and Hooker and the like, but the bridges are to lead the reader across into modern politics. That is what Strauss believed Locke succeeded in doing.[31] Jaffa may be correct to deride Bloom and others for assuming that the founders understood Locke just as Strauss did, but on the whole Bloom is more correct in his understanding that buying into even the exoteric Locke was, for Strauss, buying into Locke's modernity.

Jaffa's first line of argument on Locke is therefore not very successful in reconciling Strauss's Locke with the very un-Straussian Locke he (Jaffa) wishes to find in the founding. He seems to sense that, for he offers a quite different line of argument as well. This one drops the distinction between exoteric Locke (harmonious with Aristotle and Christianity) and esoteric Locke (harmonious with Hobbes). Instead he gives us a Locke entirely different from Strauss's Locke, without openly admitting that is what he is doing. The exoteric Locke is the real Locke, for Jaffa "concluded long ago . . . had Aristotle been called upon, in the latter half of the 17th Century, to write a guide book for constitution makers, he would have written something very closely approximating Locke's *Second Treatise*." Locke *is* Aristotelianism adapted to the new and different political needs of the Christian era, "with all its peculiar dangers of tyranny." "The Founding, which Lincoln inherited, was dominated by an Aristotelian Locke—or a Lockean Aristotle."[32]

The core of Jaffa's case for this conclusion is the observation that "Aristotle says . . . all of natural right [is] changeable." That is to say, Jaffa takes Aristotle to supply warrant for the view that the true political teaching could look very different in different political circumstances, as different as his own *Politics* and Locke's *Two Treatises*. The efforts Jaffa makes to draw connections between Lockean doctrines and Aristotle are casual and hardly definitive, however. He notices that the founders slide from speaking of "rights" (an apparently un-Aristotelian idea) to speaking of "ends" and happiness, much more Aristotle-like. He also notices that Locke speaks of a state of nature (said by Strauss to be completely alien to classical Aristotelian political philosophy) and Aristotle does not. But Jaffa reconciles them by asserting that

> Locke's state of nature is not a merely hypothetical construct. It is rather a dictate of that very prudence which is, according to Aristotle, the hallmark of all political wisdom. It arises from that fundamental transformation from . . . a world in which each city has its own God . . . to one in which there is but one God for the human race. This God, however, was not the God of any one city, or the author of its laws. The obligations of a citizen of an ancient city followed from its obligation to the god of that city. Under Christian monotheism . . . each individual is a citizen, actual or potential, of the city of God, before being a citizen of his own particular country.[33]

It is striking how unsatisfactorily this explanation gets us from Aristotle to Locke. One is hard pressed to find the point at which the state of nature becomes a response to the problem posed by Christianity. Moreover, what Jaffa says about ancient politics resonates very little with Aristotle; the Greek thinker does not speak of obligation; he does not rest his claim that man is by nature a political animal, and thus not a denizen of a state of nature, on the purported founding of cities by gods. Jaffa's explanation resonates very little with Locke also, for the state of nature is either (as Strauss would have it) an "inference from the passions" (as in Hobbes) or, as some Midwest Straussians would say, an inference from the fundamental moral condition of mankind. Nothing in Locke sounds anything like what Jaffa says here. This is not to say that Jaffa, a very intelligent, even brilliant man, might not be able to make a stronger case than he has made.

One obvious avenue forward, not yet taken by West Coasters, is to give up entirely on the Straussian Locke. Strauss's Locke, the esoteric Hobbesian, is by no means the standard Locke among scholars. Indeed one of Strauss's most controversial and controverted readings of any philosopher has been his reading of Locke. Most mainstream scholars reject Strauss's Locke root and branch and read Locke as a far more traditional, certainly as a far more Christian thinker, than Strauss did. West Coasters could find the Locke they are seeking by adopting these more standard scholarly interpretations. They have thus far not done so, although the reasons they have not are not clear. Possibly Jaffa, if not younger adherents of the West Coast position, are reluctant to break so openly with Strauss or to side with those who in many cases are avowed enemies of Strauss. The West Coast Straussian position is so far defined and definable in terms that require a minimal open deviation from Strauss: there is some warrant in Strauss for finding and emphasizing the nonmodern elements in the origin of America. To reject his Locke as a way to make good that claim requires a deeper-going and more prominent break with a central Strauss teaching. Reluctance to take that step may well account for the hitherto half-hearted effort to retrofit Locke to the needs of West Coast Straussianism.

The West Coast position, then, involves a rejection of Strauss's first proposition, "America is modern." Its prescriptions for the future of America are therefore a straightforward and patriotic return to the founders and their nineteenth-century heir, Lincoln. The evils of contemporary America, which they identify similarly to the way Bloom does, result not from the presence of the virus of modernity from the outset, but from the later invasion of bad doctrine with the American Progressives, thinkers and statesmen like Herbert Croly, Woodrow Wilson, Charles Beard, and John

Dewey. These are the founders of contemporary American liberalism—relativistic, egalitarian to the point of leveling, libertarian almost to the point of libertinism. They were, to varying degrees, critics of the founders and the founding, and it is their influence and that of their heirs, contemporary liberals, that must be overcome. West Coast Straussianism is thus the most overtly political of the various Straussian camps and the most readily identifiable on the political spectrum of contemporary American politics. Contrary to what is often said about Straussians in American politics, the West Coasters are not aligned with the neoconservatives but with traditional (especially western) conservatives and Republicans. One can even discern an emerging alliance with the so-called Christian right in America, an element of the electorate very important to George W. Bush's electoral coalition. In being so clearly political and so single-mindedly attached to a certain position on the political spectrum, the West Coast Straussians present a singularly different profile from that of Strauss himself and the other Straussian camps.

Midwest

There is no single figure associated with the Midwest branch of Straussianism as Jaffa is with the West Coast variant or even as Bloom is with the East Coast branch. While the other two are already matters for folklore and legend, the Midwest variant is hardly even recognized. Indeed, we are, so far as we are aware, the first to identify and name the Midwest Straussian position.

As we suggest in chapter 6, Diamond is the founder of Midwest Straussianism, but we see gestures toward it in several other of Strauss's first generation of students, such as the later Berns, Joseph Cropsey, and Ralph Lerner. It reaches further expression in the next generation of Strauss students.

Midwest Straussianism is constituted by the negation of, or at least a strong reservation about, Strauss's second proposition: "Modernity is bad." It is the last and most hesitant of the Straussianisms to emerge, because it is the furthest of the three from Strauss himself and represents a break with a part of Strauss's position central to his entire project. If the call for a "return to the ancients" is his signature idea, then the Midwest rapprochement with modernity can be taken to be a dissent from the Straussian project. We believe it still makes sense to classify the Midwest Straussians among the Straussians, however, for their work continues to bear the distinctive marks of Strauss's influence. This observation remains true even of some of those in the next generation, like William Galston, who apparently moved far away from the Straussian "coasts" and, arguably, from Strauss himself. Contrary to the claims of today's professional anti-Straussians, we see once again that there is no "Straussian" cult with an imposed orthodoxy, whose members are unable to think independently. Those scholars who have been touched by Strauss have treated him with respect and even reverence, but their admiration and gratitude have not prevented them from thinking through the problems of political philosophy for themselves or coming to disagree on matters large and small with each other and with Strauss himself.

The seeds of Midwest Straussianism are already (barely) visible in Diamond's early work and in that of others like the University of Chicago's Herbert Storing, but the events of the late sixties and early seventies had much to do with the germination of the seeds. The impact of this turbulent era is quite visible in Diamond's corpus. From the appearance of his *American Political Science Review* article in 1959 until the appearance of his textbook on American politics, Diamond wrote and published regularly on American topics. During this period he laid out the main lines of his interpretation of the founders and the American order: his theories on democracy (or republicanism), federalism, the role of the "new science of politics" (modern political philosophy à la Strauss), the founders' political economy, and the Madisonian theory of the extended republic as the culmination and incorporation of all these themes.[34]

Diamond's steady stream of writings on the American regime came to an abrupt halt with his coauthored textbook, however. Not until 1973 did he publish again on that subject. Between 1966 and 1973 he published remarkably little—a few essays on the study of politics and none on politics per se. His period of near silence corresponded, it should be noted, with the turn in American political life we call the sixties.

When he returned to his primary topics in 1973, the impact of the sixties on his thinking was very visible. Particularly important are the two essays "A Revolution of Sober Expectations," which we have already had occasion to notice, and "The Utopian Grounds for Pessimism and the Reasonable Grounds for Optimism." Beard and the Progressives remain important counterpoints for Diamond, but the utopian thinking of the sixties erupts into his texts as an equal or more prominent opponent. The essay on the American Revolution was explicitly addressed to "our needs today." Our needs, he implies, are different from those that prevailed in Lincoln's day to which he (and Jaffa?) responded. In the nineteenth century the chief danger lay in the severing of the Constitution from the Declaration, and

Lincoln's response was to remind his listeners that the positive provisions of the Constitution must be read in terms of the moral principles of the Declaration. Today, however, almost the reverse is needed: "Now we need to train ourselves, when hearing the Declaration's heady rhetoric of revolution and freedom, or when it is foolishly cited as authority for populistic passions, always soberly to see the Constitution as the necessary forming, constraining, and sustaining system of government that made our revolution a blessing to mankind and not a curse." We live in an age of "unbridled, utopian expectations"—the expectations of sixties politics—and for us "nothing could be more useful than to look back to the sources of the sobriety that spared us in our birth the disasters of revolution which have befallen so many others."[35]

The essay on optimism and pessimism is even more pervaded by the reaction to sixties politics. The "utopian grounds for pessimism" are nothing but the "unbridled, utopian expectations" that irrupted into American political life and first caused a revulsion against the established order, a first-order pessimism, one might say, and then caused a yet deeper pessimism when the utopian hopes failed to deliver on their promises. A marvelously illustrative instance of the hopes—and the failures of hope—was the pronouncement by the New Left radicals Jerry Rubin and Abbie Hoffman that society should be organized on the same spontaneous principles of order and goodwill as were the Beatles. That pronouncement came but a short while before the breakup of the Beatles and the increasing public evidence that love and goodwill had pretty much run out for the "Fab Four."

The criticism and hopes of the sixties led Diamond to reconsider the regime and the value of the modernity on which, he continued to believe, it rested. Unlike Bloom, Diamond did not see sixties radicalism as the fruition of the modernity on which America rested. Unlike Bloom or Strauss, Diamond never committed himself to the notion that early modernity was so fragile as to be completely vulnerable to later waves of modernity.

In an ongoing effort to make sense of Strauss's three propositions on America, Diamond's thinking moved in another direction from Bloom's. In the essay on utopian pessimism and reasonable optimism, Diamond concluded that just as utopianism was the paradoxical source of pessimism, so sobriety or "reasonableness" was the ground for optimism. Explicitly resting on modern political philosophy, the American regime supplied the "reasonable grounds for optimism: it supplied genuine goods. Diamond thus began in these 1973 essays to move beyond the restrained defense of America and modernity contained in his pre-1966 writings.

Diamond's development of an account of the goods of modernity occurred gradually over the next four years or so, culminating in his last writing, "Ethics and Politics: The American Way." The trajectory on which he was embarked was cut short by his sudden death in 1977 at the age of fifty-eight, while he was in the midst of a second great burst of writing and thinking. Against the challenge posed by Strauss and the New Left, Diamond was engaged in a persistent reconsideration of the relative merits of the ancients and moderns. He never brought himself to renounce Strauss's assessment of good ancients–bad moderns, but his thinking was clearly moving in that direction.

In his post-1973 writings, Diamond repeats Strauss's story of the coming of modernity: "the ancients," who "took their bearings from the highest possibilities of human nature," were rejected by the moderns, who "would take man as he actually *is*," which involved a "lowering of the aims and expectations of politics."[36] Yet in Diamond's presentation of ancients and moderns, new themes also begin to appear. His views of the ancients subtly evolved. He began to emphasize and endorse, as he had not earlier, the critique lodged by the moderns against the ancients. In the 1959 essay he had noticed, almost in passing, that Madison had "deprecated . . . the efficacy of the kind of moral and religious motives" on which the ancients had relied. In his later writings, however, Diamond dwelled at length on the modern critique of the premodern orientation. "But that strenuous and demanding ancient political art, the moderns charged, had been ineffective and excessive—that is, 'utopian.'" In his 1977 essay "Ethics and Politics," this point is repeated: the moderns "charged that classical and Christian political philosophy had been both misguided and ineffective, in a word, utopian."[37] Perhaps most interesting in these formulations is the echo of the earlier charges leveled against the New Left—that the classics were ineffective, excessive, utopian. Although Diamond never went so far as to identify the classical and New Left positions, there are nonetheless some striking parallels between his own critique of sixties radicalism and the moderns' critique of the ancients. In both cases, aiming for too much ends up accomplishing too little and leads to a kind of disillusionment. "Despite two millennia of such elevated teachings, man's estate had still not been relieved; greed and vainglory ruled under the guise of virtue or piety."[38] The moderns do not merely raise such accusations against the ancients, but, according to Diamond, they do so "with some justification," for "ancient and medieval political practice had not vindicated the high aims and claims of premodern thought."[39] Diamond had come to see a kind of parallel between classical and radical utopianism; his defense of the modernist American regime against the latter had implications, he seems to have seen, for the former.

The second revision in standard Straussian views that we begin to see in these late writings is a much stronger recognition of the success of modern theory. "From the point of view of the generality of mankind, the new policy delivered on its promises. In comparison with the pre-modern achievement, it raised to unprecedented heights the benefits, the freedoms, and the dignity enjoyed by the great many."[40]

Diamond remains too good a Straussian not to recognize the costs of the modern achievements. Those costs derive from the emancipation of interest, ambition, and acquisitiveness within the Madisonian modern regime. "Put bluntly, this means that in order to defuse the dangerous factional forces of opinion, passion, and class interest, Madison's policy deliberately risks magnifying and multiplying in American life the selfish, the interested, the narrow, the vulgar, and the crassly economic."[41]

In his early writings, Diamond considered these costs high and thought they substantially detracted from the value of Madison's modernist constitutional order. In the early works, Diamond affirmed the idea that something higher was needed, or at least was desirable. In "Ethics and Politics" he sees the costs differently: the costs are "the price to be paid in order to enjoy [the] many blessings" of the Madisonian order. Here is no call for moving on beyond modernism. Diamond agrees with Strauss that something is lost with the turn to modernity, but on balance Diamond thinks modernity is good enough to outweigh its costs. Among the goods modernity provides, Diamond cites "the benefits, the freedom, the dignity, enjoyed by the great many." In his earlier work Diamond saw the Madisonian regime as "little more than a clever social arrangement." The "liberalism and republicanism" of the American order, he had said, "are not the means by which men may ascend to a noble life; rather they are simply instrumentalities which solve Hobbesean problems [i.e., the disordered results of the passions] in a more moderate manner" than Hobbes himself had done. The American regime, Diamond had argued, rises no higher than the low Hobbesian foundations on which it is built.[42] "You can't make a silk purse out of a sow's ear."

But by 1977 Diamond no longer believed that. The Madisonian modernist regime is good because of its very modernist elements (i.e., not because of premodern residues). The American order produces "virtues or excellences." "While the American founders turned away from the classic enterprise regarding virtue, they did not thereby abandon the pursuit of virtue or excellence in all other possible ways. In fact, the American political order rises repeatedly high enough above the vulgar level of mere self-interest in the direction of virtue—if not to the highest reaches of the ancient perspective, still toward positive human decencies or excellences."[43] Diamond believes that the American regime produces results better than Strauss's version of modern political philosophy would produce, and he explains that belief in terms of a quite different grasp of the meaning and value of modern political philosophy. He gives the example of "acquisitiveness." Diamond sees that Madison and the Americans, following Locke, attempted to build on the basis of the emancipation of acquisitiveness. But to understand this choice it is not enough to denounce acquisitiveness as Strauss and the precedent tradition did. Acquisitiveness is genuinely different from the justly blamed avarice. Avarice is merely the desire to have, and in itself supplies no limitation to that desire, no training in virtue of any sort. Acquisitiveness is quite different: it "teaches a form of moderation to the desiring passions ... because to acquire is not primarily to have and to hold, but to get and to earn, and moreover to earn justly, at least to the extent that the acquisition must be the fruit of one's own exertions or qualities." The "acquisitive man" must "cultivate certain excellences ... as means to achieve his ends." As Locke insists, a proper modern order does not license the greedy and the covetous, but rewards the "rational and industrious." As Diamond concludes, "acquisitive man, unlike avaricious man, is likely to have what we call the bourgeois virtues." Diamond goes on to show the large number of virtues the acquisitive man must possess. In implicit response to Bloom, Diamond admits that "these may be put down as merely 'bourgeois virtues,'" but they are virtues or human excellences nonetheless.[44]

Diamond follows the lead of Tocqueville and concludes that there is a yet higher level to which the formation of American character rises. The virtues of "self-interest rightly understood" are virtues of character and cohere with the yet more impressive virtues of self-governance that accompany the egalitarian emancipation of everyman. Beyond the egalitarian virtues, the sphere of freedom and opportunity allows the formation and reward of genuinely inegalitarian excellences. Diamond points to the "natural aristocracy" affirmed by Jefferson as an indication of the moral qualities sought and made possible within the modern horizon.[45]

The American modern regime has a full claim to the title of a virtue- or excellence-producing order, even if it does not do so in the ways characteristically commended by Aristotle. In America, character and virtue formation occur not through education by the laws but through life in the private sphere. What Diamond has in mind is what a second-generation Midwest Straussian, William Galston, calls "liberal virtues."

The modern virtues, Diamond concedes, are lower than the virtues sought by the premoderns, but as opposed to those, these are achieved, and they are achieved in ways compatible with free and equal forms of life. This may sound like the typical Straussian "lowering of the sights" argument, and it surely is an echo of that, but it is quite different as well. The moderns aim at and produce *virtues*, not just the more readily achieved emancipation of the passions, self-preservation, or wealth. Diamond died before he had an opportunity to work out the Midwest Straussian position any further. That work has been done to some degree by fellow first-generation students of Strauss like Berns and Lerner and by second-generation students like Galston. Diamond left much that required development—his "Ethics and Politics" has the character of an exploratory foray, designed to bring into focus many phenomena that Strauss's view of the moderns had omitted. From the standpoint of Strauss's own position, Diamond's version of Midwest Straussianism is perhaps most incomplete in failing to address the issues raised by Strauss's "wave theory." Admitting that modernity, at least in the version of early modernity ensconced in the American order, is good in the ways Diamond suggests, what about Strauss's (and Bloom's) conviction that these orders are exceedingly vulnerable to waves of thought such as were embedded in sixties radicalism or postmodernism? That is a challenge that, we believe, the Midwest Straussians have yet to meet.

The three Straussian "schools" by no means exhaust the influence Strauss has had. It is worth reiterating that many of his most prominent students make up no part of our story, for we have limited ourselves to Strauss's impact on the study of America. Many scholars touched by Strauss have pursued quite other interests. Few if any individuals have had the range of Strauss himself, but the sum total of his influence across the range of political and philosophic fields has been substantial.

As we hope this survey of the later works of three prominent representatives of the three "schools" that developed out of the tension among Strauss's three theses has made clear, Strauss and the Straussians have been far more interested in exploring the history of political thought than in acquiring or exercising direct and immediate influence on American public policy. The differences among the Straussians are principled and philosophical more than they are partisan or personal.

As we also hope we have established, the Straussians have no party line. They do indeed have some things in common, including concern about the current health of the American polity, the preservation of a principled form of politics and public virtue, and skepticism about utopian political hopes. But they do not have so much in common as to make them a homogeneous clique. They divide along preexisting lines of cleavage or tension in Strauss's own thinking, but divide they do. Had we chosen to carry the story of the three "schools" beyond their initial emergence in Bloom, Jaffa, and Diamond, the lines of cleavage and dispersal would appear even more pronounced. What we do not see and would not see if we carried the story further is the fable-like version of "Straussianism" that has become the staple of urban (and academic) legend. There is no "sect" attempting to impose the rule of philosopher-kings by lying to the American public or its elected leaders. There is a deep-going debate and serious division of opinion about the character and meaning of American political principles—at the time of the founding and at present.

Conclusion

We may be brief. The impossible Broadway image of Strauss as Wilsonian and Machiavellian is simply false to what the man wrote and thought. He endorsed liberal democracy as the best regime possible in the modern era, but an important part of his return to the ancients was a break with the all-or-nothing principles of legitimacy characteristic of modern political philosophy and political practice. Principles of political right do not demand democracy everywhere. He would no doubt agree that the replacement of tyrannies by constitutional regimes would be a blessing for all who could have the experience, but he was very restrained in his sense of the possibility and desirability of international action to impose or export liberal democracy. Despite his affirmation of natural right and a theory of the best regime, he was always possessed of the conservative insight that circumstance was all—or nearly all—in politics. The wise statesman recognizes the limits of the possible, both in general and for any given nation. Strauss would be the last to decree war (as a practical venture) on all tyranny everywhere, or to announce a crusade on behalf of liberal democracy worldwide, because he knew that one regime does not fit all peoples. "A very imperfect regime," Strauss said, "may supply the only just solution to the problem of a given community."[1]

Moreover, although he was no cynic, Strauss was enough of a political realist to wonder whether those who announce benevolent intentions in their dealings with others are as free from self-interest as they say, or think, they are. "Know thyself" is a difficult task. One of Strauss's main insights, gleaned from his study of Plato, held that the love of one's own, a token of the peculiar nature of human beings, could never be escaped. The only remedy, so far as there is one, is philosophy. Politics is at best a partial remedy, and it remains infected with self-interest. Strauss's implicit motto was "Distrust those who claim to act on the basis of pure benevolence."

Beware of "pious cruelty." Thus Strauss also stood for the proposition that the evils of political life will never end. "The classics thought that, owing to the weakness or dependence of human nature, universal happiness is impossible."[2] In his pessimism, in his affirmation of the limits of politics, he angered some of the more hopeful of the liberals among us. Whatever the merits of their impatience with Strauss's conservative sense of the limits of political action, these liberal critics testify to the restrained and moderate character of the hopes Strauss entertained and, by implication, the policies he favored.

Strauss is as little a Machiavellian as he is a Wilsonian. His doctrine of esoteric writing has been distorted beyond recognition in current discussions. His noticing that occasionally circumstances require actions that normal decency frowns on has been misunderstood to be a legitimation of Machiavellian ruthlessness, expansionism, and elitism. He is an elitist of a sort, but it is an elitism of the aspiration to human excellence, one key part of which is the practice of justice; another is the recognition of the need to respect the demand for consent of the governed. Strauss differed from Machiavelli precisely in refusing to take necessity as the orienting principle for human life. There are a natural right and a human good that point to a kind of politics very different from Machiavellian politics. "It is the hierarchic order of men's natural constitution which supplies the basis for natural right as the classics understood it."[3] This hierarchic order leads, Strauss believed, to an understanding of "the proper work of man [as consisting in] living thoughtfully, in understanding, and in thoughtful action." The good or the natural life, according to Strauss's ancients, is a very far cry from Machiavelli's prominent declaration that "it is very natural to desire to acquire."[4] Rather, "the life according to nature is the life of human excellence or virtue . . . and not the life of pleasure as pleasure," to say nothing of the life of acquisition after acquisition. This classical conception of human nature culminates in a very un-Machiavellian notion of the nature of politics and political action. "Political activity is then properly directed if it is directed toward human perfection or virtue. . . . The city is essentially different from a gang of robbers," or a Machiavellian state, "because it is not merely an organ of collective selfishness." From all of this Strauss draws an emphatic conclusion, directly contrary to what so many in the popular press are saying of him: "Since the ultimate end of the city is the same as that of the individual, the end of the city is peaceful activity in accordance with the dignity of man, and not war and conquest."[5] Not the extreme case, with its uncontrollable temptations to preemption and aggression, but the best case, with its eros for the beautiful and the noble, is, when possible, the proper ground and orienting principle for political life. "Machiavelli denies natural right, because he takes his bearings by the extreme situation in which the demands of justice are reduced to the requirements of necessity, and not by the normal situation in which the demands of justice in the strict sense are the highest law."[6] Strauss concedes that necessity sometimes makes it impossible to do the just, to say nothing of the noble, thing, but he differs from all Machiavellianism by refusing to take the extreme as the norm. Strauss is no utopian who believes political life is or ever will be a gentle pursuit—he always emphasized the "brachial" dimension of the enterprise, but he stood foursquare against any politics of thuggishness, any politics that affirmed mastery as the good.

Strauss was as little a Nietzschean nihilist as he was a Machiavellian or a Wilsonian. Indeed, his philosophic activity ought best to be seen as an effort to rediscover the grounds on which nihilism could be resisted. He granted to Nietzsche what was Nietzsche's—a powerful critique of the modern conception (and practice) of philosophy and politics—but he insisted that we grant to Socrates what is his. What is Socrates' is the discovery of the natural good and the adumbration of the implications of that good for politics and justice. For Nietzsche, Strauss tells us, "nature has ceased to appear as lawful and merciful. The fundamental experience of existence is therefore the experience, not of bliss, but of suffering, of emptiness, of an abyss." In his own name, Strauss affirmed something quite different: "By becoming aware of the dignity of the mind, we realize the true ground of the dignity of man and therewith of the goodness of the world, whether we understand it as created or uncreated, which is the home of man because it is the home of the human mind."[7] Not an abyss, but a home.

We firmly conclude, then, that Strauss is not at all what our modern publicists and the "scholars" who stand behind them have made of him. We forbear from drawing any conclusions about whether Strauss's project of a return to the ancients succeeds. We have, we hope, laid out some of the main reasonings that led Strauss to seek to effect such a return, some of what he found by studying the ancients, and some of the conclusions and implications that he drew from those findings. We believe we have provided a sounder footing for beginning a genuine consideration and confrontation with Strauss's achievement than the mythologies about him that have become part of the political culture.

But what of the neoconservatives? Is there anything to the alleged connection between Strauss and them? There is more to it than there is to the mythologies about Strauss the Wilsonian-Machiavellian-Nietzschean that circulate through the media. Some individuals who are identified as neoconservatives do have some involvement with Strauss. Irving Kristol, one of the founders of the movement, identified Strauss as one of those who had influenced him. But he also identified the liberal literary critic Lionel Trilling as a parallel influence. Kristol's son, William, attended Harvard and studied with Harvey Mansfield, one of the prominent students of Strauss. As coeditor of the widely read conservative journal of opinion *The Weekly Standard,* the younger Kristol is an influential voice in American politics today. Having coauthored the book *The War over Iraq,* Kristol is often thought to have been influential in prompting the Bush administration toward the Iraq War.[8] Even more visible than Kristol has been Paul Wolfowitz, deputy secretary of defense when the Iraq War began and a very public partisan of the war. He studied with Strauss's student Allan Bloom as an undergraduate and very slightly (by his own account, he took two courses) with Strauss himself.

No others with Strauss connections have the visibility or prominence of these two. However, there have been others who have held important political positions during the Bush and Reagan administrations, for example, Carnes Lord (who worked at the National Security Council under Reagan and with Vice President Dan Quayle on national security issues) and Abram Shulsky (who worked in the Pentagon's intelligence shop).

Nonetheless, the Strauss links to neoconservatism have been much overstated in both the popular and the more scholarly press. For one thing, there has been a striking irresponsibility in throwing around attributions of Straussian connections. Individuals such as Richard Perle, Clarence Thomas, and Robert Bork have been said to be Straussians, but there is not a shred of merit to these claims. We believe that Thomas once had someone on his staff at the Equal Employment Opportunity Commission who had studied with a student of Strauss; Robert Bork had an office at Washington's American Enterprise Institute in the same building as Walter Berns. Richard Perle had no connection whatever so far as we can discern. These kinds of links do not "Straussians" make. Once we require some actual criteria and evidence of connection to Strauss, the numbers of "Straussians" diminishes greatly.

We believe that in the tendency to see a Straussian under every bed in Washington there is at work an optical illusion of sorts. It must be recalled that Strauss and then some of his students have taught for many years in some of the leading graduate departments of political science in America. Such departments attract young, bright, often ambitious students, many of whom aim at a life in politics or end up in Washington for a variety of accidental reasons. The current "Strauss-craze" has observers looking for "Straussians" in government, with that category very loosely defined. Whatever the actual number may be, we must take account of the fact that the leading graduate departments of political science are all likely to have their graduates in Washington in some numbers. Nobody is counting up the number of those in Washington who studied at Harvard with Carl Friedrich or Judith Sklar or Samuel Huntington, all distinguished political scientists with no whiff of Straussianism. Nobody is counting those who studied at Yale with Robert Dahl or at Cornell with Theodore Lowi. Before we get carried away with the impression that there are a lot of "Straussians" inside the beltway, we need to define more carefully what criteria gain one inclusion in that category, and we need to control for the fact that some number of the bright young graduate students from the leading departments will, almost as a matter of course, end up in government, if not for a career, at least for temporary service.

Even those neoconservatives who do have some connection to Strauss are far from clearly followers of Strauss in their politics. To take the two best known: both William Kristol and Paul Wolfowitz deny that their political views and their political advocacy owe anything in particular to Strauss. Wolfowitz identified Albert Wohlstetter (an economist and strategic thinker who barely knew Strauss and certainly was no follower or adherent of his views) as the more significant influence on his thinking about foreign policy. Perhaps Wolfowitz looks to Strauss for his views on Plato and al Farabi, but apparently not on what to do about Iraq.

One objective way to get a handle on the link between Strauss and the neoconservatives is to turn to those scholars who have studied the latter movement with no prejudice or ax to grind vis-à-vis Strauss. Probably the leading older study of the movement is Peter Steinfels's book *The Neo-Conservatives,* a study focused on the first generation of neoconservatives.[9] In light of recent rumors, it is quite surprising and significant that Strauss does not even appear in Steinfels's index. He can write an entire three-hundred-page book on the neoconservatives without once speaking of Strauss!

Steinfels focuses his attention on the Big Three of neoconservatism: Irving Kristol, Daniel Patrick Moynihan, and Daniel Bell. The last two have nothing of Strauss in them, and although Kristol does look to Strauss, the links are not so important that Steinfels saw any need to discuss them. Steinfels also mentions in passing many, many more neoconservatives. On one page he refers to thirty different writers as neoconservatives.[10] Exactly one of them, Martin Diamond, can by any stretch be considered a Straussian.

Somewhat more recently a collection called *The Essential Neo-Conservative Reader* appeared in print.[11] That collection contains twenty-six essays. Several are by Irving Kristol, one by William Kristol, and one by another scholar recognizably touched by Strauss, Leon Kass, who also served under George W. Bush as head of the Council on Bioethics. That means that all the rest of this big book has not even a slight dependence on Strauss. As with Steinfels's volume, Strauss does not appear in the index to this book.

Yet more recently (in 2005) a collection of writings by and about the neoconservatives has appeared, and finally, in it, Strauss makes an appearance. One essay is even titled "Philosophic Roots, the Role of Leo Strauss, and the War in Iraq." Strauss makes lesser appearances in several other essays. But this sudden irruption of Strauss into the neoconservative world is not evidence for the claims of those who have made Strauss into the puppet-master of the current Bush and of the neoconservatives. Strauss plays the role he does in this more recent book because the authors are responding to the literature that ties Strauss to the neoconservatives. Although the various authors acknowledge a connection between some of the neoconservatives and Strauss, they deny that he played a significant role in shaping the peculiar features of neoconservative principles or policy. Typical is the conclusion of Kenneth Weinstein, the author of the article on Strauss and the Iraq War: "In sum, those who oppose the War in Iraq, and those who would blame the influence of a relatively obscure philosopher on the Bush administration's neocon contingent, would do well to look elsewhere: perhaps even to Strauss himself and the classics he revived for support for their view that there are distinct limitations to the form that a post-Saddam Iraq might take."[12]

There is some overlap between Straussians and neoconservatives, then, but it is easy to overstate the convergence between them. We have already suggested the ground for what relationship there is—the common revulsion against "the sixties" and the utopian political immoderation and insobriety for which that decade stands. It would take us far afield from our primary topic to undertake a thorough survey of neoconservatism—something on the order of Steinfels's book, perhaps. Such a review is unnecessary, however. We have shown, we think, that Mr. Strauss did not go to Washington. He remained in body in Chicago and in mind in his beloved Athens and Jerusalem. His political thinking bears none of the marks attributed to it in the media and by Drury. Moreover, as a guide to policy, Strauss's thought is far too underdetermined for him to be the mastermind or inspiration behind Bush (father or son) or Reagan, or, for that matter, Clinton.

Mr. Strauss did not go to Washington, but, we have shown, he did on the whole support Washington as the best political alternative in the modern world. But even here, Strauss left a tense legacy for his students and others who have found his path a promising one. A number of different "schools" have resulted from the efforts to think through the perceived tensions or uncertainties in his thinking. Contrary to what is often said, those who have followed him are far from single-minded in what they take from him, except perhaps for some threshold or methodological commitments. That philosophy is important, that political philosophy is a viable enterprise, that philosophic texts must be read in a particularly attentive manner, that the distinction between the ancients and the moderns means something (although just what it means is contested in Straussian circles)— these propositions are what individuals known as Straussians mostly agree about. Perhaps they also take from Strauss a substantive commitment to moderation that tends to place them in the center-right or center-left of the American political spectrum. But even that generalization has exceptions.

Our taxonomy of the Straussian schools has revealed, we believe, that wherever the truly serious students of Strauss stand, the depictions in the media of those who are Strauss-influenced are as much caricatures as are the portrayals of Strauss himself. There may be individuals in political life who have had some slight (or even more than slight) contact with Strauss and who are Wilsonian-Machiavellians, who favor manipulation and lying, who want to spread democracy by force of arms, or who want to secure their own rule by deception and fraud; but, if there are such persons, they are not the "children of Strauss," nor are they acting on the basis of his teachings or thinking.

Notes

ABBREVIATIONS

The following abbreviations are used for frequently cited works:

CAM   Allan Bloom. *The Closing of the American Mind : How Higher Education Has Failed Democracy and Impoverished the Souls of Today's Students.* New York: Simon and Schuster, 1987.

CHD   Harry Jaffa. *Crisis of the House Divided.* Seattle: University of Washington Press, 1973.

CM   Leo Strauss. *The City and Man.* Chicago: University of Chicago Press, 1964.

FVFA   Walter Berns. *Freedom, Virtue, and the First Amendment.* Chicago: Henry Regnery, 1965.

LAM   Leo Strauss. *Liberalism: Ancient and Modern.* New York: Basic Books, 1968.

NRH   Leo Strauss. *Natural Right and History.* Chicago: University of Chicago Press, 1954.

OT   Leo Strauss. *On Tyranny.* Ed. Victor Gourevitch and Michael S. Roth. New York: Free Press, 1991.

PAW   Leo Strauss. *Persecution and the Art of Writing.* Free Press, 1952. Reprint, Chicago: University of Chicago Press, 1980. Citations are to the 1952 edition.

PILS   Shadia Drury. *The Political Ideas of Leo Strauss.* New York: St. Martin's Press, 1988.

RCPR   Leo Strauss. *The Rebirth of Classical Political Rationalism*, ed. Thomas Pangle. Chicago: University of Chicago Press, 1989.

TM   Leo Strauss. *Thoughts on Machiavelli.* Glencoe, IL: Free Press, 1958.

"WIPP"   Leo Strauss. "What Is Political Philosophy?" In *What Is Political Philosophy? And Other Studies.* Glencoe, IL: Free Press, 1959.

WIPP   Leo Strauss. *What Is Political Philosophy? And Other Essays.* Glencoe, IL: Free Press, 1959.

INTRODUCTION

1. James Atlas, "Leo-Cons; A Classicist's Legacy: New Empire Builders," *New York Times,* May 4, 2003, sec. 4, Week in Review, 1; Alain Frachon and Daniel Vernet, "The Strategist and the Philosopher," *Le Monde,* April 19, 2003 (trans. Mark K. Jensen), http://www.yubanet.com/artman/publish/article_2653.shtml, pp. 2–3; Steven Lenzner and William Kristol, "What Was Leo Strauss Up To?" *Public Interest,* Fall 2003, 10; Richard

Bernstein, "A Very Unlikely Villain (or Hero)," *New York Times*, January 29, 1995, E4. Also see Jim Lobe, "Neo-Cons Dance a Straussian Waltz," *Asia Times Online*, May 9, 2003, http://www.atimes.com.

2. Richard Lacoyo, "You've Read about Who's Influential, but Who Has the Power?" *Time*, June 17, 1996, 56, http://time-proxy.yaga.com/time/magazine/article/qpass.

3. Brent Staples, "Undemocratic Vistas: The Sinister Vogue of Leo Strauss," *New York Times,* November 28, 1994, A16; Miles Burnyeat, "The Sphinx Without a Secret," *New York Review of Books*, May 30, 1985, 30–36; Robert Devigne, *Recasting Conservatism* (New Haven, CT: Yale University Press, 1994).

4. "Philosophers and Kings," *Economist*, June 19, 2003, http://www.economist.com/printedition/displaystory.cfm?story_ID=1859009, p. 1; Jeet Heer, "The Philosopher," *Boston Globe*, May 11, 2003, H1; William Pfaff, "The Long Reach of Leo Strauss," *International Herald Tribune*, May 15, 2003, http://www.iht.com/articles/96307.html, p. 2; Atlas, "Leo-Cons," sec. 4, p. 1.

5. Atlas, "Leo-Cons," sec. 4, p. 4. This and many of the other statements in the media "name names," i.e., identify purported Straussians in government and the media. See, e.g., Robert Locke, "Leo Strauss, Conservative Mastermind," *Frontpage Magazine,* May 31, 2002.

6. Frachon and Vernet, "Strategist and Philosopher," 2; also see Renana Brooks, "The Character Myth," *Nation*, December 29, 2003, http://www.thenation.com/doc/20031229/brooks, p. 1.

7. Atlas, "Leo-Cons," H1.

8. Ibid.

9. Pfaff, "Long Reach," 1.

10. Jenny Strauss Clay, "The Real Strauss," *New York Times*, June 14, 2003, 1, http://www.nytimes.com/2003/06/07/opinion/07CLAY.html?n=top%2fopinion%2fedition. com; Frachon and Vernet, "Strategist and Philosopher," 3; see also Peter Berkowitz, "What Hath Strauss Wrought?" http://www.theweeklystandard.com/content/public/articles/000/000/002/717acusr.asp, p. 1; "Philosophers and Kings," 2; Atlas, "Leo-Cons," sec. 4, p. 2; Dinesh D'Souza, "The Legacy of Leo Strauss," *Policy Review*, Spring 1987, 36, 38, quotation on 36. See also Thomas Pangle, "Leo Strauss's Perspectives on Modern Politics," *Perspectives on Political Science* 25, no. 4 (Fall 2004), 6–8.

11. Charles Larmore, "The Secrets of Philosophy," *New Republic*, July 3, 1989, 32; Paul Gottfried, "Straussians vs. Paleo-conservatives," May 17, 2002, *Lew Rockwell*, http://www.lewrockwell.com/gottfried/gottfried29.html, p. 2.

12. "Philosophers and Kings," 2; Seymour Hersh, "Selective Intelligence," *New Yorker*, May 12, 2003, 6. A follow-up to Hersh's article is Laura Rozen, "ConTract: The Theory behind Neo-Con Self Deception," *Washington Monthly*, October 2003.

13. Frachon and Vernet, "Strategist and Philosopher," 3; see also Heer, "Philosopher," 2; Shadia Drury, *Leo Strauss and the American Right* (New York: St. Martin's Press, 1997), 4–7.

14. Pfaff, "Long Reach," 2.

15. Lenzner and Kristol, "What Was Strauss Up To?" 11. For speculations on the role of "regime-analysis" in Iraq War policy analysis, see Rozen, "ConTract," 2.

16. Frachon and Vernet, "Strategist and Philosopher," 3.

17. Pfaff, "Long Reach," 2; Heer, "Philosopher," 2–3; Berkowitz, "What Hath Strauss Wrought?" 1; "Philosophers and Kings," 2; see also Lobe, "Straussian Waltz," 2; John

Micklethwait and Adrian Wooldridge, *The Right Nation* (New York: Penguin, 2004), 15, 75, 340, quotation on 15.

18. Joseph Schumpeter, *Capitalism, Socialism, and Democracy* (New York: Harper, 1942); Robert Dahl, *A Preface to Democratic Theory* (Chicago: University of Chicago Press, 1956).

19. Heer, "Philosopher," 4; quotation in Pfaff, "Long Reach," 2; Berkowitz, "What Hath Strauss Wrought?" 1; Frachon and Vernet, "Strategist and Philosopher," 3.

20. Atlas, "Leo-Cons," 3.

21. Heer, "Philosopher," 4.

22. Hersh, "Selective Intelligence," 7; see also Heer, "Philosopher," 3; Mark Hosenball, Michael Isikoff, and Evan Thomas, "Cheney's Long Road to War," *Newsweek*, November 17, 2003, 38, 40.

23. "Philosophers and Kings," 2; see also Brooks, "Character Myth."

24. Pfaff, "Long Reach," 2.

25. Quotation in Heer, "Philosopher," 5. Lobe, "Straussian Waltz": Strauss was "elitist, amoral, and hostile to democratic government."

26. Burnyeat, "Sphinx Without a Secret," 30–36; David Lawrence Levine, "Without Malice but With Foresight: A Response to Burnyeat," *Review of Politics*, Winter 1991, 215.

27. Gordon Wood, "The Fundamentalists and the Constitution," *New York Review of Books*, February 18, 1988, 33–40. See also David Lewis Schaefer, "Leo Strauss and American Democracy: A Response to Wood and Holmes," *Review of Politics*, Winter 1991, 187–99.

28. Staples, "Undemocratic Vistas," A16.

29. Staples may also have been influenced by Robert Devigne's *Recasting Conservatism*, which argued that American conservatism had been remade by the influx of Straussian ideas into it. He was also one of the first to argue for a firm connection between Strauss and neoconservatism. We suspect Devigne did influence Staples, because he attempted to draw policy connections between Strauss and contemporary conservatism, a link very much on Staples's mind. Beyond its possible influence on Staples, Devigne's book does not seem to have played much of a role in the developing popular story of Strauss as Svengali to President Bush et al. We did not find any other tracks of it in the later versions of the story of the Straussians' ascent to power. (A possible exception is Drury's later book, *Leo Strauss and the American Right*, a book with a subject matter rather similar to Devigne's; she does cite Devigne.)

30. Bernstein, "Very Unlikely Villain," E4.

31. Robert Bartley, "Joining LaRouche in the Fever Swamps: The New York Times and The New Yorker Go Off the Deep End," *Wall Street Journal*, June 9, 2003.

32. Atlas, "Leo-Cons," 1; "Philosophers and Kings," 1.

33. Frachon and Vernet, "Strategist and Philosopher," 1.

34. Jeffrey Steinberg, "The 'Ignoble Liars' behind Bush's Deadly Iraq War," *LaRouche in 2004*, http://larouchein2004.net/pages/other/2003/030409cosart1.htm, p. 4.

35. On the denial that Wohlstetter is a Straussian, also see Anne Norton, *Leo Strauss and the Politics of American Empire* (New Haven, CT: Yale University Press, 2004), 182.

36. Quotation in Lyndon LaRouche, "The Essential Fraud of Leo Strauss," *Executive Intelligence Review*, March 21, 2003, http://larouchepub.com/lar/2003/

3011strauss_fraud.html, p. 4; Lyndon LaRouche, "Insanity as Geometry," *LaRouche in 2004,* http://larouchein2004.net/pages/writings/2003/030326insanity.htm, p. 4. I owe much of my understanding of LaRouche's ideology to Lauren Brubaker.

37. LaRouche, "Insanity as Geometry," 9, 10.

38. LaRouche, "Essential Fraud," 1, 4; LaRouche, "Insanity as Geometry," 4, 8; Steinberg, "Ignoble Liars," 3.

39. Jeffrey Steinberg, "Profile: Leo Strauss, Fascist Grandfather of the Neo-Cons," *Executive Intelligence Review,* March 21, 2003, http://larouchepub.com/other/2003/3011profile_strauss.html, p. 2.

40. Steinberg, "Ignoble Liars," 3; LaRouche, "Essential Fraud," 1.

41. Steinberg, "Profile," 2; Tony Papert, "The Secret Kingdom of Leo Strauss," *LaRouche in 2004,* http://larouchein2004.net/pages/other/2003/030409cosart2.htm, p. 4.

42. Papert, "Secret Kingdom," 4.

43. Ibid., 6.

44. Steinberg, "Ignoble Liars," 2–3.

45. Papert, "Secret Kingdom," 2–3; Steinberg, "Profile," 1.

46. See LaRouche, "Insanity as Geometry," 1, 2; Steinberg, "Profile," 2; "LaRouche Campaign Exposes 'Children of Satan,'" press release, April 17, 2003, 1, online version in *LaRouche in 2004,* http://larouchein2004.net/pages/pressreleases/2003/030417cospamphlet.htm; Lyndon LaRouche, "LaRouche Replies to Bartley Column," July 10, 2003, 1, online version in *LaRouche in 2004,* http://larouchein2004.net/pages/pressreleases/2003/030610bartley.htm; Lyndon LaRouche, "Can We Salvage This Presidency?" March 19, 2003, 1, in *Stop the Iraq War,* www.cecaust.com.au/iraq/0319.html; Tony Papert, "Where the Chicken-Hawks Got Their Love of War," *Executive Intelligence Review,* May 9, 2003, online version at http://www.larouchepub.com/other/2003/3018kojeve_strau.html. See the debate about Schmitt and Strauss in Alan Wolfe, "A Fascist Philosopher Helps Us Understand Contemporary Politics," *Chronicle of Higher Education,* April 2, May 14, 2004.

47. LaRouche, "Insanity as Geometry," 1; a detailed discussion is to be found in "A Dialogue about Leo Strauss, and the Effect of the Nihilist Philosophy Today," *Executive Intelligence Review,* June 20, 2003, http://www.larouchepub.com/other/2003/commentaries/3024lar_show_strauss.html.

48. See, e.g., Will Hutton, "Time to Stop Being America's Lap Dog," *Observer,* February 17, 2002, http://www.guardian.co.uk/print/0,3858,4357739-102273,00.html, p. 1; Lobe, "Straussian Waltz," 2.

49. Shadia Drury, "Saving America," *Evatt Foundation,* http://evatt.org.au/publications/papers/112html, p. 1 (article no longer present; accessed December 15, 2003). Consider her change of view from *The Political Ideas of Leo Strauss* (New York: St. Martin's Press, 1988), 194 (hereafter cited as *PILS*).

50. Danny Postel, "Noble Lies and Perpetual War: Leo Strauss, the Neocons, and Iraq," *Free Republic,* http://209.157.64.200/focus/f-news/10026664/posts, p. 7 (article no longer present; accessed December 18, 2003) .

51. Lobe, "Straussian Waltz," 2; quotation in Postel, "Noble Lies," 4.

52. *PILS,* 4, 193.

53. See, e.g., Drury, "Saving America," 3; also her *Strauss and the American Right,* chap. 3.

54. Drury, "Saving America," 3.

55. Ibid., 2, 1.

56. Ibid., 6.

57. Ibid., 1. A recent study of American conservatism is convinced that the Straussians in Washington have been shut out of America's "liberal universities" for political reasons. Micklethwait and Wooldridge, *Right Nation,* 22.

58. Lobe, "Straussian Waltz," 2.

59. Quotations in Drury, "Saving America," 1; Drury, *Strauss and the American Right,* 19, 78, 80–81.

60. Drury, *"Saving America,"* 4.

61. Postel, "Noble Lies," 6.

62. Drury, "Saving America," 5; Postel, "Noble Lies," 3–4.

63. Drury, "Saving America," 1, 3, quotation on 1; Postel, "Noble Lies," 4.

64. Quotation in Postel, "Noble Lies," 4. See also Lobe, "Straussian Waltz," 2.

65. Drury, *PILS,* 26; Postel, "Noble Lies," 3.

66. Drury, "Saving America," 1–2; Postel, "Noble Lies," 3.

67. Quotation in Drury, "Saving America," 2; Postel, "Noble Lies," 3.

68. Lobe, "Straussian Waltz," 2.

CHAPTER ONE

1. Leo Strauss, "A Giving of Accounts: Jacob Klein and Leo Strauss," *College,* April 1970, 2; reprinted in *Leo Strauss, Jewish Philosophy, and the Crisis of Modernity,* ed. Kenneth Hart Green (Albany: State University of New York Press, 1997), 457–67.

2. Alain Frachon and Daniel Vernet, "The Strategist and the Philosopher," *Le Monde,* April 19, 2003 (trans. Mark K. Jensen), http://www.yubanet.com/artman/publish/article_2653.shtml, p. 3.

3. Leo Strauss, "What Is Political Philosophy?" in *What Is Political Philosophy? And Other Studies,* by Strauss (Glencoe, IL: Free Press, 1959), 17. The essay is hereafter cited as "WIPP"; the book is cited as *WIPP.*

4. Strauss addressed social science positivism on many occasions in his writings, and he almost always began his classes with a review of the issues raised by positivism. His most significant writings on the subject probably are his essay "What Is Political Philosophy," his chapter on Max Weber in *Natural Right and History* (Chicago: University of Chicago Press, 1954) (hereafter cited as *NRH*), and his epilogue in the book *Essays on the Scientific Study of Politics,* ed. Herbert J. Storing (New York: Holt, Rinehart, and Winston, 1962) (which was produced by four of his students). Many of his students took up the antipositivist cudgels. Among the early statements were Walter Berns, "The Behavioral Sciences and the Study of Political Things," *American Political Science Review* 55 (September 1961): 550–59; and Harry V. Jaffa, "Comment on Oppenheim: In Defense of 'The Natural Law Thesis,'" *American Political Science Review* 51, no. 1 (March 1957): 54–64. Probably the most thorough review of Strauss's critique of modern social science is to be found in Nasser Behnegar, *Leo Strauss, Max Weber, and the Scientific Study of Politics* (Chicago: University of Chicago Press, 2003).

5. Diskin Clay, "On a Forgotten Kind of Reading," in *Leo Strauss's Thought: Toward a Critical Engagement,* ed. Alan Udoff (Boulder, CO: Lynne Rienner, 1991), 257, calls attention to the fact that Strauss's students have also produced a series of "strict new English translations" of Greek (and, we add, other) texts in the history of political philosophy.

6. Miles Burnyeat, "The Sphinx Without a Secret," *New York Review of Books*, May 30, 1985, 30–36.

7. *PILS*; Elizabeth Young-Bruehl, *Hannah Arendt: For Love of the World* (New Haven, CT: Yale University Press, 1982); Luc Ferry, *Political Philosophy I: The Ancients and the Moderns,* trans. Franklin Philip (Chicago: University of Chicago Press, 1990), 20–21.

8. Robert Devigne, *Recasting Conservatism* (New Haven, CT: Yale University Press, 1994), 49.

9. Ibid., 41.

10. *WIPP*, 17.

11. Leo Strauss, letter of June 26, 1950, reprinted in *On Tyranny*, by Strauss, ed. Victor Gourevitch and Michael S. Roth (New York: Free Press, 1991), 251 (hereafter cited in the notes as *OT*). On Strauss's reluctance to publicize the views of Heidegger, consider his comments on the Islamic Falasifa and their opponents in *Persecution and the Art of Writing* (Free Press, 1952; reprint, Chicago: University of Chicago Press, 1980) (hereafter cited in the notes as *PAW*).

12. Strauss's student Stanley Rosen, *The Question of Being* (New Haven, CT: Yale University Press, 1993), and Rosen's student Robert B. Pippin, *Modernism as a Philosophical Problem* (Cambridge, MA: Blackwell, 1991), may represent partial exceptions.

13. Quotation in Karl Loewith and Leo Strauss, "Correspondence," *Independent Journal of Philosophy* 5–6 (1988): 183. Admitting that Strauss states in this early letter that he had turned away from Nietzsche, Laurence Lampert argues in "Nietzsche's Challenge to Philosophy in the Thought of Leo Strauss," *Review of Metaphysics* 58 (March 2005): 585–619, that Strauss nevertheless agreed with Nietzsche's three "deadly truths" concerning the sovereignty of becoming; the fluidity of all concepts, types, and species; and no fundamental difference between man and the animals. We explain in more detail at the beginning of chapter 3 what we think Strauss's relation to Nietzsche was and why we disagree with Lampert. In chapter 4 we then explain why we agree with Lampert in thinking that Strauss did what he observed Lessing had not done, by bringing into the open the hidden history of philosophy and its strategies in its battle with revealed religion.

14. Leo Strauss, *Die Religionskritik Spinozas als Grundlage seine Bibelwissenschaft: Untersuchungen zu Spinozas Theologisch-politischen Traktat* (Berlin: Akademie-Verlag, 1930); trans. E. M. Sinclair as *Spinoza's Critique of Religion* (New York: Schocken Books, 1965).

15. Quotation in Leo Strauss, preface to *Spinoza's Critique of Religion*, 29. Cf. *NRH*, 75; Stanley Rosen, "Leo Strauss and the Quarrel between the Ancients and the Moderns," in Udoff, *Leo Strauss's Thought*, 159–60; Stanley Rosen, "Wittgenstein, Strauss, and the Possibility of Philosophy," in *The Elusiveness of the Ordinary : Studies in the Possibility of Philosophy*, by Rosen (New Haven, CT: Yale University Press, 2002), 150.

16. Leo Strauss, *Philosophie und Gesetz* (Berlin: Schocken Verlag, 1935); trans. Eve Adler as *Philosophy and Law: Contributions to the Understanding of Maimonides and His Predecessors* (Albany: State University of New York Press, 1995), 29–30.

17. Friedrich Nietzsche, *The Gay Science,* trans. Walter Kaufmann (New York: Vintage, 1974), sec. 125; Strauss, preface to *Spinoza's Critique of Religion*, 30.

18. Strauss, *Philosophy and Law,* 36–38.

19. In *WIPP,* 37, Strauss stated, "The difference between the classics and us with regard to democracy consists *exclusively* in a different estimate of the virtues of technology"

(emphasis added). Cf. Martin Heidegger, *The Question concerning Technology and Other Essays*, trans. William Lovitt (New York: Harper and Row, 1977), 53–112.

20. Friedrich Nietzsche, *Thus Spoke Zarathustra*, prologue.

21. Cf. Strauss, *Philosophy and Law*, 28–32; Strauss, *Spinoza's Critique of Religion*, 30–31; Rosen, "Wittgenstein, Strauss," 150–51.

22. See Leo Strauss, "Quelques remarques sur la science politique de Maimonide et de Farabi," *Revue des Etudes Juives* 100 (1936): 1–37; trans. Robert Bartlett, *Interpretation* 18 (Fall 1990): 3–15.

23. Preface to *Spinoza's Critique of Religion*, 31.

24. See Remi Brague, "Leo Strauss and Maimonides," in Udoff, *Leo Strauss's Thought*, 103. On the "Maimonidean Enlightenment," one should consult the book by Strauss's student Ralph Lerner, *Maimonides' Empire of Light: Popular Enlightenment in an Age of Belief* (Chicago: University of Chicago Press, 2000).

25. See, e.g., David Bolotin, *An Approach to Aristotle's Physics* (Albany: State University of New York Press, 1998); Larry Arnhart, *Darwinian Natural Right: The Biological Ethics of Human Nature* (Albany: State University of New York Press, 1998).

26. Three years after he published *Philosophy and Law*, Strauss wrote his close friend Jacob Klein, saying he had discovered that Maimonides was "really a free spirit." Strauss to Klein, January 20, 1938, in *Gesammelte Schriften*, ed. Heinrich Meier (Stuttgart: J. B. Metzler, 2001), 3:545. The next month (February 16) he added, "One does not *easily* understand Maimonides, if one does not reckon with the possibility that he was an 'Averroist.' If one does, one immediately solves all difficulties in principle" (3:549). At that point, Strauss told Klein, he had not written a word. The exigencies of emigrating and obtaining employment interfered with a smooth process of publication. Strauss first published an article "Persecution and the Art of Writing" in *Social Research* 8, no. 4 (November 1941): 488–504. He first published his essay "The Literary Character of *The Guide for the Perplexed*" in *Essays on Maimonides*, ed. S. W. Baron (New York: Columbia University Press, 1941), 37–91. He published his explanation "How to Begin to Study *The Guide of the Perplexed*" as an introductory essay to *The Guide of the Perplexed*, by Moses Maimonides (Chicago: University of Chicago Press, 1963), xi–lvi.

27. Cf. *NRH*, 32; "WIPP," 11.

28. On Strauss's view of the limits of science, see Leo Strauss, "Existentialism," *Interpretation* 22, no. 3 (Spring 1995): 309: "Science does no longer conceive of itself as the perfection of the human understanding; it admits that it is based on fundamental hypotheses which will always remain hypotheses"; and "Progress or Return?" in *An Introduction to Political Philosophy: Ten Essays by Leo Strauss*, ed. Hilail Gildin (Detroit: Wayne State University Press, 1989), 266–67.

29. Leo Strauss, "Farabi's Plato," in *Louis Ginzburg: Jubilee Volume*, ed. Saul Lieberman, Shalom Spiegel, Solomon Zeitlin, and Alexander Marx (New York: American Academy for Jewish Research, 1945), 359–83, Strauss quotations on 381; *PAW*, 15. Cf. Leo Strauss, "The Problem of Socrates," in *The Rebirth of Classical Political Rationalism*, by Strauss, ed. Thomas Pangle (Chicago: University of Chicago Press, 1989), 161 (hereafter cited in the notes as *RCPR*).

30. "Farabi's Plato," 369–72.

31. Ibid., 375. Strauss, it has been noted, much more resembles Farabi than, say, Plato or Aristotle, in that he too appears in the guise of a commentator on the thought of earlier thinkers. Does this mean he too "avails himself of the specific immunity of the commentator"? This is a topic to which we return at some length in chapter 4.

32. Quotation in Plato *Apology of Socrates* 38a, in *Four Texts on Socrates*, by Plato and Aristophanes, trans. Thomas G. West and Grace Starry West (Ithaca, NY: Cornell University Press, 1984), 92. Cf. Strauss, "Progress or Return?" 300.

33. In *WIPP*, Strauss cautions: "It is of the essence of devices of this kind that, while they are helpful up to a certain point, they are never sufficient and are never meant to be sufficient: they are merely hints" (166). Leo Strauss, "A Forgotten Kind of Writing," in *WIPP*, 221–32.

34. *PAW*, 33.

35. *PAW*, 32. It is worth noting that Shadia Drury, in her accusation that Strauss covertly presents his own views, Farabi-like in the guise of being a commentator, does not meet the Straussian test for attributing esotericism to writers. He has put forward, she says, not the genuine view of Plato and other ancients, but his own views, Machiavellian or Nietzschean in character, while hiding behind the commentator role. But in order to prove that Strauss's presentation of the ancients is a disguised presentation of modern and nihilistic doctrines, she would have to show that Strauss leaves out such obviously important aspects of Plato's teaching (as Strauss said Farabi did) without pointing out that he is doing so. She does not and cannot show that, like Farabi, Strauss ignored central Platonic teachings about the ideas and the immortality of the soul, because Strauss explicitly writes about both in his own essays on Plato.

36. Michael P. Zuckert, *Launching Liberalism: On Lockean Political Philosophy* (Lawrence: University Press of Kansas, 2002), chap. 2.

37. *PAW*, 35–37; Leo Strauss, *The City and Man* (Chicago: University of Chicago Press, 1964), 52–54 (hereafter cited as *CM*).

38. *PAW*, 34; Alexis de Tocqueville, *Democracy in America*, vol. 2, part 2, chap. 2.

39. *PAW*, 35.

40. Cf. Strauss, "Problem of Socrates," 171.

41. *OT*, 197–203; *CM*, 122–27.

42. *OT*, 196. Cf. *WIPP*, 116; *NRH*, 32. Thus, in explicating Strauss's understanding of esoteric writing, Lampert notes that "even a writer like Descartes, bent on crushing the persecution that made it impossible for him to say openly what he thought, still held that it was useful to hide his conclusions and to hide the way to his conclusions because to do so was a service to his best readers: only by becoming its codiscoverers could his readers make their own what was already Descartes' own." *Leo Strauss and Nietzsche* (Chicago: University of Chicago Press, 1996), 14.

43. *OT*, 196. Cf. *WIPP*, 116; *NRH*, 32. In "Philosophy and History: Tradition and Interpretation in the Work of Leo Strauss," *Polity* 16 (Fall 1983): 5–29, Nathan Tarcov emphasizes both the nontraditional and the open-ended character of Strauss's arguments in his response to John Gunnell, "Myth of the Tradition," *American Political Science Review* 72 (May 1978): 122–34.

44. Strauss, "Progress or Return?" 289. Strauss's emphasis on the importance of retaining and reviving the conflict between reason and revelation in order to retain and revive the Western philosophical tradition is one reason for the problematic nature of Lampert's contention in "Nietzsche's Challenge," 618–19, that, like Nietzsche, Strauss wanted "unbelief" to dictate "belief." If philosophy is to rule religion, as Lampert argues, religion becomes subordinate. There is no longer an unresolved tension.

45. Victor Gourevitch, "Philosophy and Politics, I," *Review of Metaphysics* 22 (1968): 60–61; *PILS*, 170–81; also Devigne, *Recasting Conservatism*, 41.

46. Leo Strauss, "What Is Liberal Education," in *Liberalism: Ancient and Modern*, by Strauss (New York: Basic Books, 1968), 7–8 (hereafter cited in the notes as *LAM*). For a fuller account of Strauss's argument, see Walter Nicgorski, "Leo Strauss and Liberal Education," *Interpretation* 13 (May 1985): 233–49.

47. Charles Larmore, "The Secrets of Philosophy," *New Republic*, July 3, 1989, 30–35.

48. Cf. Leo Strauss, "Philosophy as Rigorous Science and Political Philosophy," in *Studies in Platonic Political Philosophy*, by Strauss, ed. Thomas L. Pangle (Chicago: University of Chicago Press, 1983), 32–34.

49. *OT*, 183–84.

50. Leo Strauss, *Thoughts on Machiavelli* (Glencoe, IL: Free Press, 1958), 83–84 (hereafter cited in the notes as *TM*).

51. Ibid., 226–31. Cf. *PAW*, 15. Earlier in *TM*, Strauss argued that Machiavelli was not a "pagan," but one of the "wise of the world" who, Savonarola complained, "do not wish to believe anything except what rational discourse proves,... [and] who transcend[ing] the limits of political cleverness reject not only the myths of the pagans but above all revelation.... They are *falasifa* or 'Averroists'" (175). Later Strauss observed that "the fundamental tenets of Averroism were as well known to intelligent men of Machiavelli's age as the fundamental tenets of, say, Marxism are in the present age" (202–3).

52. In fact, Strauss knew, in *Discourses* 2.2.2 Machiavelli blamed the imperialistic expansion of the Roman republic that he seemed to praise in *Discourses* 1.2–4 for the destruction of free polities.

53. Strauss, *Philosophy and Law*, 29.

54. Cf. Leo Strauss, "On Classical Political Philosophy," in *WIPP*, 91. Strauss's emphasis on Machiavelli's ignoring of the Socratic side or half of Xenophon should make it difficult for readers to accept Drury's claim that Strauss read the ancients—Plato, Aristotle, and Xenophon—as if they said the same thing Machiavelli did, the only difference being, in his opinion, that he was more open about it.

55. *OT*, 211.

56. *NRH*, 120. See also Strauss, "Problem of Socrates," 168; Leo Strauss, "Social Science and Humanism," in *RCPR*, 6; *NRH*, 121–25.

57. Quotations in *OT*, 199. Much of the animus Shadia Drury expresses against Strauss arises from her belief that he thought the lives of all human beings, and the point of all political societies, were merely to serve a few philosophers. Her belief is quite mistaken, however. She commits the fallacy of thinking that since Strauss argues that morality is necessary for the maintenance of political order, and political order is a prerequisite of philosophy, he therefore thinks that the moral virtues are only for the sake of the philosophical life.

58. *CM*, 131; cf. "WIPP," 36–37.

59. Quotation in *CM*, 131–32; cf. Rosen, "Strauss and the Quarrel," 163.

60. Strauss, "Problem of Socrates," 163.

61. Leo Strauss, "Pleasure and Virtue," in *OT*, 92–108.

62. According to Drury in *PILS*, "His idea of philosophy as eros is a splendid excuse for being one of the Hugh Hefners of the philosophical set" (202). See also 82, 83, 91.

63. *OT*, 193–94.

64. Strauss, *CM*, 128. Strauss observes here the same abstraction in the account of the ascent from the "cave" to the light of the sun, which is given solely in terms of compulsion (*Republic* 515c5–516a1) without any indication of a desire to learn.

65. Strauss, *CM,* 128, citing the *Apology of Socrates* 30a3–4.

66. G. R. F. Ferrari, in "Strauss's Plato," *Arion* 5, no. 2 (Fall 1997): 36–63, gives a very detailed reading of this part of *The City and Man* in response to Burnyeat's critique of Strauss's reading of Plato's *Republic* in the *New York Review of Books.*

67. *OT,* 205. This is also the position, one might recall, that Strauss attributed to Farabi.

68. *OT,* 193–94.

69. See Rosen, "Wittgenstein, Strauss," 135, 137, 145, 147.

70. Although he did not remain a Zionist, Strauss did proclaim the establishment of the state of Israel to be a blessing for all Jews, everywhere, whether they admitted it or not. Preface to *Spinoza's Critique of Religion,* 5.

71. *Federalist* 10, in *The Federalist,* by Alexander Hamilton, James Madison, and John Jay (Middleton, CT: Wesleyan University Press, 1961), 60.

72. In *The Human Condition* (Chicago: University of Chicago Press, 1958), 22–78, Hannah Arendt gave a similar critique of modern political philosophy and the social science it spawned.

73. Preface to *Spinoza's Critique of Religion,* 1.

74. Leo Strauss, "An Epilogue," in *LAM,* 205–6.

CHAPTER TWO

1. Strauss's relative silence on America was no doubt related to the commonly noted fact that he seldom said much about current politics. See, e.g., Alain Frachon and Daniel Vernet, "The Strategist and the Philosopher," *Le Monde,* April 19, 2003 (trans. Mark K. Jensen), http://www.yubanet.com/artman/publish/article_2653.shtml, p. 2.

2. John G. Gunnell, "Political Theory and Politics: The Case of Leo Strauss and Liberal Democracy," in *The Crisis of Liberal Democracy,* ed. Kenneth L. Deutsch and Walter Soffer (Albany: State University of New York Press, 1987), 68.

3. *NRH,* 120; *CM,* 13.

4. Catherine H. Zuckert, "The Socratic Turn," *History of Political Thought* 25, no. 1 (Summer 2004): 189.

5. *NRH,* 120–34; *WIPP,* 10–12, 27–28, 38–40, 92–94; Leo Strauss, "The Problem of Socrates," in *RCPR,* 126.

6. *NRH,* 153–64.

7. See *PAW.*

8. "WIPP," 44.

9. See, e.g., *WIPP,* 40–55; Leo Strauss, "The Three Waves of Modernity," in *An Introduction to Political Philosophy: Ten Essays,* by Leo Strauss, ed. Hilail Gildin (Detroit: Wayne State University Press, 1989), 81–98.

10. "WIPP," 57; cf. Dana Villa, *Socratic Citizenship* (Princeton, NJ: Princeton University Press, 2001), 282.

11. Friedrich Nietzsche, *Twilight of the Idols,* trans. R. J. Hollingdale (New York: Viking Press, 1990); Neil G. Robertson, "The Closing of the Early Modern Mind: Leo Strauss and Early Modern Political Thought," http://www.mun.ca/animus/1998vol3/robert3.htm, p. 1.

12. Martin Heidegger, *What Is Called Thinking?* trans. J. Glenn Gray (New York: Harper, 1968).

13. See Leo Strauss, "On Classical Political Philosophy," in *WIPP,* 78–94; Leo Strauss, "An Epilogue," in *LAM,* 205–7.

14. *CM*, 138; Thomas Pangle, "Leo Strauss's Perspectives on Modern Politics," *Perspectives on Political Science* 25, no. 4 (Fall 2004), 1–2.

15. *CM*, 122–38; *LAM*, 19; Nathan Tarcov and Thomas L. Pangle, "Epilogue: Leo Strauss and the History of Political Philosophy," in *History of Political Philosophy*, ed. Leo Strauss and Joseph Cropsey, 3rd ed. (Chicago: University of Chicago Press, 1987), 917.

16. "WIPP," 45–47.

17. Thomas Jefferson to Roger Weightman, June 24, 1826, in Jefferson, *Writings*, ed. Merrill Peterson (New York: Library of America, 1984).

18. Strauss, "Three Waves," 88–89; Machiavelli, *Prince*, ed. and trans. Harvey Mansfield (Chicago: University of Chicago Press, 1985), chap. 15.

19. Strauss, "Classical Political Philosophy," in *WIPP*, 85–91; "WIPP," 3; quotation in *CM*, 127.

20. "WIPP," 43–44, 55; quotation in Machiavelli, *Prince*, chap. 15.

21. "WIPP," 39–41, 53, 55–57.

22. Quotation in *NRH*, 178; *TM*, 285.

23. Strauss, "Three Waves," 85.

24. "WIPP," 44, 47.

25. Leo Strauss, "Political Philosophy and the Crisis of Our Time," in *Post-Behavioral Era: Perspectives on Political Science*, ed. George Graham and George Carey (New York: David McKay, 1972), 222; *TM*, 281; *NRH*, 248.

26. Strauss, "Three Waves," 88–89.

27. *NRH*, 179; Tarcov and Pangle, "Epilogue," 917.

28. Somewhat more controversially, Strauss saw successive rights doctrines within modern philosophy as resting on the same foundation of the passions. For a discussion of the controversy arising in the case of one such successor, Locke, see Michael P. Zuckert, *Launching Liberalism: On Lockean Political Philosophy* (Lawrence: University Press of Kansas, 2002), chaps. 1–4; James Stoner, "Was Leo Strauss Wrong about John Locke?" *Review of Politics* 66 (Fall 2004): 553–64; quotation in *NRH*, 180; Robertson, "Closing of the Early Modern Mind," 7.

29. *NRH*, chap. 4; Nasser Behnegar, "The Liberal Politics of Leo Strauss," in *Political Philosophy and the Human Good,* ed. Michael Palmer and Thomas Pangle (Lanham, MD: Roman and Littlefield, 1995), 262.

30. See esp. *Federalist*, no. 10, in *The Federalist*, by Alexander Hamilton, James Madison, and John Jay, ed. Jacob E. Cooke (Middleton, CT: Wesleyan University Press, 1961), 51.

31. *NRH*, 245.

32. Strauss, preface to *Spinoza's Critique of Religion*, by Strauss, trans. E. M. Sinclair (New York: Schocken Books, 1965), 1–31.

33. William Butler Yeats, "The Second Coming," line 3, in *Selected Poems and Two Plays of William Butler Yeats*, ed. M. L. Rosenthal (New York: Collier Books, 1962), 91.

34. See the reflection by Strauss's friend and dialogic partner Alexander Kojeve, "Tyranny and Wisdom," in *OT*, 135–76.

35. "WIPP," 57.

36. Originally published in 1930 as *Die Religionskritik Spinozas als Grundlage seine Bibelwissenschaft: Untersuchungen zu Spinozas Theologisch-politischen Traktat* (Berlin: Akademie-Verlag, 1930).

37. Leo Strauss, *The Political Philosophy of Hobbes: Its Basis and Genesis*, trans. Elsa M. Sinclair (Chicago: University of Chicago Press, 1952), 110. Cf. Michael Oakeshott, *Hobbes on Civil Association* (Indianapolis: Liberty Fund, 1975), 146, 156.

38. Strauss later modified his judgment about the role of the new science in Hobbes's thought. See Leo Strauss, "On the Basis of Hobbes's Political Philosophy," in *WIPP*, 170–196.

39. *CM*, 28; "WIPP," 51.

40. *TM*, 232. Here is a point on which Strauss's critique converges with that of Alasdair McIntyre, *After Virtue*, 2nd ed. (Notre Dame, IN: University of Notre Dame Press, 1984), 52.

41. On the transition from happiness and thus virtue and nobility as the end of politics to the conditions for individual, variable "pursuit of happiness" as the end, see *CM*, 31; *OT*, 210.

42. Strauss, "Liberal Education and Responsibility," in *LAM*, 19.

43. This is not to say, as is sometimes said of Strauss, that he saw no room for virtue in modern political philosophy. See *CM*, 32.

44. Leo Strauss, "Relativism," in *RCPR*, 21.

45. Leo Strauss, "What Is Liberal Education," in *LAM*, 5; "WIPP," 20, 36–37; cf. Behnegar, "Liberal Politics of Leo Strauss," 256.

46. *CM*, 2

47. "WIPP," 57.

48. Ibid.

49. "WIPP," 48.

50. Strauss, "Three Waves," 89.

51. Ibid., 89, quotations on 90.

52. Ibid., 93, quotations on 94.

53. Ibid., 96–97.

54. *CM*, 2, 6–7.

55. Quotation in Strauss, "Political Philosophy and the Crisis of Our Time," 223; *CM*, 3, 42–43.

56. *TM*, 297.

57. Quotation in Strauss, "Political Philosophy and the Crisis of Our Time," 224; *CM*, 3–4; Strauss, "Three Waves," 87–88; "WIPP," 48; cf. Robertson, "Closing of the Early Modern Mind," 5.

58. Strauss, "Political Philosophy and the Crisis of Our Time," 232.

59. Strauss, "Three Waves," 89.

60. *OT*, 23, 27.

61. *OT*, 270. Strauss here expresses great doubts about the Enlightenment project of spreading liberal democracy throughout the world, and this indicates clearly the distance between him and the American policymakers who are allegedly acting on his theories.

62. See *OT*, 23–27; quotation in Strauss, "Political Philosophy and the Crisis of Our Time," 221.

63. Strauss, "Classical Political Philosophy," 81–83; Strauss, "Epilogue," in *LAM*, 205–6.

64. *CM*, 7; cf. Villa, *Socratic Citizenship*, 287.

65. Strauss, "Three Waves," 81–83; quotation in *CM*, 4.

66. Strauss, "Three Waves," 98.

67. Cf. Alfred Jules Ayer, *Language, Truth, and Logic* (New York: Dover, 1952), 5–15.

68. "WIPP," 23.

69. Strauss, "Relativism," 17.

70. Behnegar, "Liberal Politics of Leo Strauss," 253.

71. Strauss, "Epilogue," in *LAM*, 219–21.

72. "By exposing the Hobbesean and hedonistic foundations of Locke's thought, Strauss's study may undermine the respectability of Locke and consequently put in question the status of American founding fathers. In fact, a strong case can be made that *Natural Right and History* ultimately questions the soundness of our founding principles." Behnegar, "Liberal Politics of Leo Strauss," 258.

73. Frachon and Vernet, "Strategist and Philosopher," 2; Gregory B. Smith, "Athens and Washington: Leo Strauss and the American Regime," in *Leo Strauss, the Straussians, and the American Regime*, ed. Kenneth L. Deutsch and John A. Murley (Lanham, MD: Rowman and Littlefield, 1999), 122.

74. "WIPP," 27.

75. Smith, "Athens and Washington," 122; Strauss, "Three Waves," 98.

76. "WIPP," 56.

77. "WIPP," 57.

78. Robert Pippin, "The Modern World of Leo Strauss," *Political Theory* 20, no. 3 (August 1992): 451; "WIPP," 55; Strauss, "Three Waves," 90.

79. *LAM*, vi.

80. Cf. Pangle, "Strauss's Perspectives on Modern Politics," 6: Strauss recognized "the practical humane superiority of . . . 'the first wave of modernity.' "

81. *NRH*, 139.

82. Strauss, "Liberal Education and Responsibility," 24.

83. Quotation in Strauss, "Three Waves," 98; *LAM*, 15–16; Behnegar, "Liberal Politics of Leo Strauss," 259.

84. "WIPP," 35; *CM*, 35.

85. "WIPP," 37.

86. *CM*, 22–23; "WIPP," 37.

87. Cf. Stanley Rosen, "Wittgenstein, Strauss, and the Possibility of Philosophy," in *The Elusiveness of the Ordinary: Studies in the Possibility of Philosophy*, by Stanley Rosen (New Haven, CT: Yale University Press, 2002), 145.

88. *NRH*, 1–2.

CHAPTER THREE

1. Stanley Rosen, "Leo Strauss and the Quarrel between the Ancients and the Moderns," in *Leo Strauss's Thought: Toward a Critical Engagement*, ed. Alan Udoff (Boulder, CO: Lynne Rienner, 1991), 166.

2. Clayton Koelb, ed., *Nietzsche as Postmodernist: Essays Pro and Contra* (Albany: State University of New York Press, 1990).

3. Quotation in Leo Strauss, "Correspondence," *Independent Journal of Philosophy* 5–6 (1988): 183; Leo Strauss, "Correspondence concerning *Wahrheit und Methode*," *Independent Journal of Philosophy* 2 (1978): 5–12.

4. Leo Strauss, *Socrates and Aristophanes* (New York: Basic, 1968), 6; Robert Devigne, "Plato, Nietzsche, and Strauss," *Political Science Reviewer* 26, no. 4 (1997): 416.

5. Aristotle *Metaphysics* 1078b9–16.

6. *OT*, 204.

7. Cf. *CM*, 13–23, 50–138; Leo Strauss, *Xenophon's Socratic Discourse: An Interpretation of the Oeconomicus* (Ithaca, NY: Cornell University Press, 1970); Leo Strauss, *Xenophon's Socrates* (Ithaca, NY: Cornell University Press, 1972).

8. *WIPP*, 38–40. Thus in his "Restatement on Xenophon's *Hiero*," Strauss writes:

> Philosophy as such is nothing other than the real consciousness of the problems, that is to say, of the fundamental and comprehensive problems. It is impossible to think about these problems without being attracted toward . . . one or the other of certain rare typical solutions. However, as long as there is no wisdom, but only the search for wisdom, the evidence of all these solutions is necessarily smaller than the evidence of the problems. As a result, the philosopher ceases to be a philosopher from the moment that his "subjective certitude" of the truth of a solution becomes stronger than the consciousness that he may have of the problematical character of this solution. (*OT,* 116)

9. Cf. *CM*, 62; quotation in *OT,* 196.

10. Cf. Friedrich Nietzsche, "On the Prejudices of Philosophers," part 1 of *Beyond Good and Evil*, in *Basic Writings of Nietzsche*, trans. and ed. Walter Kaufmann (New York: Modern Library, 1968); and "How the 'Real World' at Last Became a Myth," in *Twilight of the Idols* (New York: Viking Press, 1990).

11. See Leo Strauss, "Note on the Plan of Nietzsche's *Beyond Good and Evil,*" in *Studies in Platonic Political Philosophy,* ed. Thomas L. Pangle (Chicago: University of Chicago Press, 1983), 189.

12. *WIPP*, 39.

13. *TM*, 13. Stanley Rosen, "Wittgenstein, Strauss, and the Possibility of Philosophy," in *The Elusiveness of the Ordinary: Studies in the Possibility of Philosophy*, by Stanley Rosen (New Haven, CT: Yale University Press, 2002), 139–40, also points out Strauss's fondness for this observation.

14. *NRH*, 123.

15. Cf. Strauss, "Note on the Plan," 184–85.

16. Leo Strauss, "What Is Liberal Education?" in *LAM,* 8.

17. Quoted phrases in Leo Strauss, "An Epilogue," in *LAM*, 211–13; Leo Strauss, "Philosophy as Rigorous Science and Political Philosophy," in Strauss, *Studies*, 29–37; cf. Nasser Behnegar, *Leo Strauss, Max Weber, and the Scientific Study of Politics* (Chicago: University of Chicago Press, 2003), 179–88.

18. See, e.g., Richard Rorty, *Contingency, Irony, Solidarity* (Cambridge: Cambridge University Press, 1989); quotation in *WIPP*, 40.

19. Strauss, "Note on the Plan," 174.

20. Ibid., 190–91; quotation in Leo Strauss, "An Introduction to Heideggerian Existentialism," in *RCPR,* 41.

21. Strauss, "Note on the Plan," 174–91, quotation on 186.

22. Strauss, "Epilogue," in *LAM*, 207; cf. "WIPP," 32; Behnegar, *Strauss, Weber, and the Study of Politics*, 164; "WIPP," 54.

23. "WIPP," 54–55.

24. Strauss, "The Three Waves of Modernity," in *An Introduction to Political Philosophy: Ten Essays*, by Strauss, ed. Hilail Gildin (Detroit: Wayne State University Press, 1989), 98.

25. Strauss, "Heideggerian Existentialism," 41.

26. "WIPP," 55.

27. *CM*, 241; Leo Strauss, "Progress or Return?" in Strauss, *Introduction to Political Philosophy*, 276, quotation on 274.

28. Leo Strauss, "Relativism," in *RCPR*, 26.

29. In *Philosophical Apprenticeships*, trans. Robert R. Sullivan (Cambridge, MA: MIT Press, 1985), 38–39, 49, Hans Georg Gadamer admitted that he had not understood that Heidegger's apparently sympathetic rereading of Aristotle in the 1920s had merely represented the beginning of a more fundamental critique of the entire Western philosophical tradition. Heidegger spoke of the "new beginning" in his infamous Rector's Address in 1933, "The Self-Assertion of the German University," trans. Karsten Harries, *Review of Metaphysics* 38 (March 1985): 471–73, and the "leap" in his posthumously published *Beiträge zur Philosophie, Gesamtausgabe* (Frankfurt: Vittorio Klostermann, 1989), vol. 65.

30. Luc Ferry, *Political Philosophy I: The Ancients and the Moderns,* trans. Franklin Philip (Chicago: University of Chicago Press, 1990); quotation in Strauss, "Heideggerian Existentialism," 29.

31. Strauss, "Philosophy as Rigorous Science," 31.

32. Strauss, "Heideggerian Existentialism," 29.

33. Martin Heidegger, *An Introduction to Metaphysics,* trans. Ralph Manheim (Garden City, NY: Doubleday Anchor, 1961).

34. Martin Heidegger, "The Word of Nietzsche: 'God Is Dead,' " in *The Question concerning Technology and Other Essays*, by Heidegger, trans. William Lovitt (New York: Harper, 1977), 53–112.

35. Strauss, "Heideggerian Existentialism," 42.

36. Martin Heidegger, "The Question concerning Technology" and "The Turning," in *The Question concerning Technology*, 3–49.

37. Martin Heidegger, *What Is Called Thinking?* trans. J. Glenn Gray (New York: Harper, 1968); Martin Heidegger, "The Spiegel Interview," in *Martin Heidegger and National Socialism: Questions and Answers,* ed. Günther Neske and Emil Kettering (New York: Paragon, 1990), 61–62.

38. Cf. Martin Heidegger, *On the Way to Language,* trans. Peter D. Hertz (San Francisco: Harper and Row, 1959).

39. Strauss, "Heideggerian Existentialism," 43–44.

40. Strauss, "Philosophy as Rigorous Science," 33–34; Strauss, "Heideggerian Existentialism," 42–46.

41. Strauss restates the

thesis of radical historicism . . . as follows. All understanding, all knowledge, however limited and "scientific," presupposes a frame of reference; it presupposes a horizon, a comprehensive view within which understanding and knowing take place. Only such a comprehensive vision makes possible any seeing, any observation, any orientation. The comprehensive view of the whole cannot be validated by reasoning, since it is the basis of all reasoning. Accordingly, there is a variety of such comprehensive views, each as legitimate as any other. . . . Strictly speaking, we cannot choose among different views. A single comprehensive view is imposed on us by fate. . . . Yet the support of the horizon produced by fate is ultimately the choice of the individual, since that fate has to be accepted by the individual. We are free ... either to choose in anguish the world view and the standards imposed on us by fate or else to lose ourselves in illusory security or in despair. (*NRH*, 27)

42. Strauss, "Heideggerian Existentialism," 38.

43. Ibid.

44. Leo Strauss, "The Problem of Socrates," the second of the two lectures published in *Interpretation* 22, no. 3 (Spring 1995): 321–38. It was delivered April 17, 1970, at St. John's College, Annapolis, MD.

45. Martin Heidegger, "What Is Metaphysics?" in *Basic Writings,* by Heidegger, ed. David Farrell Krell (New York: Harper, 1993), 89–110.

46. Strauss, "Heideggerian Existentialism," 46.

47. Leo Strauss, "Jerusalem and Athens," in Strauss, *Studies,* 147–73; Strauss, "Progress or Return?" 265–67, 276–310.

48. Although Strauss does not name Heidegger, he wrote his friend Alexander Kojeve on June 26, 1950, "I have once again been dealing with Historicism, that is to say, with Heidegger, the only radical historicist." *OT,* 251.

49. Cf. Steven B. Smith, "Destruktion or Recovery?" *Review of Metaphysics* 51 (December 1997): 374; quotation in *NRH,* 31–32.

50. Strauss, "Heideggerian Existentialism," 35–36.

51. Quotation in *NRH,* 6; Cf. Strauss, "Relativism," 13–26.

52. *NRH,* 6, 5.

53. Nietzsche, *Beyond Good and Evil* and *Genealogy of Morals,* in *Basic Writings of Nietzsche,* 179–599.

54. Heidegger, "Word of Nietzsche," 53–112.

55. Cf. Leo Strauss to Gerhard Krueger, January 7, 1930, reprinted in *Gesammelte Schriften,* by Strauss, ed. Heinrich Meier (Stuttgart: J. B. Metzler, 2001), 3:380.

56. Strauss, "Heideggerian Existentialism," 33.

57. *NRH,* 23.

58. Quotation in Strauss, "Three Waves," 98; Gregory B. Smith, "The Post-Modern Leo Strauss?" *History of European Ideas* 19, no. 1 (1994): 192, also emphasizes Strauss's fervent defense of liberal democracy in contrast to Heidegger's continued insistence on the "inner truth and greatness of National Socialism."

59. *NRH,* 32.

60. Strauss, "Heideggerian Existentialism," 34.

61. *NRH,* 32.

62. *NRH,* 33.

63. Strauss, "Problem of Socrates," *Interpretation,* 326.

64. Cf. Leo Strauss, "Political Philosophy and History," in *WIPP,* 66; Jacques Derrida, *Of Grammatology,* trans. Gayatri Chakravorty Spivak (Baltimore: Johns Hopkins University Press, 1974), 1–94.

65. Cf. Leo Strauss, "The Problem of Socrates," in *RCPR,* 103–83; Jacques Derrida, "Plato's Pharmacy," in *Dissemination,* by Derrida, trans. Barbara Johnson (Chicago: University of Chicago Press, 1981), 86; Jacques Derrida, *Khora,* in *On the Name,* by Derrida, ed. Thomas Dutoit, trans. David Wood, John P. Leavey Jr., and Ian McLeod (Stanford, CA: Stanford University Press, 1995), 100–104.

66. Jacques Derrida, "The Principle of Reason," *diacritics* 13 (Fall 1983): 3–20; Jacques Derrida, "No Apocalypse, Not Now," *diacritics* 14 (Summer 1984): 20–31.

67. Leo Strauss, preface to *Spinoza's Critique of Religion,* by Strauss, trans. E. M. Sinclair (New York: Schocken Books, 1965), 1–31; Jacques Derrida, "Like the Sound of

the Sea Deep within a Shell: Paul de Man's War," trans. Peggy Kamuf, *Critical Inquiry* 14 (Spring 1988): "I am Jewish, I was persecuted as a child during the war" (648).

68. See, e.g., Stanley Rosen, *Hermeneutics as Politics* (New York: Oxford University Press, 1987); Susan Handelman, *The Slayers of Moses: The Emergence of Rabbinic Interpretation in Modern Literary Theory* (Albany: State University of New York Press, 1982).

69. *PAW,* 22–37; Derrida, "Plato's Pharmacy," 148.

70. Paul A. Cantor, "Leo Strauss and Contemporary Hermeneutics," in Udoff, *Leo Strauss's Thought,* 279.

71. Leo Strauss, "On Plato's *Apology of Socrates* and *Crito,*" in Strauss, *Studies,* 38–66; "WIPP," 33, Derrida, "Plato's Pharmacy," 148–53.

72. Strauss, "Three Waves," 54–55; Strauss, *Studies,* 30; Jacques Derrida, *The Ear of the Other,* trans. Peggy Kamuf (New York: Schocken, 1985); Jacques Derrida, *Of Spirit,* trans. Geoffrey Bennington and Rachel Bowlby (Chicago: University of Chicago Press, 1987).

73. Cf. Jacques Derrida, *Speech and Phenomena and Other Essays on Husserl's Theory of Signs,* trans. David Allison (Evanston, IL: Northwestern University Press, 1973).

74. Cf. Jacques Derrida, *Edmund Husserl's Origin of Geometry: An Introduction,* trans. John P. Leavey Jr. (Boulder, CO: Nicolas Hays, 1978).

75. In *Of Grammatology*, Derrida thus urges:

> To save Nietzsche from a reading of the Heideggerian type [in terms primarily of the "will to power"], it seems that we must above all not attempt to restore or make explicit a less naive "ontology" [which, we believe, is what Derrida would think Strauss is doing]. . ... Rather than protect Nietzsche from the Heideggerian reading, we should perhaps offer him up to it completely, underwriting that interpretation without reserve; in a certain way and up to the point where, the content of the Nietzschean discourse being almost lost for the question of being, its form regains its absolute strangeness ... [and] invokes a different type of reading, more faithful to his type of writing: Nietzsche has written ... that writing—and first of all his own—is not originarily subordinate to the logos and to truth." (19)

76. The common ancient Greek definition of political associations in terms of "friends" and "enemies" raised several times in the Platonic dialogues (e.g., *Republic* 332a–335e, *Clitophon* 410b, *Lysis* 213a–c) differs from the definition of politics in terms of friends and enemies more recently advocated by Carl Schmitt in *The Concept of the Political,* inasmuch as the ancients, on the one hand, understood the "they," strangers (*xenoi*) or "enemies," (*polemios* or *echthros*) to be those who did not share the characteristics, ethnic or political (e.g., the barbarians), of the "we." Schmitt, on the other hand, defines "friends" primarily in terms of their common "enemies." Since Strauss takes Socrates as his model, it is important to note that Socrates criticized the proposition that one ought to be good to one's friends and bad to one's enemies by arguing that one should not harm anyone. For more on the relation between Strauss and Schmitt, see chapter 5.

77. Jacques Derrida, *The Other Heading: Reflections on Today's Europe,* trans. Pascale-Anne Brault and Michael B. Naas (Bloomington: Indiana University Press, 1992); quotation in Derrida, "Like the Sound of the Sea," 648, where he reminds his readers that he was arrested, interrogated, and imprisoned by the "totalitarian police" in what was then Czechoslovakia.

78. Derrida, *Other Heading*, 17–19.

79. Jacques Derrida, *Of Hospitality*, trans. Rachel Bowlby (Stanford, CA: Stanford University Press, 2000).

80. Derrida, *Other Heading*, 56.

81. Jacques Derrida, "Force of Law," in *Deconstruction and the Possibility of Justice*, ed. Drucilla Cornell, Michel Rosenfeld, and David Gray Carlson (New York: Routledge, 1992), 3–67.

82. Cf. Derrida, "Principle of Reason," 16–19.

83. Derrida, *Other Heading*, 76–77.

84. Cf. Jacques Derrida, "Passions," in *On the Name*, 9–24.

85. Jacques Derrida, "*Sauf le nom*," in *On the Name*, 35–85.

86. Cf. *Theaetetus* 152c–e.

87. Jacques Derrida, "Violence and Metaphysics: An Essay on the Thought of Emmanuel Levinas," in *Writing and Difference*, by Derrida, trans. Alan Bass (Chicago: University of Chicago Press, 1978), 79–153.

88. Cf. Jacques Derrida, "*Admiration de Nelson Mandela sur les lois de la reflexion*," in *Psyche*, by Derrida (Paris: Galilee, 1987), 453–76. Strauss speaks of Asian great books in "What Is Liberal Education," in *LAM*, 3–8.

89. In "How to Avoid Speaking: Denials," trans. Ken Frieden, in *Derrida and Negative Theology*, by Derrida, ed. Harold Coward and Toby Foshay (Albany: State University of New York Press, 1992), 135n13, Derrida admits that "for lack of capacity, competence, or self-authorization, I have never yet been able to speak of what my birth . . . should have made closest to me: the Jew, the Arab." And in 1981 he told Richard Kearney, "I often feel that the questions I attempt to formulate on the outskirts of the Greek philosophical tradition have as their 'other' the model of the Jew. . . . And yet the paradox is that I have never actually invoked the Jewish tradition in any 'rooted' or direct manner. Though I was born a Jew, I do not work or think within a living Jewish tradition." Jürgen Habermas, *Philosophical-Political Profiles*, trans. Frederick G. Lawrence (Cambridge, Mass.: MIT Press, 1983), 33.

90. Strauss, "Heideggerian Existentialism," 43–44.

91. Cf. Strauss, *Studies*; Leo Strauss, *Jewish Philosophy and the Crisis of Modernity* (Albany: State University of New York Press, 1997).

92. Emil Fackenheim, "Straussians in the News," September 28, 2003, *Straussian.net*, http://www.Straussian.net (this article no longer on site; accessed September 2003).

CHAPTER FOUR

1. *PILS*, ix. For the record, we might note that this is a false claim. Strauss believed that the art of philosophic concealment died with Kant, but that Kant and many of his successors qualify as great philosophers (see *OT*, 27). (In this chapter, citations of *PILS* are in most cases placed in the text.)

2. Shadia Drury, *Leo Strauss and the American Right* (New York: St. Martin's Press, 1997), 231; cf. *TM*, 29–35; *PAW*, 144; Irene Harvey, "The Rhetoric of Esotericism: The 'Challenge' to Deconstruction," in *Law and Semiotics*, ed. Roberta Kevelson (New York: Plenum Press, 1987), 1:218, 228, 232–3.

3. *PILS*, xi, 14, quotation on xi.

4. Cf. Harvey, "Rhetoric," 224.

5. *PILS*, 27, quoting Strauss, *PAW*, 14; cf. Laurence Lampert, *Leo Strauss and Nietzsche* (Chicago: University of Chicago Press, 1996), 146; Kenneth Hart Green,

"Religion, Philosophy, and Morality: How Leo Strauss Read Judah Halevi's *Kuzari*," *Journal of the American Academy of Religion* 61, no. 2 (Summer 1993): 256–57; Michael Frazer, "Esotericism Ancient and Modern: Strauss contra Straussianism on the Art of Political-Philosophical Writing," paper presented at the American Political Science Association Annual Meetings, Philadelphia, August 28, 2003, 1.

6. Leo Strauss, "How Farabi Read Plato's Laws," in *WIPP*, 136.

7. Ibid., 137.

8. A more nuanced version of our argument would have to take account of Maimonides, who is more open about his esotericism than any other writer. He both announces it and indicates his resolve to continue to practice it. There are more than a few important differences between Maimonides and Strauss, however, which would warrant a fuller explanation than we can provide here. First, Maimonides explicitly connects himself to maintaining the esoteric tradition in his own book; Strauss nowhere does so, despite the frequent claim by his readers that he does. Second, Maimonides refuses to reveal the secrets in earlier esoteric books, especially those in Torah; Strauss reveals the secrets. Third, as we detail subsequently, the circumstances in which the two discuss esotericism are much different. Fourth, despite the fact that Maimonides is explicit about esotericism, he does not highlight it to anything like the degree Strauss does. Strauss brings it much more into the open, makes it more obtrusive, and thus makes it harder to overlook or forget.

9. Cf. Stanley Rosen, *Hermeneutics as Politics* (New York: Oxford University Press, 1987), 113.

10. Cf. Lampert, *Strauss and Nietzsche*, 125.

11. *PAW*, 36, 22.

12. *PAW*, 32; cf. Rosen, *Hermeneutics*, 113.

13. Harvey, "Rhetoric," 218.

14. *PAW*, 27.

15. *PAW*, 30; cf. Harvey, "Rhetoric," 228–39; and Paul A. Cantor, "Leo Strauss and Contemporary Hermeneutics," in *Leo Strauss's Thought: Toward a Critical Engagement*, ed. Alan Udoff (Boulder, CO: Lynne Rienner, 1991), 270.

16. But see Michael P. Zuckert, *Launching Liberalism: On Lockean Political Philosophy* (Lawrence: University Press of Kansas, 2002), part 1.

17. Cf. Rosen, *Hermeneutics*, 113.

18. *PAW*, 27.

19. *NRH*, 12.

20. "WIPP," 26.

21. *NRH*, 19; Leo Strauss, "Political Philosophy and History," in *WIPP*, 63.

22. Cf. Laurence Lampert, "Nietzsche's Challenge to Philosophy in the Thought of Leo Strauss," *Review of Metaphysics* 58 (March 2005): 604, 608; Strauss, "Political Philosophy and History," 63.

23. *OT*, 27–28.

24. Cf. Lampert, *Strauss and Nietzsche*, 125; Harvey, "Rhetoric," 217; Peter Levine, *Nietzsche and the Modern Crisis of the Humanities* (Albany: State University of New York Press, 1995), 161; Frazer, "Esotericism," 9.

25. Vaclav Havel, *Disturbing the Peace*, trans. Paul Wilson (New York: Alfred Knopf, 1999), 13; Robert Howse, "Reading between the Lines: Exotericism, Esotericism, and the Philosophical Rhetoric of Leo Strauss," *Philosophy and Rhetoric* 32, no. 1 (1999): 64.

26. *WIPP*, 136; cf. David Lewis Schaefer, "Shadia Drury's Critique of Leo Strauss," *Political Science Reviewer* 23 (1994): 90–91.

27. *PAW*, 137.

28. *PAW*, 121–22; "WIPP," 29, 33; Leo Strauss, "On the Euthyphron," in *RCPR*, 204.

29. *PAW*, 36, 111–12, quotation on 36; *OT*, 27

30. See *PAW*, 35; Neil G. Robertson, "The Closing of the Early Modern Mind: Leo Strauss and Early Modern Political Thought," http://www.mun.ca/animus/1998vol3/robert3.htm, p. 4.

31. Lampert, *Strauss and Nietzsche*, 11; Cantor, "Strauss and Contemporary Hermeneutics," 273; cf. *OT*, 61.

32. Rosen, *Hermeneutics*, 109, 112.

33. Ibid., 109. Also cf. 112: Strauss devoted "virtually his entire professional career to the exposé of the political rhetoric of philosophers, or the distinction between their exoteric and esoteric teachings."

34. Cf. Ibid., 113.

35. *RCPR*, 64 (emphasis added).

36. Cf. Rosen, *Hermeneutics*, 137, on Strauss's "persistence in publicizing the dangerous esoteric doctrines of the philosophers."

37. *OT*, 76.

38. *Republic* 415a–b.

39. See *CM*, 102–3.

40. *TM*, 13, 14; see *NRH*, 130.

41. *LAM*, 21.

42. Cf. *TM,* 120, 31; *OT*, 31.

43. *TM*, 294.

44. See Remi Brague, "Leo Strauss and Maimonides," in Udoff, *Leo Strauss's Thought*, 97; Lampert, *Strauss and Nietzsche*; Frazer, "Esotericism," 14; Levine, *Nietzsche*, 153; Earl Shorris, "Ignoble Liars," *Harper's Magazine*, June 2004, 68; Diskin Clay, "On a Forgotten Kind of Reading," in Udoff, *Leo Strauss's Thought*, 263; James Rhodes, *Eros, Wisdom, and Silence* (Columbia: University of Missouri Press, 2003), 72.

45. Levine, *Nietzsche.*

46. *OT,* 27; Frazer, "Esotericism," 6.

47. *PAW,* 34.

48. We thus disagree with a common claim made by many readers of Strauss (Brague, "Leo Strauss and Maimonides"; Green, "Religion, Philosophy, and Morality"; Lampert, *Strauss and Nietzsche*; Rosen, *Hermeneutics,* 117).

49. See *PAW*, 22, 55–60; cf. Frazer, "Esotericism," 6, 9.

50. Cf. *PAW*, 49, 55–56.

51. Frazer, "Esotericism," 22.

52. Cf. Green, "Religion, Philosophy, and Morality," 237–38n1.

53. Cf. Schaefer, "Shadia Drury's Critique," 13; Rosen, *Hermeneutics,* 115.

54. *PAW*, 37.

55. Allan Bloom, "Leo Strauss," *Political Theory* 2, no. 4 (November 1974): 390–91.

56. *OT*, 27. We find Howse's skepticism about the educative function of philosophical reticence in "Reading between the Lines," 71, quite unpersuasive.

57. Our thesis should not be confused with that of Michael Frazer in "Esotericism," even though some of the conclusions that follow from our analysis are similar to some of his. He argues that the doctrine about esotericism is actually an exoteric doctrine,

"designed to seduce students into a life of philosophy" (3). In his interesting essay on the implications of Strauss's theory of "a forgotten kind of writing" for his own writing, Frazer starts off from a strong distinction between two kinds of esotericism, that which is persecution-driven, that is, responsive to contingent facts about the social and intellectual climate; and that which is inherent in the inevitable disproportion between philosophy and society. Frazer separates the two more than Strauss normally does, and labels the first "modern esotericism," for it is a milder form of esotericism aimed at protecting the philosopher from persecution but at the same time aimed at transforming opinion toward the truth. The "essential" kind of esotericism is called by Frazer "ancient"; there was no ultimate aim in this kind of writing to make the philosophic truth generally available to the public. The ancient esotericism is thus deeper in the sense that the truth is more hidden, or less revealed, than in modern esotericism. The modern esotericism is thus in some ways more difficult to practice, however, for although both must combine concealing and revealing, the modern esotericism puts these dual imperatives in greater tension with each other: the desire to reveal goes further toward undercutting the ability to conceal. Frazer makes the interesting argument that despite the haste with which many readers attribute to Strauss the practice of ancient esotericism, he in fact is a practitioner of modern esotericism. On this view, Strauss's apparent preference for ancient esotericism is an exoteric doctrine, an aspect of his practice of modern esotericism.

Frazer's hypothesis leads him to almost the opposite conclusion from ours. He endorses the view that Strauss "wrote esoterically about esotericism" (16). The central disagreement between Frazer and us is that Frazer finds that Strauss commits himself to the practice of "ancient esotericism." We do not find such a commitment.

We and Frazer do agree, however, that Strauss's own way of writing and his exposure of esotericism in past writers result from his attempt to lure students to the philosophic life (esp. 28–29).

58. *PAW*, 37.

59. Michael Kochin, "Morality, Nature, and Esotericism in Strauss's Persecution and the Art of Writing," *Review of Politics* 64, no. 2 (Spring 2002): 261. See *PAW*, 36.

60. For a related account of a related difference, see Howse, "Reading between the Lines," 69.

61. Levine, *Nietzsche*, 153; see, e.g. "WIPP," 54–55; Leo Strauss, "The Three Waves of Modernity," in Strauss, *An Introduction to Political Philosophy: Ten Essays by Leo Strauss*, ed. Hilail Gildin (Detroit: Wayne State University Press, 1989), 95–98.

62. Levine, *Nietzsche*, 154, 156, 161–62, quotation on 162.

63. See Larry Peterman, "Approaching Leo Strauss: Some Comments on *Thoughts on Machiavelli*," *Political Science Reviewer* 16 (Fall 1986): 322.

64. Ibid., 325. Consider also Harvey Mansfield's identification of the paradox. Quoted ibid.

65. Cf. *PAW*, 155.

66. Peterman, "Approaching Leo Strauss," 348; see, e.g. Leo Strauss, "Preliminary Observations on the Gods in Thucydides' Work," in *Studies in Platonic Political Philosophy,* by Strauss, ed. Thomas L. Pangle (Chicago: University of Chicago Press, 1983), 89–104.

67. Peterman, "Approaching Leo Strauss," 351, 323.

68. Green, "Religion, Philosophy, and Morality," 225–73; see Leo Strauss, "Jerusalem and Athens," in Strauss, *Studies*. A reading of Strauss's essay in conformity with ours is Kochin, "Morality, Nature, and Esotericism," 276–77.

69. Rosen, *Hermeneutics,* 109. Lampert, "Nietzsche's Challenge," 604.

70. Rosen, *Hermeneutics*, 113.

71. Ibid., 125; Stanley Rosen, *The Elusiveness of the Ordinary: Studies in the Possibility of Philosophy* (New Haven, CT: Yale University Press, 2002), 135; also 137, 145.

72. Quotation in Rosen, *Hermeneutics,* 136; Stanley Rosen, "Leo Strauss and the Quarrel between the Ancients and the Moderns," in Udoff, *Leo Strauss's Thought,* 163.

73. Rosen, *Hermeneutics,* 125; Carnes Lord, *Education and Culture in the Political Thought of Aristotle* (Ithaca, NY: Cornell University Press, 1982); Henry Fielding, *Tom Jones;* Strauss, "Liberal Education and Responsibility," in *LAM.*

74. Rosen, *Elusiveness*, 157.

75. Rosen, *Hermeneutics,"* 124; also see Rosen, *Elusiveness*, 148–49.

76. Rosen, *Hermeneutics,"* 129.

77. Rosen, *Elusiveness*, 157.

78. Ibid., 137, 145.

79. For insight and helpful discussion of Rosen's position, we'd like to credit our student Alex Duff, who wrote a very searching paper on Rosen's various treatments of Strauss. Rosen, *Hermeneutics,* 122.

80. Rosen, *Elusiveness*, 145–46. Strauss's views on the solution of the reason-revelation problem are intelligently teased out in Thomas Pangle's *Political Philosophy and the God of Abraham* (Baltimore: Johns Hopkins University Press, 2003).

81. Rosen, *Elusiveness*, 145, 146; cf. Rosen, *Hermeneutics,* 125.

82. Rosen, *Elusiveness*, 147.

83. Rosen, *Hermeneutics*, 139.

84. Ibid., 109, 111.

85. Ibid., 109, quoting Strauss, *OT*, 205–6.

86. "WIPP," 11.

87. Alexander Duff, "Rosen's Strauss: An Introductory Consideration of Stanley Rosen's Critique of Leo Strauss" (unpublished paper, University of Notre Dame, 2005), 23.

88. See esp. Leo Strauss, "On Classical Political Philosophy," in *WIPP*, 78–94; "An Epilogue," in *LAM*, 204–8.

89. *TM*, 13.

90. Duff, "Rosen's Critique of Strauss," 18.

91. "WIPP," 11.

92. Leo Strauss, "The Problem of Socrates," in *RCPR*, 142.

93. Strauss, "Political Philosophy and History," 73–77; *PAW*, 155–56.

94. *NRH*, 74–76.

95. Rosen, *Elusiveness*, 151.

96. Quotations in Strauss, "Reason and Revelation," lecture delivered at Hartford Theological Seminary, January 8, 1948, in *Leo Strauss and the Theologico-Political Problem*, ed. Heinrich Meier (New York: Cambridge University Press, 2006), 161, 19; Leo Strauss, "Progress or Return?" in Strauss, *Introduction to Political Philosophy*, 261–65, 269.

97. Strauss, "Progress or Return?" 266–69.

98. Ibid., 269.

99. Ibid., 269, 270.

100. Ibid., 269.

101. Ibid., 259; Strauss, preface to *Spinoza's Critique of Religion*, by Strauss, trans. E. M. Sinclair (New York: Schocken Books, 1965), 30.

102. Strauss, "Progress or Return?" 259.

103. Ibid., 260; see also 269.

104. Ibid., 262.

105. Ibid., 270.

CHAPTER FIVE

1. *TM*, 9; see Isaiah Berlin, "A Special Supplement: The Question of Machiavelli," *New York Review of Books*, November 7, 1971; Earl Shorris, "Ignoble Liars," *Harper's Magazine*, June 2004, 65.

2. See, e.g., J. G. A. Pocock, "Prophet or Inquisitor, or Church Built upon Bayonets Cannot Stand: A Comment on Mansfield's 'Strauss's Machiavelli,'" *Political Theory* 3 (1975): 385–401.

3. Schaefer, "Drury's Critique of Leo Strauss," *Political Science Reviewer* 23 (1994): 80.

4. *OT*, 177; cf. Clifford Orwin, "Leo Strauss, Moralist or Machiavellian?" *Vital Nexus* 1, no. 1 (May 1990): 105.

5. Danny Postel, "Noble Lies and Perpetual War: Leo Strauss, the Neocons, and Iraq," *Free Republic*, http://209.157.64.200/focus/f-news/10026664/posts, p. 4 (article no longer present; accessed December 18, 2003); quotations in Shadia Drury, "Saving America," *Evatt Foundation*, http://evatt.org.au/publications/papers/112html, pp. 2–3 (article no longer present; accessed December 15, 2003).

6. *PILS*, 97; cf. Dana Villa's somewhat more moderate endorsement of the same view in *Socratic Citizenship* (Princeton, NJ: Princeton University Press, 2001), 291.

7. *PILS*, 96.

8. *LAM*, 3–26.

9. *PILS*, 96, 102.

10. *OT*, 25.

11. *OT*, 22.

12. *OT*, 69; cf. *CM*, 80.

13. *OT*, 68.

14. Aristotle *Politics* 1279a32–b10.

15. *OT*, 99.

16. *OT*, 41.

17. *PILS*, 103 (emphasis in original).

18. *OT*, 101.

19. *LAM*, 7–8; cf. *OT*, 102.

20. *OT*, 35.

21. *OT*, 101. See Drury's scandalous account of "Socratic hedonism" (her term), ostensibly based on this discussion in *OT*. She not only leaves out the specific character of the analysis of the philosophic pleasure, but she omits Strauss's denial that the analysis is at bottom a hedonistic one. Drury says of "Socratic hedonism": "This highbrow hedonism continues to regard pleasure as the ultimate criterion, and identifies it with the good." *PILS*, 81. Strauss had quite explicitly rejected this interpretation, however. "If we understand by hedonism the thesis that the pleasant is identical with the good, Xenophon's Simonides is not a hedonist.... He makes it clear that he considers the

pleasant and the good fundamentally different from each other." *OT,* 95. So far is Strauss from affirming the hedonistic doctrine Drury attributes to him that he quite explicitly presents an alternate theory of the good: "What [Simonides] praises most highly is pleasant indeed, but pleasure alone does not define it sufficiently; it is pleasant on a certain level, and that level is determined, not by pleasure, but by the hierarchy of beings." *OT,* 101.

22. Leo Strauss, "What Is Liberal Education," in *LAM,* 14.

23. *CM,* 124. Subsequent citations of *CM* in this chapter are, in most cases, placed in the text.

24. *OT,* 91, 89; Plato *Apology of Socrates* 37e–38b.

25. *PILS,* 30. Even less is the message of *On Tyranny* what Nicholas Xenos takes it to be: "The tyranny [Strauss] is talking about when he is writing in 1948 is the tyranny that he experiences, or thinks he experiences, in the West." Nicholas Xenos, "Leo Strauss and the Rhetoric of the War on Terror, *Logos* 3, no. 2 (Spring 2004): 8. Apart from the fact that Xenos presents no evidence whatsoever to support this claim, it runs counter both to what Strauss explicitly says tyranny is, "lawless monarchic rule," and to the point of *On Tyranny* as a whole, to bring the reader to see that the rule-of-law regimes like those in the West, despite their limitations, are justified and validated by the Xenophontic political science that Strauss explicates.

26. Plato *Republic* 338c.

27. Postel, "Noble Lies," 3; Shadia Drury, *Leo Strauss and the American Right* (New York: St. Martin's Press, 1997), 99; James Rhodes, *Eros, Wisdom, and Silence* (Columbia: University of Missouri Press, 2003), 90–93. Rhodes connects his identification of Strauss's "secret" with the Thrasymachean thesis (following Drury). He asks, "Why does Strauss appear to torpedo esotericism by disclosing its existence, its methods, and its first three layers of pseudo and real secrets to any minimally capable person who can read?" (93). Rhodes's answer is that Strauss is thereby hiding a yet deeper secret, the secret of Thrasymachus, or a variant thereof, that is, that natural right enjoins the rule of philosophers over others as shepherds rule sheep, for the good of the shepherd. Our reply to Drury on the Thrasymachean thesis is a sufficient reply to Rhodes insofar as he follows her and insofar as he extends her argument to the affirmation of a Straussian esoteric doctrine.

28. Quotation in Postel, "Noble Lies," 3; *PILS,* 26.

29. Quotation in *PILS,* 78, citing *CM,* 88; *NRH,* 106.

30. *PILS,* 78, 76, 79.

31. *PILS,* 76, citing *CM,* 84.

32. *PILS,* 77, citing *CM,* 77.

33. *PILS,* 77. Similar to Drury's account of Thrasymachus is Laurence Lampert in his *Leo Strauss and Nietzsche* (Chicago: University of Chicago Press, 1996). Lampert, unlike Drury, is friendly to Strauss and believes that the analysis Drury presents is not only basically true to Strauss's position, but true altogether. He says, for example, "Socrates has a view of justice not unlike Thrasymachus's and . . . Socrates is prudent enough not to flaunt it" (150). We believe Lampert is mistaken in this claim for exactly the same reason Drury is. Although he agrees with Drury about Strauss on justice, Lampert has a somewhat different emphasis in his presentation of Strauss's interpretation of the *Republic.* He attends much more to the "taming" of Thrasymachus, the "befriending" of Thrasymachus by Socrates, and the enlistment of Thrasymachus's rhetorical art in an effort by the philosophers to rule. This emphasis conforms with Lampert's Nietzschean notion that philosophers are essentially legislators. He thus sees the main action of the *Republic* to be

the merging of the philosopher and the rhetorician to produce a form of philosophic po-etry capable of laying down new orders through public teaching (18). Lampert attributes to Strauss a view Strauss found in Farabi: that Plato "combines the way of Socrates and Thrasymachus." *PAW*, 16. Whether Strauss accepted that view in the 1940s remains to be seen, but in the 1960s when he wrote *The City and Man*, Strauss said that he did not recognize a difference between Socrates and Plato. "Jerusalem and Athens," in *Studies in Platonic Political Philosophy,* by Strauss, ed. Thomas L. Pangle (Chicago: University of Chicago Press, 1983), 168. Strauss does indeed pay much attention to the dynamic of the relation between Socrates and Thrasymachus, but Lampert goes astray in several places. Most generally, he attributes to Strauss a conception of philosophy that Strauss does not share (see chapter 3, this volume). More specifically to the point of the analysis of Strauss on the *Republic,* Lampert hardly notices Strauss's explicitly negative judgment on the project Lampert attributes to him. Lampert follows Strauss through his analysis of the importance of Thrasymachus's rhetorical art, but he (like Drury) checks out before the end of the analysis. "The *Republic* repeats, in order to overcome it, the errors of the Sophists regarding the power of speech." Or, as Strauss puts it most pithily: "It is against nature that rhetoric should have the power ascribed to it: that it should be able to over-come the resistance rooted in men's love of their own and ultimately in the body." *CM,* 127. The flirtation with Thrasymachus and with his idea that the right kind of rhetoric could engineer the rule of philosophy is part of the thought experiment that is the *Republic,* as Strauss reads it (123). Also cf. Xenos, "Strauss and the Rhetoric of the War on Terror," who cannot seem to get straight who stands for what in the *Republic:* "The way of the world is the way of Thrasymachus. And the argument for justice that Thrasymachus makes in Plato's *Republic* is that justice is helping friends and hurting enemies" (13).

34. *CM,* 73, 124, quotation on 73; cf. Lampert, *Strauss and Nietzsche,* 18, 146–47.

35. Leo Strauss, "The Problem of Socrates," in *RCPR,* 156, 170, quotation on 156.

36. Ibid., 170, 159–60.

37. Cf. ibid., 156.

38. Ibid., 125.

39. Ibid., 156, 157.

40. Ibid., 152.

41. *NRH,* 124.

42. *PILS,* 77.

43. Strauss, "Problem of Socrates," in *RCPR,* 157. Consider Marx: "to each according to his needs."

44. Cf. *CM,* 89.

45. *CM,* 127; cf. 109.

46. *PILS,* 78, 77.

47. Quotation in Strauss, "Problem of Socrates," in *RCPR,* 163; *CM,* 109.

48. Strauss, "Problem of Socrates," in *RCPR,* 163.

49. Ibid., 164.

50. Ibid.; see also Strauss to Kojeve, May 28, 1957, in *OT,* 276–80.

51. Strauss, "Problem of Socrates," in *RCPR,* 164.

52. *NRH,* 323.

53. *PILS,* 117.

54. As Thomas Pangle rightly noted, "Strauss was too deeply penetrated by Thucy-dides' dissection of all that is implied in the immoderation of Pericles' funeral oration to be able to celebrate the splendors of imperialistic Athens." *RCPR,* xxiv.

55. *PILS*, 115, 116, 115, 117.

56. *PILS*, 117.

57. Quotations ibid.; Robert Devigne, *Recasting Conservatism* (New Haven, CT: Yale University Press, 1994), 42, 45. Devigne's attempt to identify Strauss's politics with Machiavelli's is a particularly egregious instance of misrepresentation. He quotes an extensive passage from *Natural Right and History,* which he presents as making that point, but the passage in question is Strauss's summary of the views of the ancient conventionalists, whose views the Socratic philosophers refuted. It is very clear this is not the view Strauss is endorsing. See *NRH*, 106.

58. *PILS*, 118–19; Devigne, *Recasting Conservatism*, 46–47.

59. *PILS*, 127.

60. *PILS*, 126.

61. *PILS*, 116.

62. *OT*, 196.

63. *WIPP*, 40.

64. *WIPP*, 43, 47.

65. *WIPP*, 43.

66. *TM*, 120; cf. *PILS,* 115–16, 231n6: neither of the pages Drury cites in her note supports the point she makes in her text, so it is difficult to know for sure what she means to say. We have selected the passage most praising of Machiavelli nearest to her citation.

67. *PILS*, 115.

68. Machiavelli, *Discourses*, Epistle Dedicatory; *Prince*, chap. 15.

69. John Graville Agard Pocock, *The Machiavellian Moment: Florentine Political Thought and the Atlantic Republican Tradition* (Princeton, NJ: Princeton University Press, 1975); Vickie Sullivan, "Machiavelli's Momentary 'Machiavellian Moment': A Reconsideration of Pocock's Treatment of the *Discourses*," *Political Theory* 20, no. 2 (May 1992): 309–18.

70. *WIPP*, 45.

71. *PILS*, 125.

72. *PILS*, 126.

73. *NRH*, 159–61. Devigne, *Recasting Conservatism*, 43, thus seriously misunderstands Strauss's position when he blurs together Strauss's endorsement of the changeability of natural right and the Machiavellian position.

74. *NRH*, 162.

75. Cf. the different reading in Villa, *Socratic Citizenship*, 290.

76. See esp. Strauss's clear articulation of the difference between Machiavelli and Aristotle in *NRH*, 161–63.

77. See, e.g., Drury, *Strauss and the American Right*; Anne Norton, *Leo Strauss and the Politics of American Empire* (New Haven, CT: Yale University Press, 2004), 123 (Norton revises the triumvirate slightly by excluding Heidegger and including Kojeve); Villa, *Socratic Citizenship*, 290.

78. *WIPP*, 57. A clear recognition of Strauss's rejection of Nietzsche's politics is Stanley Rosen, "Wittgenstein, Strauss, and the Possibility of Philosophy," in *The Elusiveness of the Ordinary : Studies in the Possibility of Philosophy*, by Rosen (New Haven, CT: Yale University Press, 2002), 135, 145.

79. Leo Strauss, "The Three Waves of Modernity," in *An Introduction to Political Philosophy: Ten Essays*, by Strauss, ed. Hilail Gildin (Detroit: Wayne State University Press, 1989), 98.

80. Drury, *Strauss and the American Right*, 69.

81. Strauss, "Three Waves," 98.

82. *WIPP*, 57; cf. *RCPR*, 31, 40.

83. *WIPP*, 23–24.

84. Strauss, preface to *Spinoza's Critique of Religion*, by Strauss, trans. E. M. Sinclair (New York: Schocken Books, 1965), 31. Cf. Susan Shell, "Taking Evil Seriously," in *Leo Strauss: Political Philosopher and Jewish Thinker*, ed. Kenneth L. Deutsch and Walter Nicgorski (Lanham, MD: Rowman and Littlefield, 1994), 175.

85. Mark Lilla, *The Restless Mind: Intellectuals in Politics* (New York: New York Review of Books, 2001), 50–51.

86. Ibid., 53.

87. Heinrich Meier, *Carl Schmitt and Leo Strauss: The Hidden Dialogue*, trans. J. Harvey Lomax (Chicago: University of Chicago Press, 1995), 8n7.

88. Xenos, "Strauss and the Rhetoric of the War on Terror," 3; *PILS*, 128; Stephen Holmes, *The Anatomy of Antiliberalism* (Cambridge, MA: Harvard University Press, 1996), 60, 68–69.

89. Leo Strauss, "Notes on Carl Schmitt, in *The Concept of the Political*," trans. J. Jarvey Lomax (Chicago: University of Chicago Press, 1996), 107, para. 35.

90. Ibid., 83, para. 2, quoting Schmitt.

91. Ibid., 100–101, para. 27.

92. See Ronald J. Tercheck, "Locating Leo Strauss in the Liberal-Communitarian Debate," in *Leo Strauss, the Straussians, and the American Regime*, ed. Kenneth L. Deutsch and John A. Murley (Lanham, MD: Rowman and Littlefield, 1999).

93. *NRH*, 137.

94. Cf. the different reading in Norton, *Leo Strauss*, 40–41: she claims that Schmitt "shaped the term ... the political" for Strauss. However, she gives no evidence to support this claim.

95. *NRH*, 136.

96. Cf. Shell, "Taking Evil Seriously": "Both Schmitt and Strauss see in the idea of the 'political' an answer to the deficiencies of liberalism. ... They differ fundamentally, however, in their understanding of what politics is" (185).

97. *NRH*, 129.

98. *NRH*, 130.

99. *NRH*, 132, 133, quotation on 132.

100. *NRH*, 130–131.

CHAPTER SIX

1. "WIPP," 15–16; cf. Leo Strauss, "On Classical Political Philosophy," in *WIPP*, 81–82.

2. Leo Strauss, "An Epilogue," in *LAM*, 206–27, quotation on 206; cf. Strauss, "On Classical Political Philosophy," 79–82.

3. Leo Strauss, "The Three Waves of Modernity," in *An Introduction to Political Philosophy: Ten Essays*, by Strauss, ed. Hilail Gildin (Detroit: Wayne State University Press, 1989).

4. Ibid., 98.

5. *NRH*, 134–35.

6. Leo Strauss, "Liberal Education and Responsibility," in *LAM*, 23.

7. Martin Diamond, *As Far as Republican Principles Will Admit: Essays,* ed. William A. Schambra (Washington: AEI Press, 1992), dust jacket.

8. Walter Berns, *Freedom, Virtue and the First Amendment* (Chicago: Henry Regnery, 1965), ix (hereafter cited in text as *FVFA*).

9. See, e.g., Walter Berns, *Taking the Constitution Seriously* (New York: Simon and Schuster, 1987); and Walter Berns, *In Defense of Liberal Democracy* (Chicago: Regnery Gateway, 1984).

10. See *CM*, which treats Aristotle as ingress to Plato.

11. Gordon Wood, "A Straussian Bicentennial," *New York Review of Books,* February 18, 1988; Martin Diamond, "The Federalist," in *History of Political Philosophy*, ed. Leo Strauss and Joseph Cropsey (Chicago: University of Chicago Press, 1987). This and the other writings by Diamond cited here have been republished in a collection of Diamond's essays: Diamond, *As Far as Republican Principles.*

12. Martin Diamond, "On the Study of Politics in a Liberal Education," in *As Far as Republican Principles*, 276–77; Martin Diamond, "Teaching about Politics," ibid., 286–92, quotations on 305.

13. Diamond, "Teaching about Politics," 305.

14. Martin Diamond, "The Dependence of Fact upon 'Value,'" in *As Far as Republican Principles*, 317.

15. Diamond, "On the Study of Politics," 278.

16. Martin Diamond, "Democracy and *The Federalist*," 31, 35–36; Martin Diamond, "*The Federalists*' View of Federalism," 111; Martin Diamond, "*The Federalist*," 47, all in *As Far as Republican Principles.*

17. Martin Diamond, "The American Idea of Equality," in *As Far As Republican Principles*, 248. Also see Martin Diamond, "Separation of Powers and the Mixed Regime," ibid., 62; Martin Diamond, "The Declaration and the Constitution: Liberty, Democracy, and the Founders," ibid., 232, 286n9.

18. Diamond, "American Idea of Equality," 248–49.

19. Martin Diamond, *The Founding of the Democratic Republic* (Itasca, DE: F. E. Peacock, 1981), 5. Also see Martin Diamond, "Revolution of Sober Expectations," in *As Far as Republican Principles*, 214; Diamond, "Declaration and Constitution," 234–35. Cf. *NRH*, 232.

20. Diamond, "Democracy and *The Federalist*," 20–27; Diamond, "Declaration and Constitution," 231–34; Diamond, "American Idea of Equality," 243–44.

21. Diamond, "Democracy and *The Federalist*," 30.

22. Quotation ibid.; Diamond, "American Idea of Equality," 249; Diamond, "Separation of Powers," 63.

23. Diamond, "Democracy and *The Federalist*," 30.

24. Martin Diamond, "Ethics and Politics: The American Way," in *As Far As Republican Principles*, 352.

25. Diamond, "Declaration and Constitution," 386.

26. Diamond, "Ethics and Politics," 353; Diamond, "*The Federalist*," 54.

27. Diamond, "Democracy and *The Federalist*," 31, 32, 34.

28. Ibid., 34.

29. Ibid., 29.

30. Ibid., 35, 36.

31. Diamond, "Declaration and Constitution," 228; Diamond, "American Idea of Equality," 242.

32. Diamond, "Democracy and *The Federalist*," 27; cf. Diamond, "American Idea of Equality," 243–44.

33. Quotation in Diamond, "Democracy and *The Federalist,*" 17–18; see Diamond's version of the Progressive's "four act drama" in "Declaration and Constitution," 229; also see Diamond, "American Idea of Equality," 242–43.

34. Diamond, "American Idea of Equality," 244.

35. Diamond, "Democracy and *The Federalist,*" 18.

36. Consider Jaffa's judgment: "The issue between Lincoln and Douglas was identical in principle with that between Socrates and Thrasymachus." "Humanizing Certitudes and Impoverishing Doubts," *Interpretation* 16, no. 1 (Fall 1988), reprinted in *Essays on the Closing of the American Mind,* ed. Robert Stone (Chicago: Chicago Review Press, 1989), 143.

37. Harry Jaffa, *Crisis of the House Divided* (Seattle: University of Washington Press, 1973), 308–9 (hereafter cited in text and notes as *CHD*).

38. John Locke, *Two Treatises of Government,* II 4.

39. Ibid., 54.

40. Abraham Lincoln, speech at Springfield, June 26, 1857, in *Lincoln,* ed. Donald Fehrenbacher (New York: Library of America, n.d.) 1:398.

41. *CHD,* 318.

42. *CHD,* 222; and see esp. 341.

43. Susan Shell, "Idealism," in *Confronting the Constitution,* ed. Allan Bloom (Washington, DC: AEI Press, 1990), 258–83.

44. Aristotle *Politics* III.

45. Aristotle *Ethics* IV.

46. Charles Kesler, "A New Birth of Freedom: Harry V. Jaffa and the Study of America," in *Leo Strauss, the Straussians, and the American Regime,* ed. Kenneth L. Deutsch and John A. Murley (Lanham, MD: Rowman and Littlefield, 1999), 270.

47. See *CHD,* 213–25. For a more textually grounded interpretation, see Glen Thurow, *Lincoln and American Political Religion* (Albany: State University of New York Press, 1976).

48. Harry Jaffa, *The Conditions of Freedom* (Claremont, CA: Claremont Institute, 2000), 7, quoted phrase on 8.

CHAPTER SEVEN

1. Cf. Anne Norton, *Leo Strauss and the Politics of American Empire* (New Haven, CT: Yale University Press, 2004), 161–62; Robert Devigne, *Recasting Conservatism* (New Haven, CT: Yale University Press, 1994), 55.

2. Allan Bloom, *The Closing of the American Mind: How Higher Education Has Failed Democracy and Impoverished the Souls of Today's Students* (New York: Simon and Schuster, 1987), 312 (hereafter cited in text and notes as *CAM*).

3. For comments on the effect of the events at Cornell on Bloom, see Norton, *Leo Strauss,* 47–49.

4. Cf. *CAM,* 195–96, 201.

5. Contra Peter Levine, *Nietzsche and the Modern Crisis of the Humanities* (Albany: State University of New York Press, 1995), 165.

6. Richard M. Weaver, *Ideas Have Consequences* (Chicago: University of Chicago Press, 1948).

7. David Rieff, "The Colonel and the Professor," in *Essays on the Closing of the American Mind,* ed. Robert L. Stone (Chicago: Chicago Review Press, 1989), 293.

8. Walter Berns, "Letter to the Editor," *This World,* Spring–Summer 1984, 7.

9. Quoted in Jaffa, *How to Think*, 22 (emphasis in original); see also 33.

10. Harry Jaffa, *The Conditions of Freedom* (Claremont, CA: Claremont Institute, 2000), 6–7.

11. Ibid., 4.

12. Ibid., 5.

13. Jaffa took another approach to the same question in a 1974 polemic he wrote against the institution by the American Political Science Association of a Leo Strauss prize for the best dissertation in political philosophy. "All of Strauss' work," Jaffa observed, "took place within the setting of what he called the crisis of the West.... Yet he never seems to have thought that his work would alter the course of that crisis—except as that crisis was also a crisis within the souls of those whom he taught." Harry V. Jaffa, *How to Think about the American Revolution: A Bicentennial Cerebration* (Durham, NC: Carolina Academic Press, 1978), 172–73. Strauss was a "quietist," Jaffa seems to be saying. Even if he did not undermine healthy regimes, as Jaffa implied in his eulogy, he also did not help produce public health. Jaffa's political science was more ambitious. Witness the Claremont Institute for the Study of Statesmanship and Political Philosophy, a Jaffa-inspired organization devoted to the immediacy of contemporary politics in a way Strauss never was.

14. Jaffa, *How to Think*, 37, 38.

15. Jaffa, *Conditions of Freedom*, 152; Jaffa, *How to Think*, 111.

16. Jaffa, *Conditions of Freedom*, 152, 153.

17. Ibid., 153.

18. Jaffa, *How to Think*, 25.

19. Ibid., 20.

20. Ibid., x.

21. Ibid., x–xi.

22. Ibid., 34.

23. Martin Diamond, "The Declaration and the Constitution: Liberty, Democracy, and the Founders," in *As Far as Republican Principles Will Admit: Essays,* ed. William A. Schambra (Washington: AEI Press, 1992), 223.

24. Ibid., 223, 214–15 (emphasis added).

25. Ibid., 214; Jaffa, *Conditions of Freedom*, 157–58; quotations in Jaffa, *How to Think*, x.

26. Harry Jaffa, "Aristotle and Locke in the American Founding," *Claremont Review of Books*, Winter 2001, 10.

27. Thomas West, "Allan Bloom and America," in Stone, *Essays on the Closing*, 166.

28. Ibid., 170.

29. Jaffa, "Aristotle and Locke," 10; West, "Bloom and America," 168–69.

30. Jaffa, "Aristotle and Locke," 10.

31. "WIPP," 49–50; *NRH*, 246–51.

32. Jaffa, "Aristotle and Locke," 10.

33. Ibid..

34. As influential as Diamond's early work has proved to be, it must be noted that it did not escape serious and often well-aimed criticism. On Diamond's notion of federalism, see, e.g., Vincent Ostrom, *The Meaning of American Federalism* (San Francisco: ICS Press, 1991), chap. 4. On Diamond's views of the Madisonian extended republic and the political economy he attributed to Madison, see Alan Gibson, "The Commercial Republic and the Pluralist Critique of Marxism: An Analysis of Martin Diamond's

Interpretation of *Federalist* 10," *Polity* 25, no. 4 (Summer 1993): 497–528. Diamond's textbook is *The Democratic Republic*, by Martin Diamond, Winston Mills Fisk, and Herbert Garfinkel (Chicago: Rand McNally, 1966).

35. Martin Diamond, "Revolution of Sober Expectations," in *As Far as Republican Principles*, 222, 223.

36. Martin Diamond, "The American Idea of Equality," in *As Far As Republican Principles*, 248–49.

37. Martin Diamond, "Democracy and *The Federalist*," in *As Far as Republican Principles*, 34; Diamond, "American Idea of Equality," 268; Martin Diamond, "Ethics and Politics: The American Way," in *As Far as Republican Principles*, 344.

38. Diamond, "American Idea of Equality," 248, cf. Martin Diamond, "Separation of Powers and the Mixed Regime," in *As Far as Republican Principles*, 62–63.

39. Diamond, "Ethics and Politics," 355.

40. Ibid.

41. Ibid.

42. Ibid.; Diamond, "Democracy and *The Federalist*," 29.

43. Diamond, "Ethics and Politics," 359. That Diamond's thought had taken a surprising turn in this, his last completed essay, is evident in the reactions to it by his good friend the historian Marvin Meyers and by his former student Thomas Scorza. Both found Diamond's praise of the American regime inconsistent with the general line of his earlier analyses in terms of the ancient-modern theme, with its emphasis on the modern "lowering of the sights." Meyers and Scorza attempt to account for that incompatibility in different ways, but neither considers the explanation we supply: Diamond had come to doubt Strauss's second proposition ("modernity is bad") and was tentatively moving toward a new construal of the American regime. See Marvin Meyers, "The Least Imperfect Government: On Martin Diamond's 'Ethics and Politics,'" *Interpretation* 8, nos. 2–3 (May 1980): 5–15; and Thomas Scorza, "Comment: The Politics of Martin Diamond's Science," *Interpretation* 8, nos. 2–3 (May 1980): 16–21.

44. Ibid., 360.

45. Ibid., 363.

CONCLUSION

1. *NRH*, 140.

2. *OT*, 210.

3. *NRH*, 127.

4. Machiavelli, *Prince*, chap. 3.

5. *NRH*, 134.

6. Ibid., 162.

7. "WIPP," 54; *LAM*, 8.

8. Lawrence F. Kaplan and William Kristol, *The War over Iraq: Saddam's Tyranny and America's Mission* (San Francisco: Encounter Books, 2003).

9. Peter Steinfels, *The Neo-Conservatives: The Men Who Are Changing American Politics* (New York: Simon and Schuster, 1979).

10. Ibid., 5.

11. Mark Gerson, ed., *The Essential Neo-Conservative Reader* (Reading, MA: Addison-Wesley, 1996).

12. Kenneth R. Weinstein, "Philosophic Roots, the Role of Leo Strauss, and the War in Iraq," in *The Neocon Reader*, ed. Irwin Stelzer (New York: Grove Press, 2005), 207.

Index